PHD
PHANTASY DEGREE

6

Episode 6: Master Tower

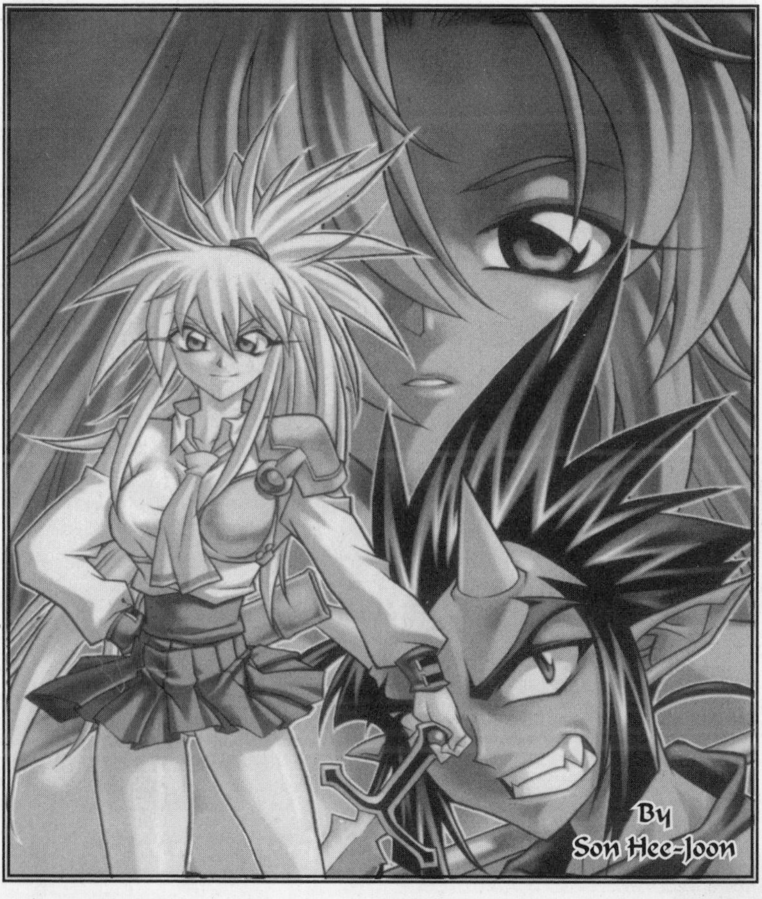
By
Son Hee-Joon

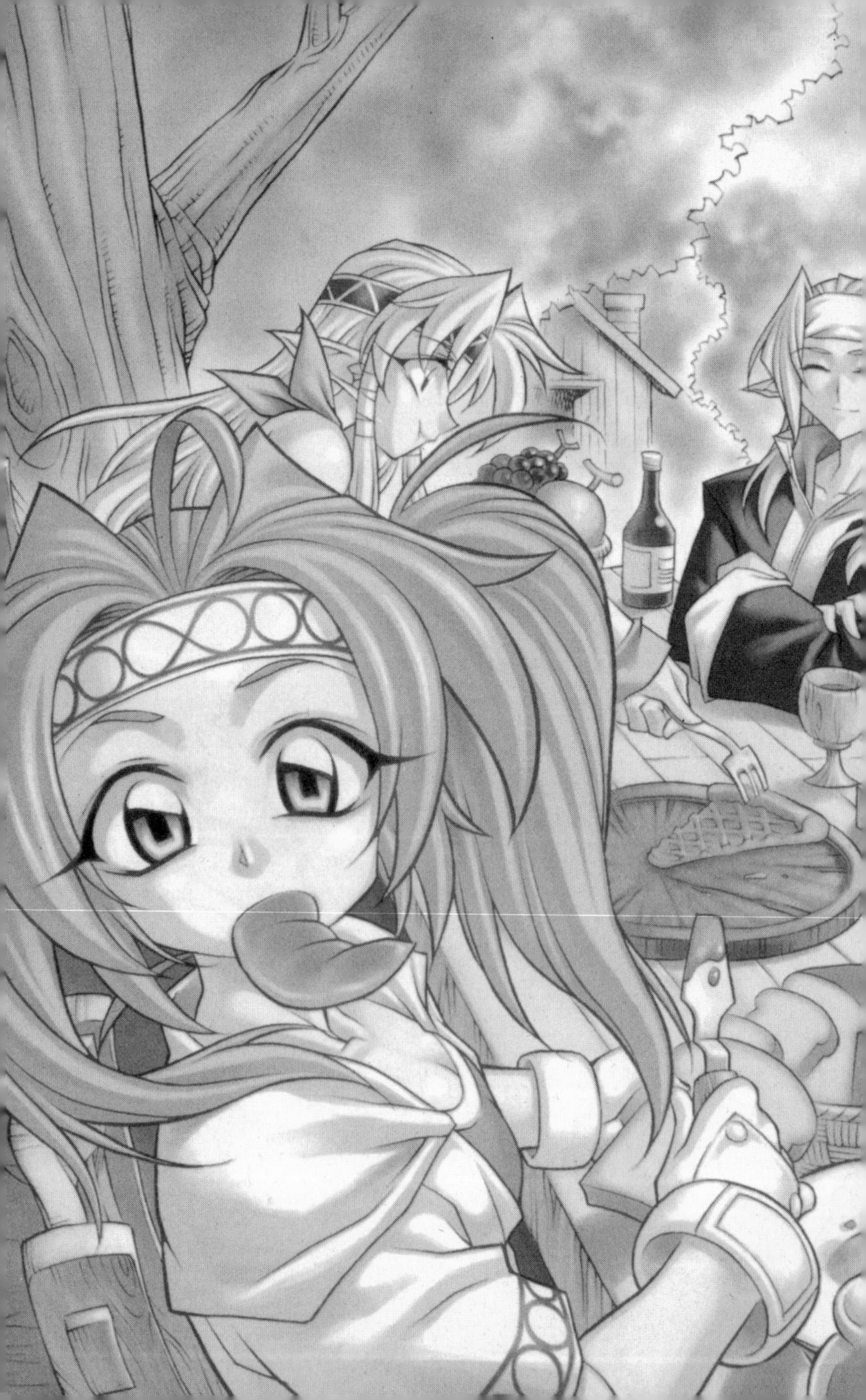

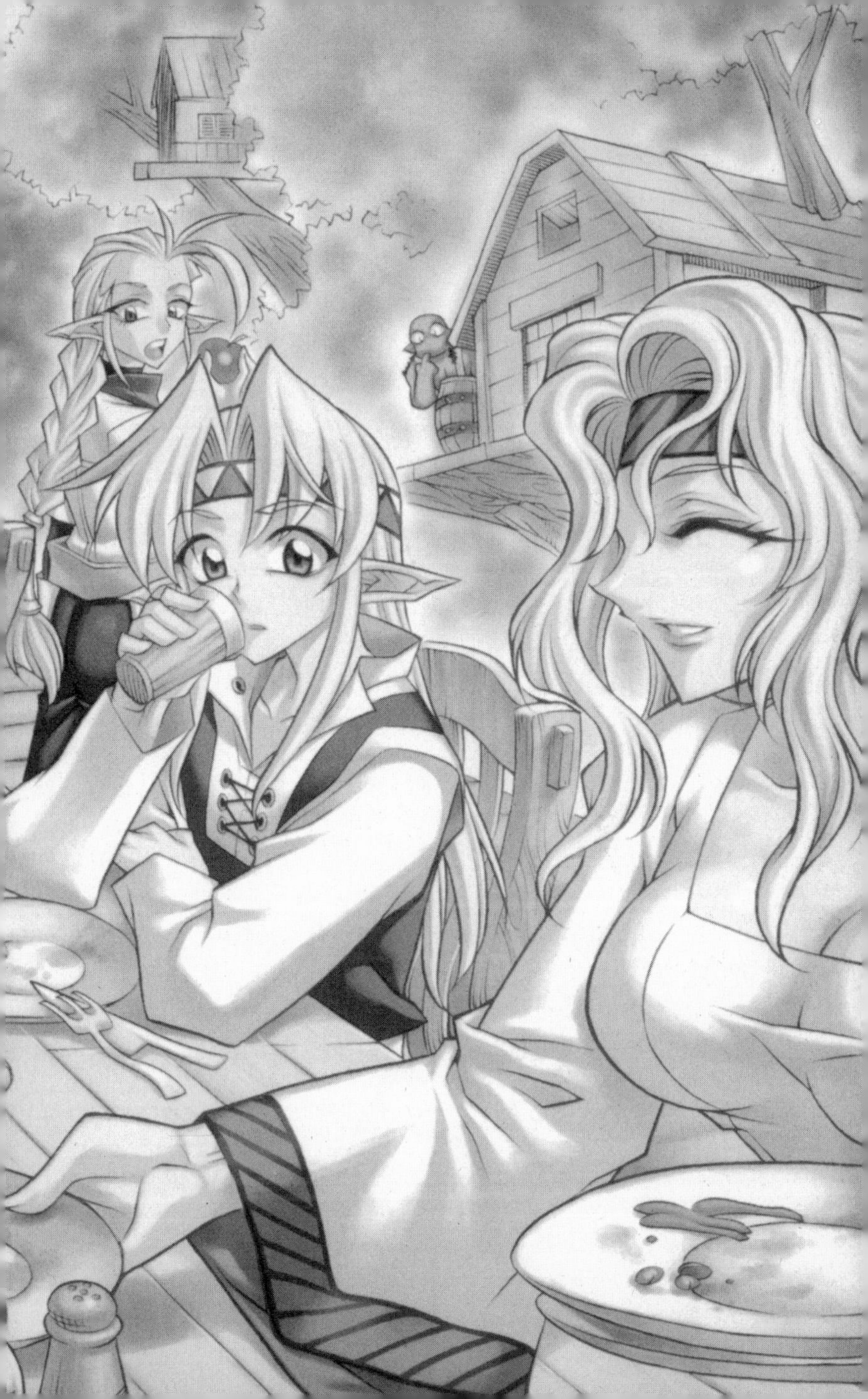

PhD: Phantasy Degree Vol. 6
Created by Son Hee-Joon

Translation - Sarah Kim
English Adaptation - Aaron Sparrow
Retouch and Lettering - Lucas Rivera and Erika Terriquez
Production Artist - Fawn Lau
Cover Design - Seth Cable

Editor - Paul Morrissey
Digital Imaging Manager - Chris Buford
Managing Editor - Lindsey Johnston
VP of Production - Ron Klamert
Editor-In-Chief - Rob Tokar
Publisher - Mike Kiley
President and C.O.O. - John Parker
C.E.O. and Chief Creative Officer - Stuart Levy

A  Manga

TOKYOPOP Inc.
5900 Wilshire Blvd. Suite 2000
Los Angeles, CA 90036

E-mail: info@TOKYOPOP.com
Come visit us online at www.TOKYOPOP.com

ISBN: 1-59532-324-4

First TOKYOPOP printing: May 2006
10 9 8 7 6 5 4 3 2 1
Printed in the USA

PHANTASY DEGREE

Volume 6

By
SON HEE-JOON

HAMBURG // LONDON // LOS ANGELES // TOKYO

Previously in...

PhD

PHANTASY DEGREE

A spunky, ring-wearing girl named Sang searches for the Demon School Hades...and a legendary ring contained within its walls. When she encounters a group of misfit monsters that are playing hooky from school, her hunt is over. They reluctantly take her to Hades, where Sang meets Notra, a female monster who's wearing a very special ring! But before Sang can snatch Notra's ring, a group of humans from the Madosa Guild attack the school! A deadly battle ensues, and Sang fights alongside her new beastly buddies...

The body count rises as the Madosa Guild continues its ruthless attack on the Demon School Hades. During the conflict, the power of Sang's rings is revealed: Not only does her jewelry make her stronger, but they can change the gender of their wearer. In Sang's case, when she takes off her rings, she becomes a muscular and powerful man! Holy gender-bender defender!

Despite a valiant effort by the denizens of the Demon School, the Madosa Guild emerges victorious. In the aftermath of all the fighting, the Demon School students bury their dead and search for a faraway land rumored to be inhabited by creatures like them. Sang, meanwhile, begins another adventure.

In a dark forest, Sang meets a girl swordmaster named Chun-Lang. A ring on Chun-Lang's finger piques Sang's curiosity. Lost, the two try to make their way out of the woods and come across Alcan, a villainous warlock from the Madosa Guild, who has unleashed a behemoth named Gigantes. With the aid of forest elves Shumiro and Hexion, Sang foils Alcan's plan...but not without a price: Sang awakens after an epic battle to shockingly discover that she has a bad case of amnesia!

Now nicknamed "Limbo," Sang recuperates in Hexion's village. As Sang struggles to remember her identity, she joins Hexion in search of a young girl named Iris who has gone missing in the troll-infested Forest of the Ants! Along the way, they encounter trolls, students from the Magic Academy Athena...and old friends Dev and Notra! Will they be able to help Sang recover her lost memories?

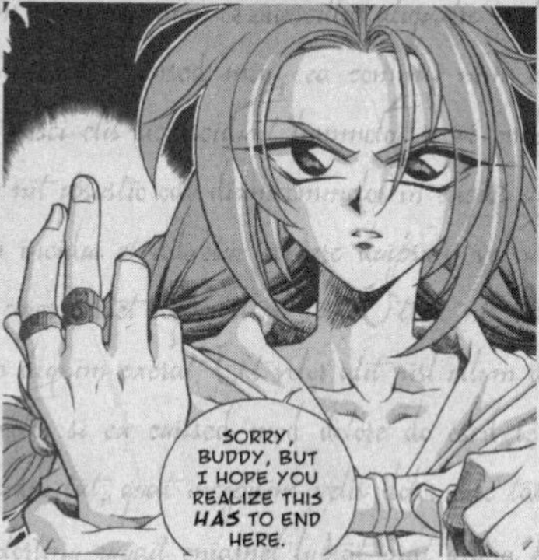
SORRY, BUDDY, BUT I HOPE YOU REALIZE THIS HAS TO END HERE.

Sang as a woman

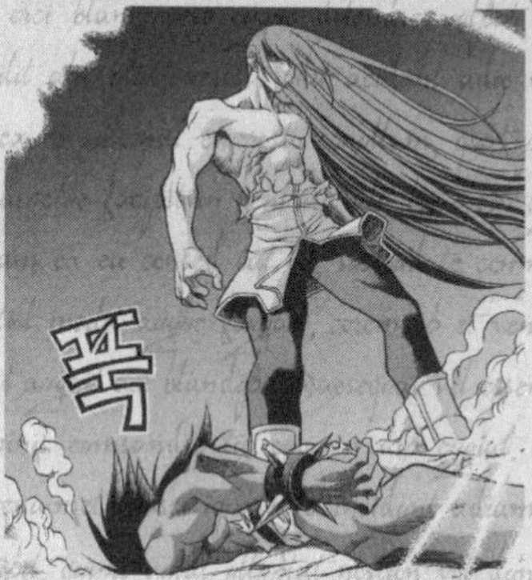

Sang as a man

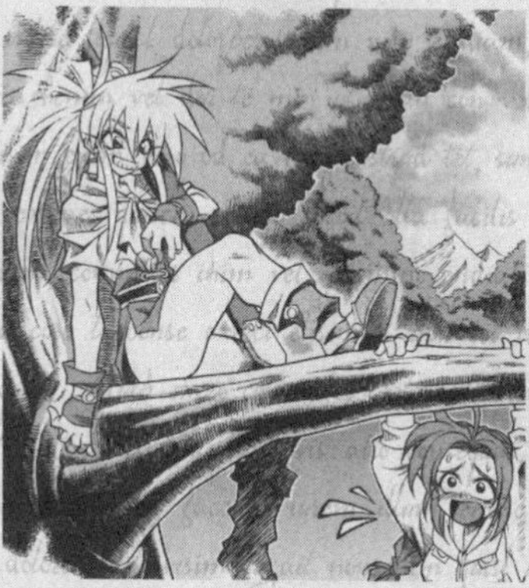

Chun-Lang & Sang

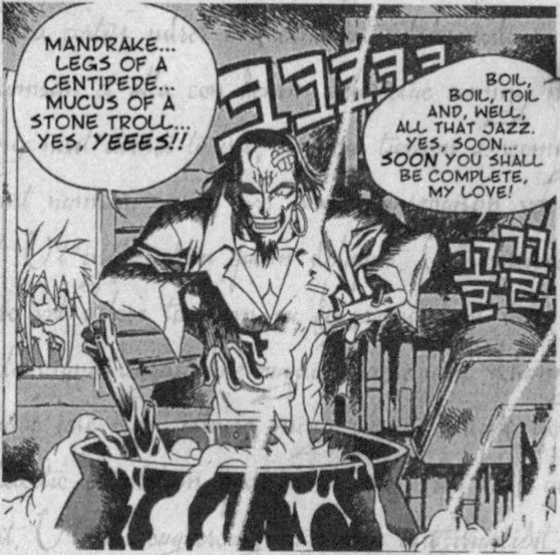
MANDRAKE... LEGS OF A CENTIPEDE... MUCUS OF A STONE TROLL... YES, YEEES!!
BOIL, BOIL, TOIL AND, WELL, ALL THAT JAZZ. YES, SOON... SOON YOU SHALL BE COMPLETE, MY LOVE!

Alcan

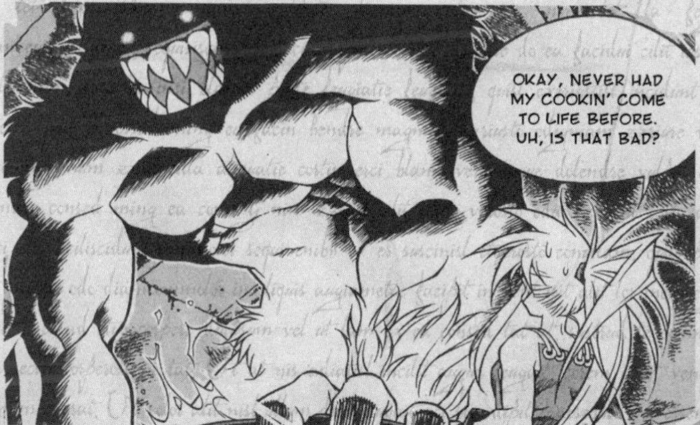
OKAY, NEVER HAD MY COOKIN' COME TO LIFE BEFORE. UH, IS THAT BAD?

Gigantes

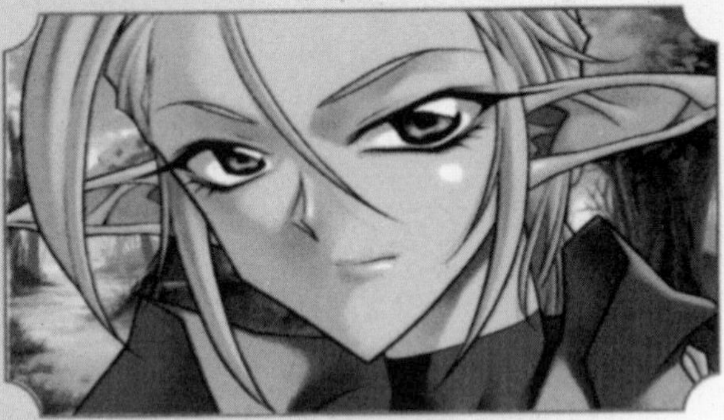

Table of Contents

Master Tower

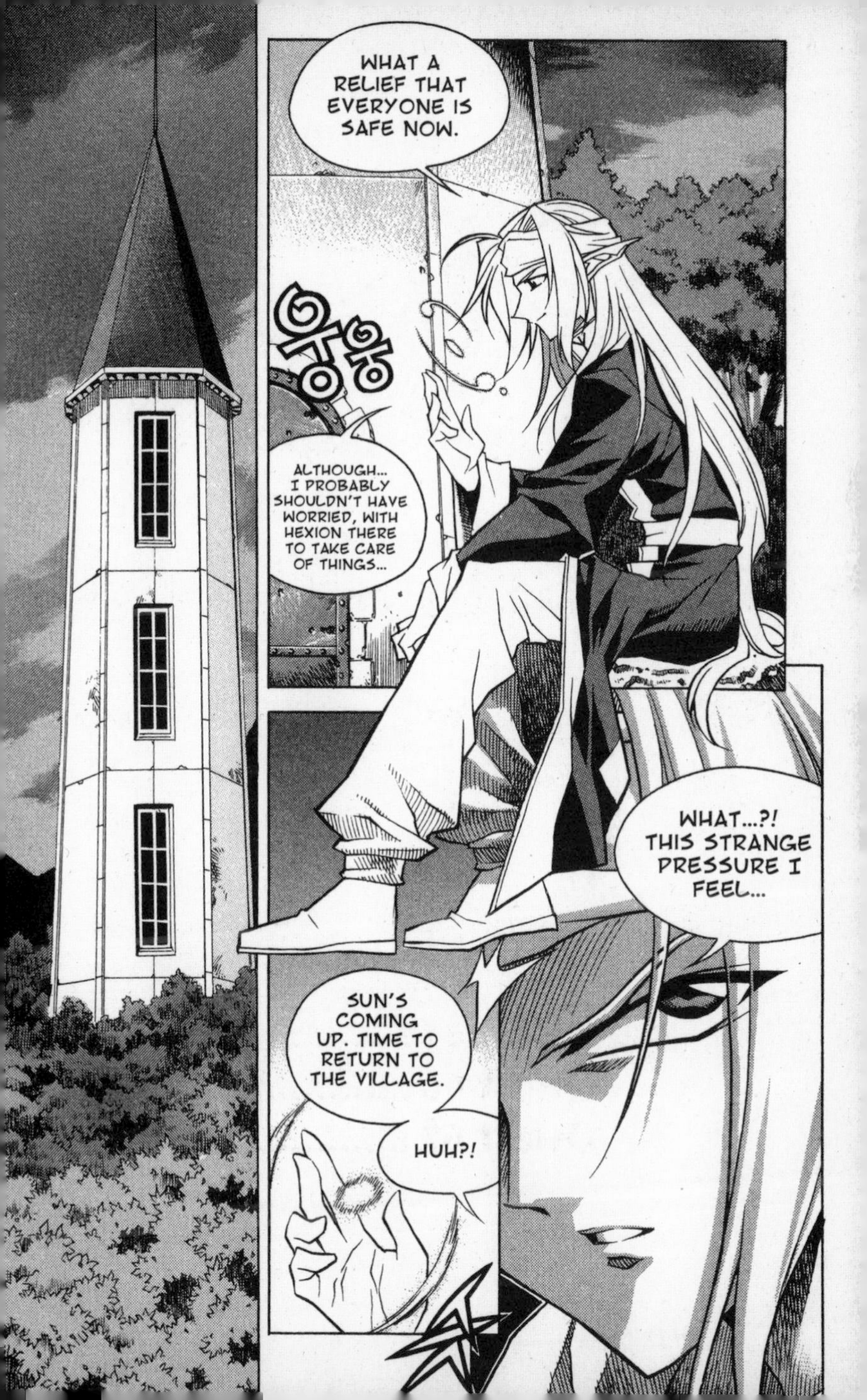
WHAT A RELIEF THAT EVERYONE IS SAFE NOW.
ALTHOUGH... I PROBABLY SHOULDN'T HAVE WORRIED, WITH HEXION THERE TO TAKE CARE OF THINGS...
WHAT...?! THIS STRANGE PRESSURE I FEEL...
SUN'S COMING UP. TIME TO RETURN TO THE VILLAGE.
HUH?!

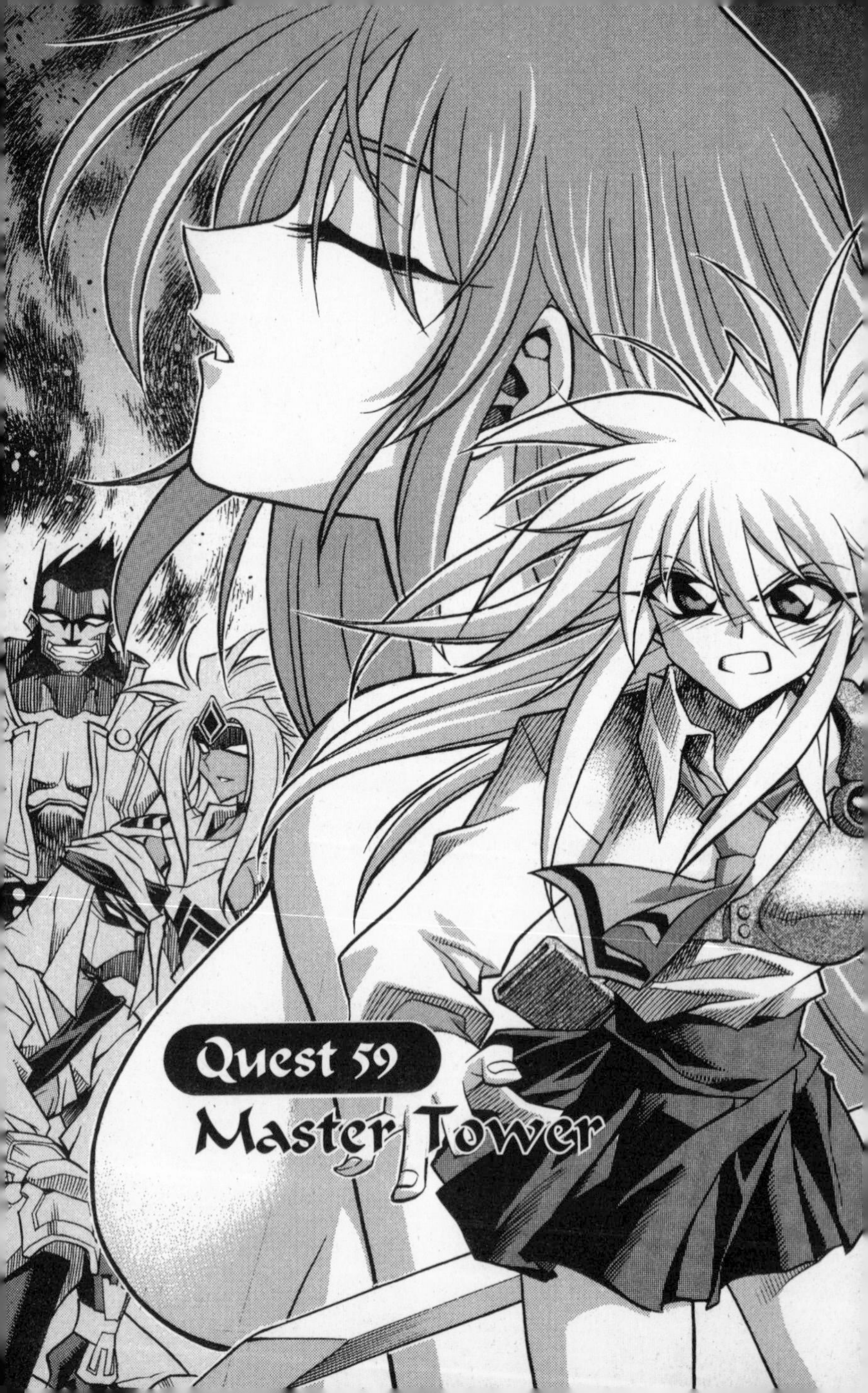
Quest 59
Master Tower

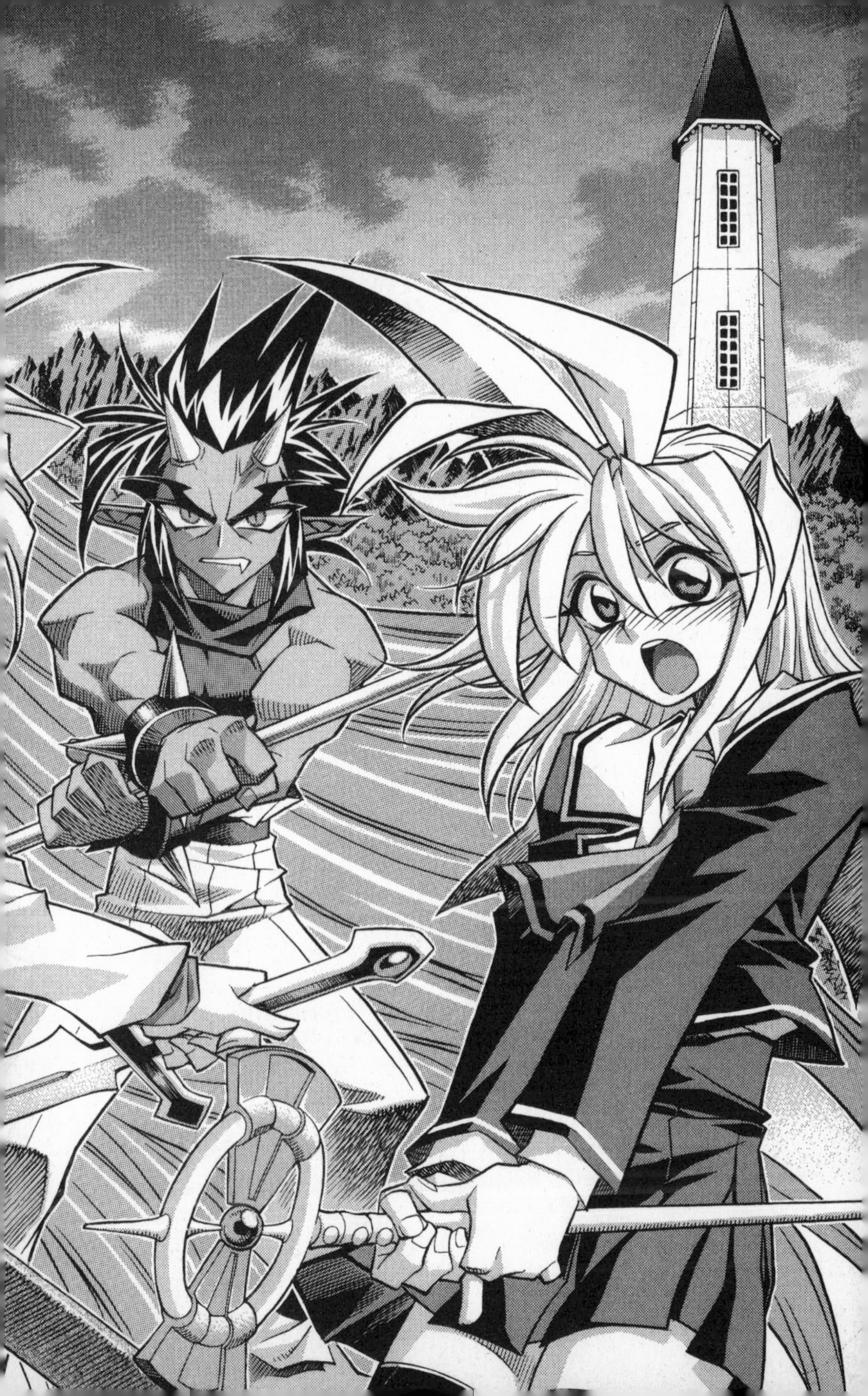

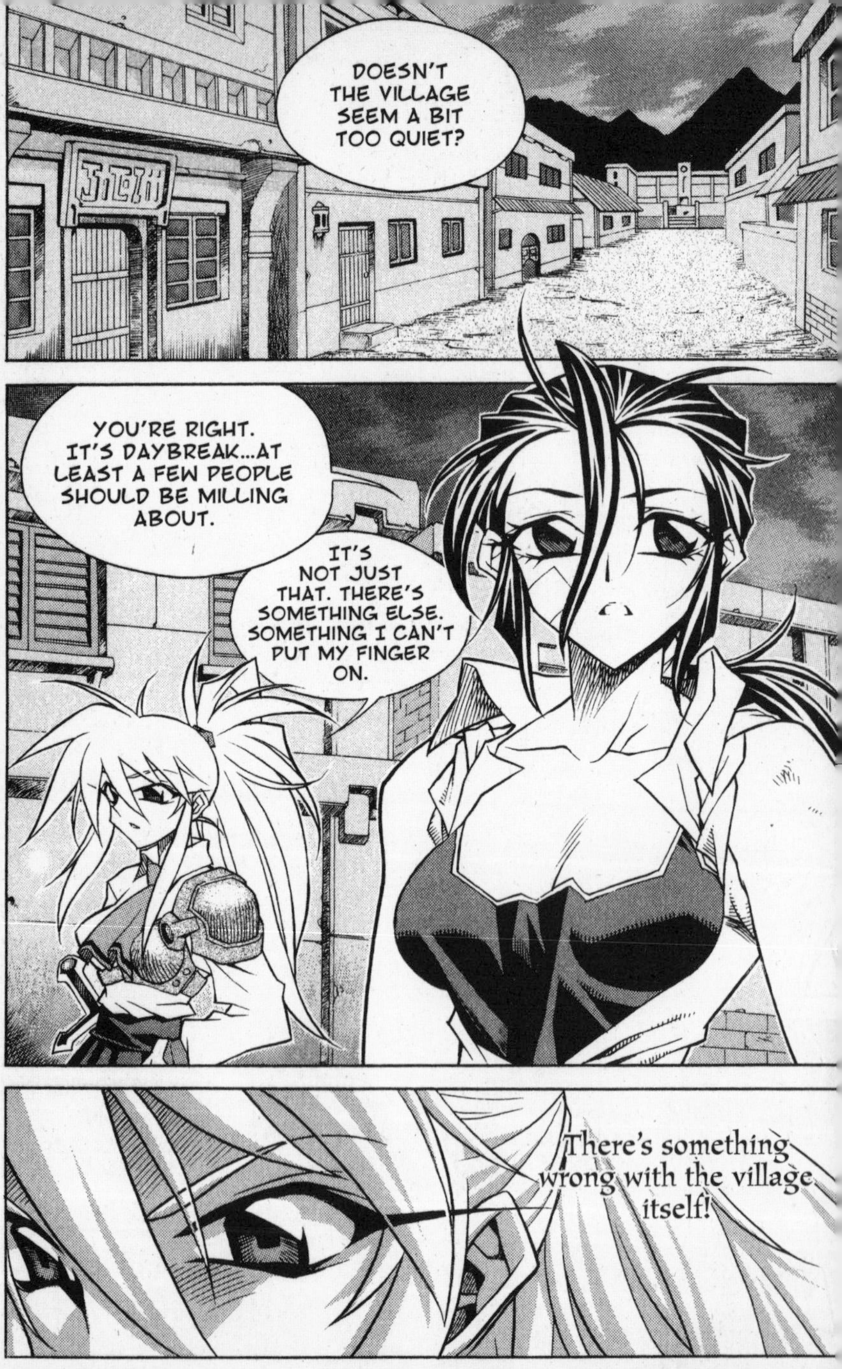
DOESN'T THE VILLAGE SEEM A BIT TOO QUIET?
YOU'RE RIGHT. IT'S DAYBREAK...AT LEAST A FEW PEOPLE SHOULD BE MILLING ABOUT.
IT'S NOT JUST THAT. THERE'S SOMETHING ELSE. SOMETHING I CAN'T PUT MY FINGER ON.
There's something wrong with the village itself!

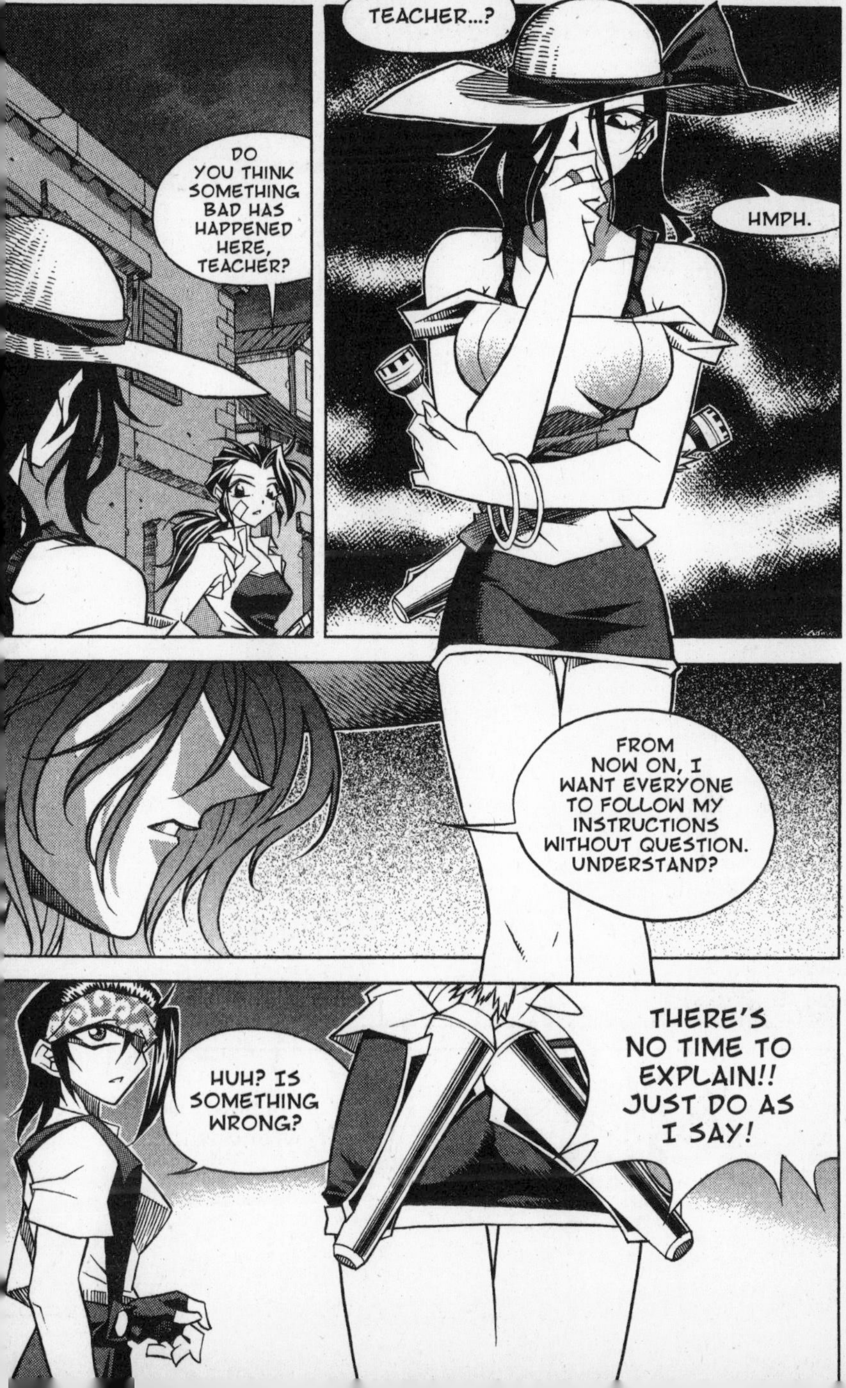

DO YOU THINK SOMETHING BAD HAS HAPPENED HERE, TEACHER?
TEACHER...?
HMPH.
FROM NOW ON, I WANT EVERYONE TO FOLLOW MY INSTRUCTIONS WITHOUT QUESTION. UNDERSTAND?
HUH? IS SOMETHING WRONG?
THERE'S NO TIME TO EXPLAIN!! JUST DO AS I SAY!

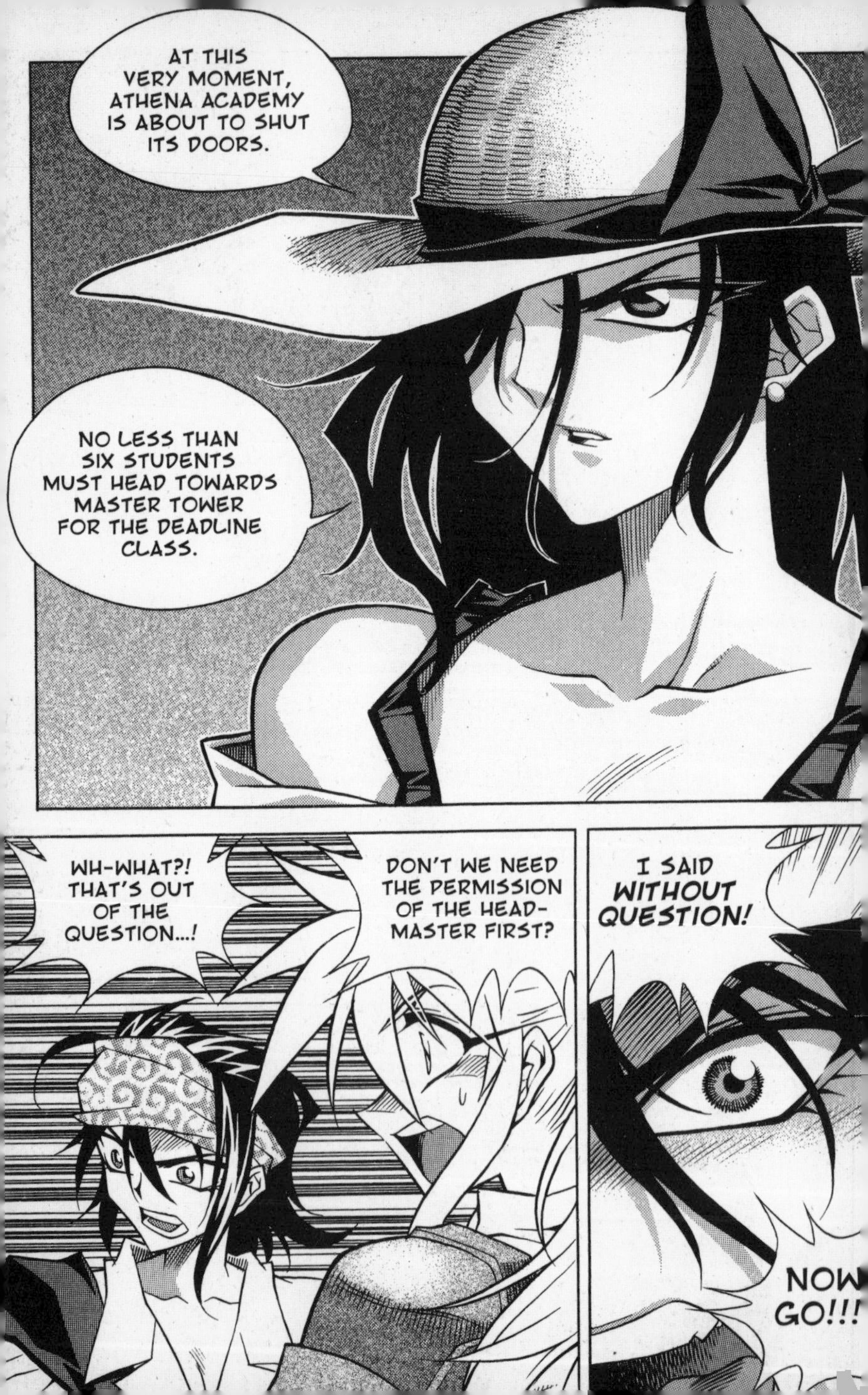
AT THIS VERY MOMENT, ATHENA ACADEMY IS ABOUT TO SHUT ITS DOORS.
NO LESS THAN SIX STUDENTS MUST HEAD TOWARDS MASTER TOWER FOR THE DEADLINE CLASS.
WH-WHAT?! THAT'S OUT OF THE QUESTION...!
DON'T WE NEED THE PERMISSION OF THE HEAD-MASTER FIRST?
I SAID WITHOUT QUESTION!
NOW GO!!!

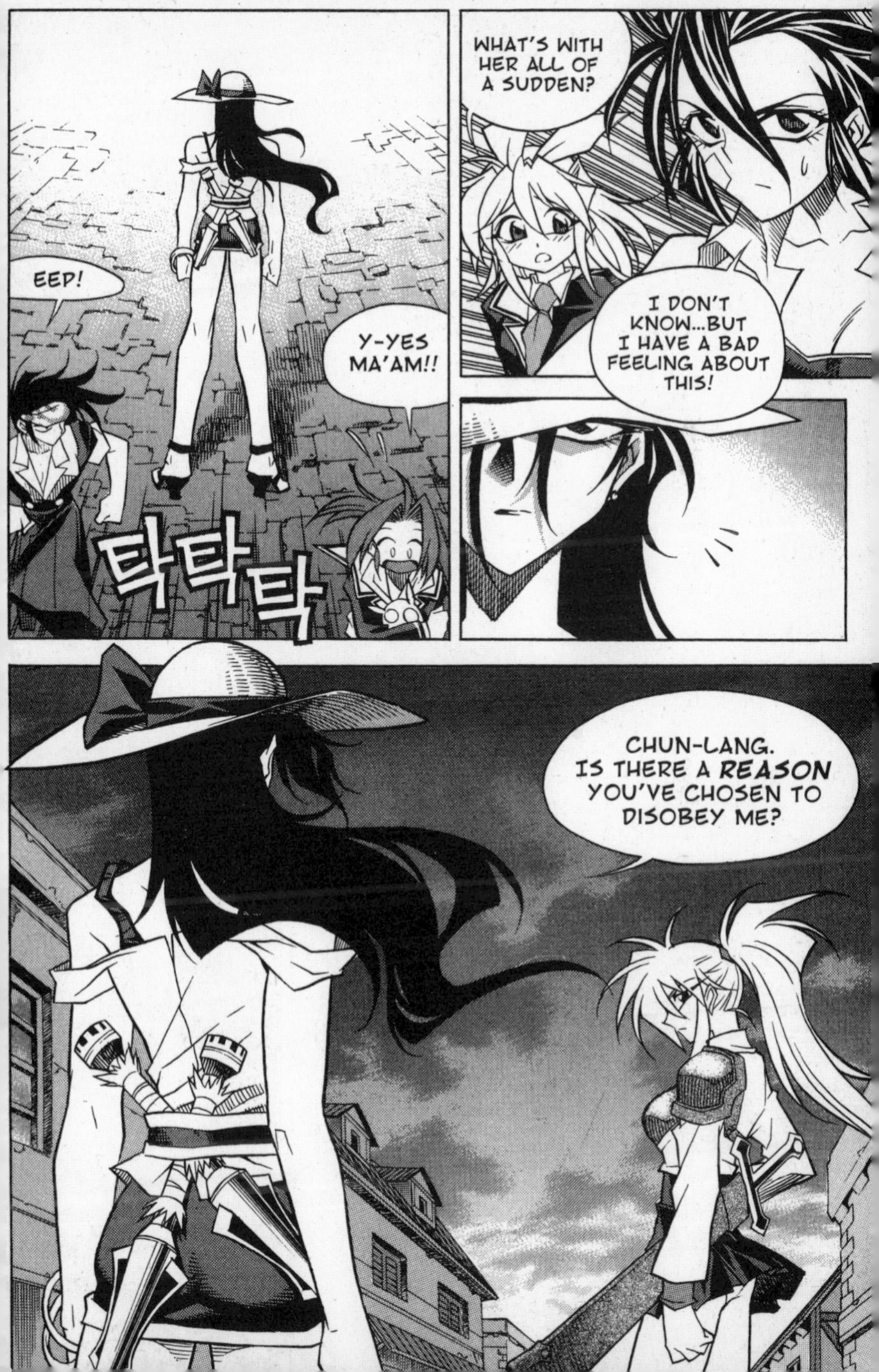
EEP!
Y-YES MA'AM!!
타타타
WHAT'S WITH HER ALL OF A SUDDEN?
I DON'T KNOW...BUT I HAVE A BAD FEELING ABOUT THIS!
CHUN-LANG. IS THERE A *REASON* YOU'VE CHOSEN TO DISOBEY ME?

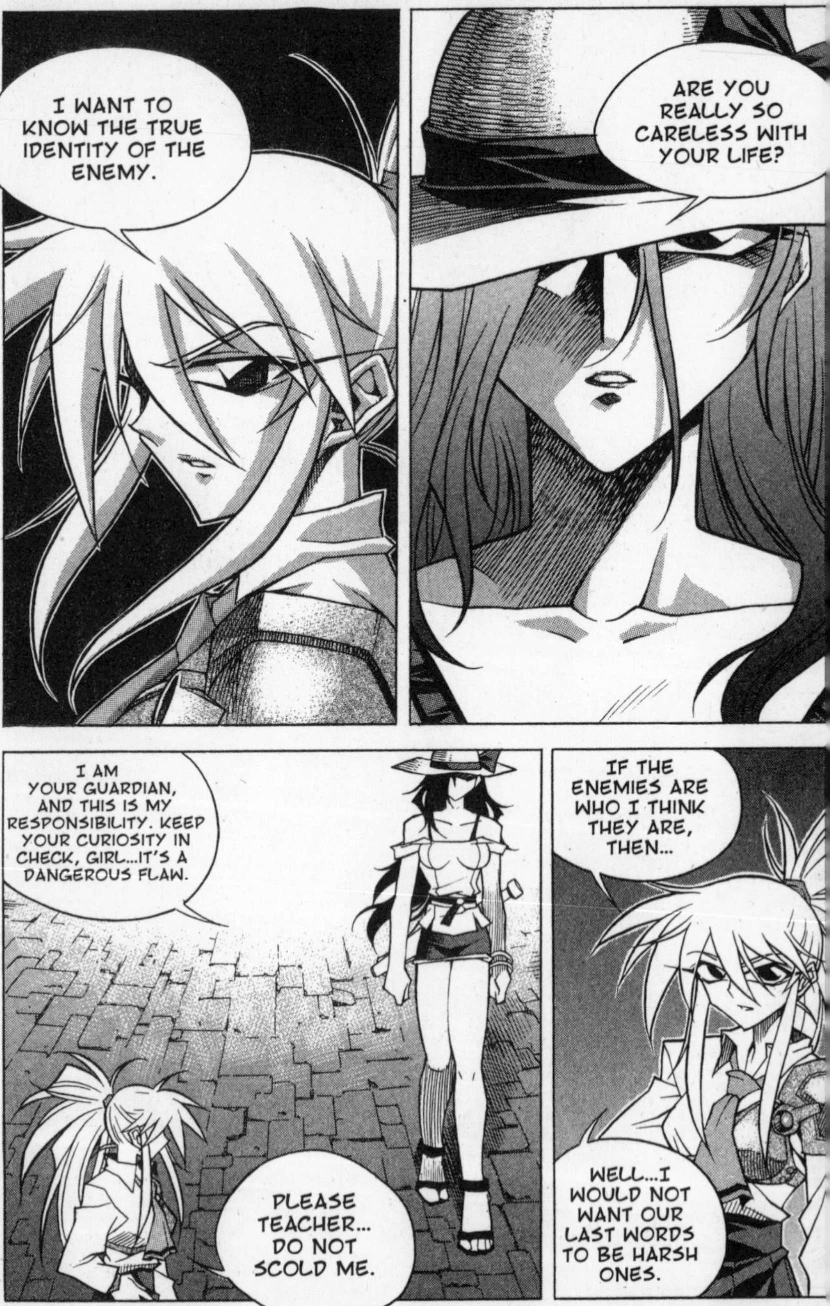
I WANT TO KNOW THE TRUE IDENTITY OF THE ENEMY.
ARE YOU REALLY SO CARELESS WITH YOUR LIFE?
I AM YOUR GUARDIAN, AND THIS IS MY RESPONSIBILITY. KEEP YOUR CURIOSITY IN CHECK, GIRL...IT'S A DANGEROUS FLAW.
PLEASE TEACHER... DO NOT SCOLD ME.
IF THE ENEMIES ARE WHO I THINK THEY ARE, THEN...
WELL...I WOULD NOT WANT OUR LAST WORDS TO BE HARSH ONES.

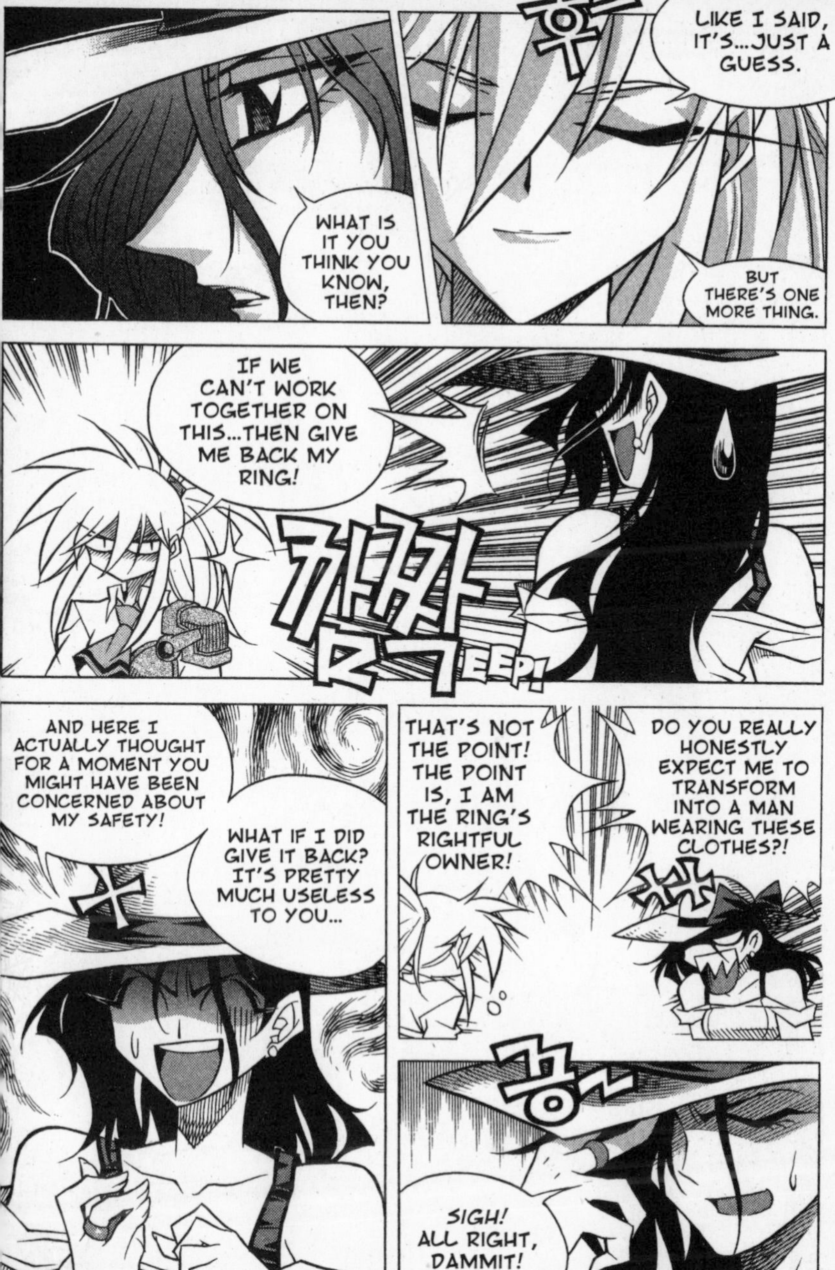
WHAT IS IT YOU THINK YOU KNOW, THEN?
LIKE I SAID, IT'S...JUST A GUESS.
BUT THERE'S ONE MORE THING.
IF WE CAN'T WORK TOGETHER ON THIS...THEN GIVE ME BACK MY RING!
EEP!
AND HERE I ACTUALLY THOUGHT FOR A MOMENT YOU MIGHT HAVE BEEN CONCERNED ABOUT MY SAFETY!
WHAT IF I DID GIVE IT BACK? IT'S PRETTY MUCH USELESS TO YOU...
THAT'S NOT THE POINT! THE POINT IS, I AM THE RING'S RIGHTFUL OWNER!
DO YOU REALLY HONESTLY EXPECT ME TO TRANSFORM INTO A MAN WEARING THESE CLOTHES?!
SIGH! ALL RIGHT, DAMMIT!

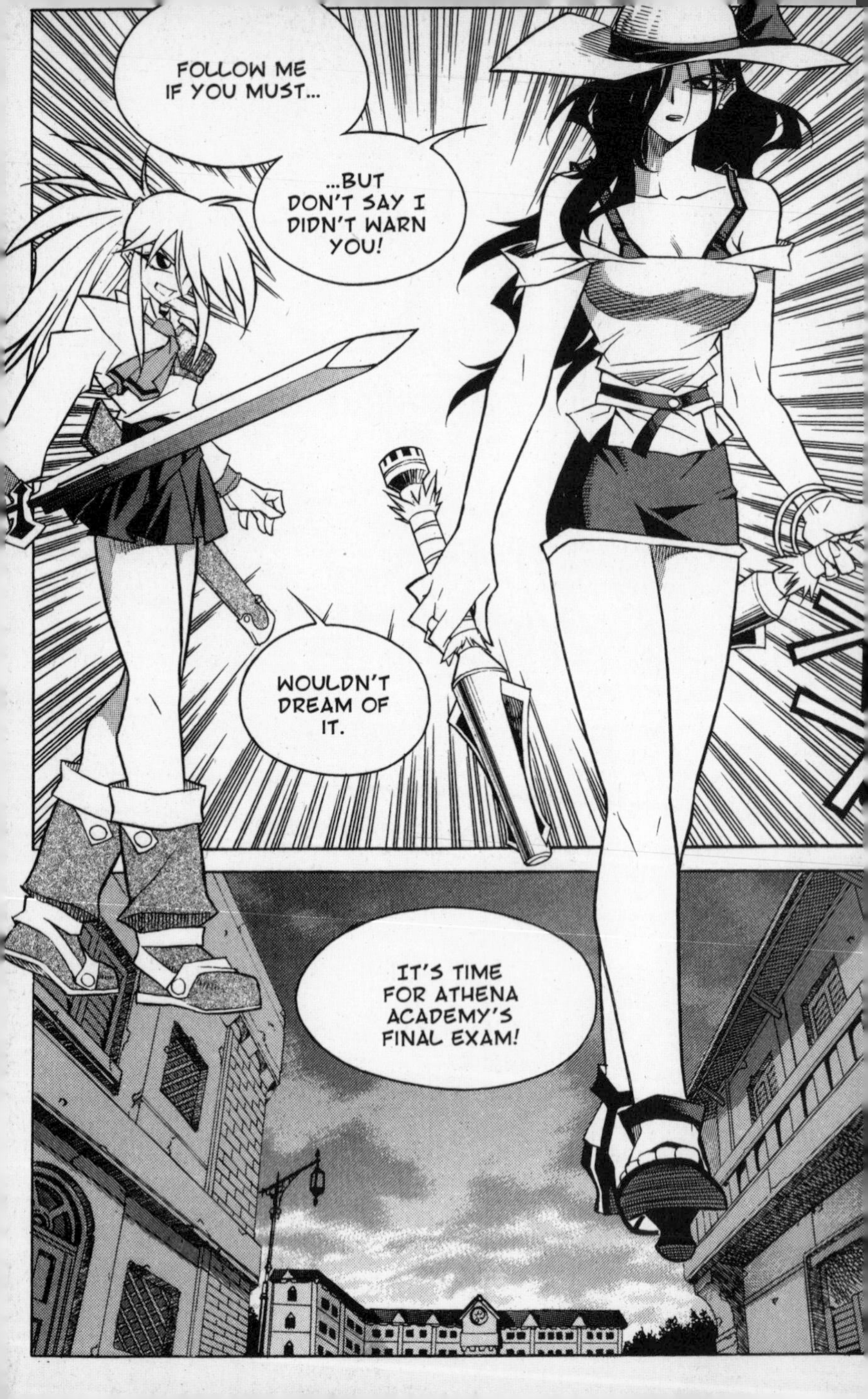
FOLLOW ME IF YOU MUST...
...BUT DON'T SAY I DIDN'T WARN YOU!
WOULDN'T DREAM OF IT.
IT'S TIME FOR ATHENA ACADEMY'S FINAL EXAM!

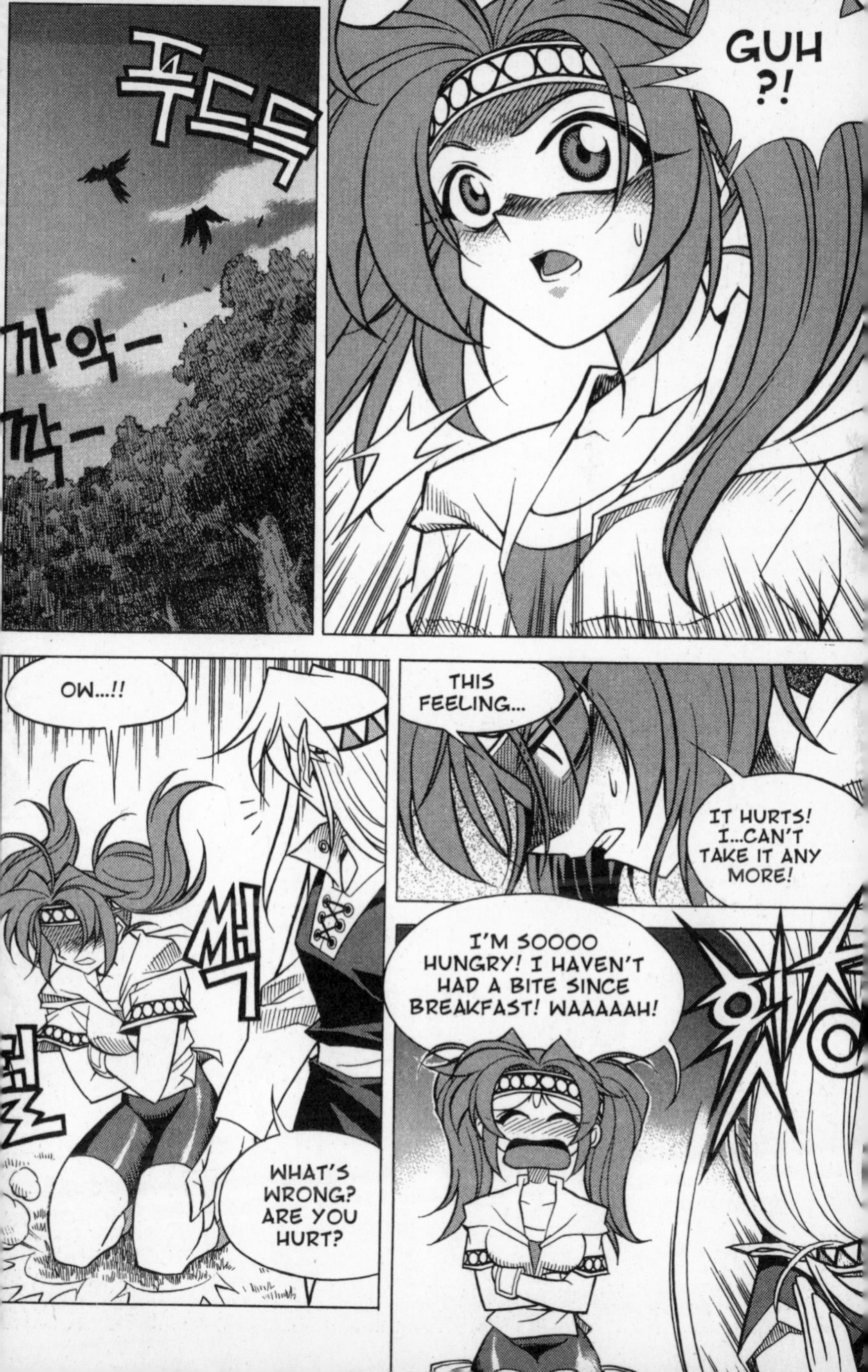

푸드득
까악—
깍—
GUH ?!
OW...!!
WHAT'S WRONG? ARE YOU HURT?
THIS FEELING...
IT HURTS! I...CAN'T TAKE IT ANY MORE!
I'M SOOOO HUNGRY! I HAVEN'T HAD A BITE SINCE BREAKFAST! WAAAAAH!

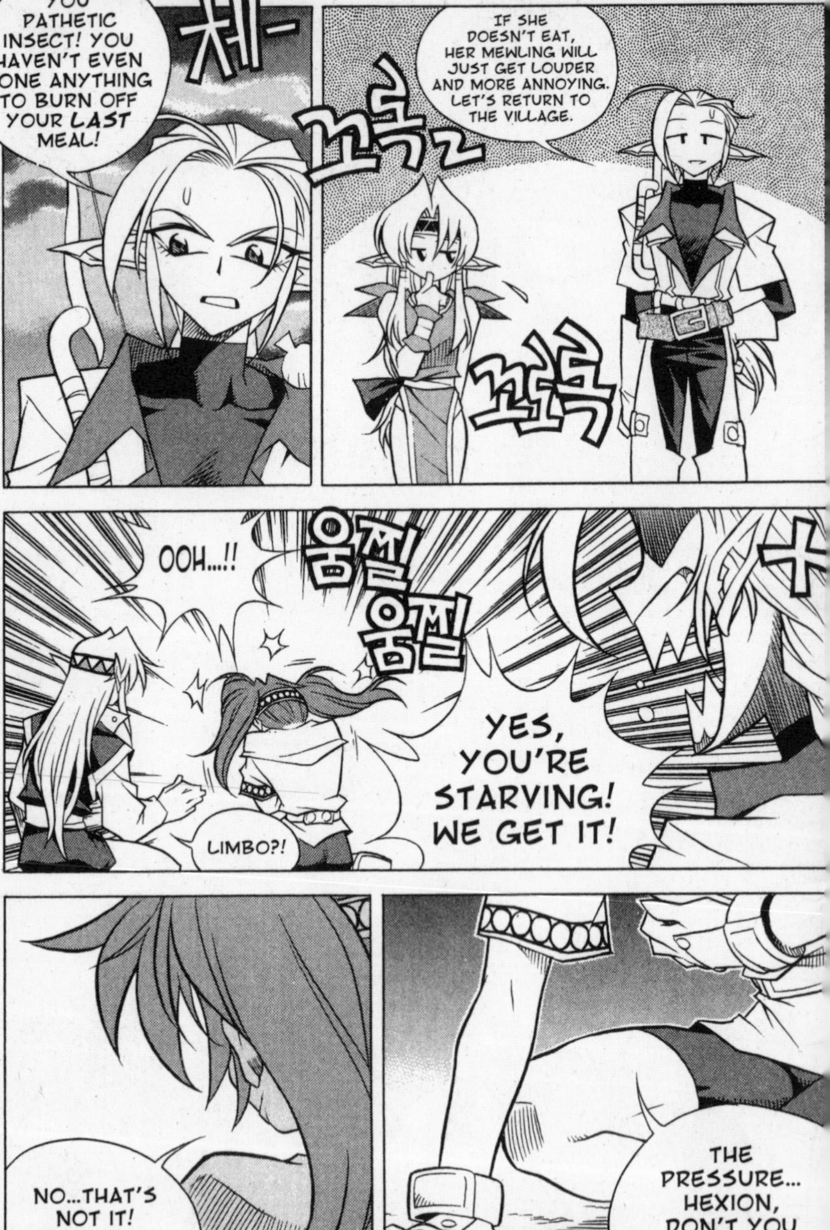

YOU PATHETIC INSECT! YOU HAVEN'T EVEN DONE ANYTHING TO BURN OFF YOUR **LAST** MEAL!
체-
IF SHE DOESN'T EAT, HER MEWLING WILL JUST GET LOUDER AND MORE ANNOYING. LET'S RETURN TO THE VILLAGE.
OOH...!!
움찔
움찔
LIMBO?!
YES, YOU'RE STARVING! WE GET IT!
NO...THAT'S NOT IT! SOMETHING ELSE...
THE PRESSURE... HEXION, DON'T YOU FEEL IT?

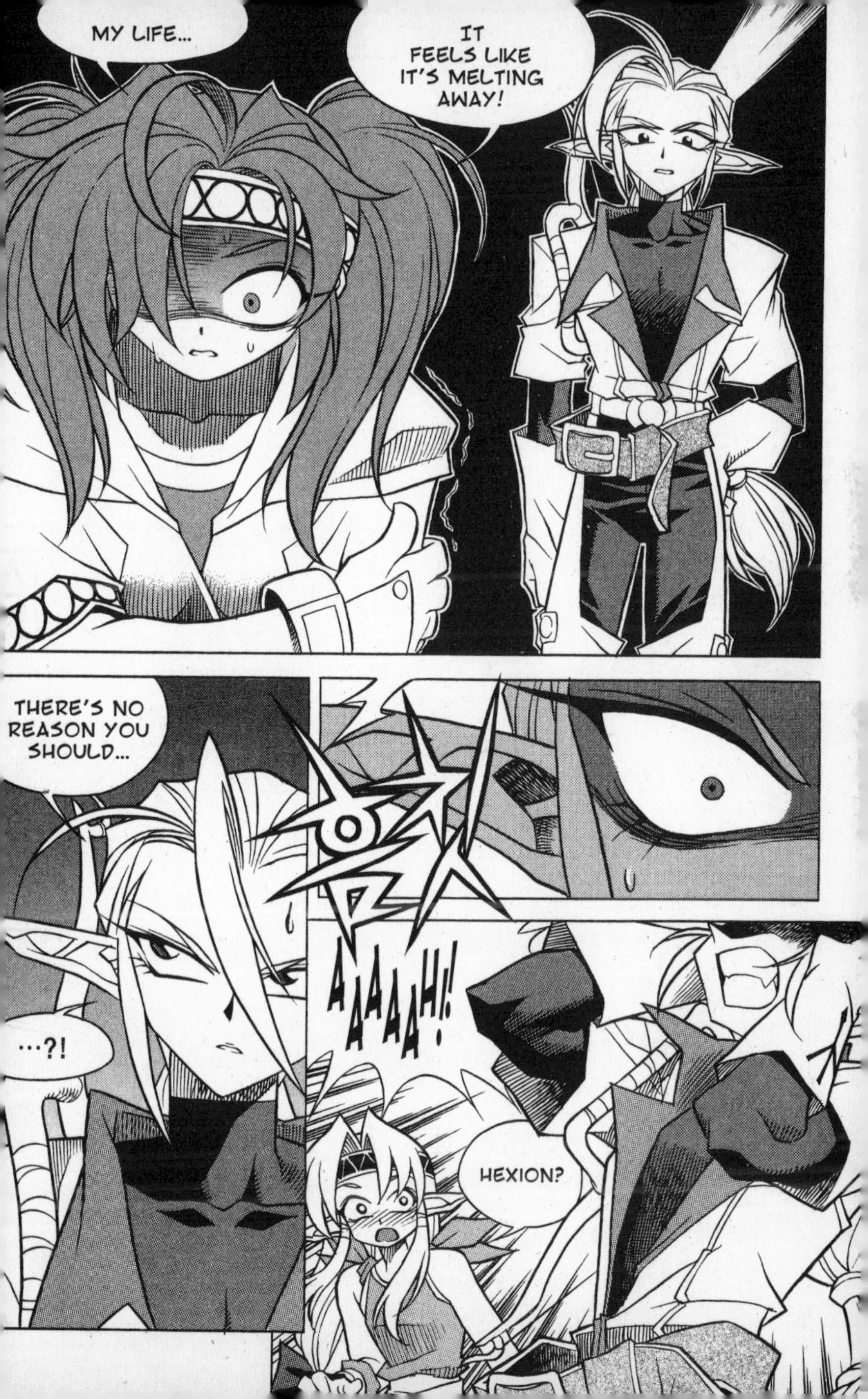
MY LIFE...
IT FEELS LIKE IT'S MELTING AWAY!
THERE'S NO REASON YOU SHOULD...
...?!
AAAAAH!!
HEXION?

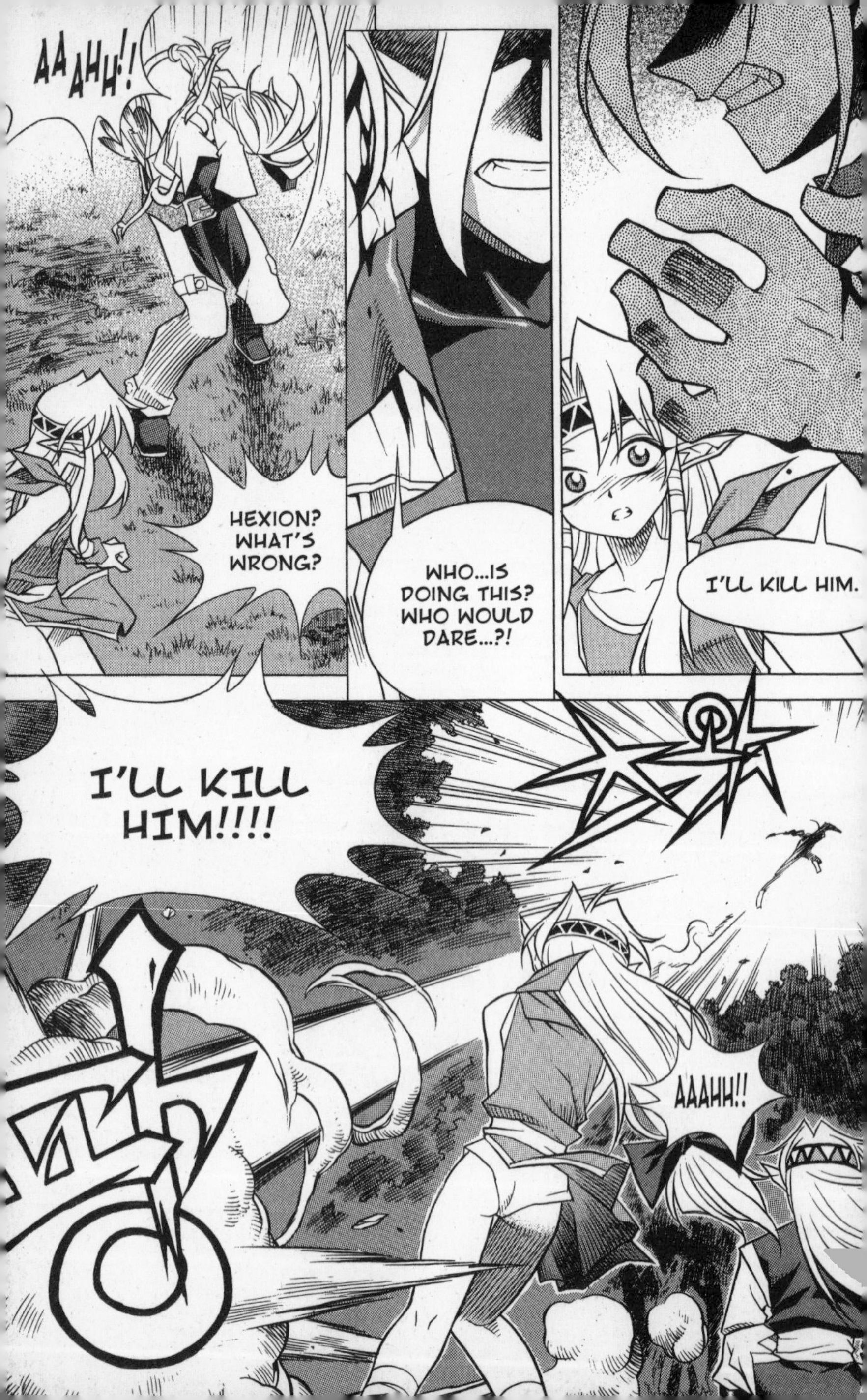
AA AHH!!
HEXION? WHAT'S WRONG?
WHO...IS DOING THIS? WHO WOULD DARE...?!
I'LL KILL HIM.
I'LL KILL HIM!!!!
AAAHH!!

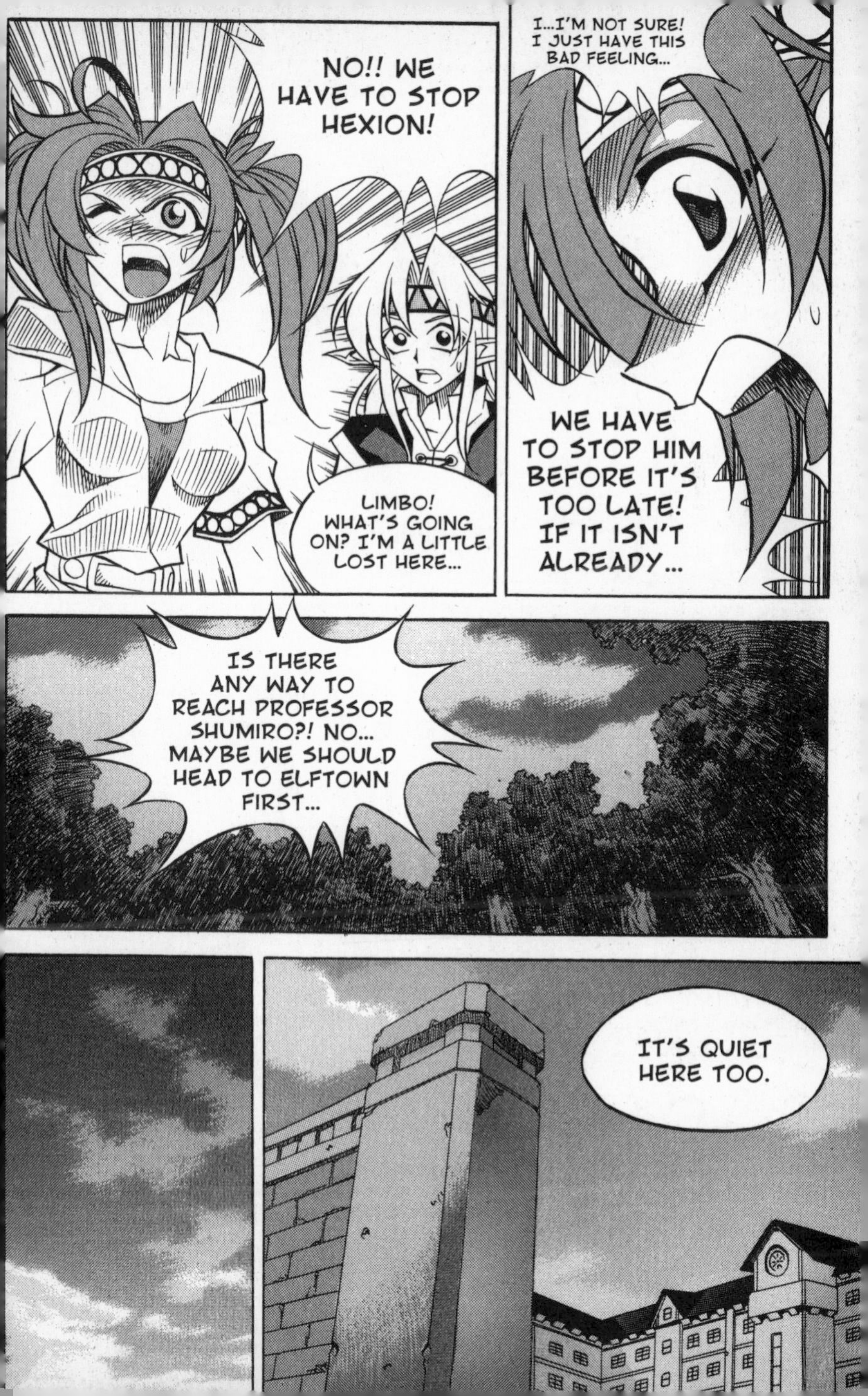
NO!! WE HAVE TO STOP HEXION!
LIMBO! WHAT'S GOING ON? I'M A LITTLE LOST HERE...
I...I'M NOT SURE! I JUST HAVE THIS BAD FEELING...
WE HAVE TO STOP HIM BEFORE IT'S TOO LATE! IF IT ISN'T ALREADY...
IS THERE ANY WAY TO REACH PROFESSOR SHUMIRO?! NO... MAYBE WE SHOULD HEAD TO ELFTOWN FIRST...
IT'S QUIET HERE TOO.

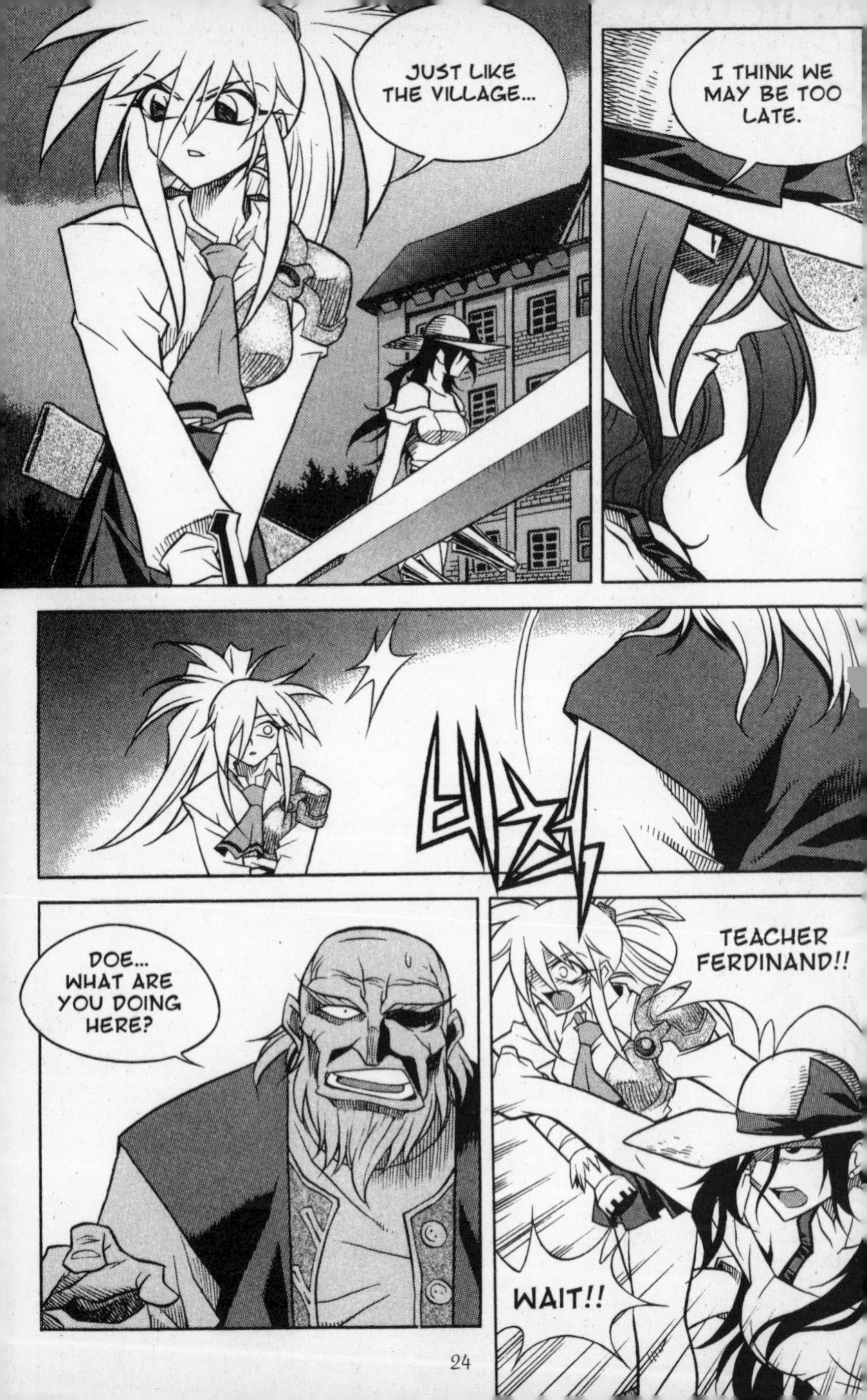
JUST LIKE THE VILLAGE...
I THINK WE MAY BE TOO LATE.
DOE... WHAT ARE YOU DOING HERE?
TEACHER FERDINAND!!
WAIT!!

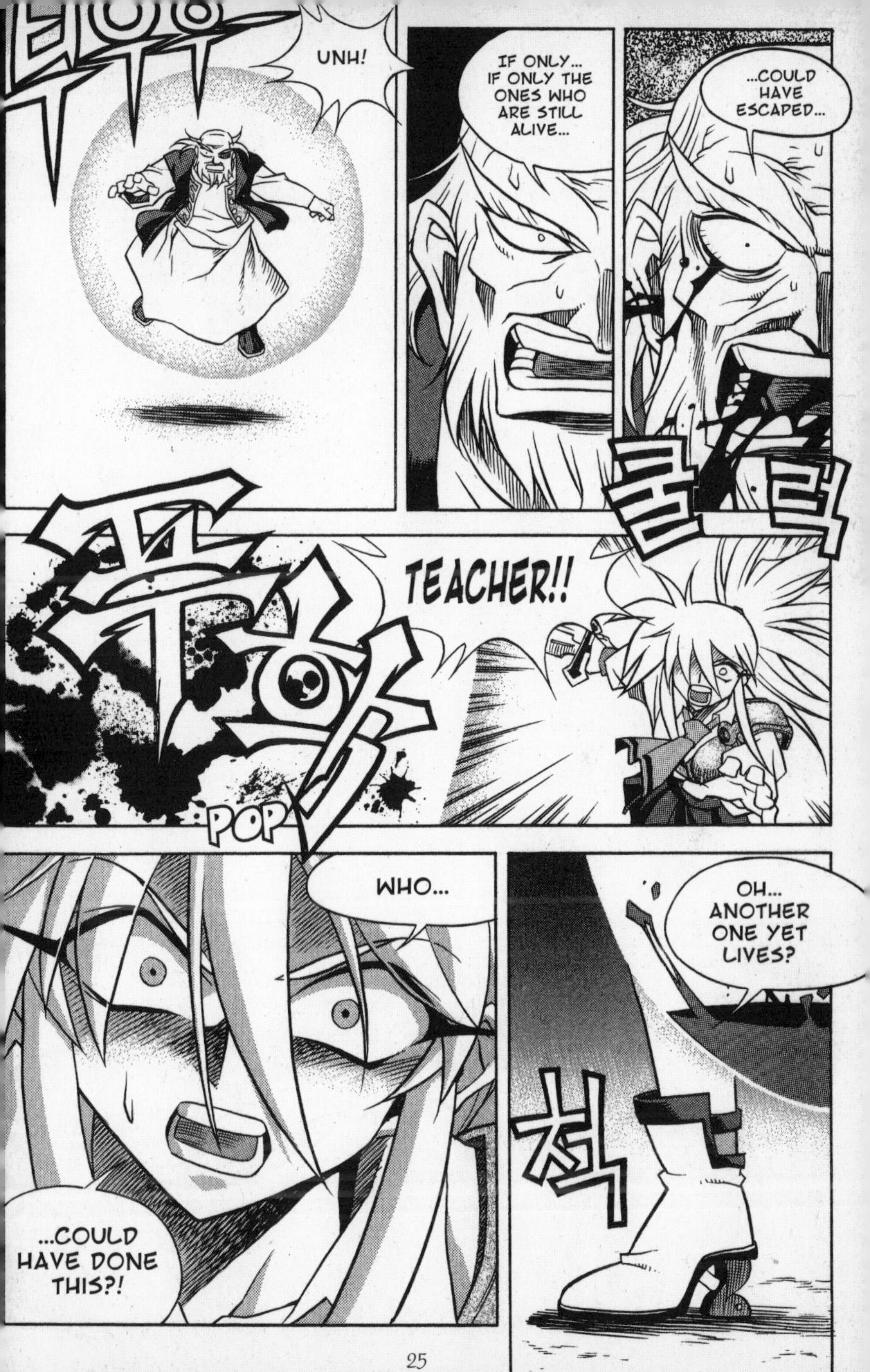
UNH!
IF ONLY... IF ONLY THE ONES WHO ARE STILL ALIVE...
...COULD HAVE ESCAPED...
POP
TEACHER!!
WHO...
...COULD HAVE DONE THIS?!
OH... ANOTHER ONE YET LIVES?
척

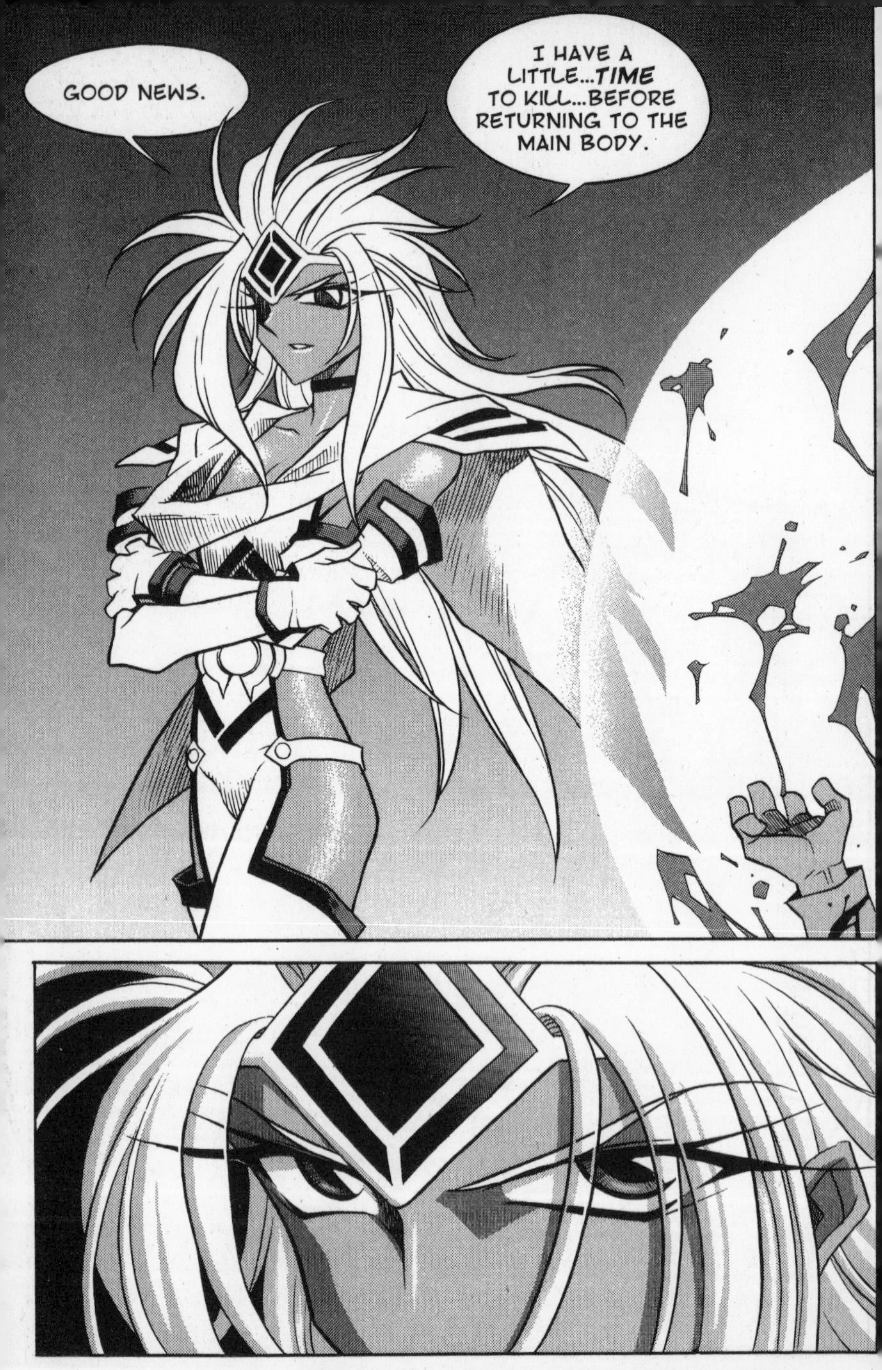
GOOD NEWS.
I HAVE A LITTLE...TIME TO KILL...BEFORE RETURNING TO THE MAIN BODY.

Quest 60

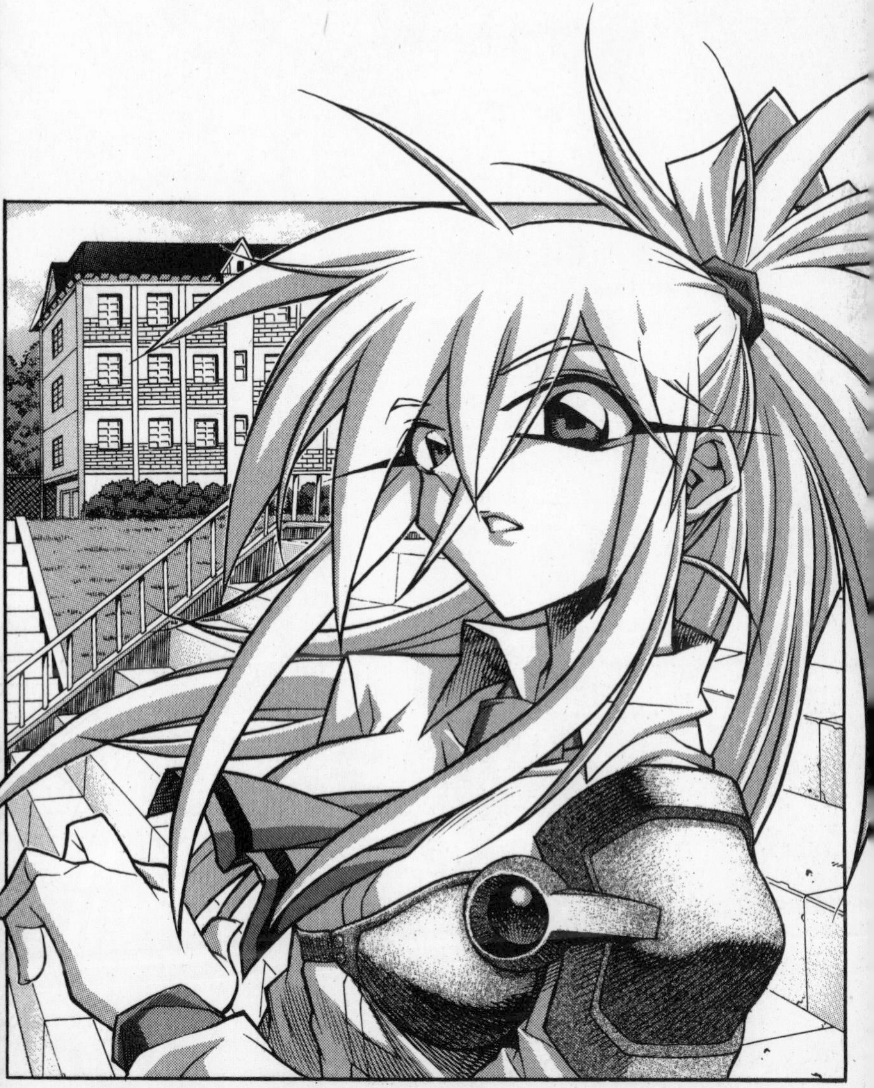

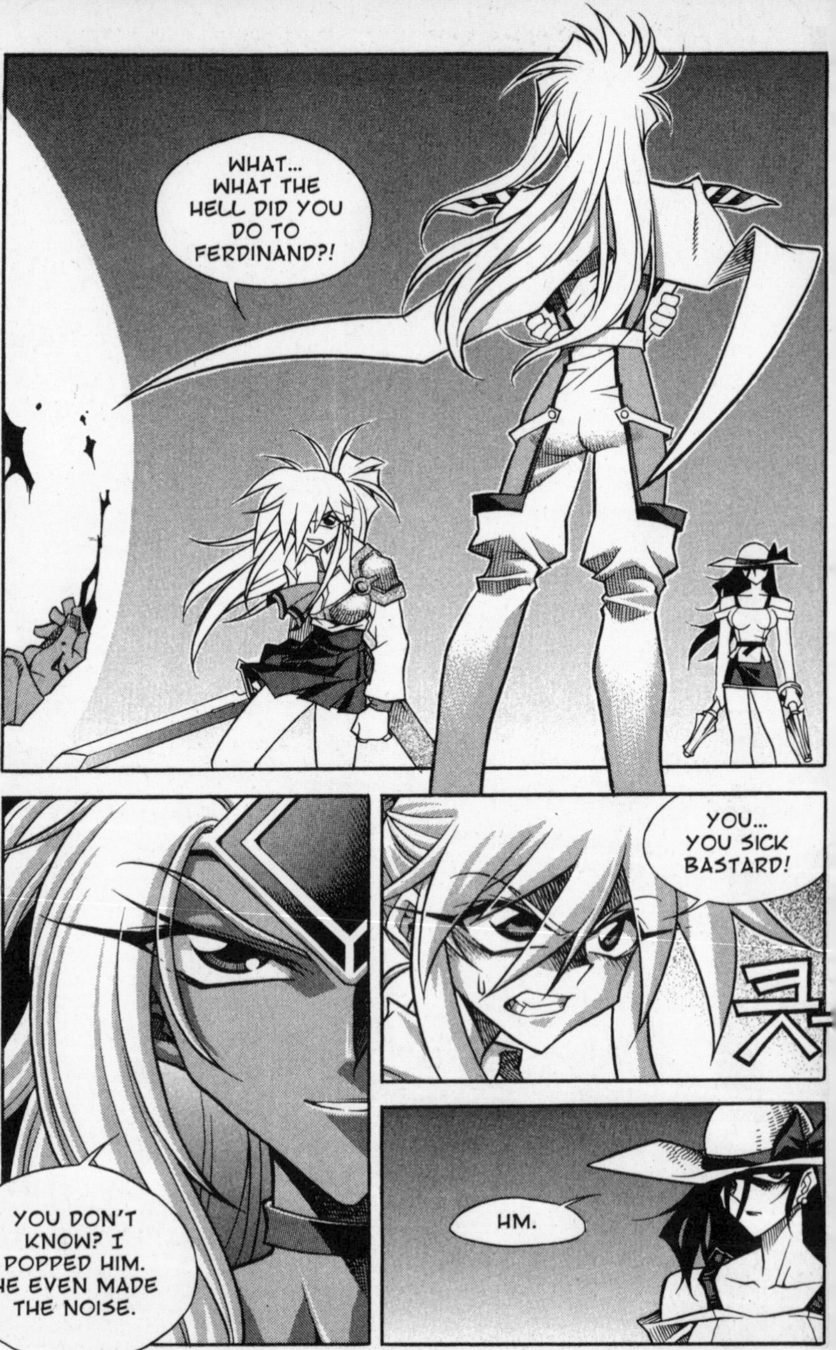
WHAT... WHAT THE HELL DID YOU DO TO FERDINAND?!
YOU DON'T KNOW? I POPPED HIM. HE EVEN MADE THE NOISE.
YOU... YOU SICK BASTARD!
HM.

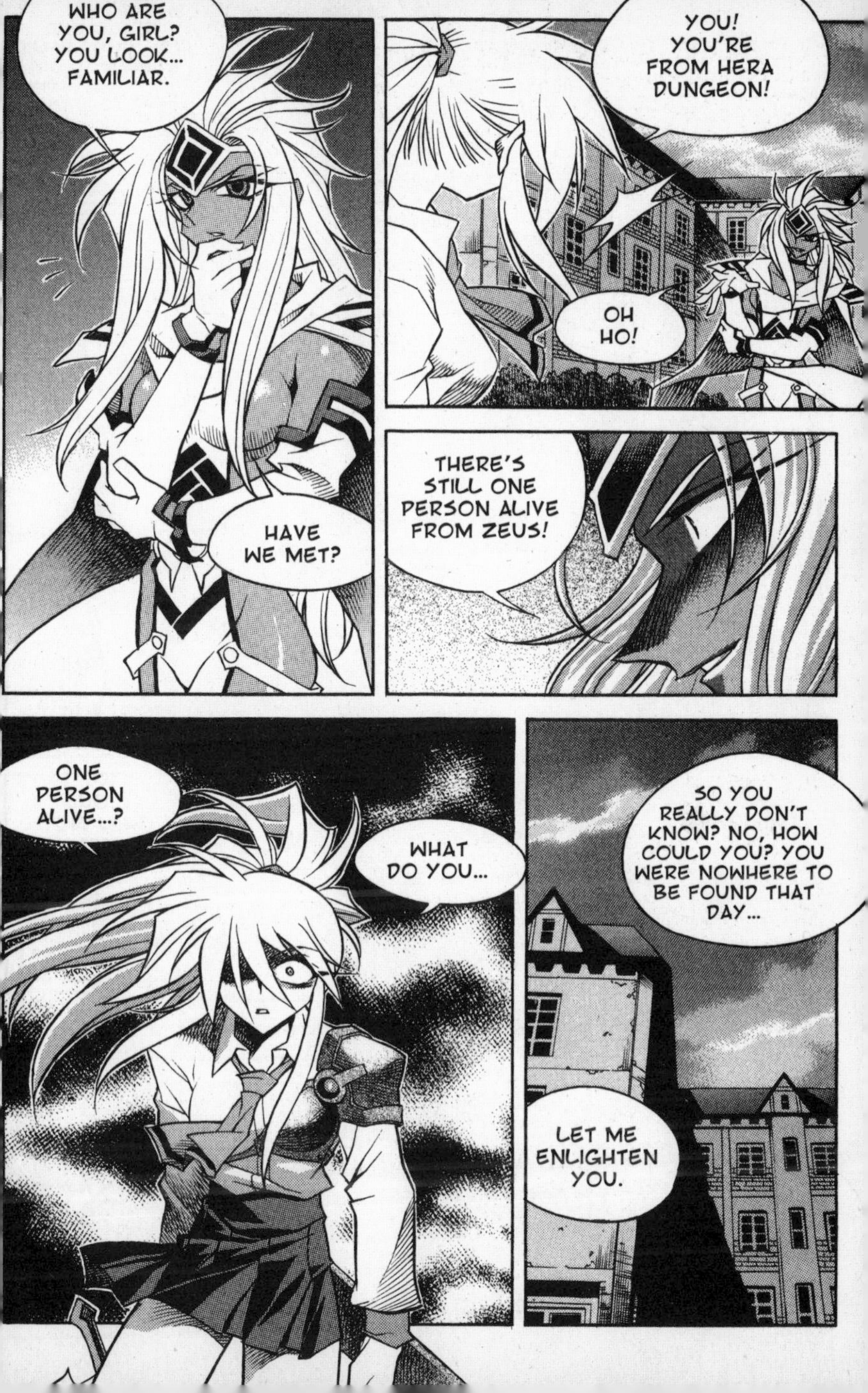
WHO ARE YOU, GIRL? YOU LOOK... FAMILIAR.
HAVE WE MET?
YOU! YOU'RE FROM HERA DUNGEON!
OH HO!
THERE'S STILL ONE PERSON ALIVE FROM ZEUS!
ONE PERSON ALIVE...?
WHAT DO YOU...
SO YOU REALLY DON'T KNOW? NO, HOW COULD YOU? YOU WERE NOWHERE TO BE FOUND THAT DAY...
LET ME ENLIGHTEN YOU.

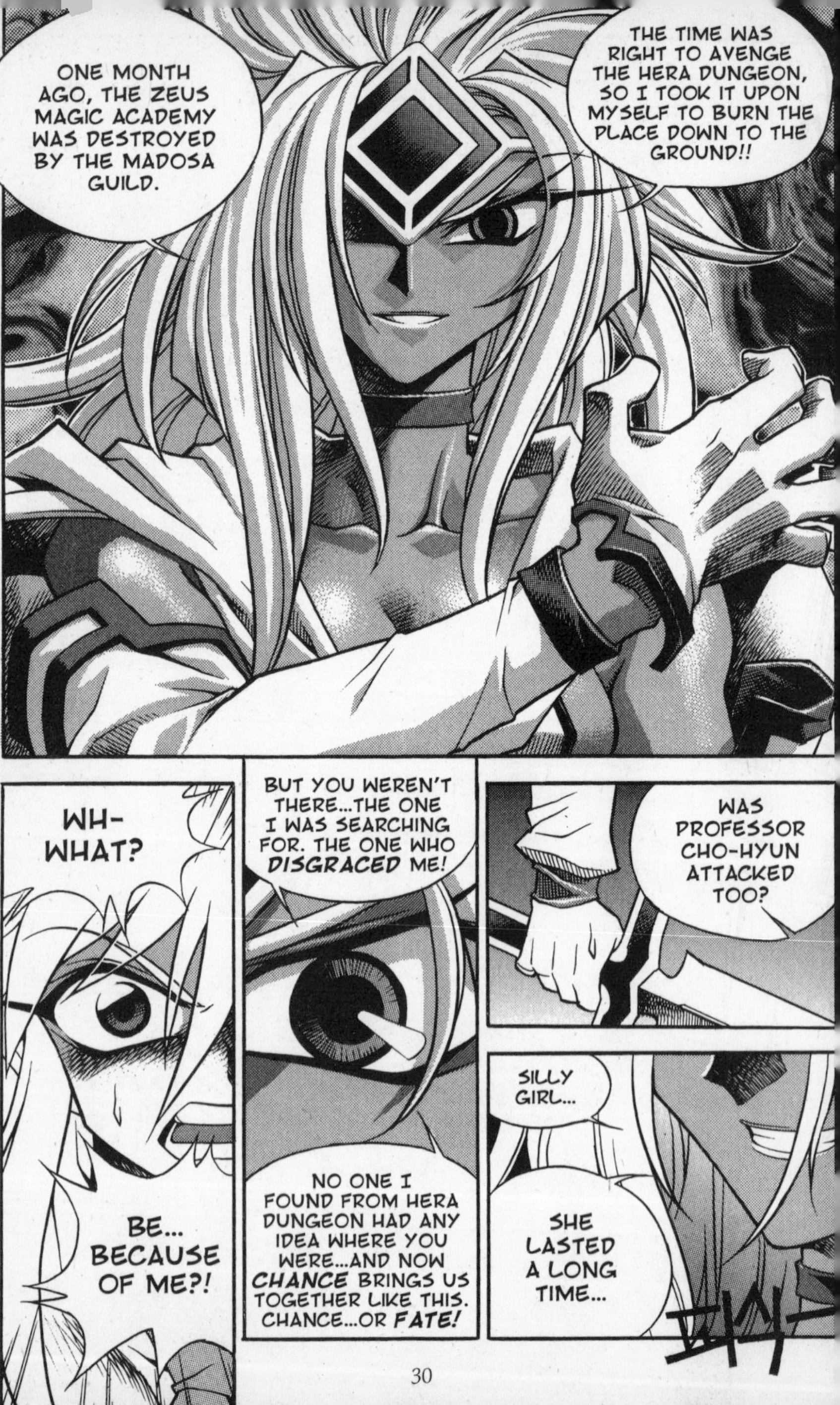
ONE MONTH AGO, THE ZEUS MAGIC ACADEMY WAS DESTROYED BY THE MADOSA GUILD.
THE TIME WAS RIGHT TO AVENGE THE HERA DUNGEON, SO I TOOK IT UPON MYSELF TO BURN THE PLACE DOWN TO THE GROUND!!
WH- WHAT?
BE... BECAUSE OF ME?!
BUT YOU WEREN'T THERE...THE ONE I WAS SEARCHING FOR. THE ONE WHO *DISGRACED* ME!
NO ONE I FOUND FROM HERA DUNGEON HAD ANY IDEA WHERE YOU WERE...AND NOW *CHANCE* BRINGS US TOGETHER LIKE THIS. CHANCE...OR *FATE!*
WAS PROFESSOR CHO-HYUN ATTACKED TOO?
SILLY GIRL...
SHE LASTED A LONG TIME...

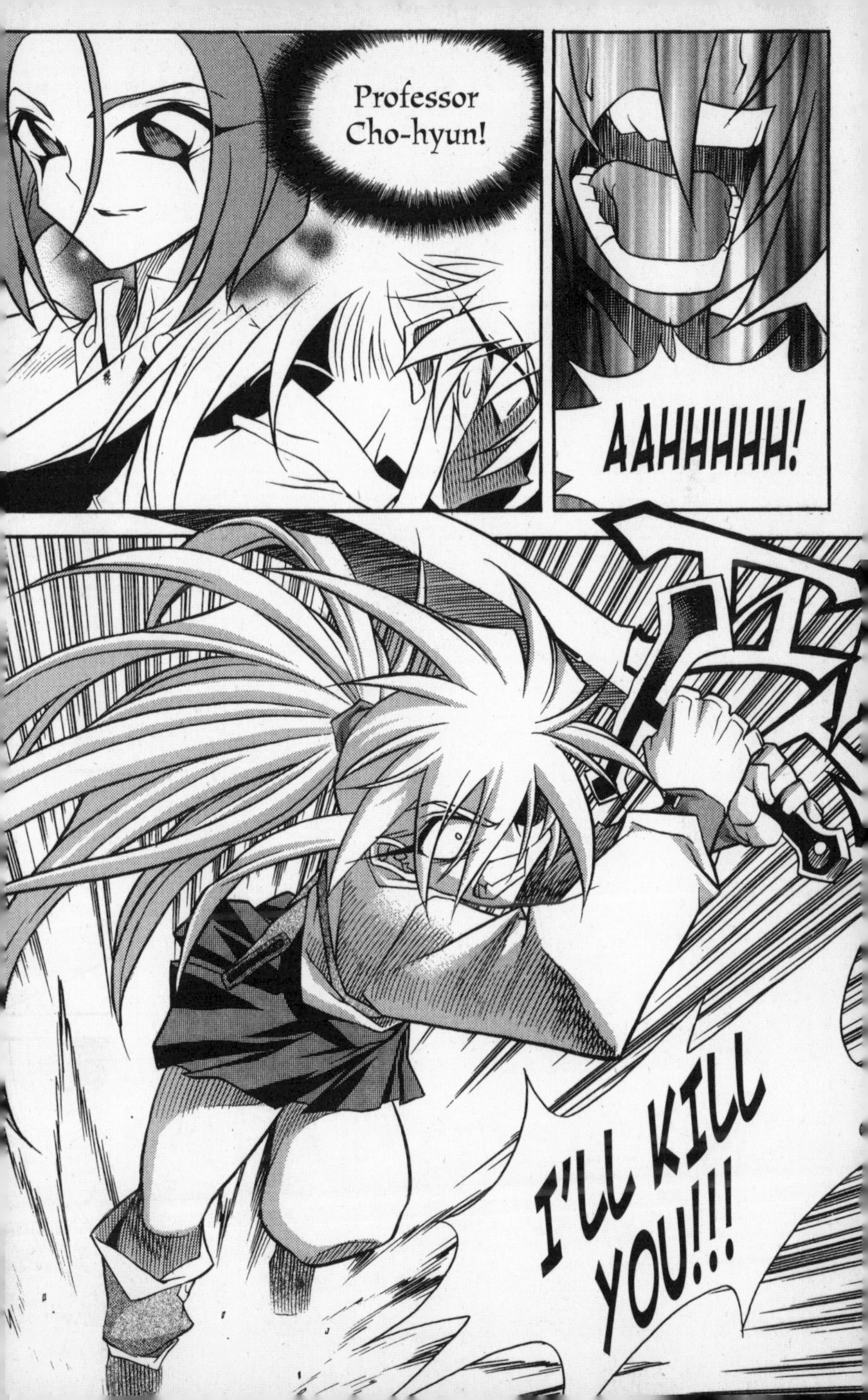
Professor Cho-hyun!
AAHHHHH!
I'LL KILL YOU!!!

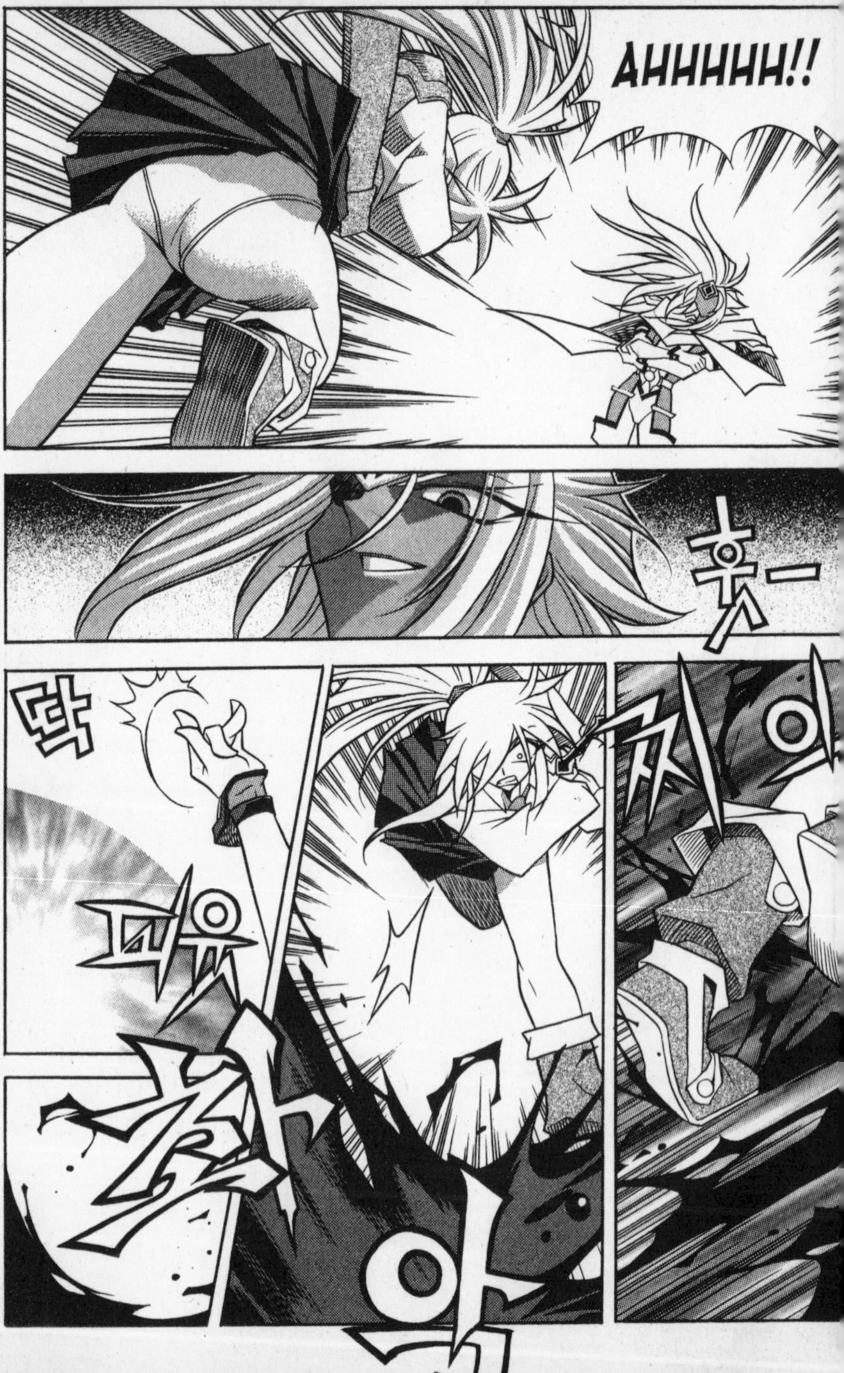
AHHHHH!!
딱

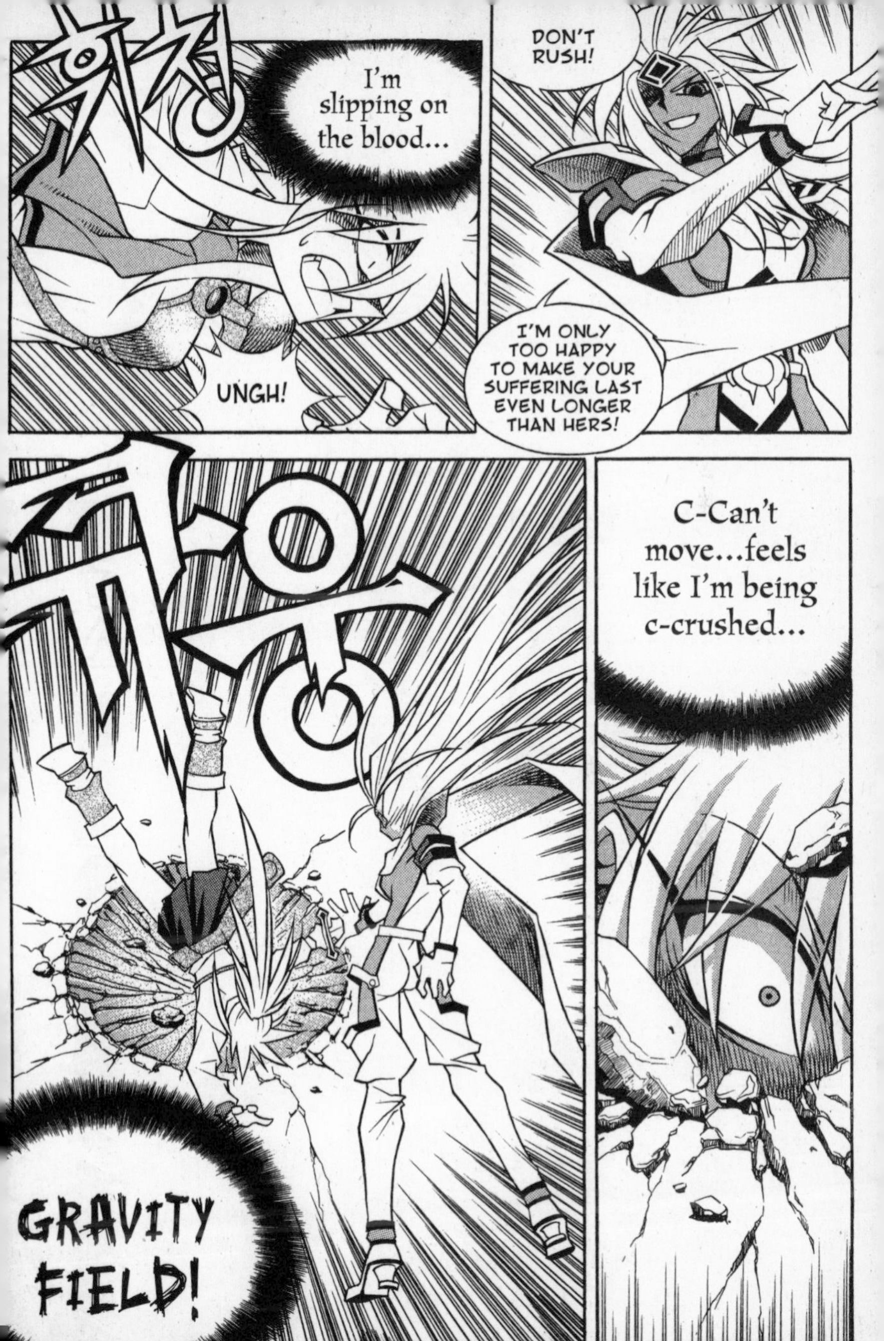
I'm slipping on the blood...
UNGH!
DON'T RUSH!
I'M ONLY TOO HAPPY TO MAKE YOUR SUFFERING LAST EVEN LONGER THAN HERS!
GRAVITY FIELD!
C-Can't move...feels like I'm being c-crushed...

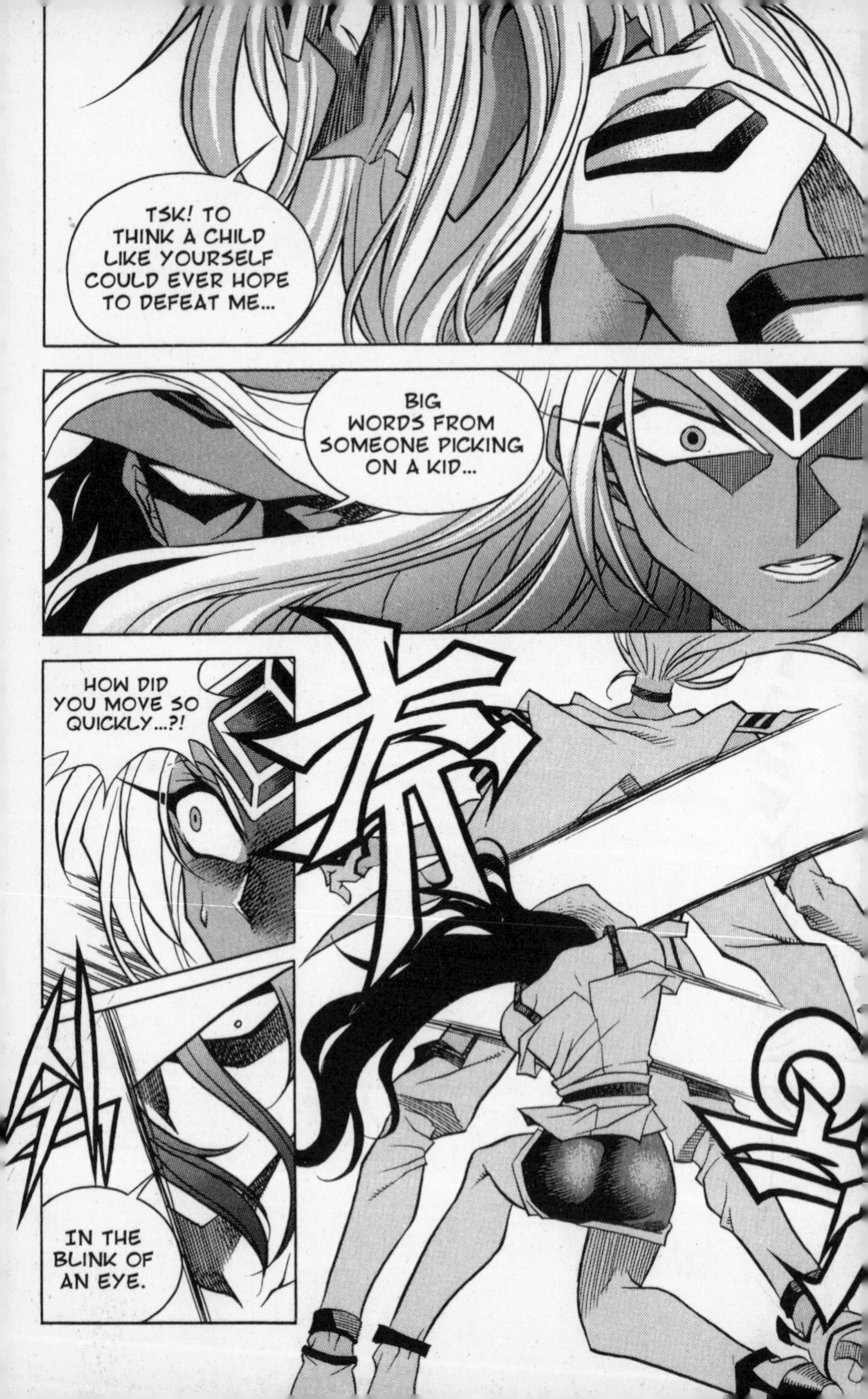
TSK! TO THINK A CHILD LIKE YOURSELF COULD EVER HOPE TO DEFEAT ME...
BIG WORDS FROM SOMEONE PICKING ON A KID...
HOW DID YOU MOVE SO QUICKLY...?!
IN THE BLINK OF AN EYE.

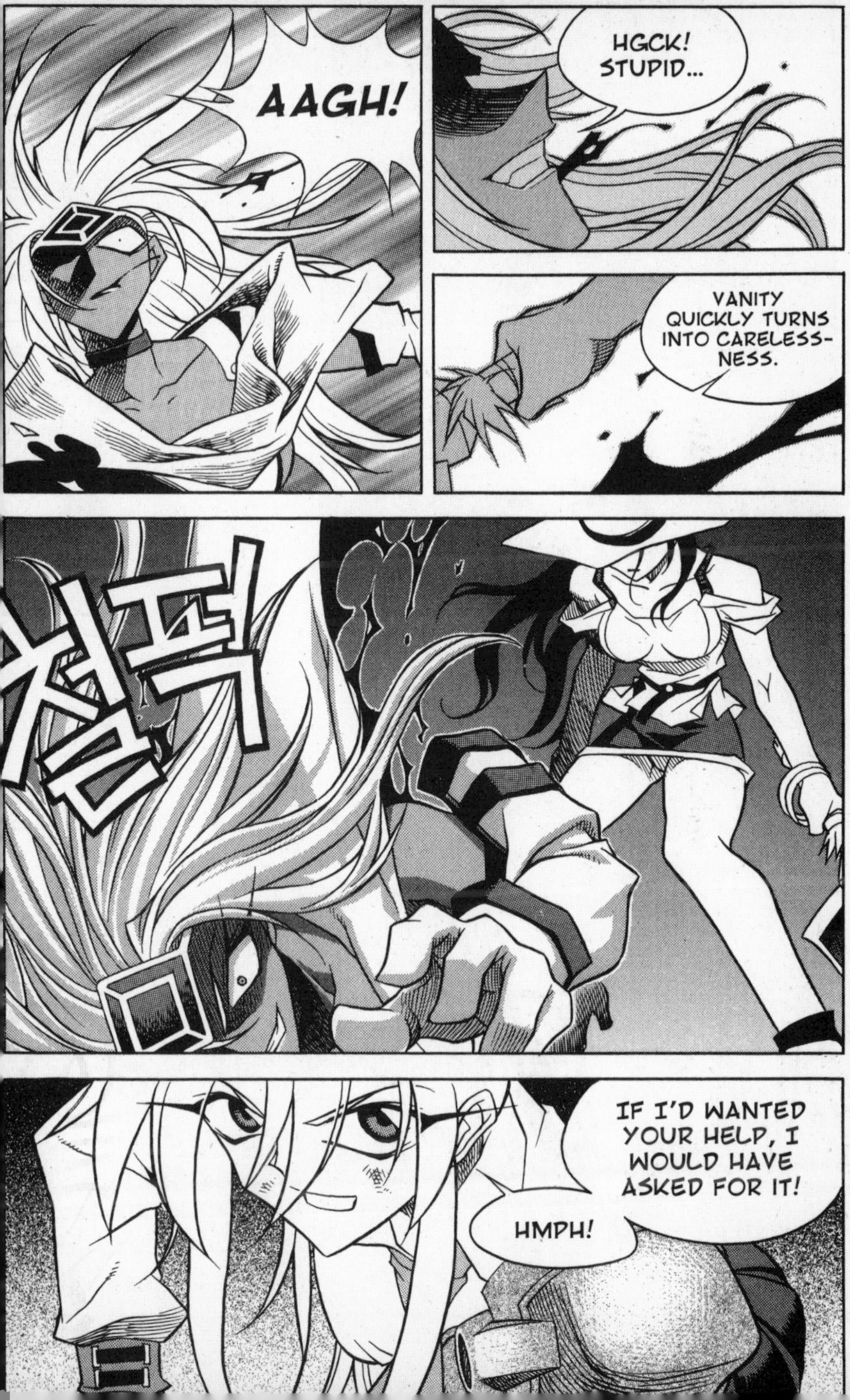
AAGH!
HGCK! STUPID...
VANITY QUICKLY TURNS INTO CARELESS-NESS.
IF I'D WANTED YOUR HELP, I WOULD HAVE ASKED FOR IT!
HMPH!

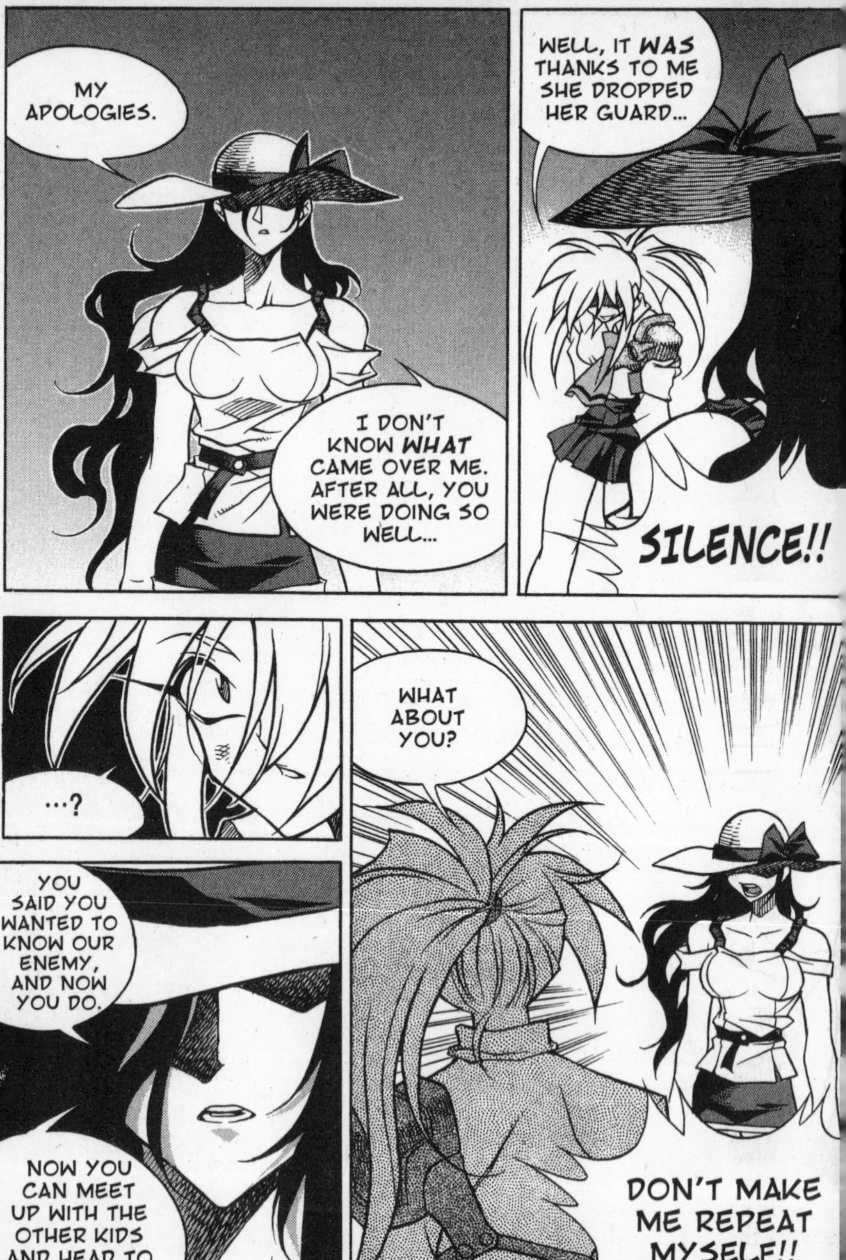
MY APOLOGIES.
I DON'T KNOW WHAT CAME OVER ME. AFTER ALL, YOU WERE DOING SO WELL...
WELL, IT WAS THANKS TO ME SHE DROPPED HER GUARD...
SILENCE!!
...?
WHAT ABOUT YOU?
YOU SAID YOU WANTED TO KNOW OUR ENEMY, AND NOW YOU DO.
NOW YOU CAN MEET UP WITH THE OTHER KIDS AND HEAD TO THE MASTER TOWER!
DON'T MAKE ME REPEAT MYSELF!! GO!!

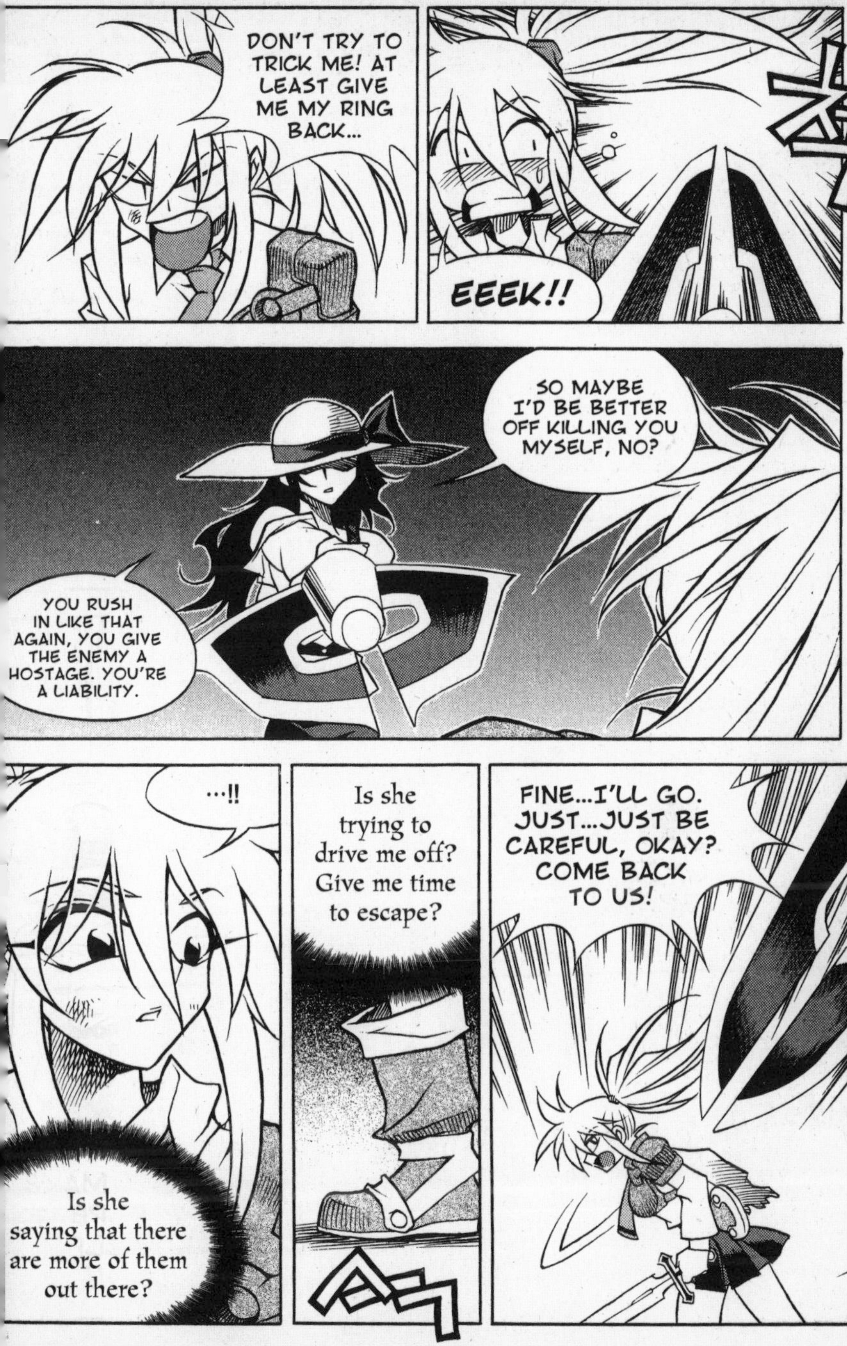
DON'T TRY TO TRICK ME! AT LEAST GIVE ME MY RING BACK...
EEEK!!
YOU RUSH IN LIKE THAT AGAIN, YOU GIVE THE ENEMY A HOSTAGE. YOU'RE A LIABILITY.
SO MAYBE I'D BE BETTER OFF KILLING YOU MYSELF, NO?
...!!
Is she saying that there are more of them out there?
Is she trying to drive me off? Give me time to escape?
FINE...I'LL GO. JUST...JUST BE CAREFUL, OKAY? COME BACK TO US!

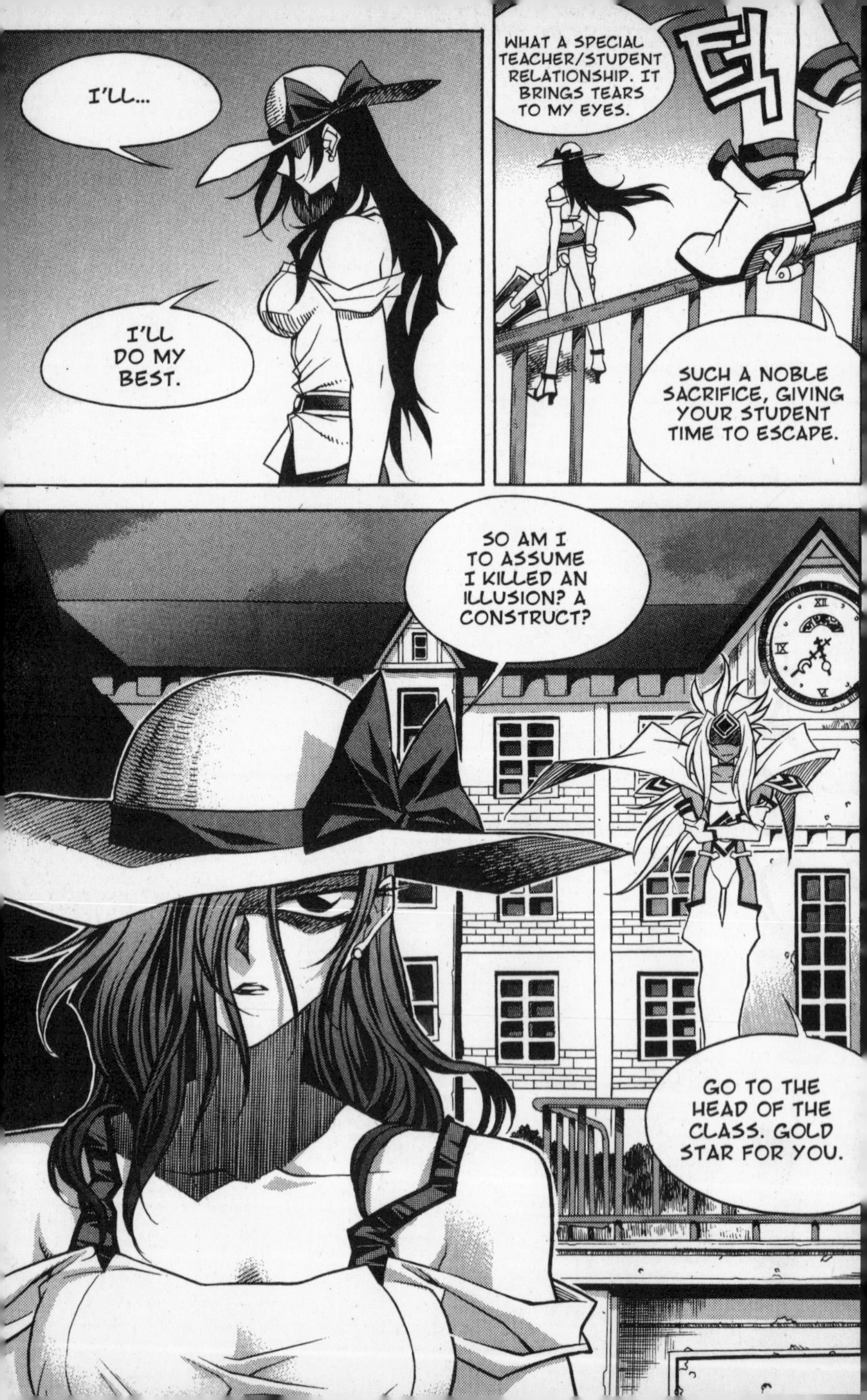
I'LL...
I'LL DO MY BEST.
WHAT A SPECIAL TEACHER/STUDENT RELATIONSHIP. IT BRINGS TEARS TO MY EYES.
SUCH A NOBLE SACRIFICE, GIVING YOUR STUDENT TIME TO ESCAPE.
SO AM I TO ASSUME I KILLED AN ILLUSION? A CONSTRUCT?
GO TO THE HEAD OF THE CLASS. GOLD STAR FOR YOU.

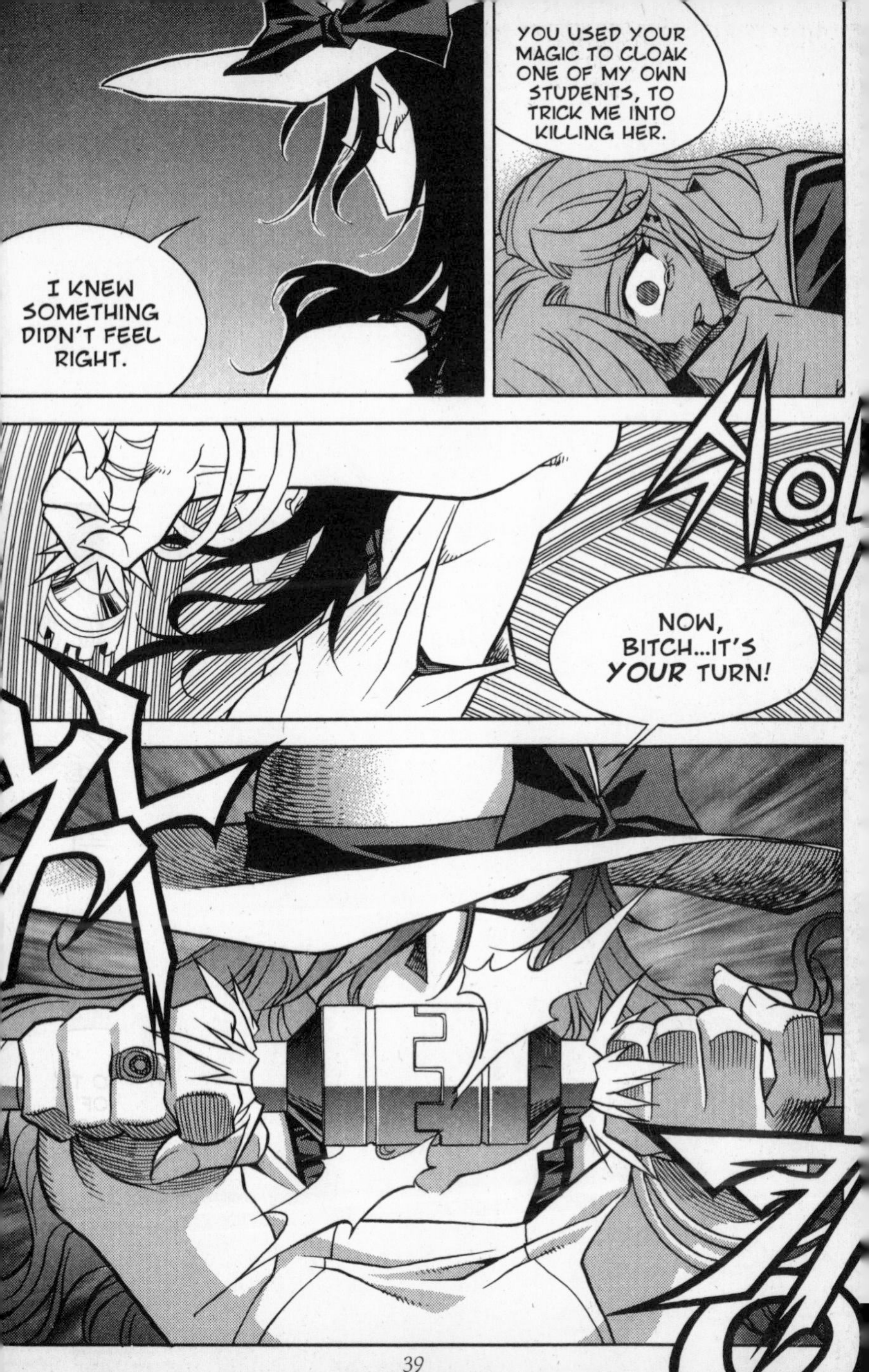
I KNEW SOMETHING DIDN'T FEEL RIGHT.
YOU USED YOUR MAGIC TO CLOAK ONE OF MY OWN STUDENTS, TO TRICK ME INTO KILLING HER.
NOW, BITCH...IT'S *YOUR* TURN!

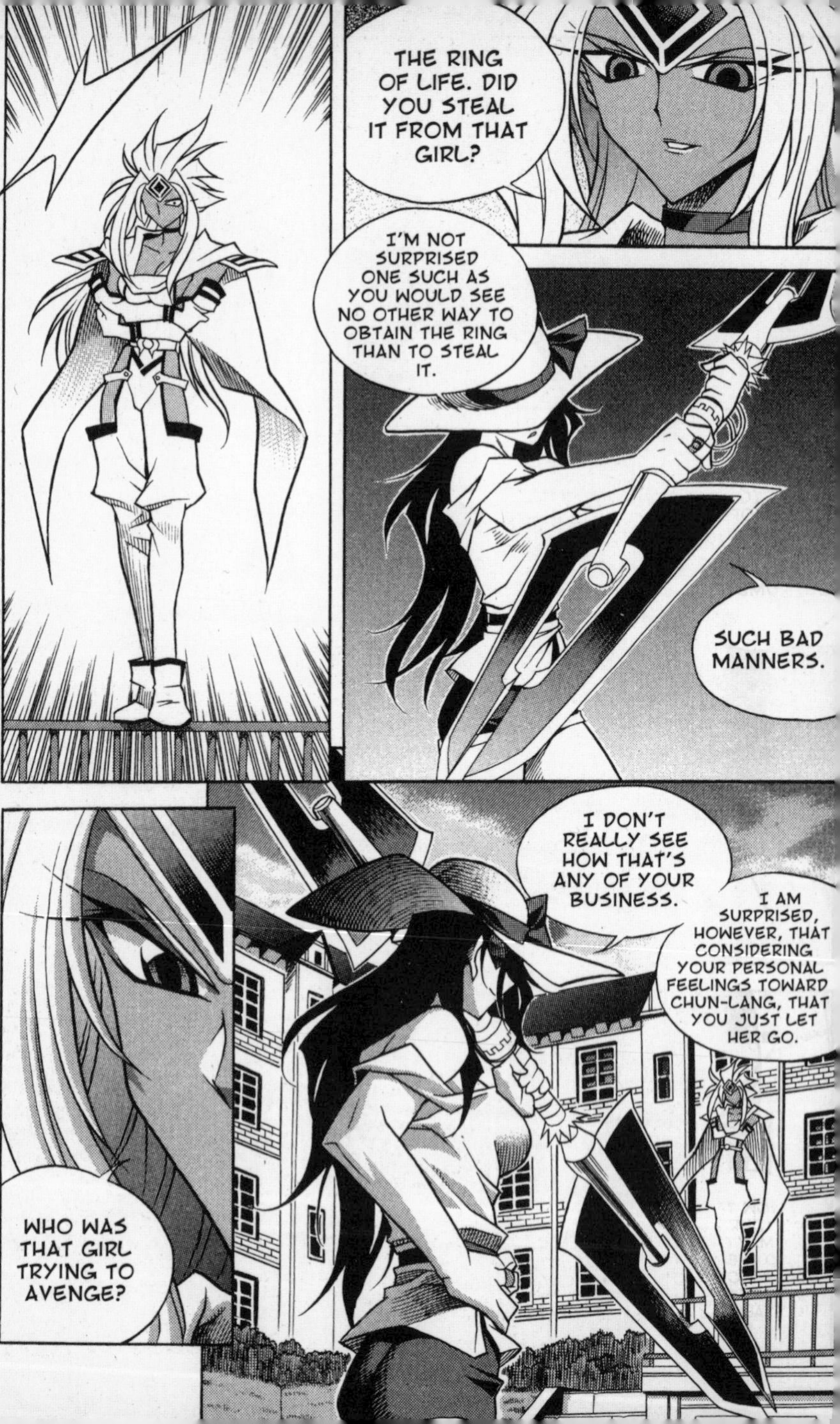
THE RING OF LIFE. DID YOU STEAL IT FROM THAT GIRL?
I'M NOT SURPRISED ONE SUCH AS YOU WOULD SEE NO OTHER WAY TO OBTAIN THE RING THAN TO STEAL IT.
SUCH BAD MANNERS.
WHO WAS THAT GIRL TRYING TO AVENGE?
I DON'T REALLY SEE HOW THAT'S ANY OF YOUR BUSINESS.
I AM SURPRISED, HOWEVER, THAT CONSIDERING YOUR PERSONAL FEELINGS TOWARD CHUN-LANG, THAT YOU JUST LET HER GO.

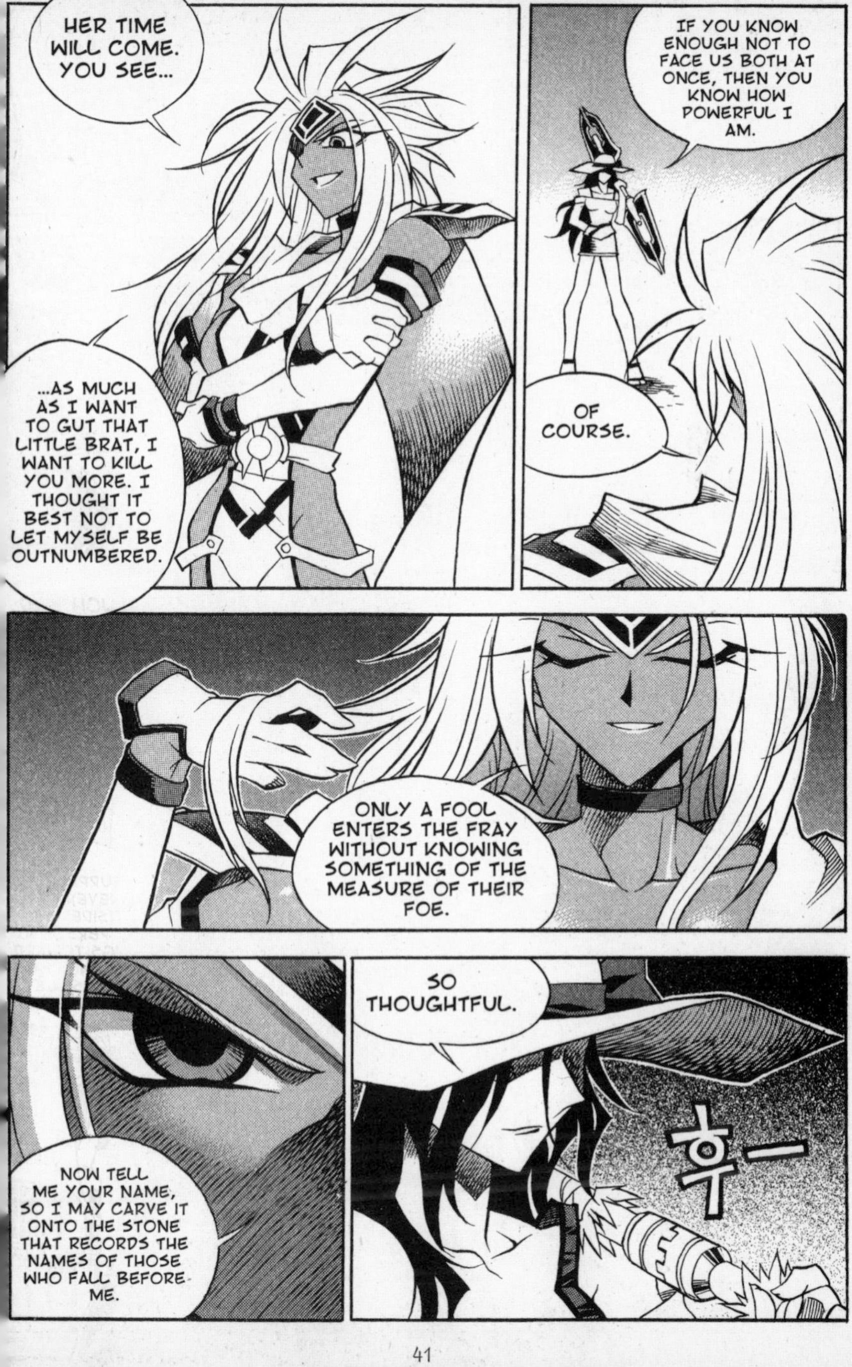
HER TIME WILL COME. YOU SEE...
...AS MUCH AS I WANT TO GUT THAT LITTLE BRAT, I WANT TO KILL YOU MORE. I THOUGHT IT BEST NOT TO LET MYSELF BE OUTNUMBERED.
IF YOU KNOW ENOUGH NOT TO FACE US BOTH AT ONCE, THEN YOU KNOW HOW POWERFUL I AM.
OF COURSE.
ONLY A FOOL ENTERS THE FRAY WITHOUT KNOWING SOMETHING OF THE MEASURE OF THEIR FOE.
NOW TELL ME YOUR NAME, SO I MAY CARVE IT ONTO THE STONE THAT RECORDS THE NAMES OF THOSE WHO FALL BEFORE ME.
SO THOUGHTFUL.
후ー

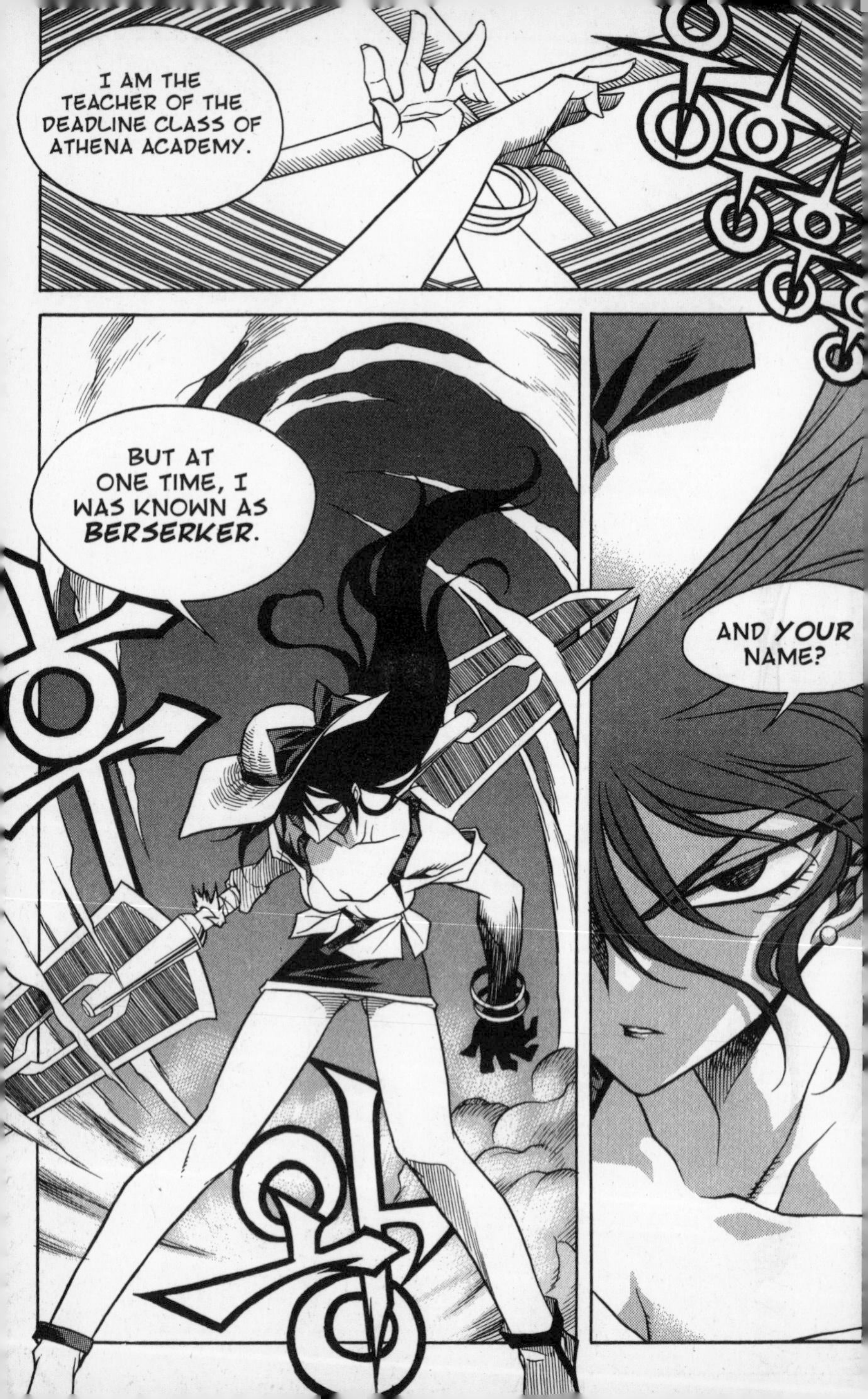
I AM THE TEACHER OF THE DEADLINE CLASS OF ATHENA ACADEMY.
BUT AT ONE TIME, I WAS KNOWN AS *BERSERKER*.
AND *YOUR* NAME?

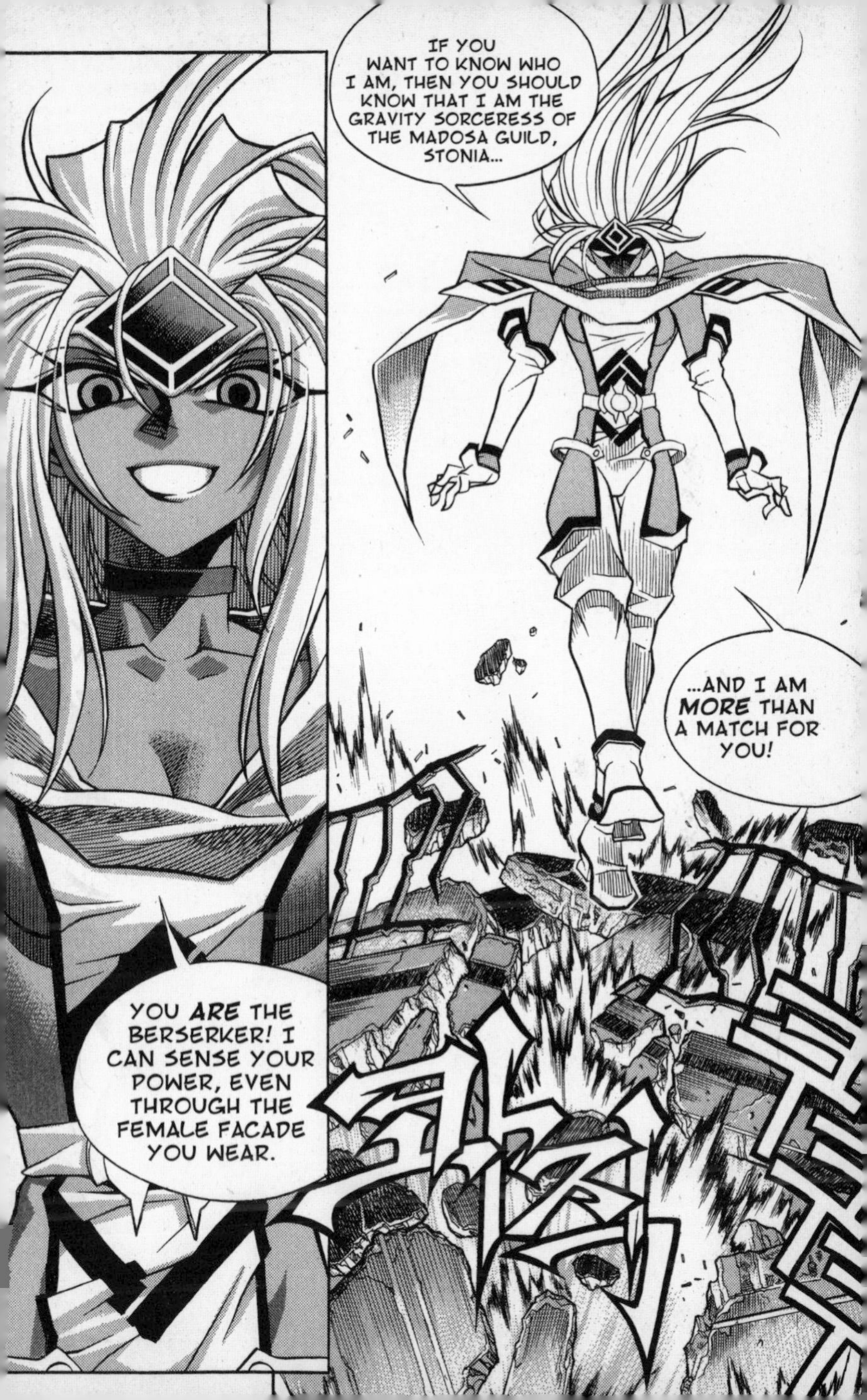
YOU **ARE** THE BERSERKER! I CAN SENSE YOUR POWER, EVEN THROUGH THE FEMALE FACADE YOU WEAR.
IF YOU WANT TO KNOW WHO I AM, THEN YOU SHOULD KNOW THAT I AM THE GRAVITY SORCERESS OF THE MADOSA GUILD, STONIA...
...AND I AM **MORE** THAN A MATCH FOR YOU!

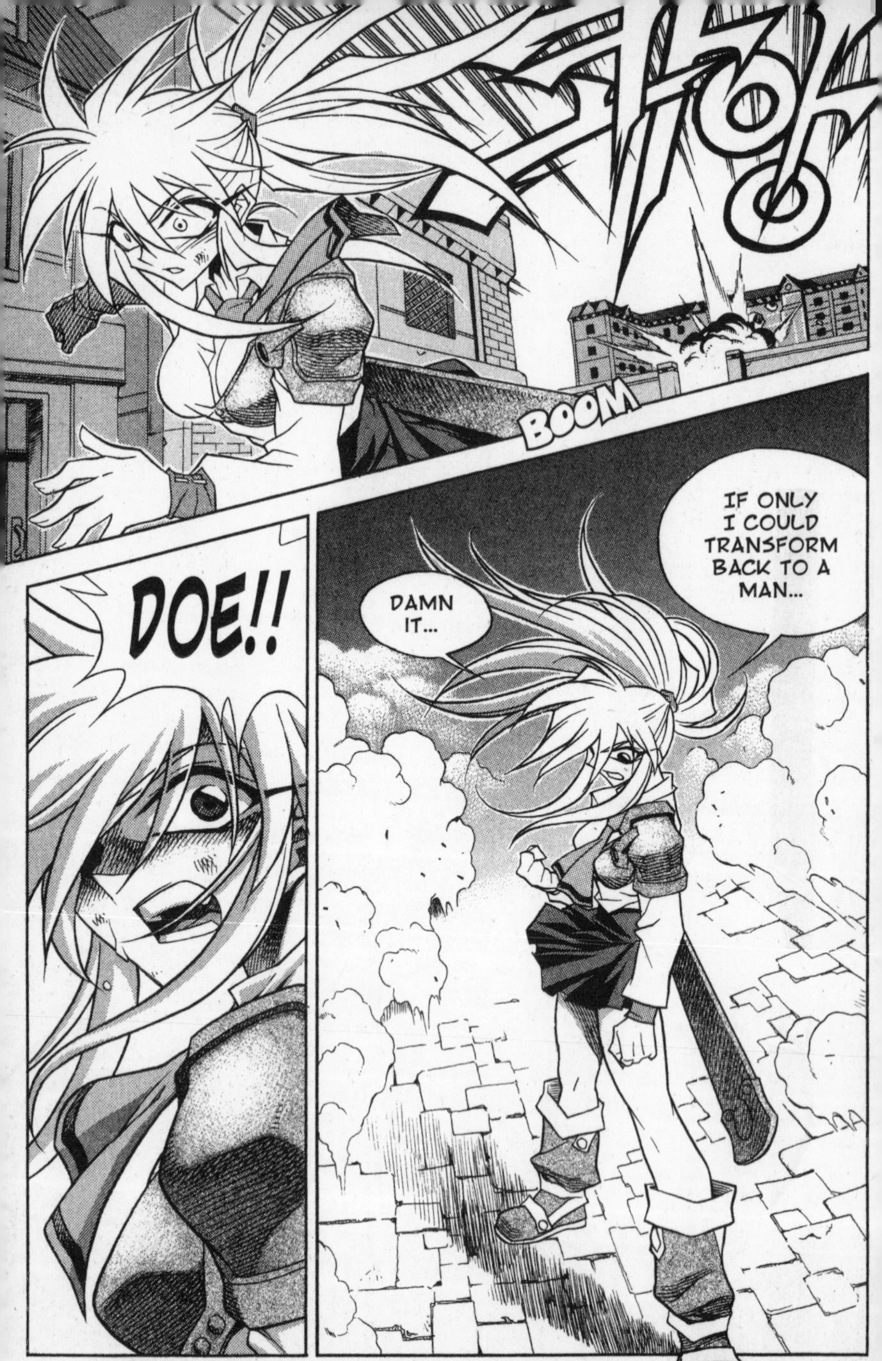
BOOM
DOE!!
DAMN IT...
IF ONLY I COULD TRANSFORM BACK TO A MAN...

Quest 61

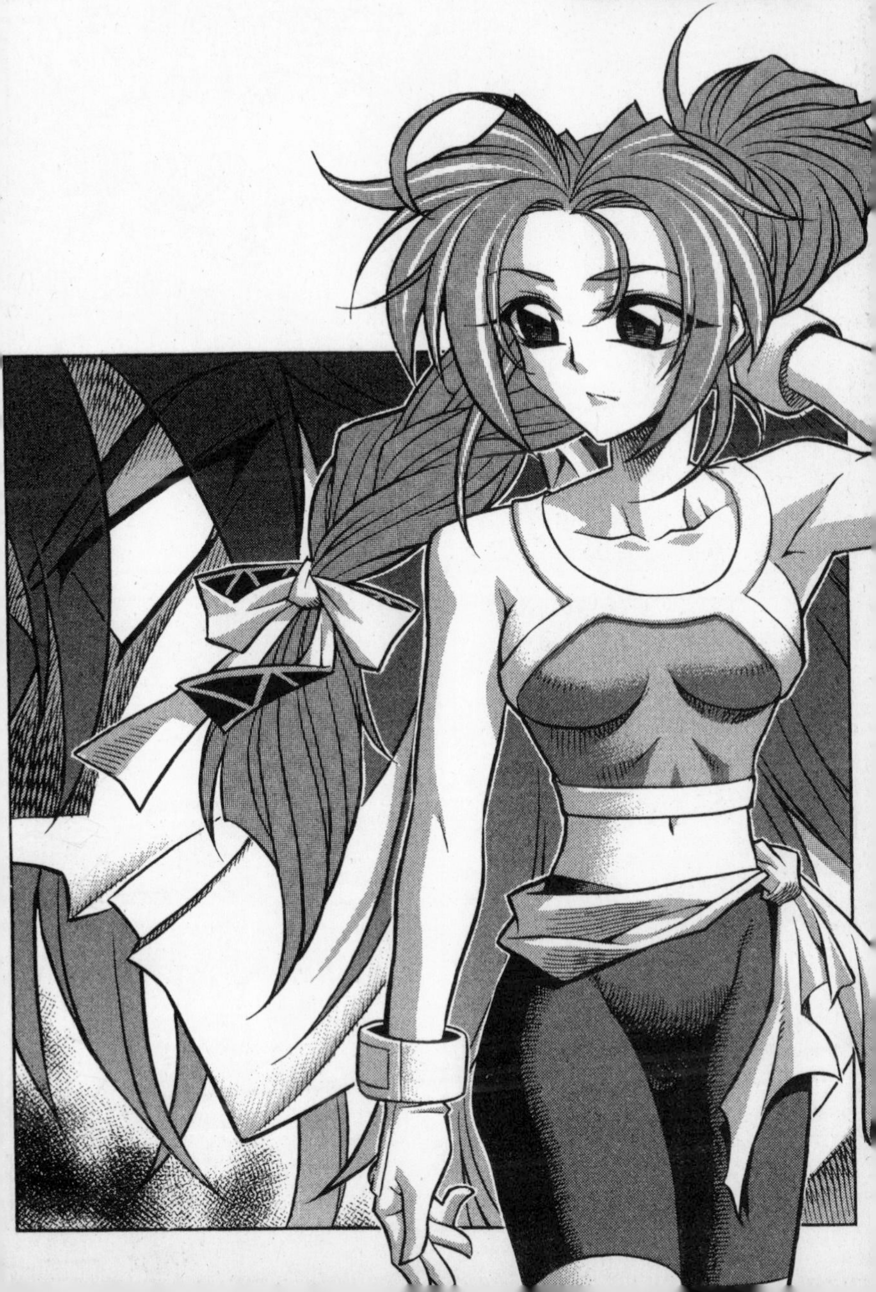

WE'RE ALMOST THERE! I CAN SEE THE VILLAGE!
Wah! You're going too fast!!
WE...WE MIGHT ALREADY BE TOO LATE. I CAN BARELY SENSE ANY LIVING ENERGY.
HEXION MIGHT ALREADY BE....
NOT SOUND OR SMELL... WHAT DOES SHE MEAN BY ENERGY? WHAT THE HECK IS SHE SENSING?
AAAHHH!! LOOK AT THAT!

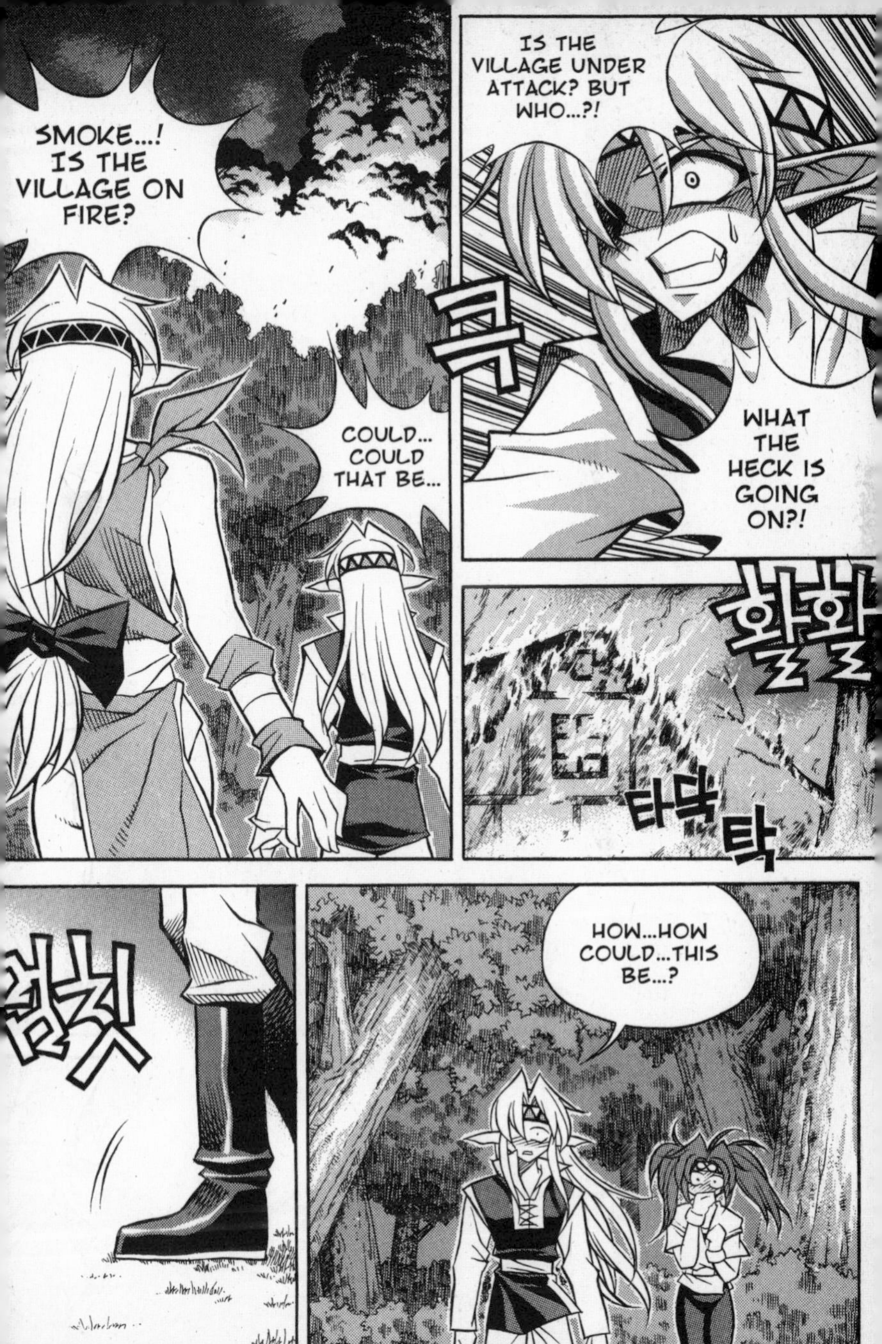
SMOKE...! IS THE VILLAGE ON FIRE?
COULD... COULD THAT BE...
IS THE VILLAGE UNDER ATTACK? BUT WHO...?!
크
WHAT THE HECK IS GOING ON?!
활활
타닥 탁
HOW...HOW COULD...THIS BE...?

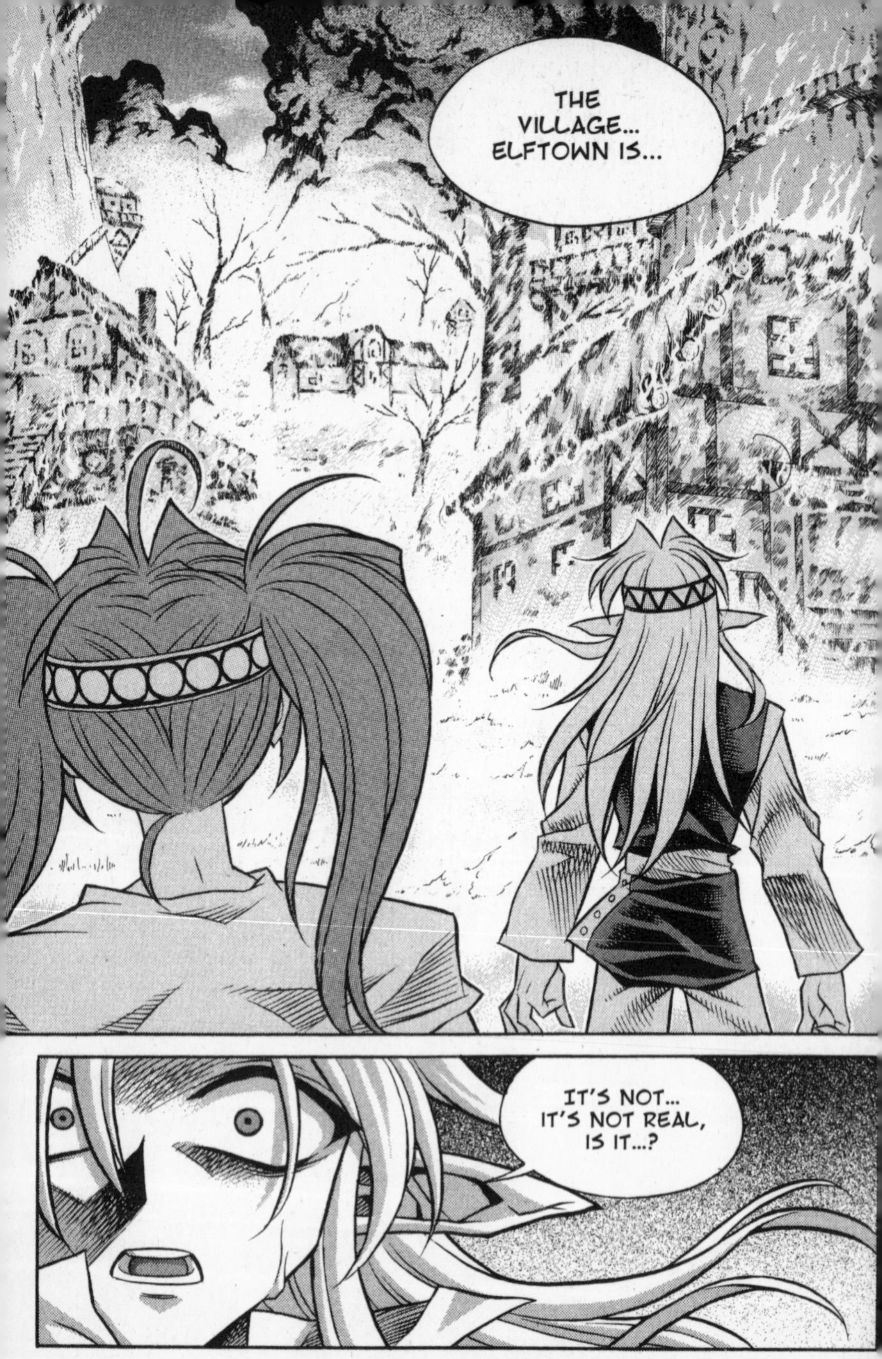
THE VILLAGE... ELFTOWN IS...
IT'S NOT... IT'S NOT REAL, IS IT...?

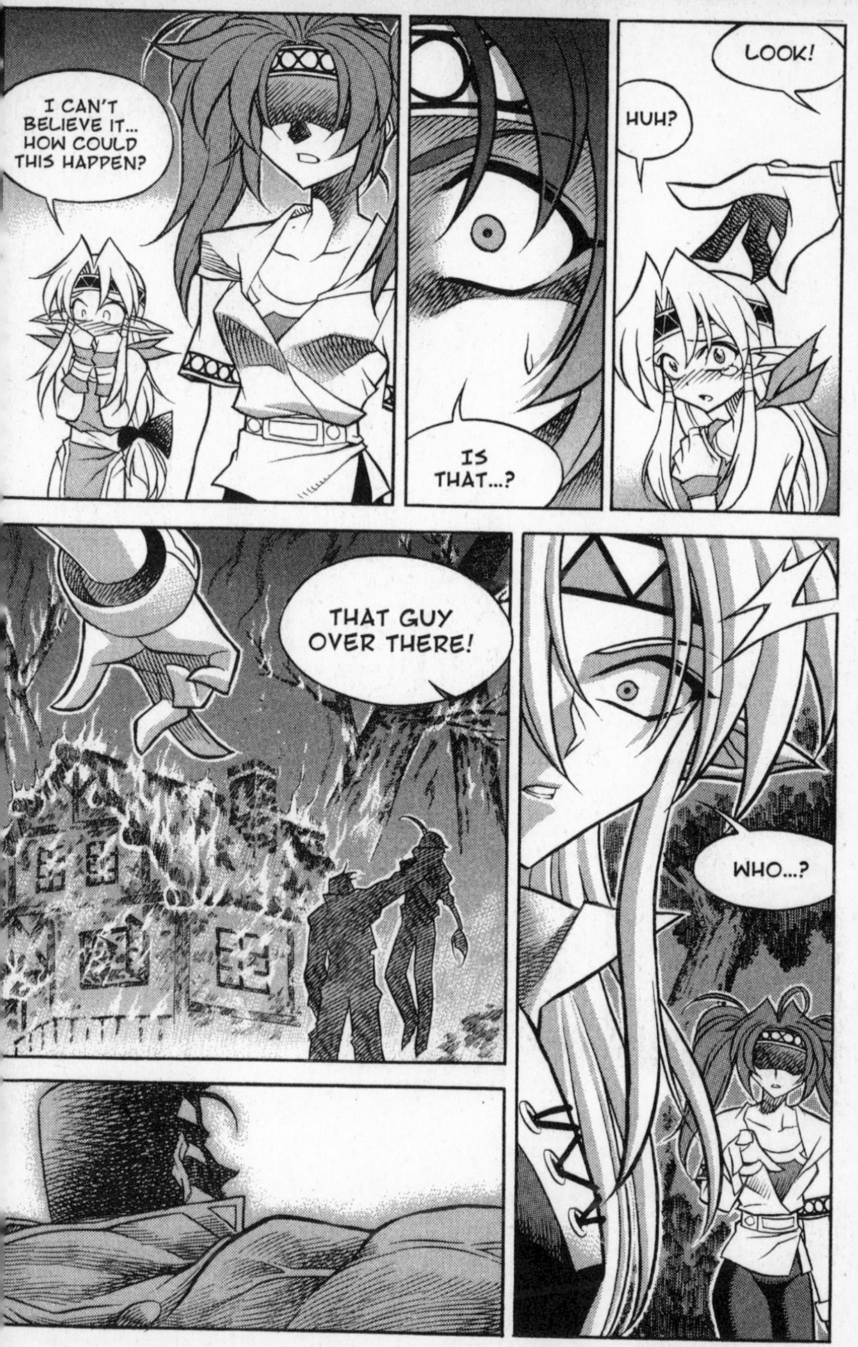
I CAN'T BELIEVE IT... HOW COULD THIS HAPPEN?
IS THAT...?
HUH?
LOOK!
THAT GUY OVER THERE!
WHO...?

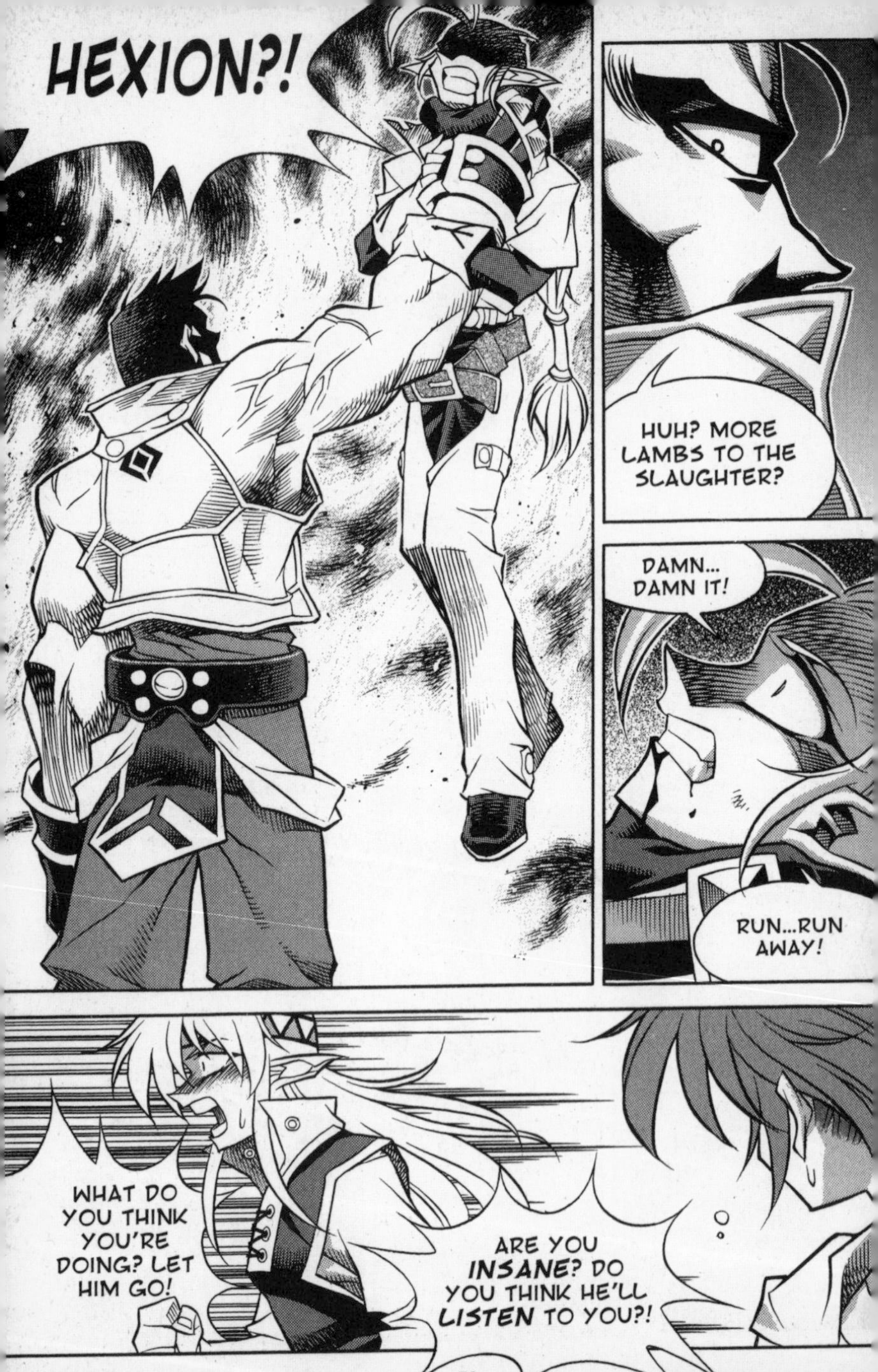
HEXION?!
HUH? MORE LAMBS TO THE SLAUGHTER?
DAMN... DAMN IT!
RUN...RUN AWAY!
WHAT DO YOU THINK YOU'RE DOING? LET HIM GO!
ARE YOU INSANE? DO YOU THINK HE'LL LISTEN TO YOU?!

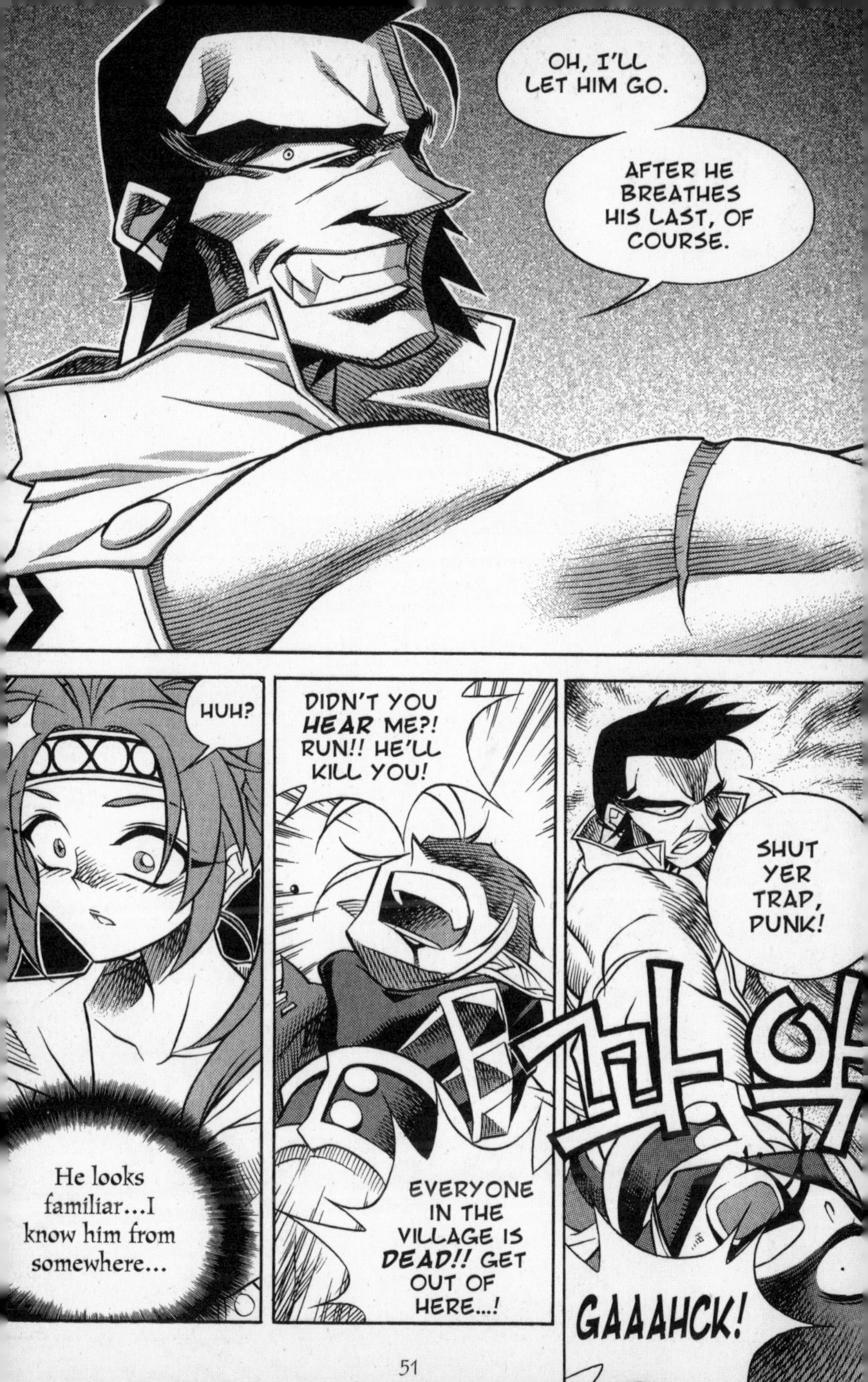
OH, I'LL LET HIM GO.
AFTER HE BREATHES HIS LAST, OF COURSE.
HUH?
He looks familiar...I know him from somewhere...
DIDN'T YOU *HEAR* ME?! RUN!! HE'LL KILL YOU!
EVERYONE IN THE VILLAGE IS *DEAD!!* GET OUT OF HERE...!
SHUT YER TRAP, PUNK!
GAAAHCK!

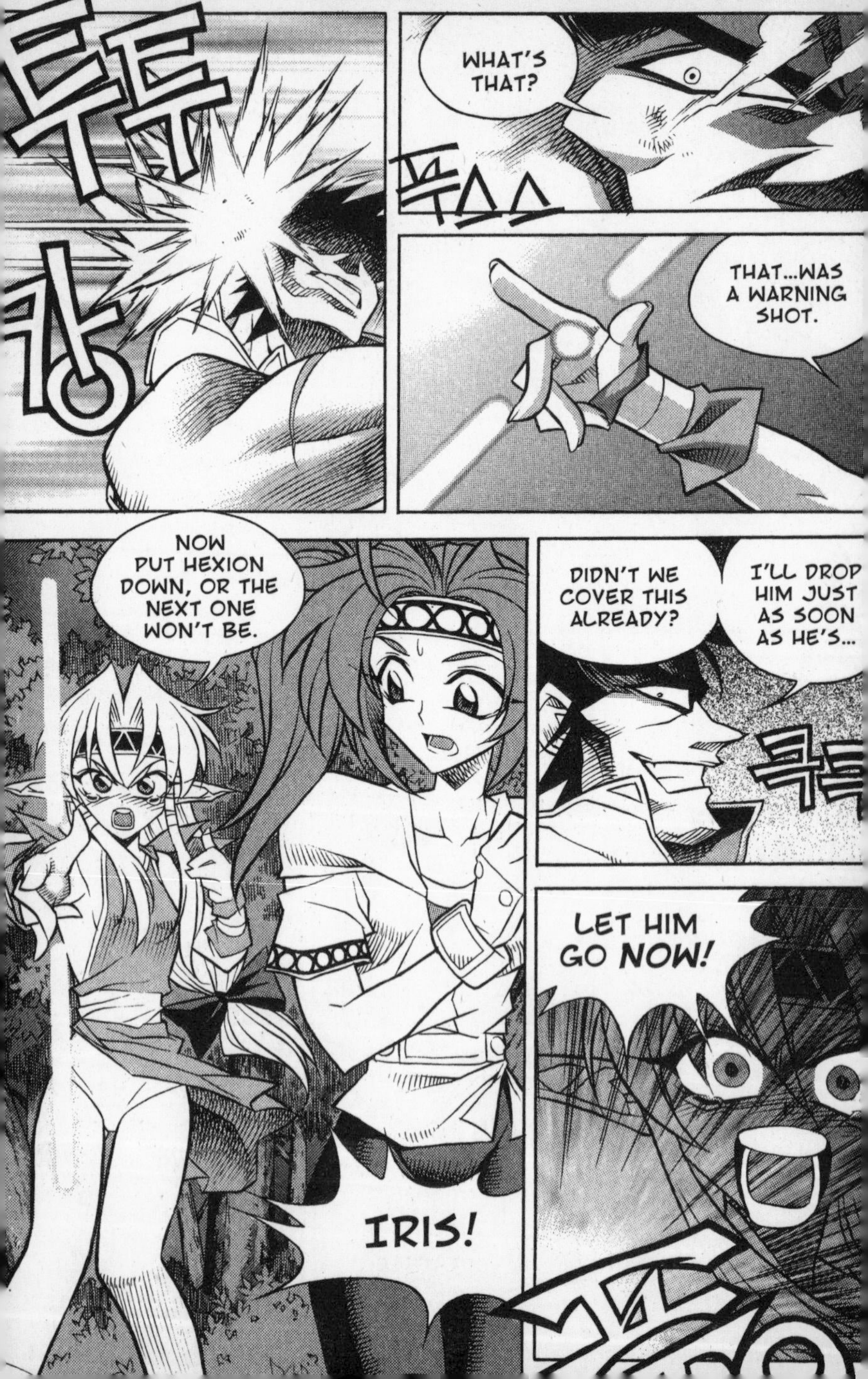
WHAT'S THAT?
THAT...WAS A WARNING SHOT.
NOW PUT HEXION DOWN, OR THE NEXT ONE WON'T BE.
IRIS!
DIDN'T WE COVER THIS ALREADY?
I'LL DROP HIM JUST AS SOON AS HE'S...
LET HIM GO NOW!

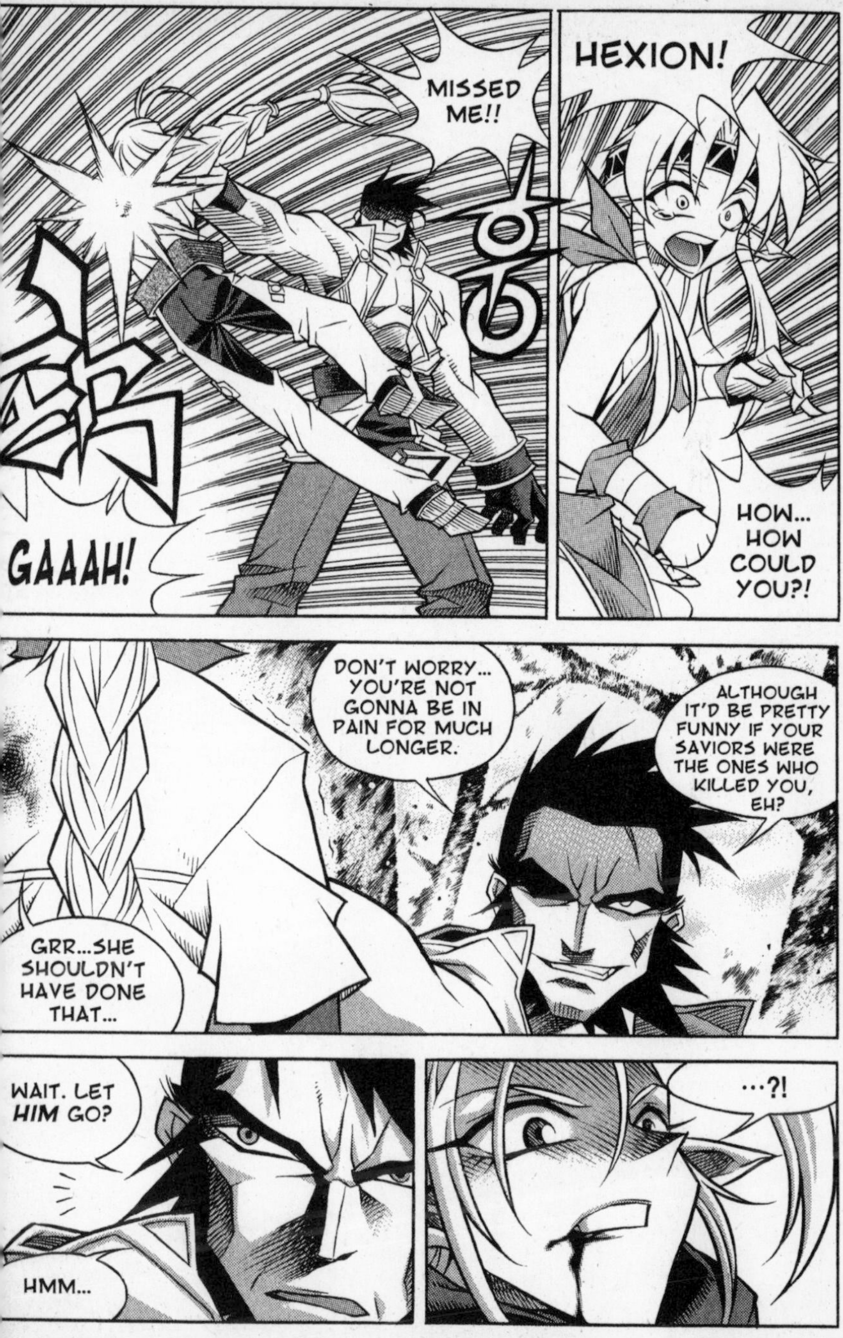
GAAAH!
MISSED ME!!
HEXION!
HOW... HOW COULD YOU?!
DON'T WORRY... YOU'RE NOT GONNA BE IN PAIN FOR MUCH LONGER.
ALTHOUGH IT'D BE PRETTY FUNNY IF YOUR SAVIORS WERE THE ONES WHO KILLED YOU, EH?
GRR...SHE SHOULDN'T HAVE DONE THAT...
WAIT. LET *HIM* GO?
HMM...
...?!

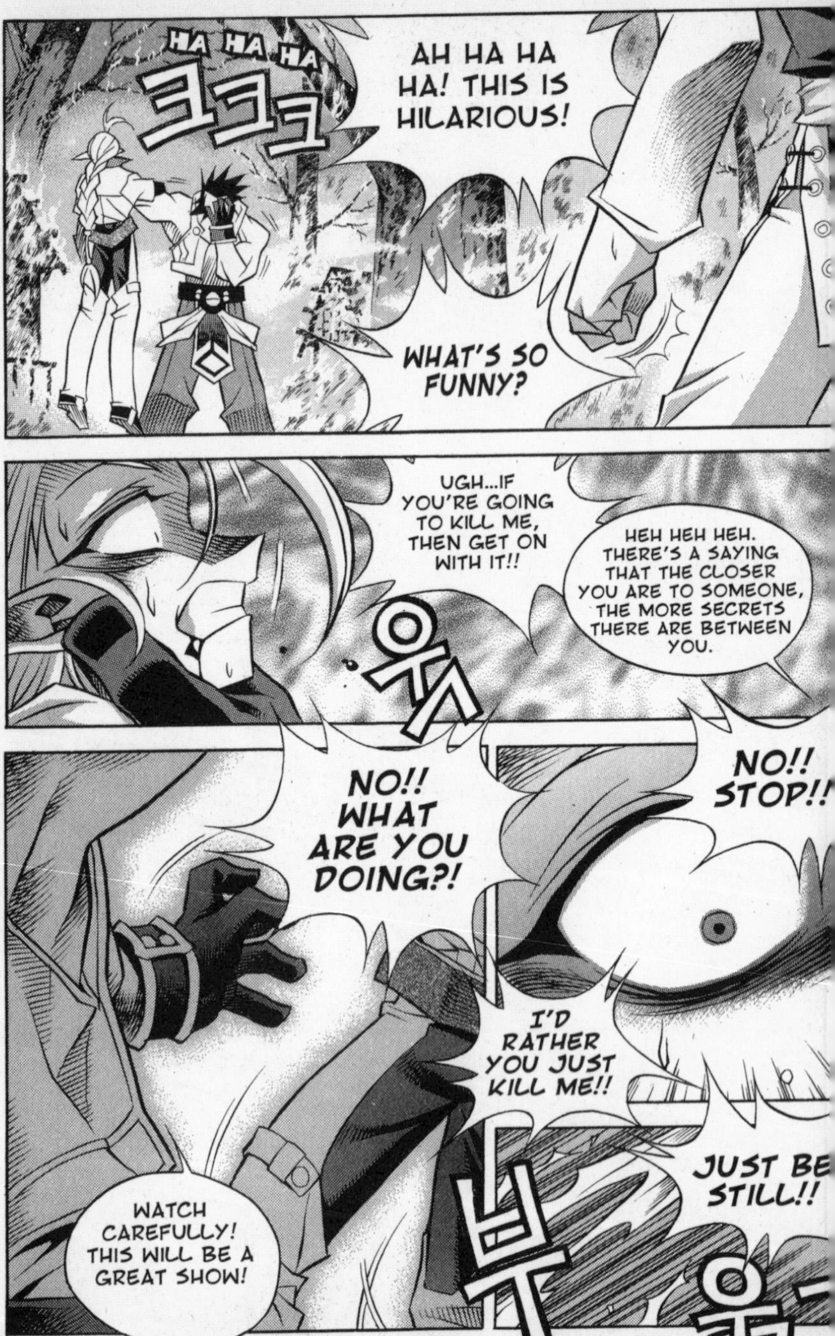
HA HA HA
AH HA HA HA! THIS IS HILARIOUS!
WHAT'S SO FUNNY?
UGH...IF YOU'RE GOING TO KILL ME, THEN GET ON WITH IT!!
HEH HEH HEH. THERE'S A SAYING THAT THE CLOSER YOU ARE TO SOMEONE, THE MORE SECRETS THERE ARE BETWEEN YOU.
NO!! WHAT ARE YOU DOING?!
NO!! STOP!!
I'D RATHER YOU JUST KILL ME!!
WATCH CAREFULLY! THIS WILL BE A GREAT SHOW!
JUST BE STILL!!

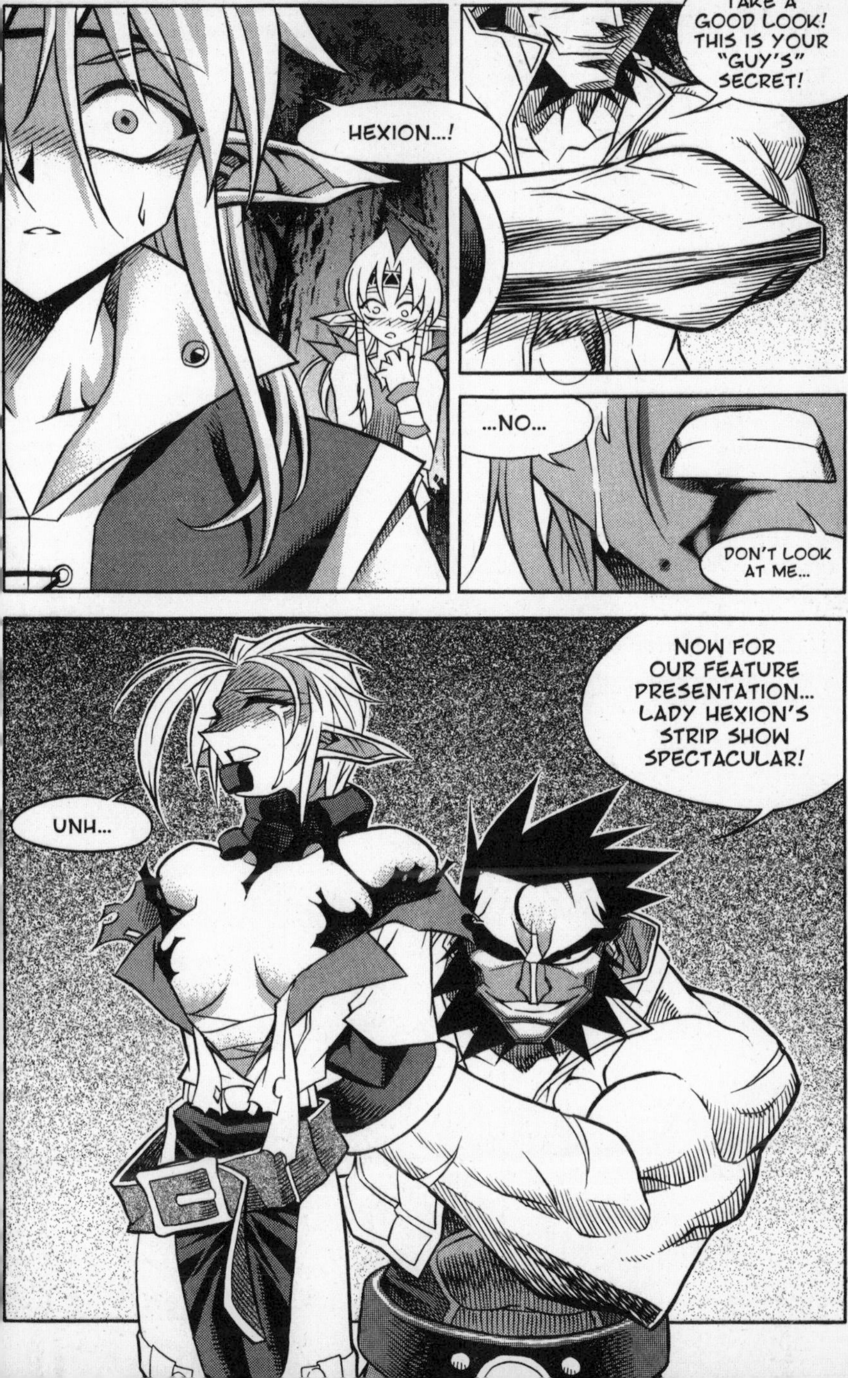
HEXION...!
TAKE A GOOD LOOK! THIS IS YOUR "GUY'S" SECRET!
...NO...
DON'T LOOK AT ME...
NOW FOR OUR FEATURE PRESENTATION... LADY HEXION'S STRIP SHOW SPECTACULAR!
UNH...

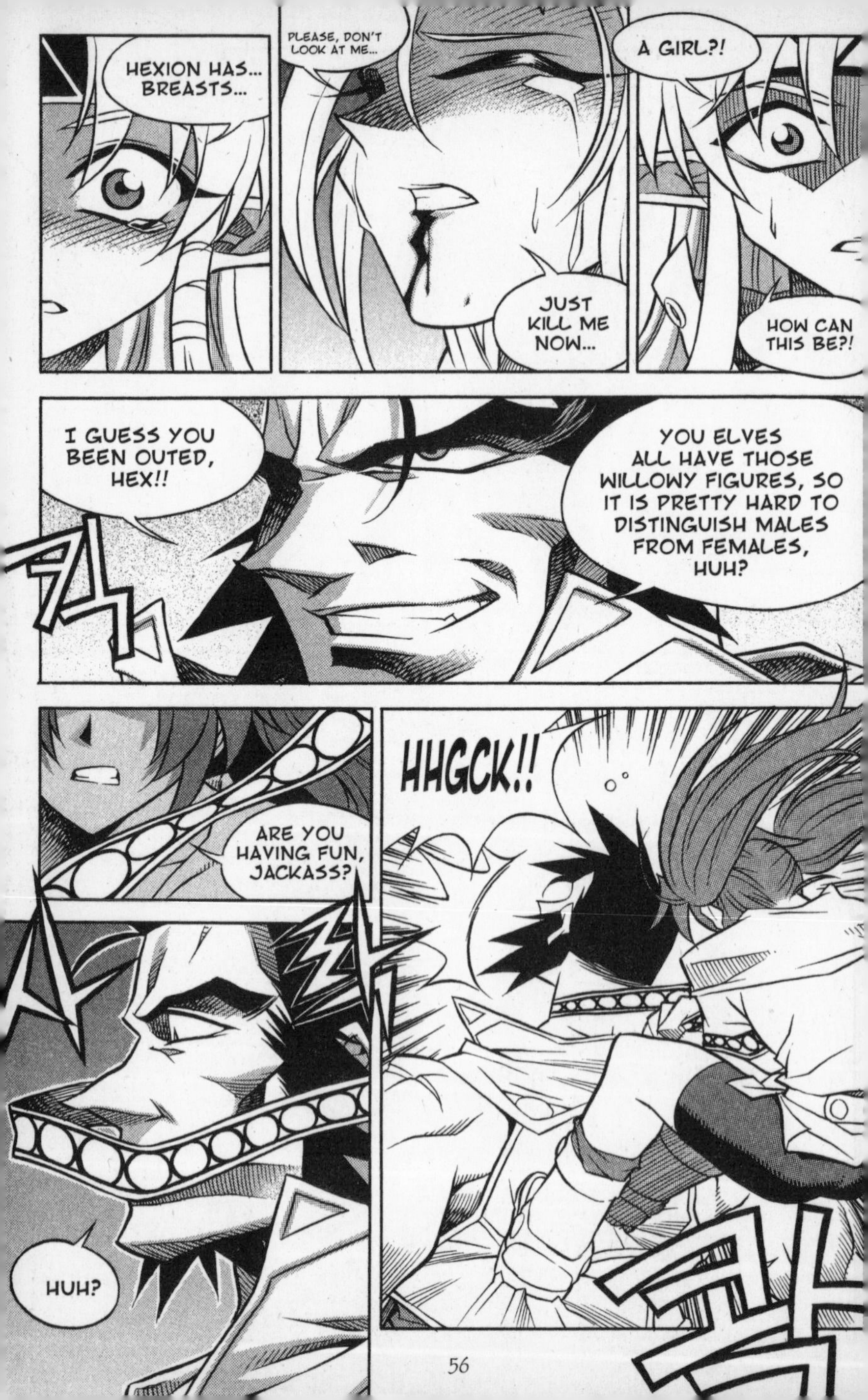
HEXION HAS... BREASTS...
PLEASE, DON'T LOOK AT ME...
JUST KILL ME NOW...
A GIRL?!
HOW CAN THIS BE?!
I GUESS YOU BEEN OUTED, HEX!!
YOU ELVES ALL HAVE THOSE WILLOWY FIGURES, SO IT IS PRETTY HARD TO DISTINGUISH MALES FROM FEMALES, HUH?
ARE YOU HAVING FUN, JACKASS?
HUH?
HHGCK!!

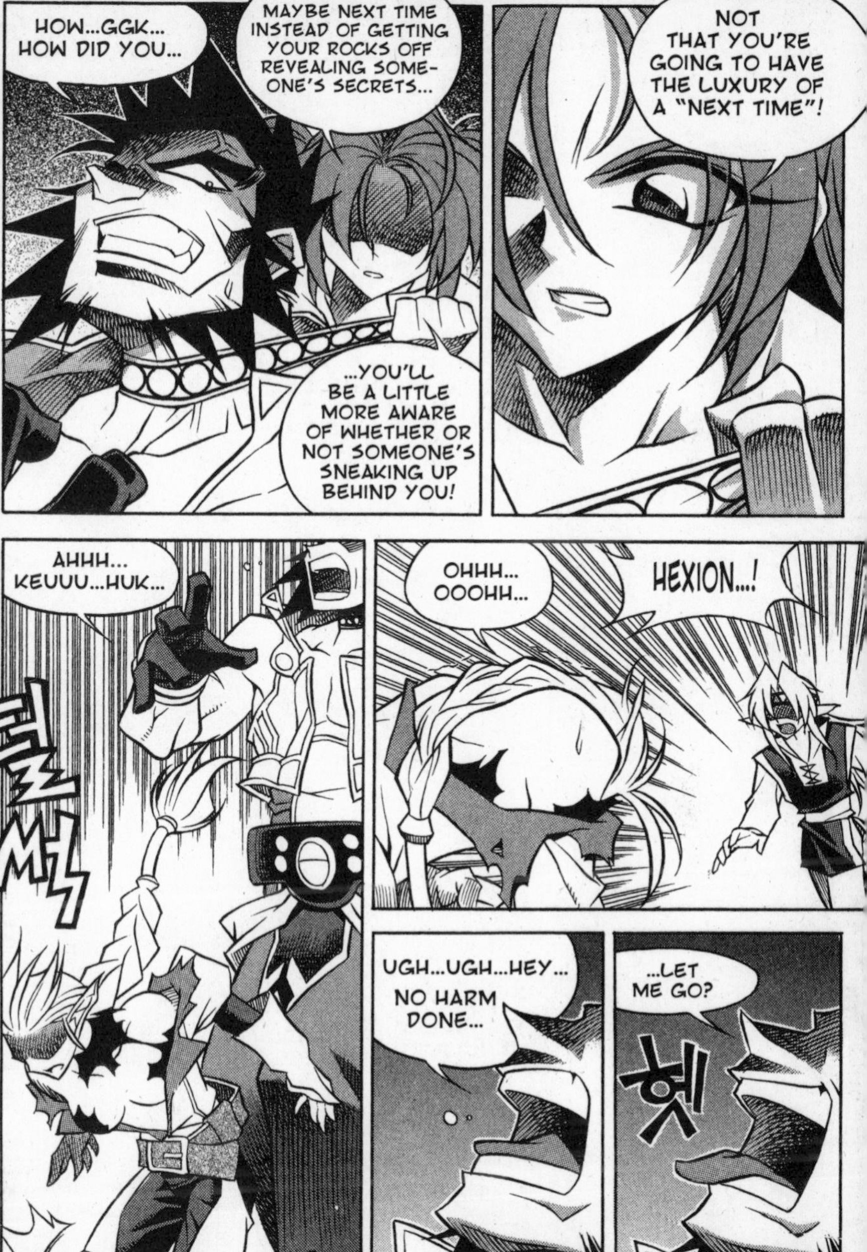
HOW...GGK... HOW DID YOU...
MAYBE NEXT TIME INSTEAD OF GETTING YOUR ROCKS OFF REVEALING SOME-ONE'S SECRETS...
...YOU'LL BE A LITTLE MORE AWARE OF WHETHER OR NOT SOMEONE'S SNEAKING UP BEHIND YOU!
NOT THAT YOU'RE GOING TO HAVE THE LUXURY OF A "NEXT TIME"!
AHHH... KEUUU...HUK...
OHHH... OOOHH...
HEXION...!
UGH...UGH...HEY... NO HARM DONE...
...LET ME GO?

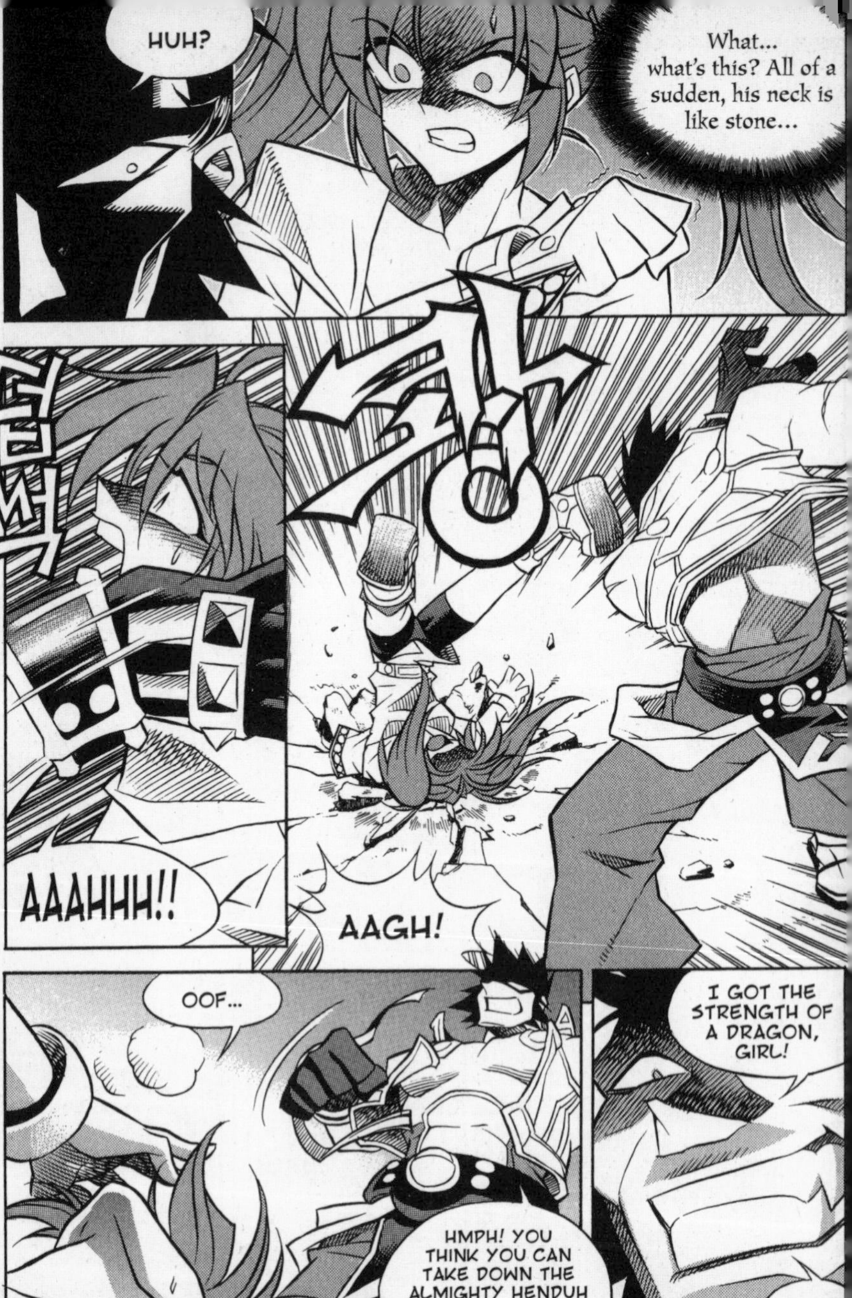
HUH?
What... what's this? All of a sudden, his neck is like stone...
THWM
AAAHHH!!
AAGH!
OOF...
HMPH! YOU THINK YOU CAN TAKE DOWN THE ALMIGHTY HENDUH WITH THIS SCRAP OF COTTON? WHAT A JOKE!
I GOT THE STRENGTH OF A DRAGON, GIRL!
HUH?

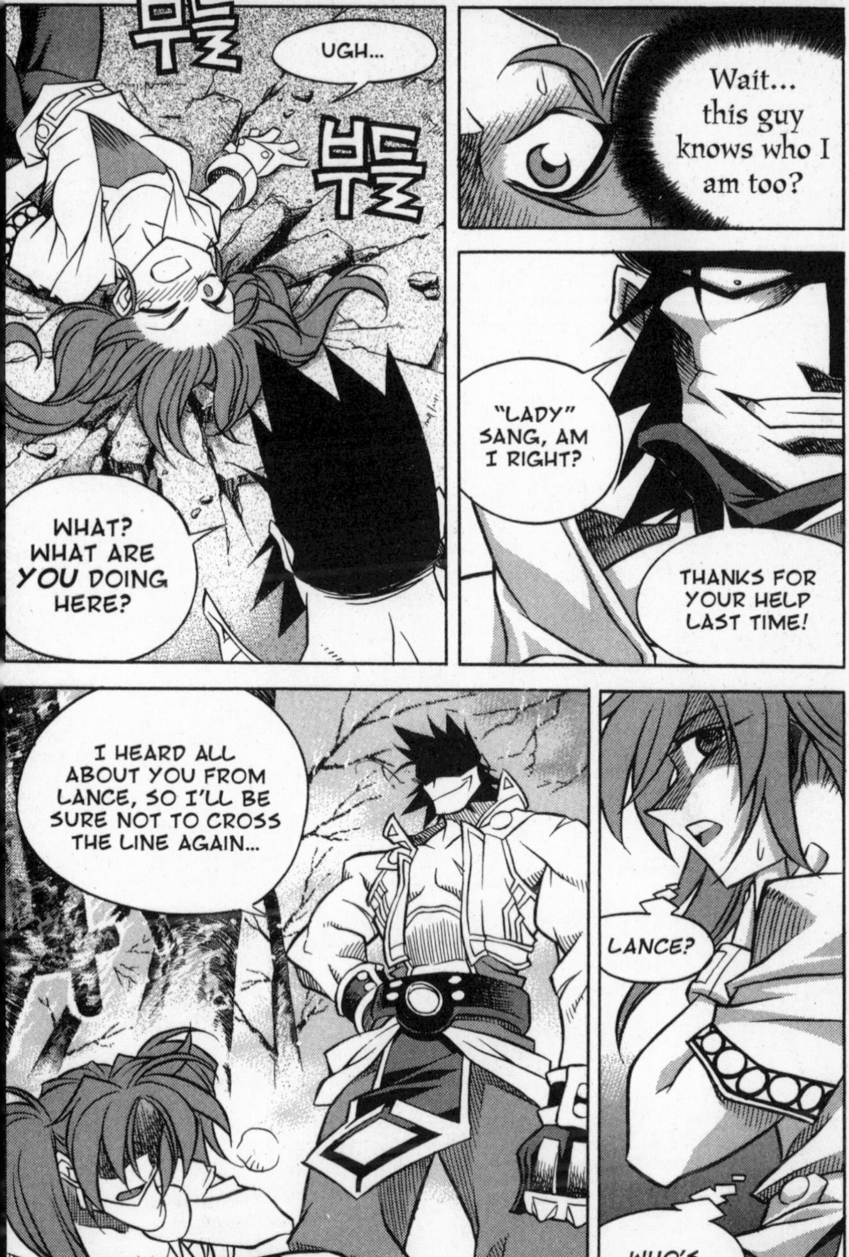
UGH...
WHAT? WHAT ARE *YOU* DOING HERE?
Wait... this guy knows who I am too?
"LADY" SANG, AM I RIGHT?
THANKS FOR YOUR HELP LAST TIME!
I HEARD ALL ABOUT YOU FROM LANCE, SO I'LL BE SURE NOT TO CROSS THE LINE AGAIN...
LANCE?
WHO'S LANCE?!

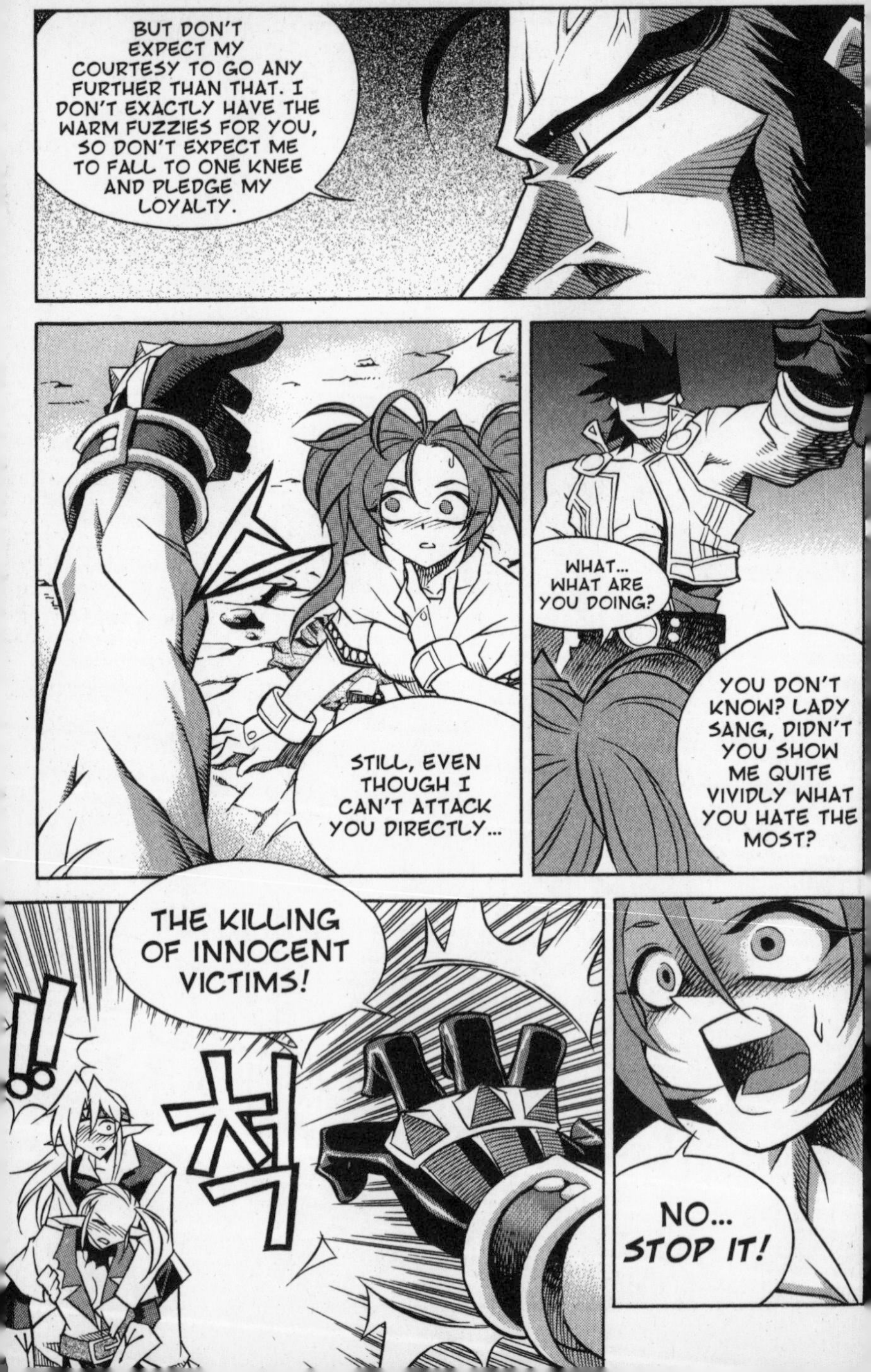
BUT DON'T EXPECT MY COURTESY TO GO ANY FURTHER THAN THAT. I DON'T EXACTLY HAVE THE WARM FUZZIES FOR YOU, SO DON'T EXPECT ME TO FALL TO ONE KNEE AND PLEDGE MY LOYALTY.
STILL, EVEN THOUGH I CAN'T ATTACK YOU DIRECTLY...
WHAT... WHAT ARE YOU DOING?
YOU DON'T KNOW? LADY SANG, DIDN'T YOU SHOW ME QUITE VIVIDLY WHAT YOU HATE THE MOST?
THE KILLING OF INNOCENT VICTIMS!
!!
척
NO... STOP IT!

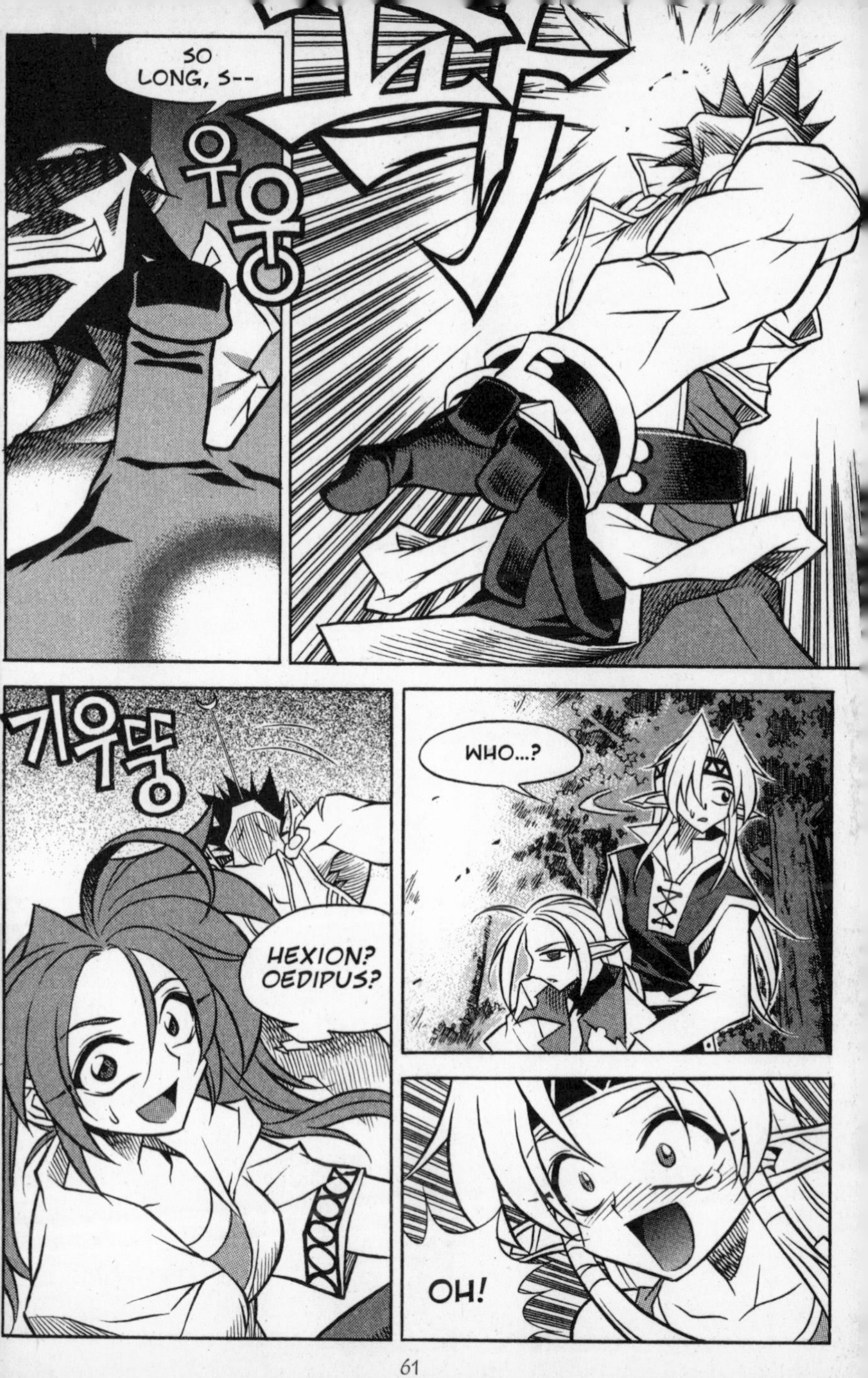
SO LONG, S--
우웅
기우뚱
HEXION? OEDIPUS?
WHO...?
OH!

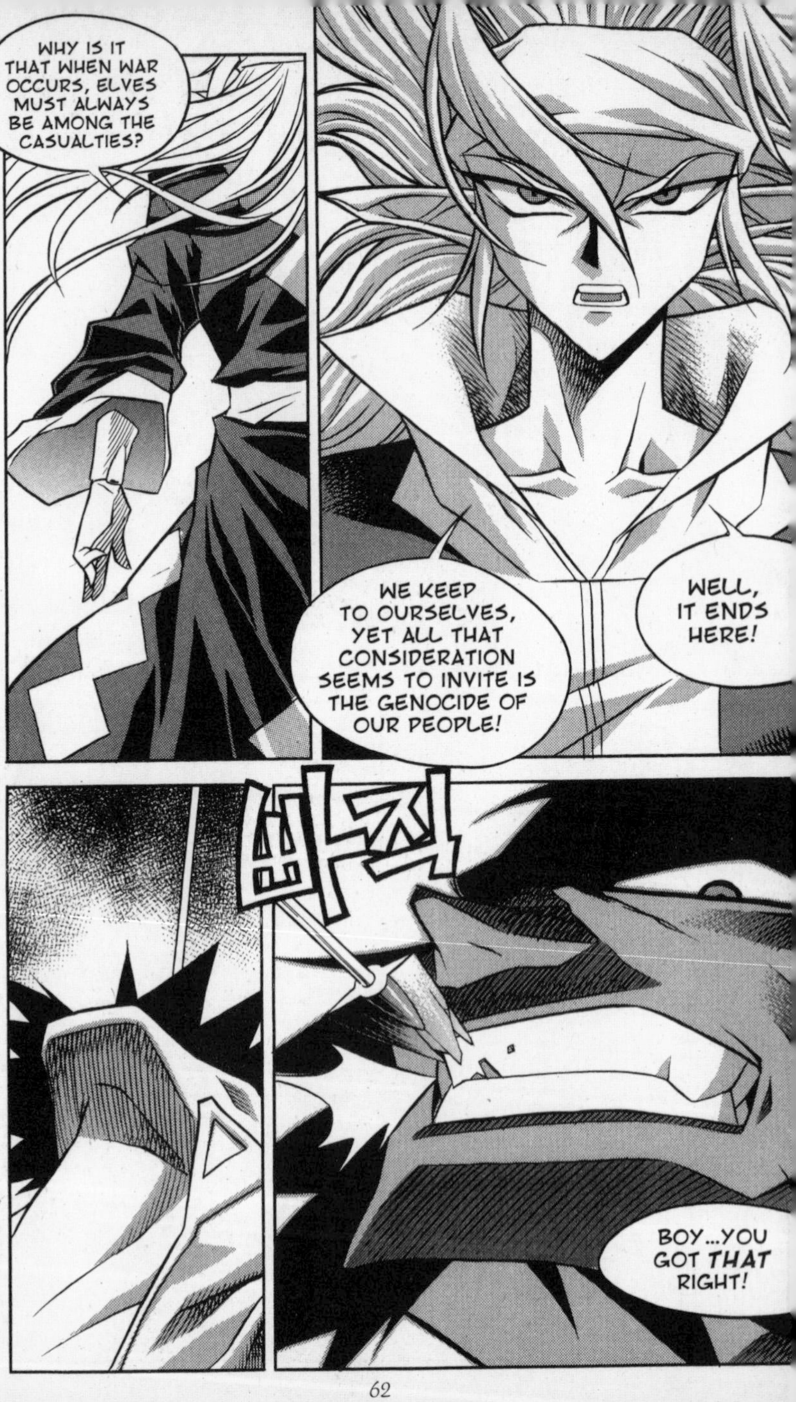
WHY IS IT THAT WHEN WAR OCCURS, ELVES MUST ALWAYS BE AMONG THE CASUALTIES?
WE KEEP TO OURSELVES, YET ALL THAT CONSIDERATION SEEMS TO INVITE IS THE GENOCIDE OF OUR PEOPLE!
WELL, IT ENDS HERE!
빠직
BOY...YOU GOT *THAT* RIGHT!

Quest 62

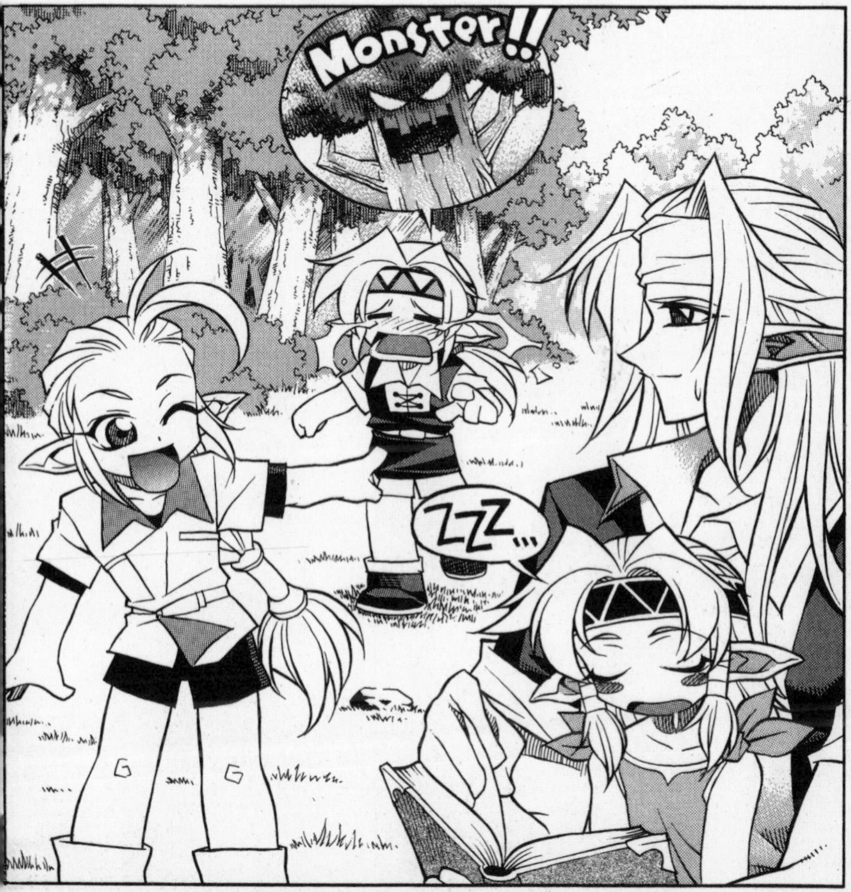

Monster!!
ZZZ...

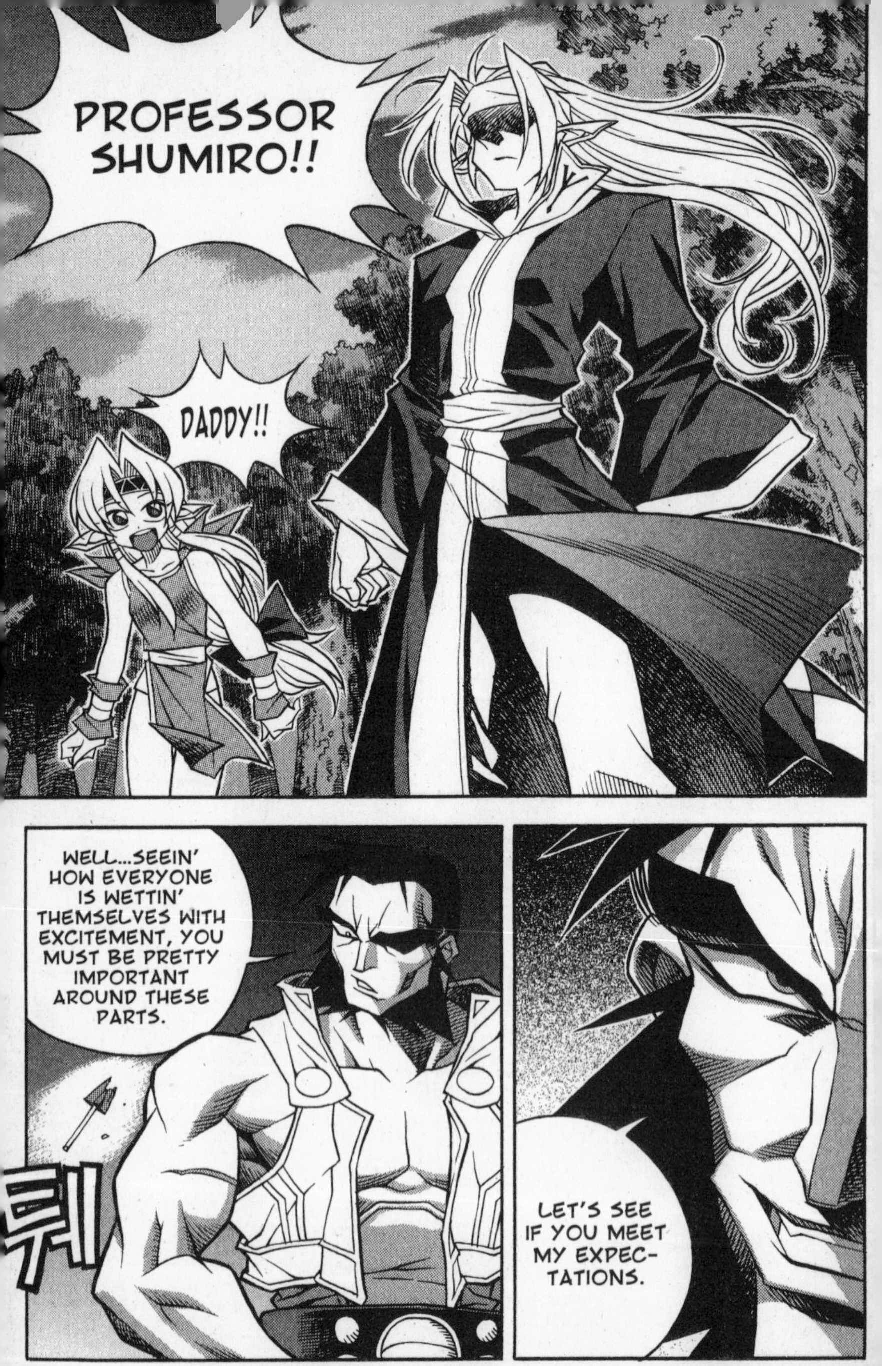
PROFESSOR SHUMIRO!!
DADDY!!
WELL...SEEIN' HOW EVERYONE IS WETTIN' THEMSELVES WITH EXCITEMENT, YOU MUST BE PRETTY IMPORTANT AROUND THESE PARTS.
LET'S SEE IF YOU MEET MY EXPEC-TATIONS.

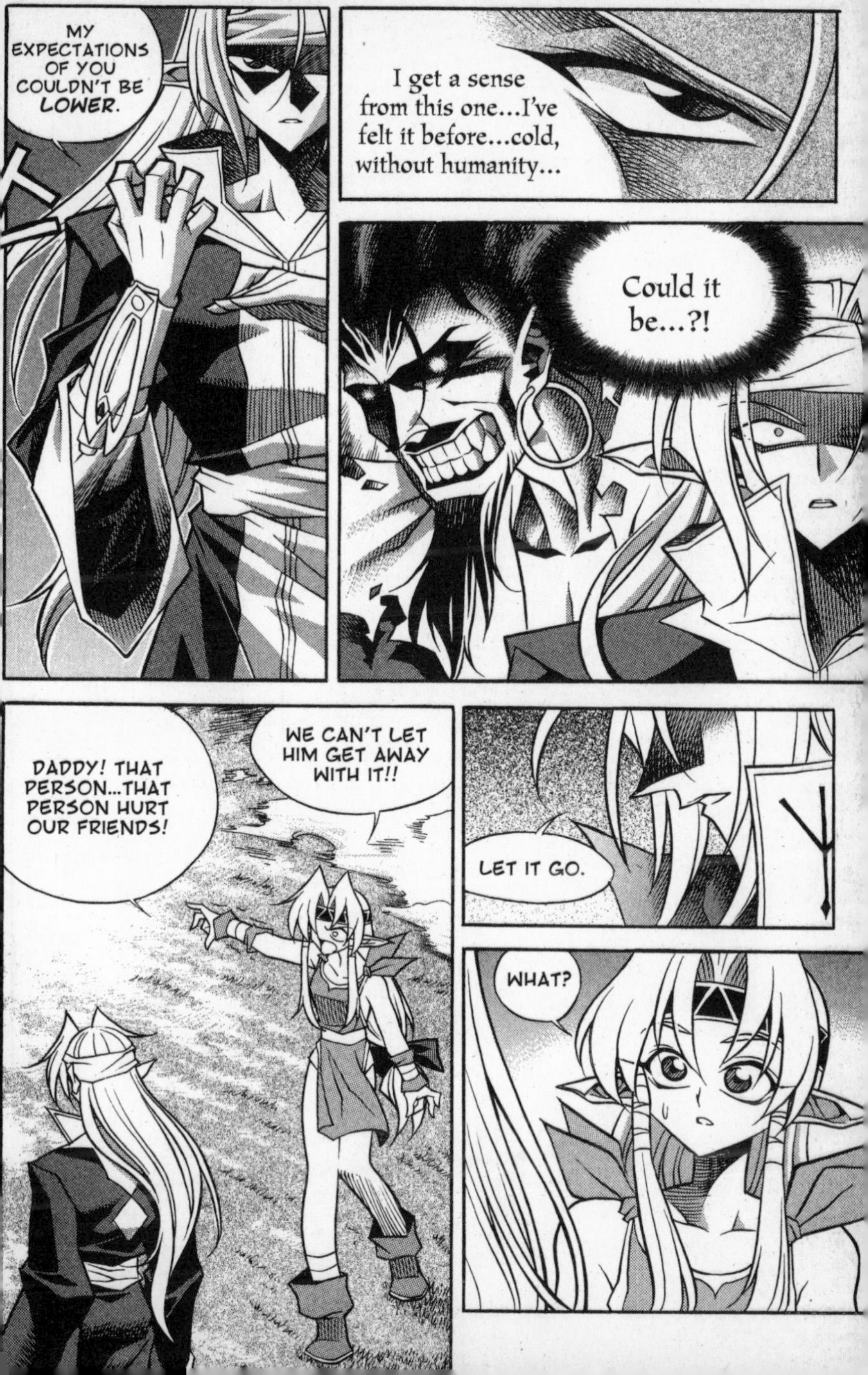
MY EXPECTATIONS OF YOU COULDN'T BE LOWER.
I get a sense from this one...I've felt it before...cold, without humanity...
Could it be...?!
DADDY! THAT PERSON...THAT PERSON HURT OUR FRIENDS!
WE CAN'T LET HIM GET AWAY WITH IT!!
LET IT GO.
WHAT?

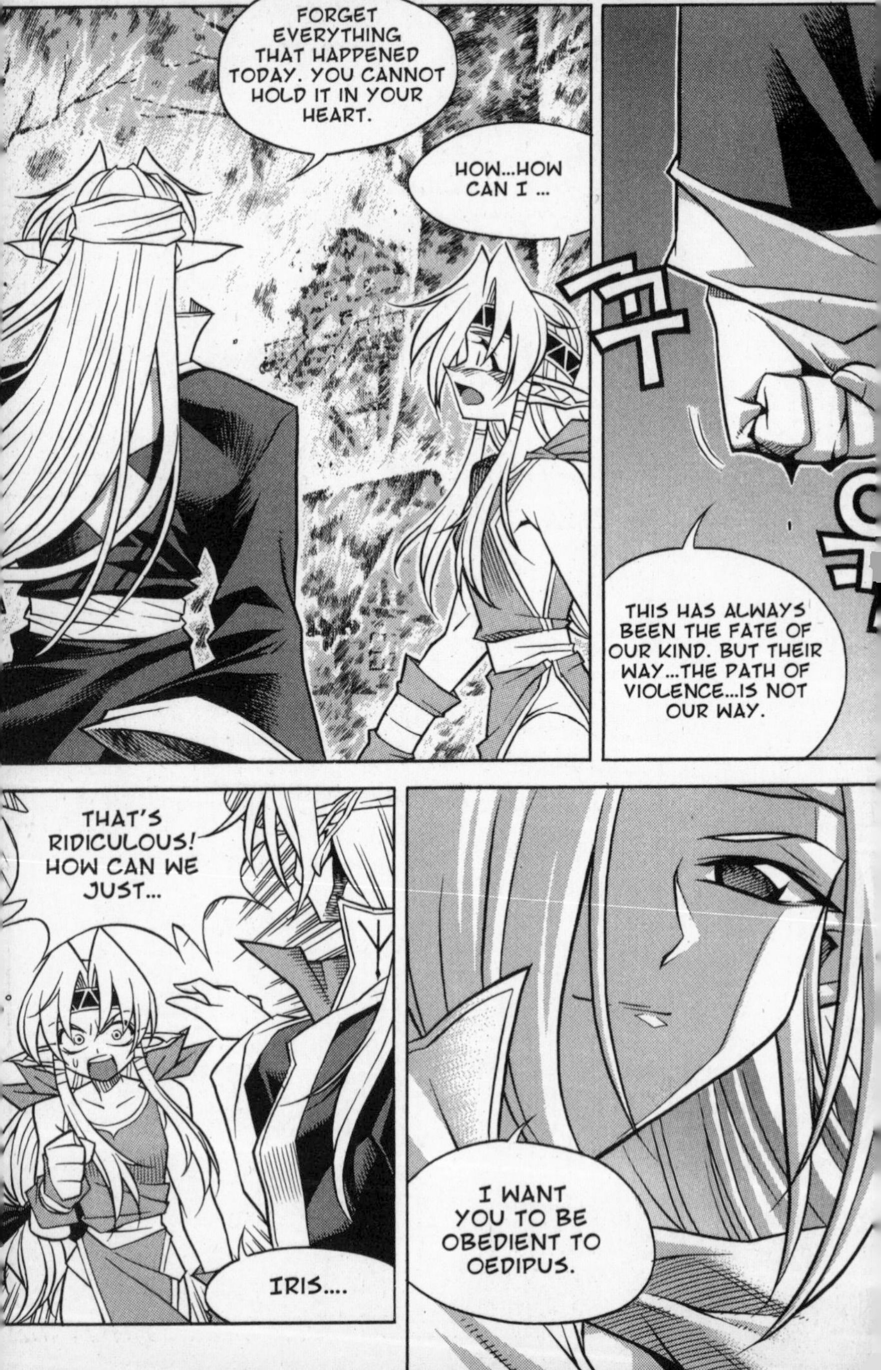
FORGET EVERYTHING THAT HAPPENED TODAY. YOU CANNOT HOLD IT IN YOUR HEART.
HOW...HOW CAN I ...
THIS HAS ALWAYS BEEN THE FATE OF OUR KIND. BUT THEIR WAY...THE PATH OF VIOLENCE...IS NOT OUR WAY.
THAT'S RIDICULOUS! HOW CAN WE JUST...
IRIS....
I WANT YOU TO BE OBEDIENT TO OEDIPUS.

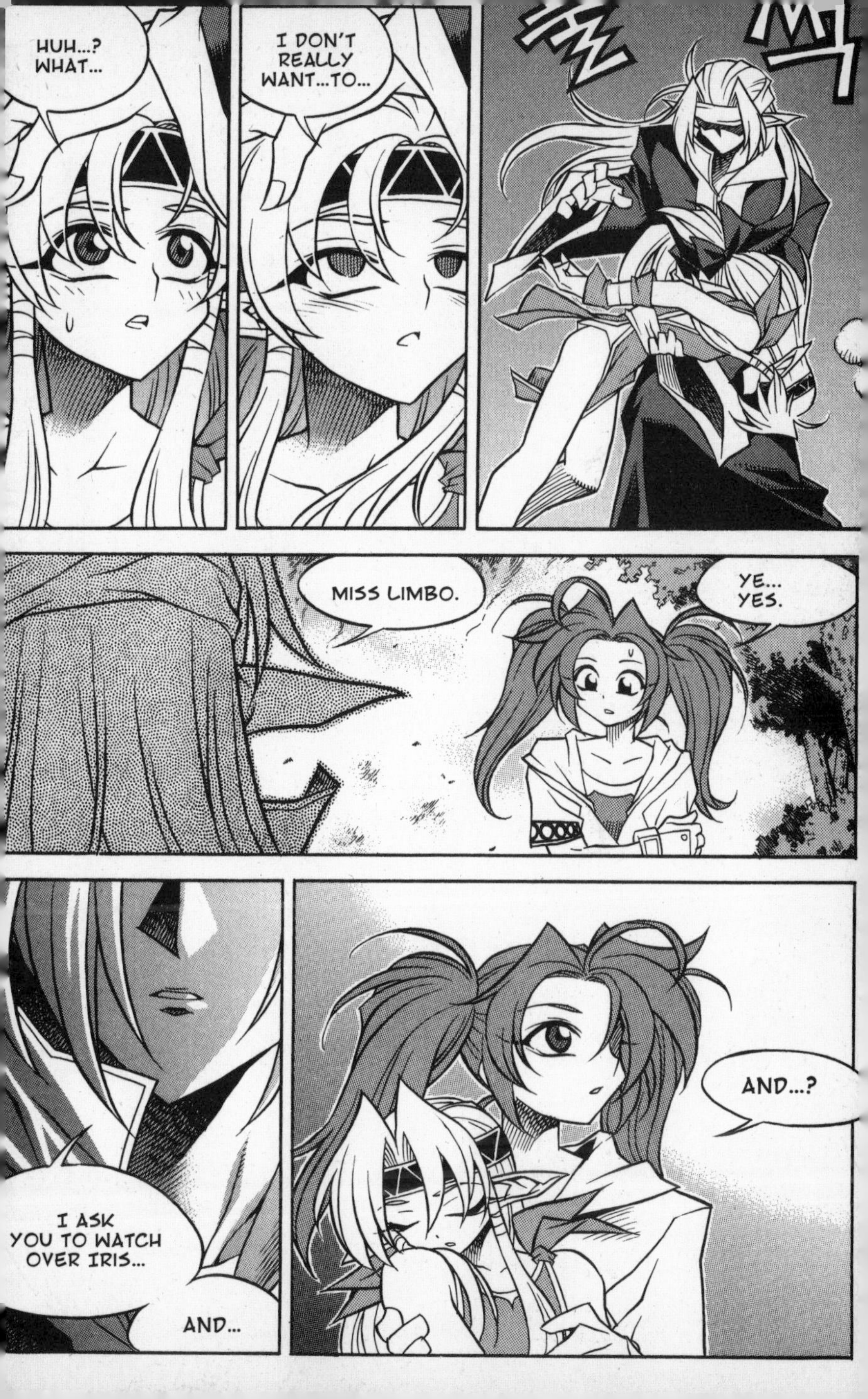
HUH...? WHAT...
I DON'T REALLY WANT...TO...
MISS LIMBO.
YE... YES.
I ASK YOU TO WATCH OVER IRIS...
AND...
AND...?

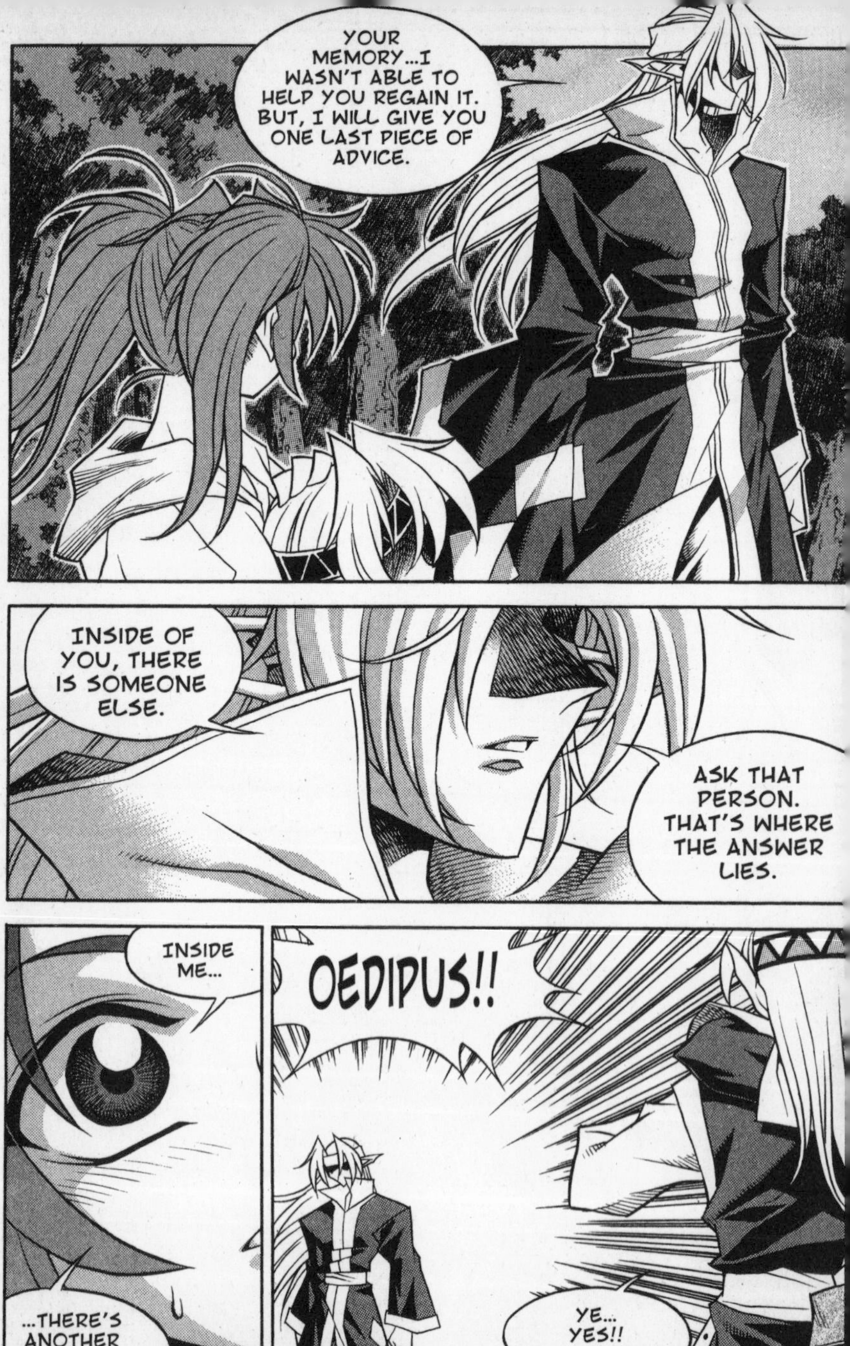

YOUR MEMORY...I WASN'T ABLE TO HELP YOU REGAIN IT. BUT, I WILL GIVE YOU ONE LAST PIECE OF ADVICE.
INSIDE OF YOU, THERE IS SOMEONE ELSE.
ASK THAT PERSON. THAT'S WHERE THE ANSWER LIES.
INSIDE ME...
...THERE'S ANOTHER PERSON?
OEDIPUS!!
YE... YES!!

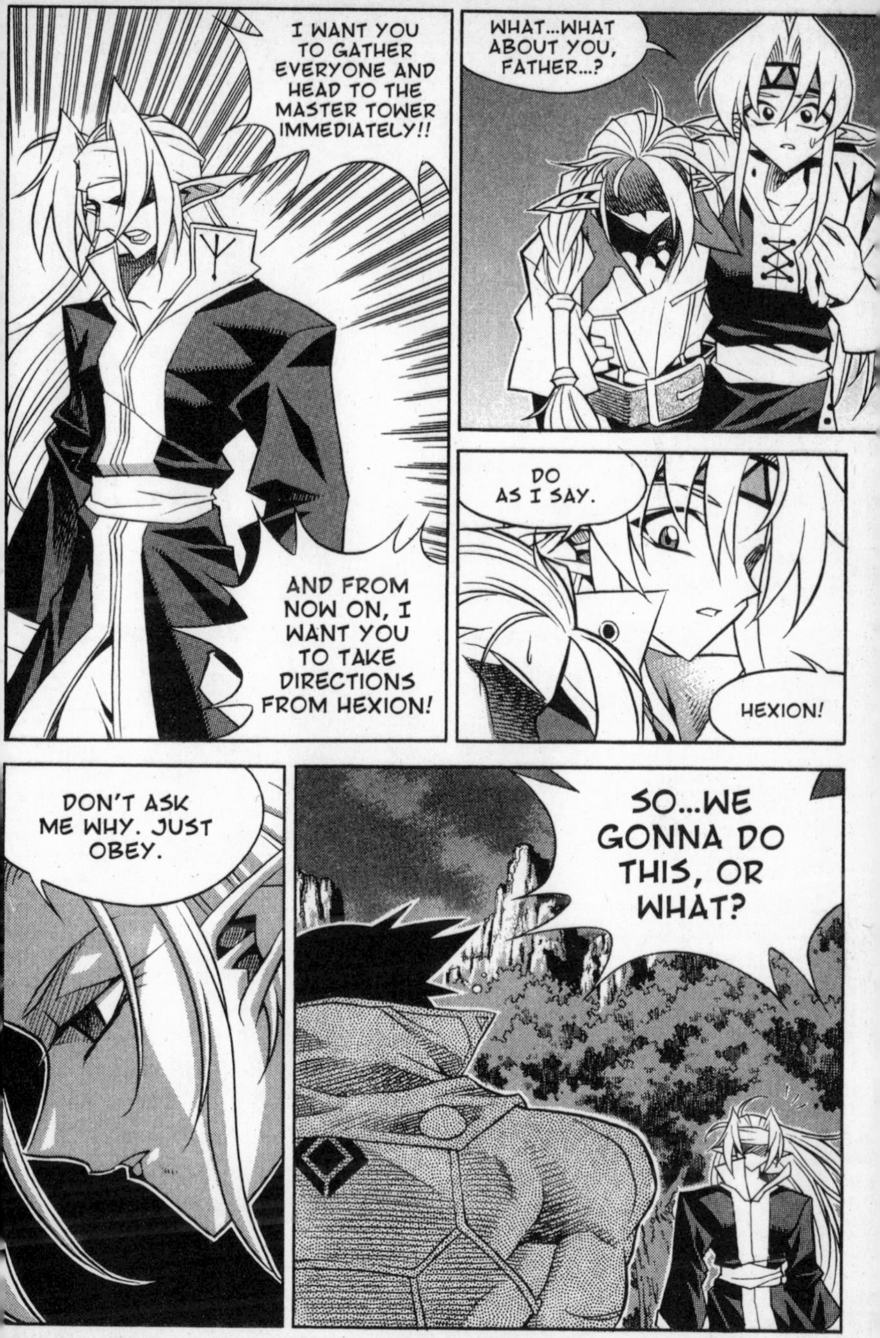
I WANT YOU TO GATHER EVERYONE AND HEAD TO THE MASTER TOWER IMMEDIATELY!!
AND FROM NOW ON, I WANT YOU TO TAKE DIRECTIONS FROM HEXION!
WHAT...WHAT ABOUT YOU, FATHER...?
DO AS I SAY.
HEXION!
DON'T ASK ME WHY. JUST OBEY.
SO...WE GONNA DO THIS, OR WHAT?

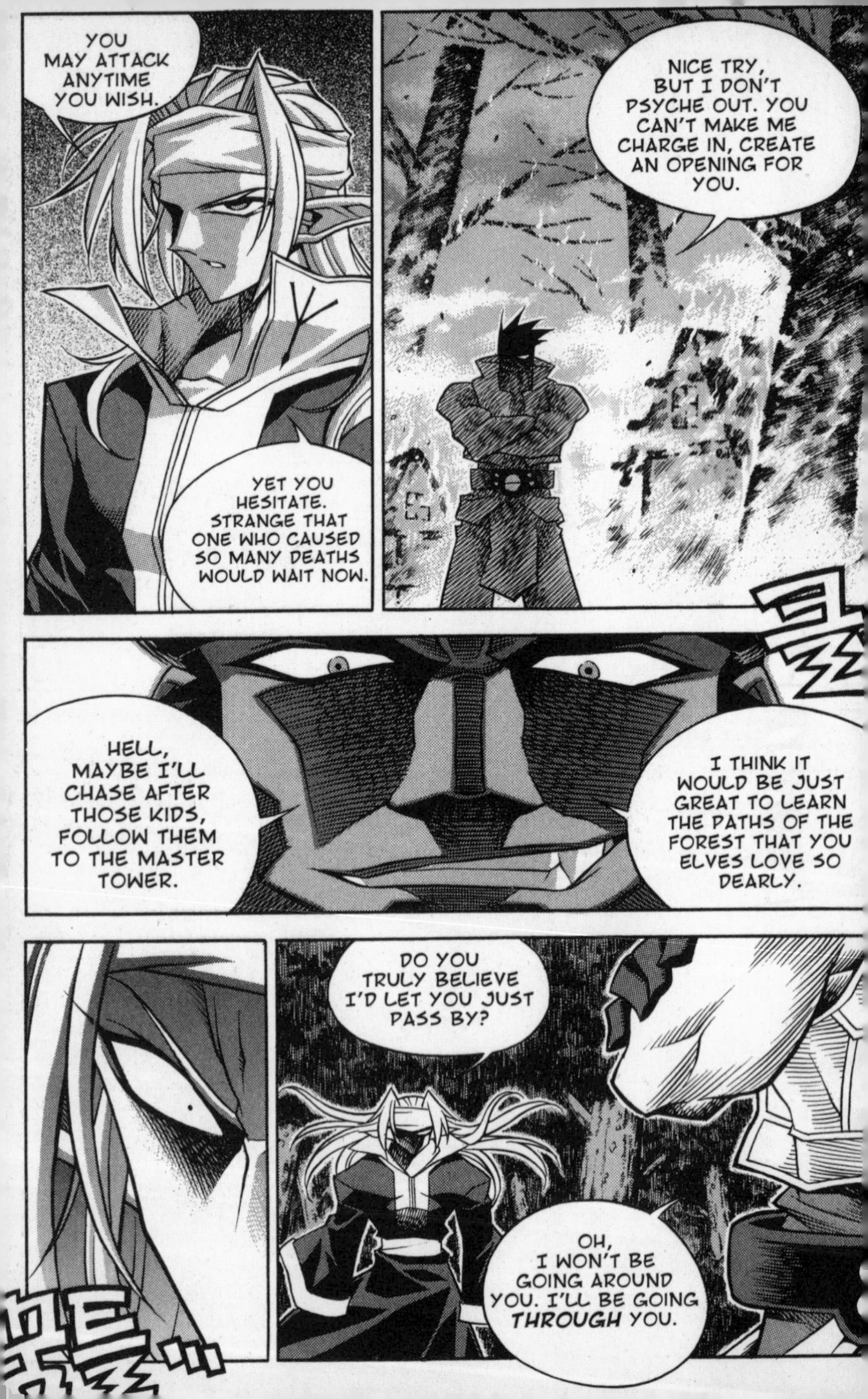

YOU MAY ATTACK ANYTIME YOU WISH.
YET YOU HESITATE. STRANGE THAT ONE WHO CAUSED SO MANY DEATHS WOULD WAIT NOW.
NICE TRY, BUT I DON'T PSYCHE OUT. YOU CAN'T MAKE ME CHARGE IN, CREATE AN OPENING FOR YOU.
HELL, MAYBE I'LL CHASE AFTER THOSE KIDS, FOLLOW THEM TO THE MASTER TOWER.
I THINK IT WOULD BE JUST GREAT TO LEARN THE PATHS OF THE FOREST THAT YOU ELVES LOVE SO DEARLY.
DO YOU TRULY BELIEVE I'D LET YOU JUST PASS BY?
OH, I WON'T BE GOING AROUND YOU. I'LL BE GOING *THROUGH* YOU.

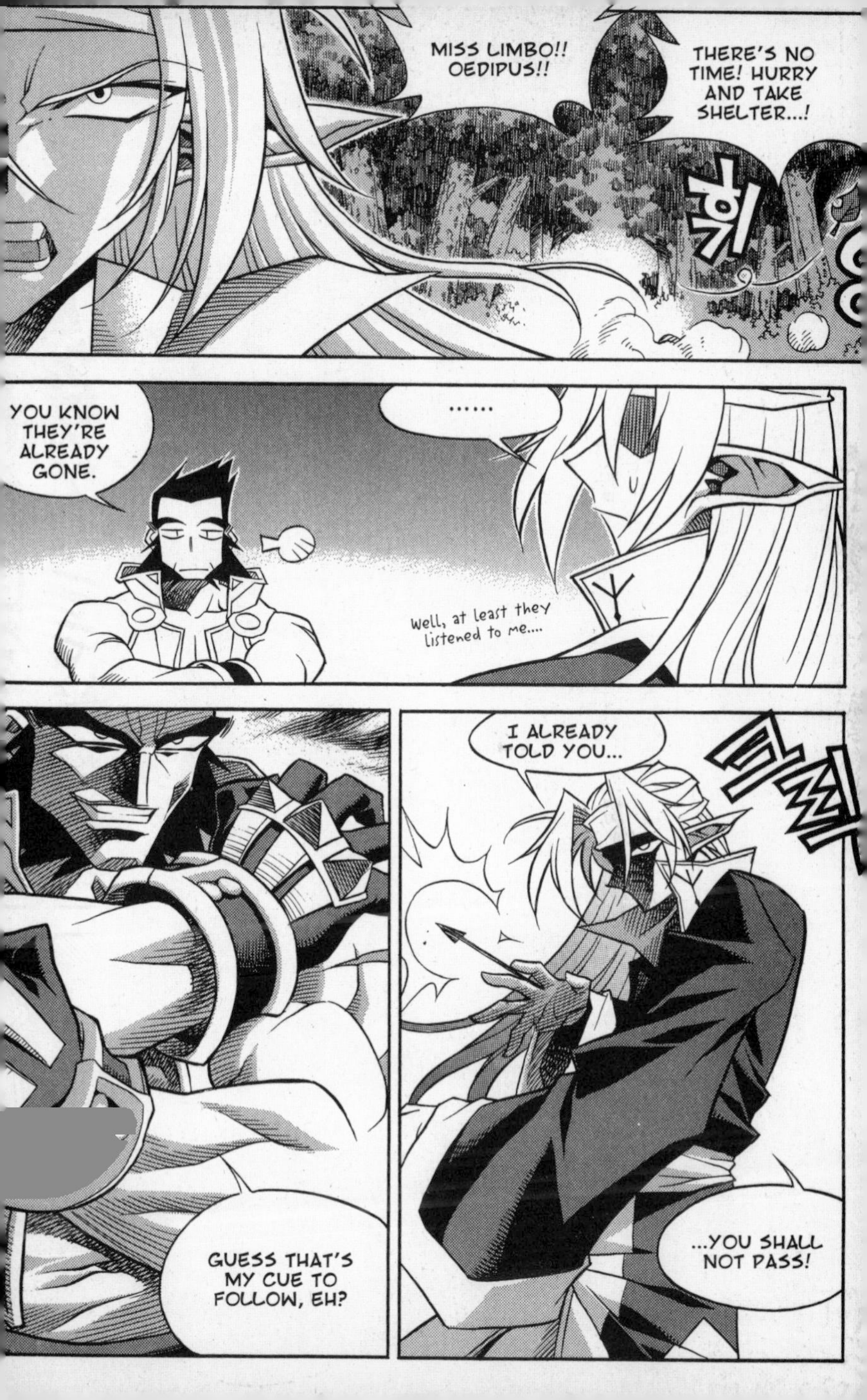
MISS LIMBO!! OEDIPUS!!
THERE'S NO TIME! HURRY AND TAKE SHELTER...!
YOU KNOW THEY'RE ALREADY GONE.
......
Well, at least they listened to me....
GUESS THAT'S MY CUE TO FOLLOW, EH?
I ALREADY TOLD YOU...
...YOU SHALL NOT PASS!

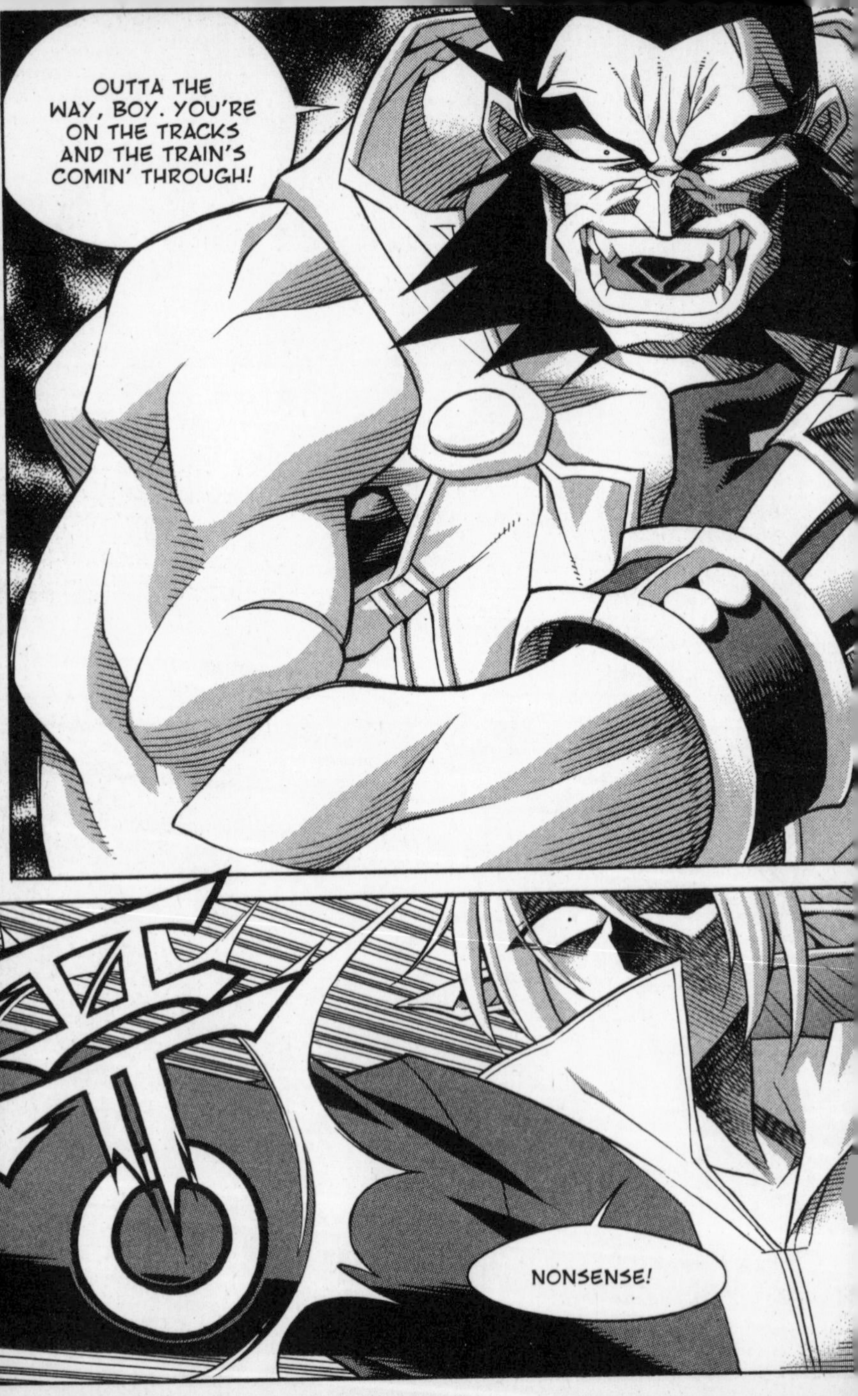
OUTTA THE WAY, BOY. YOU'RE ON THE TRACKS AND THE TRAIN'S COMIN' THROUGH!
NONSENSE!

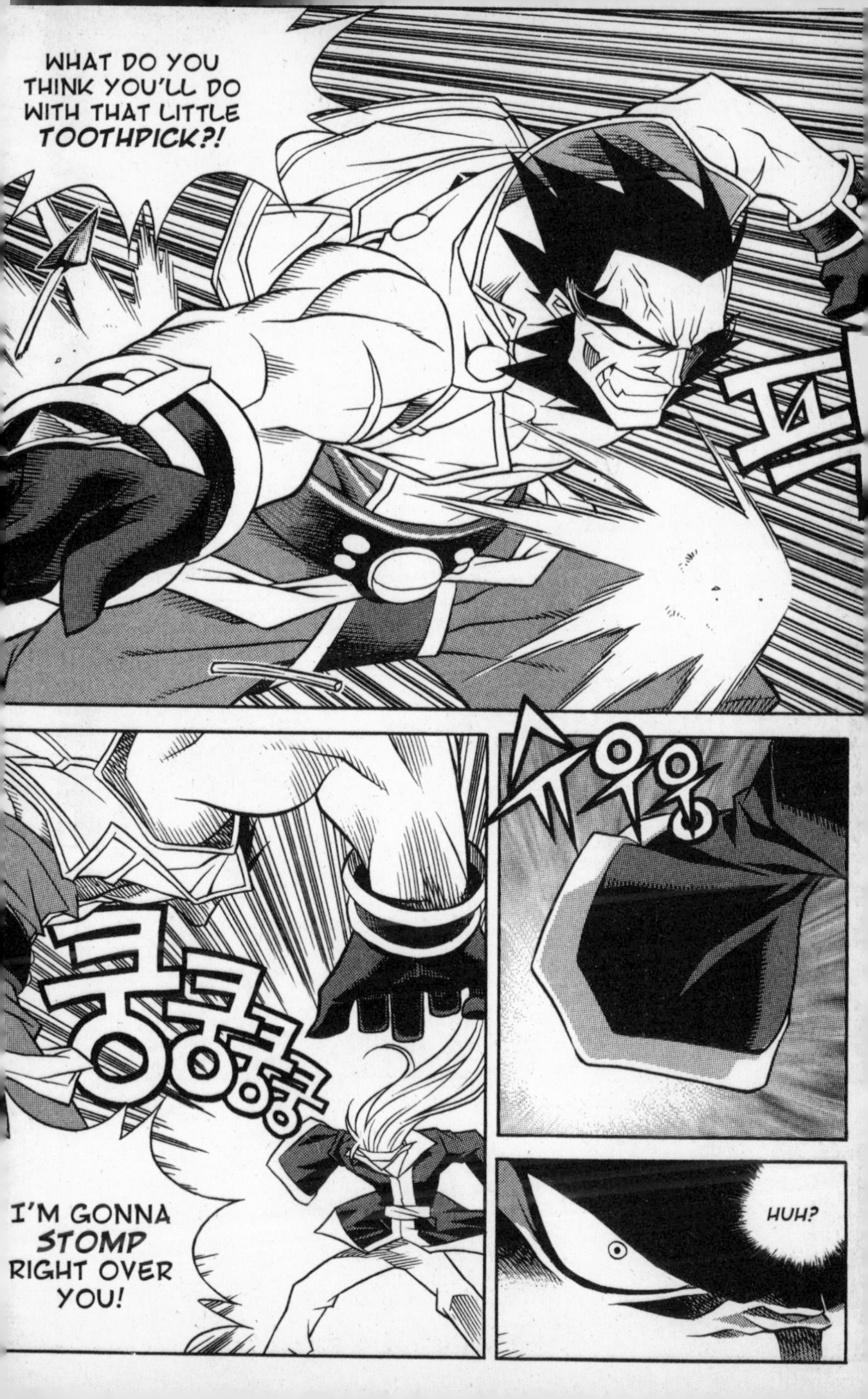
WHAT DO YOU THINK YOU'LL DO WITH THAT LITTLE TOOTHPICK?!
쿵쿵쿵
I'M GONNA STOMP RIGHT OVER YOU!
HUH?

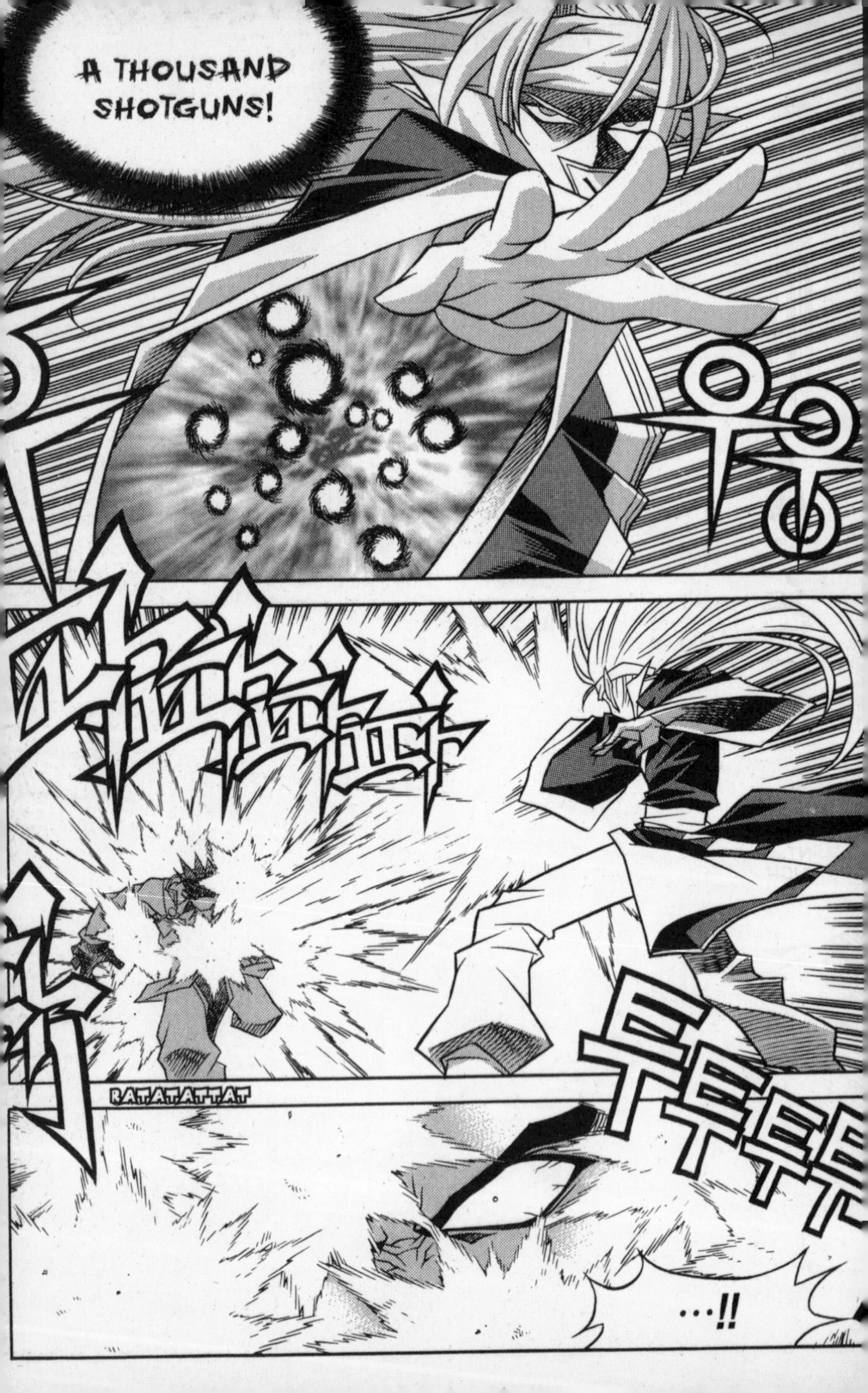
A THOUSAND SHOTGUNS!
RATATATTAT
...!!

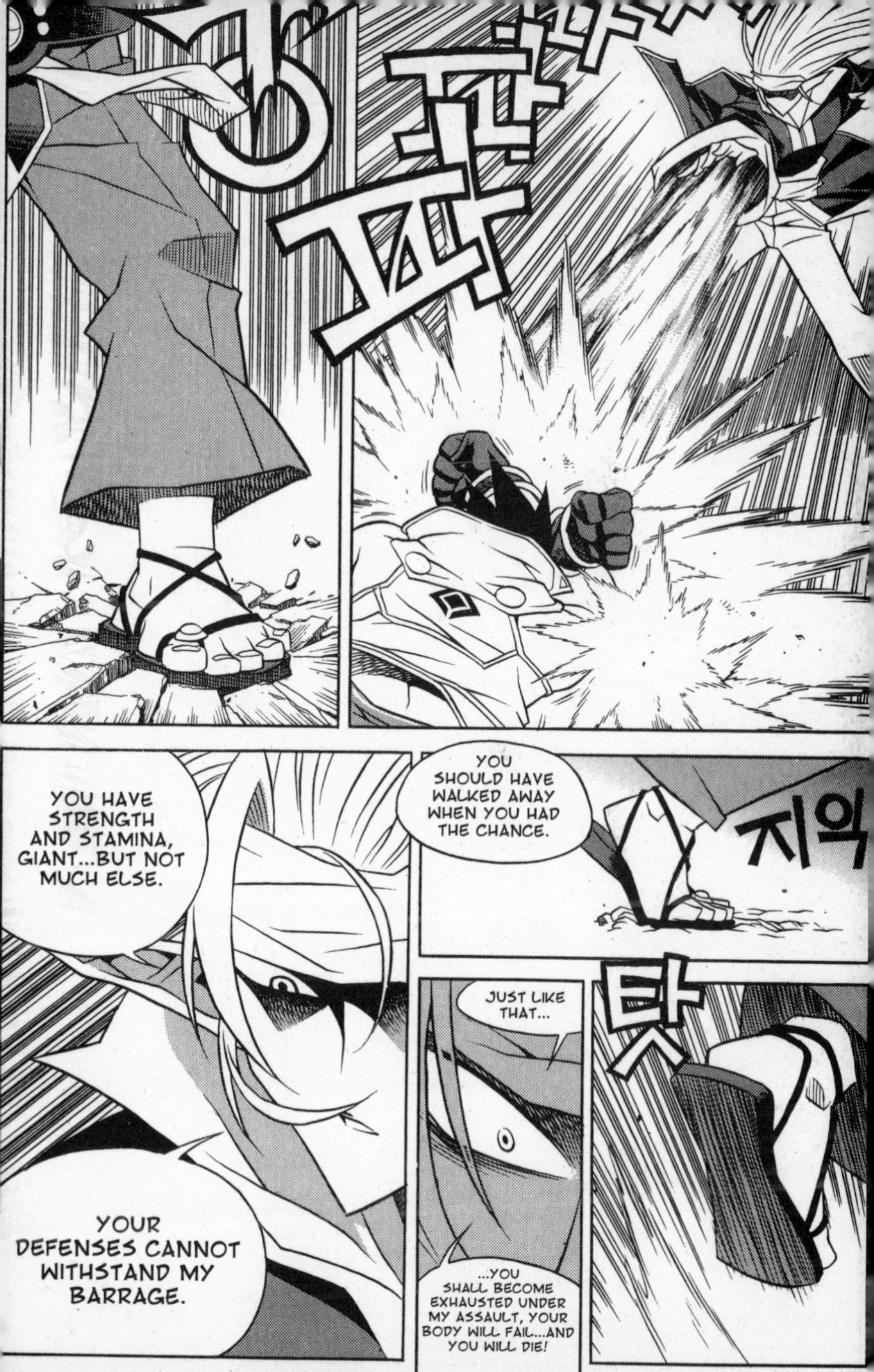
YOU HAVE STRENGTH AND STAMINA, GIANT...BUT NOT MUCH ELSE.
YOUR DEFENSES CANNOT WITHSTAND MY BARRAGE.
YOU SHOULD HAVE WALKED AWAY WHEN YOU HAD THE CHANCE.
지익
JUST LIKE THAT...
...YOU SHALL BECOME EXHAUSTED UNDER MY ASSAULT, YOUR BODY WILL FAIL...AND YOU WILL DIE!
탓

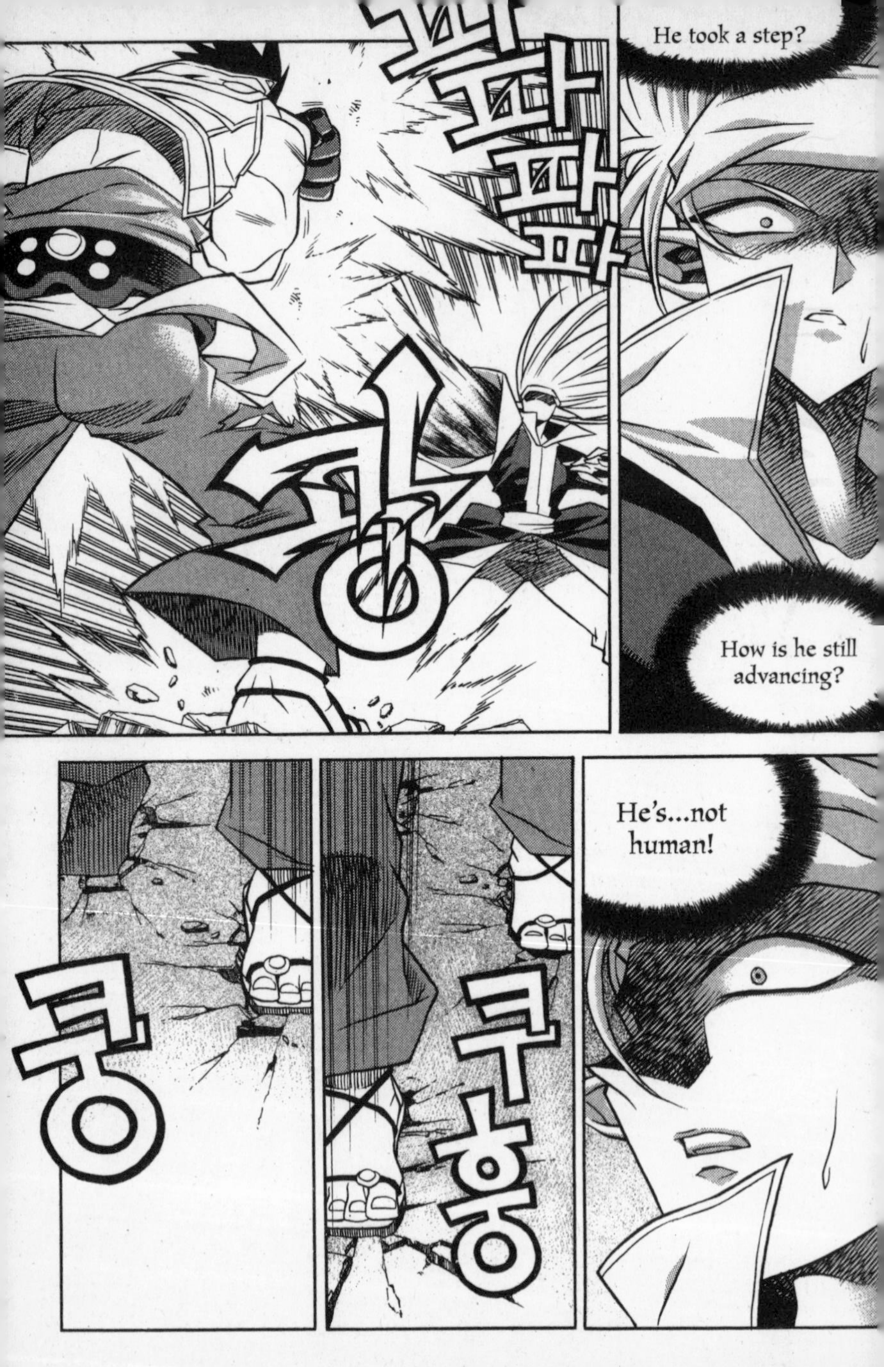
He took a step?
How is he still advancing?
쿵
He's...not human!

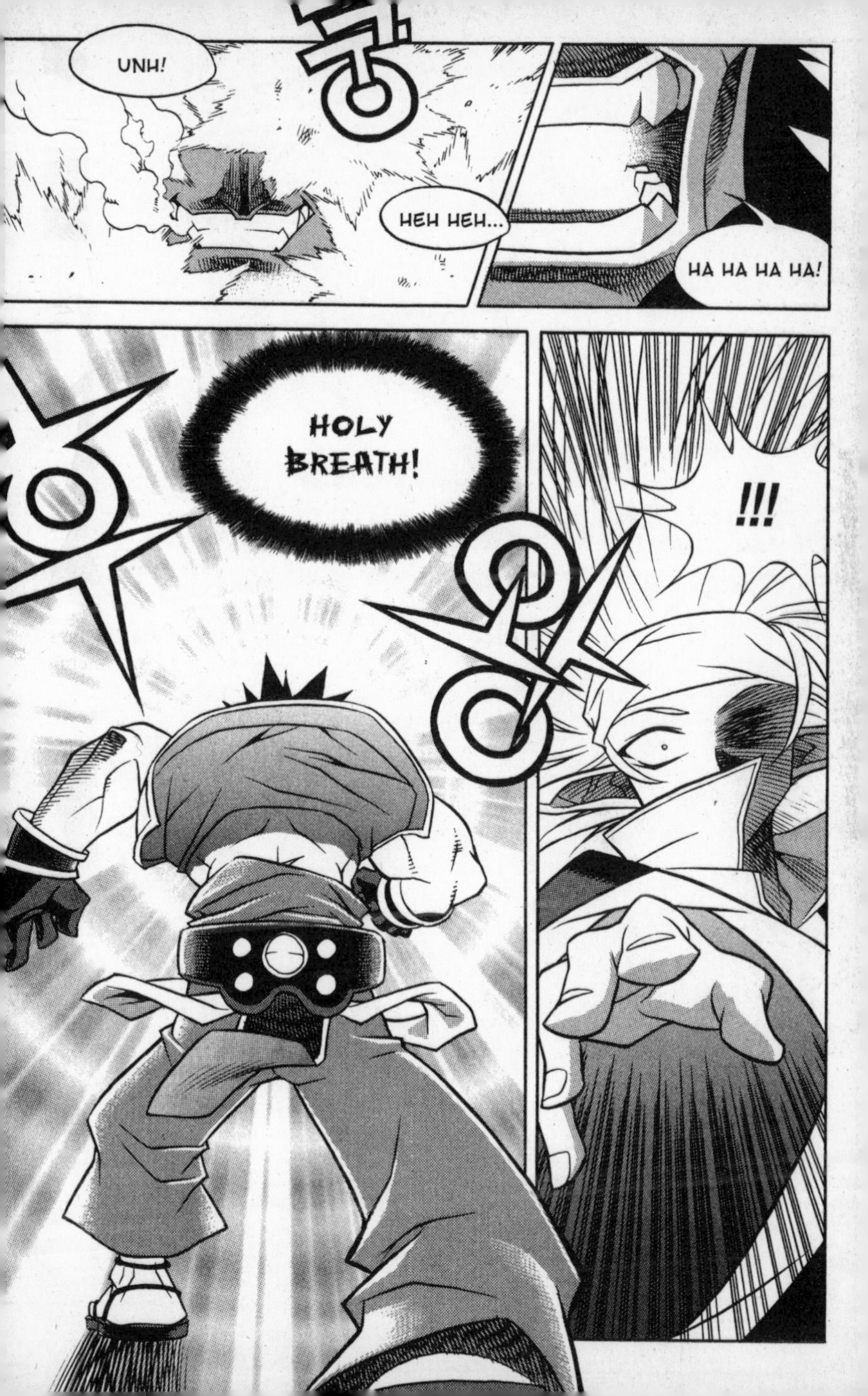
UNH!
HEH HEH...
HA HA HA HA!
HOLY BREATH!
!!!

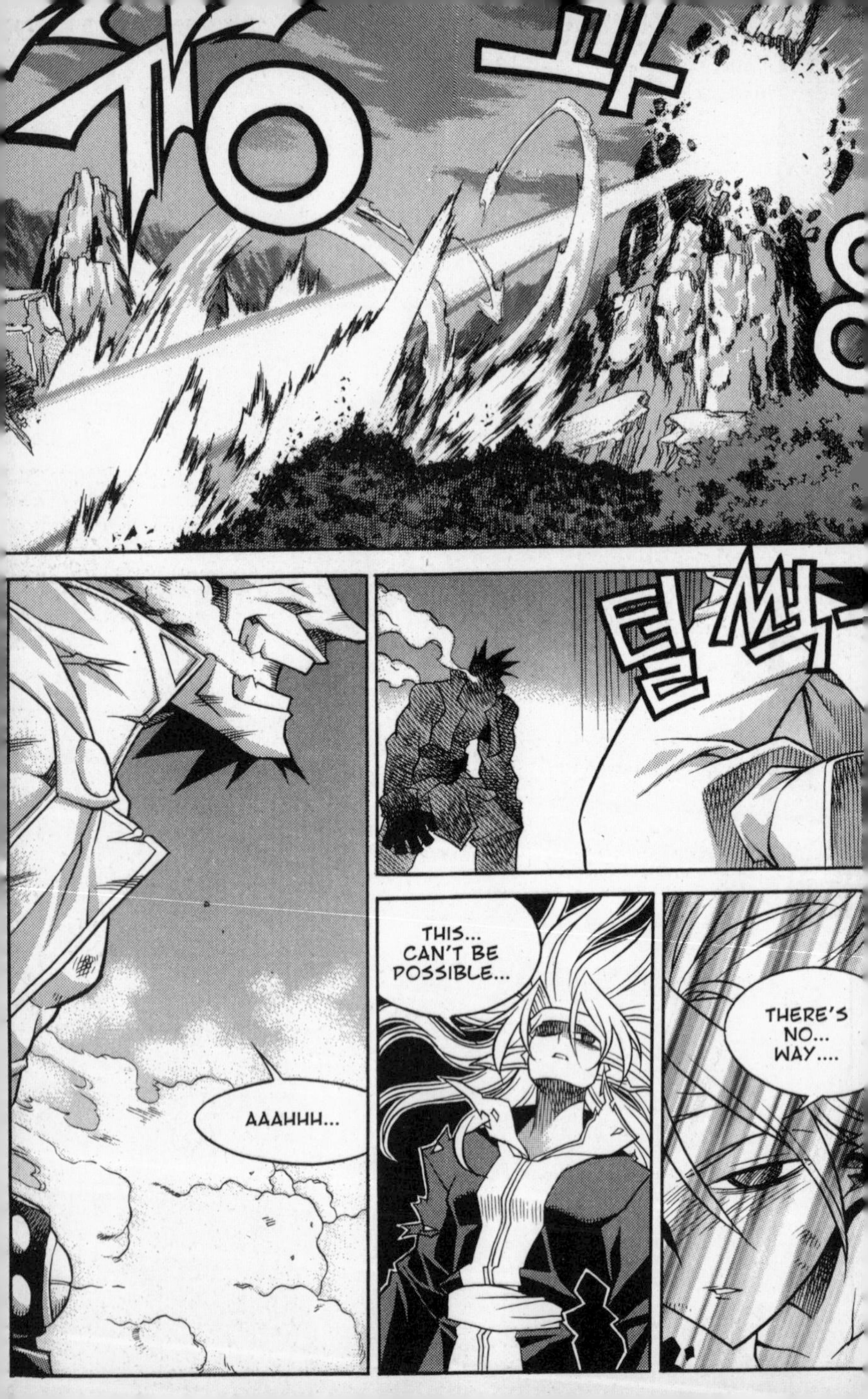
AAAHHH...
털썩
THIS... CAN'T BE POSSIBLE...
THERE'S NO... WAY....

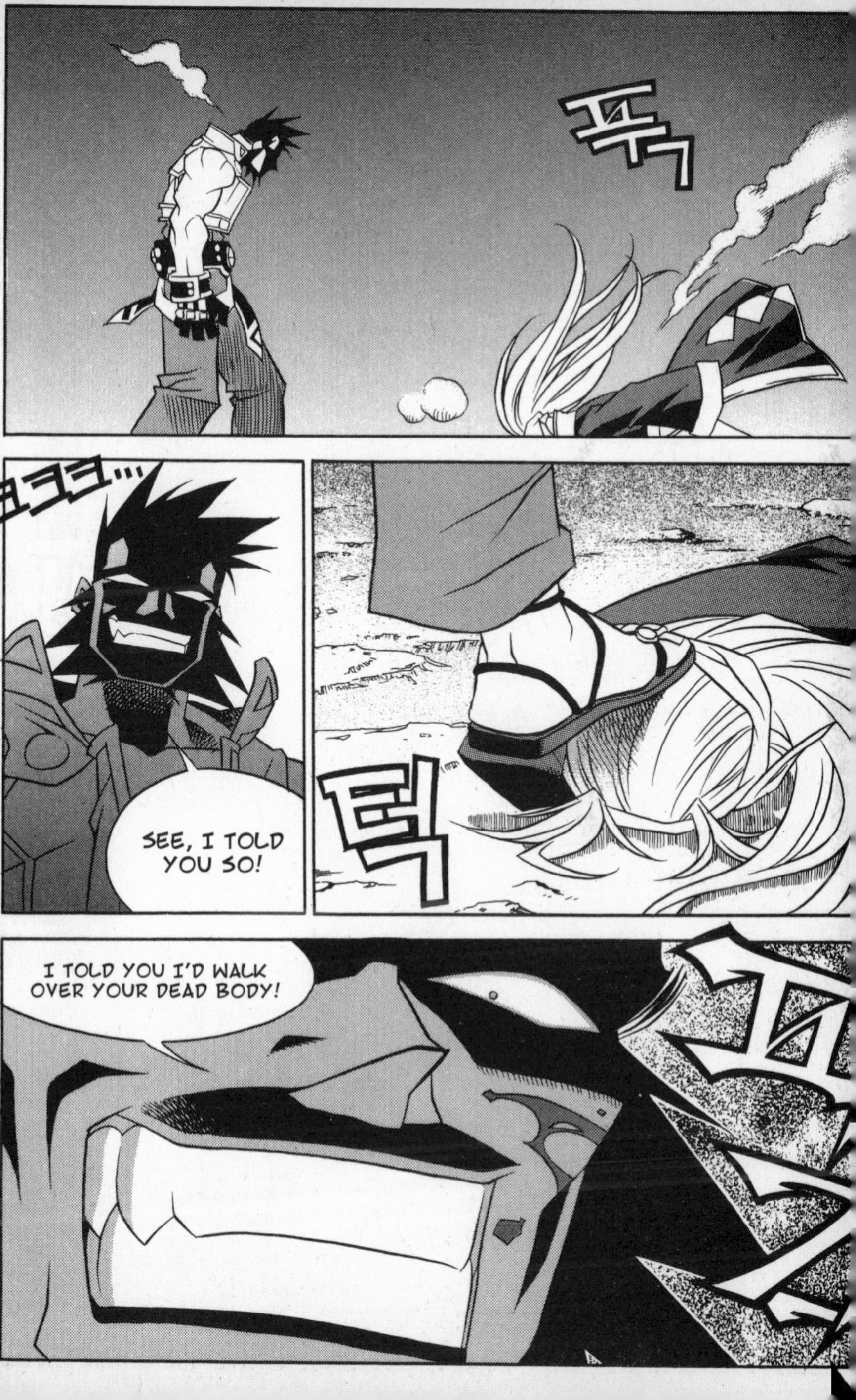
퍽
크크크...
SEE, I TOLD YOU SO!
턱
I TOLD YOU I'D WALK OVER YOUR DEAD BODY!

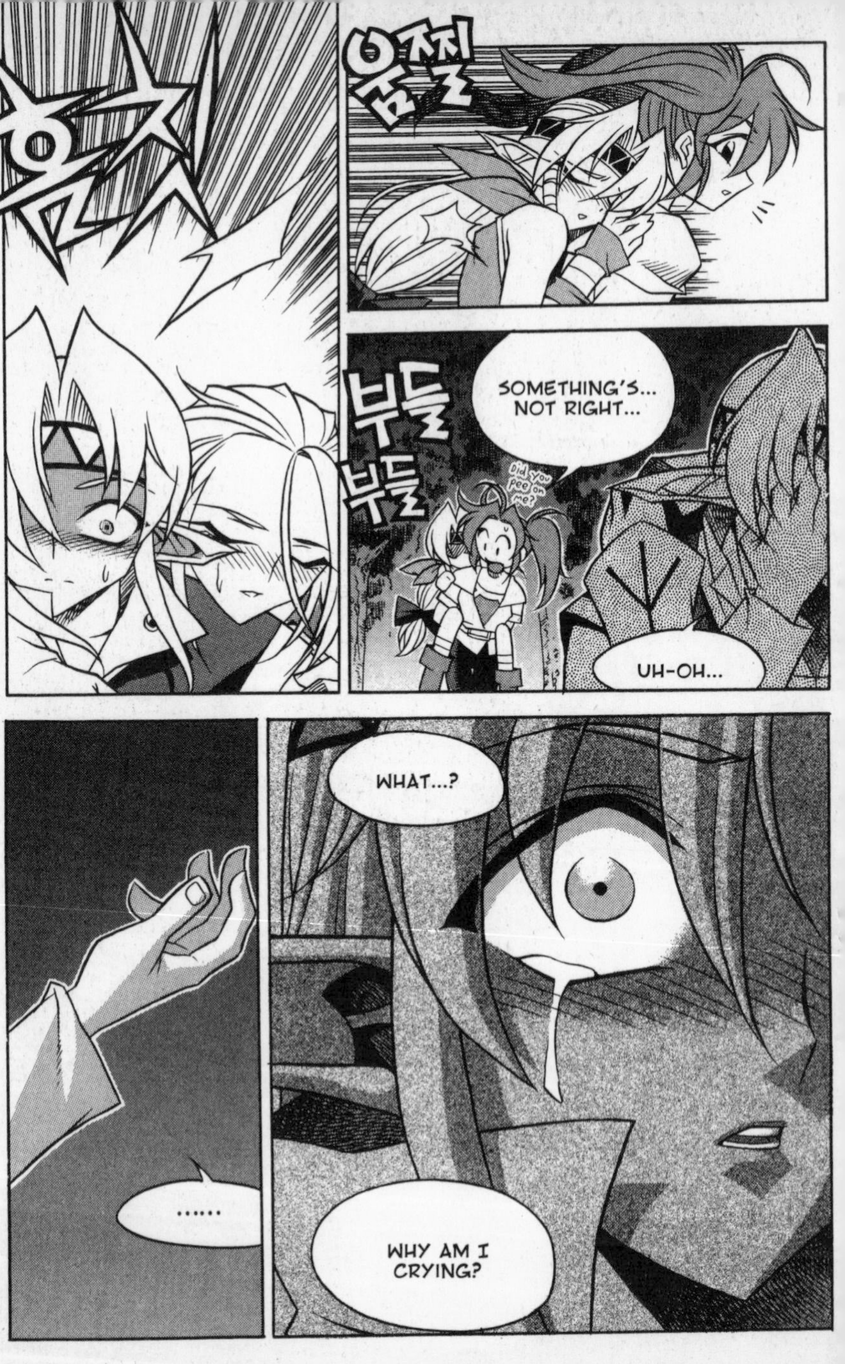
부들
부들
SOMETHING'S... NOT RIGHT...
Did you pee on me?
UH-OH...
......
WHAT...?
WHY AM I CRYING?

Quest 63

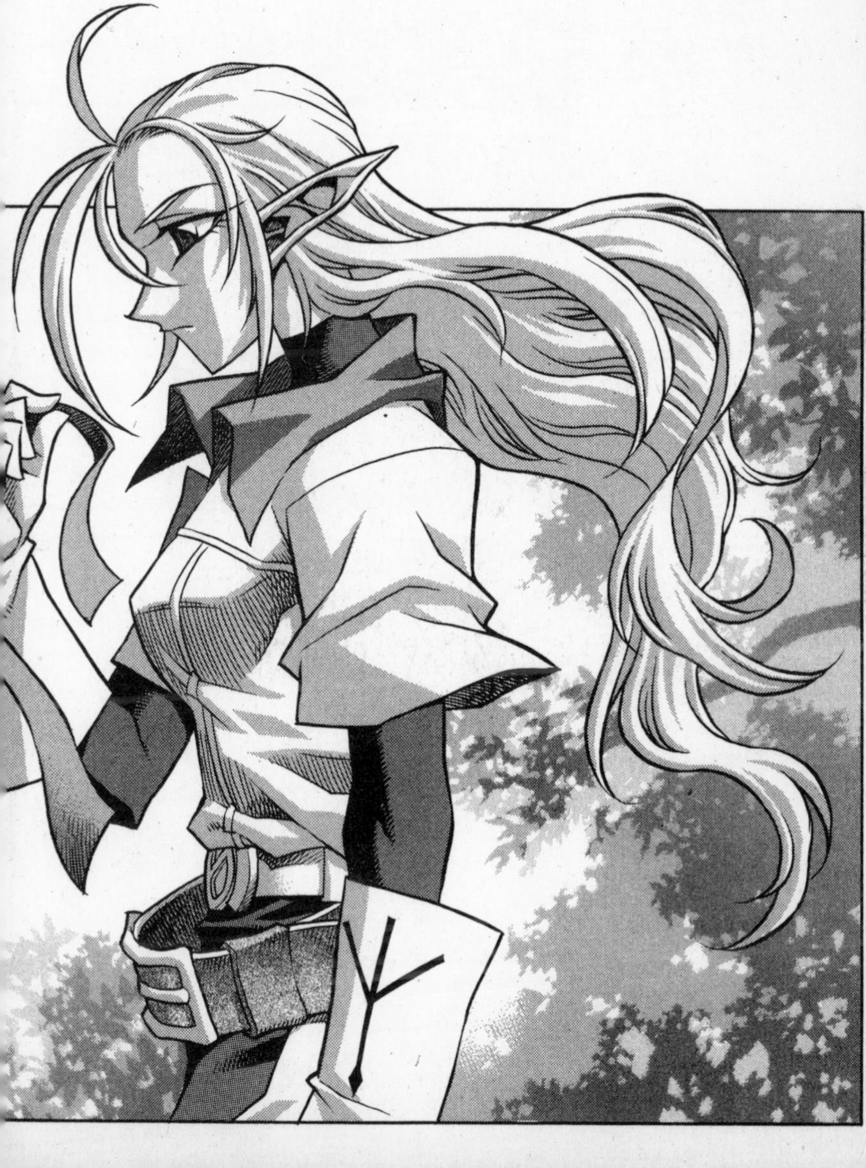

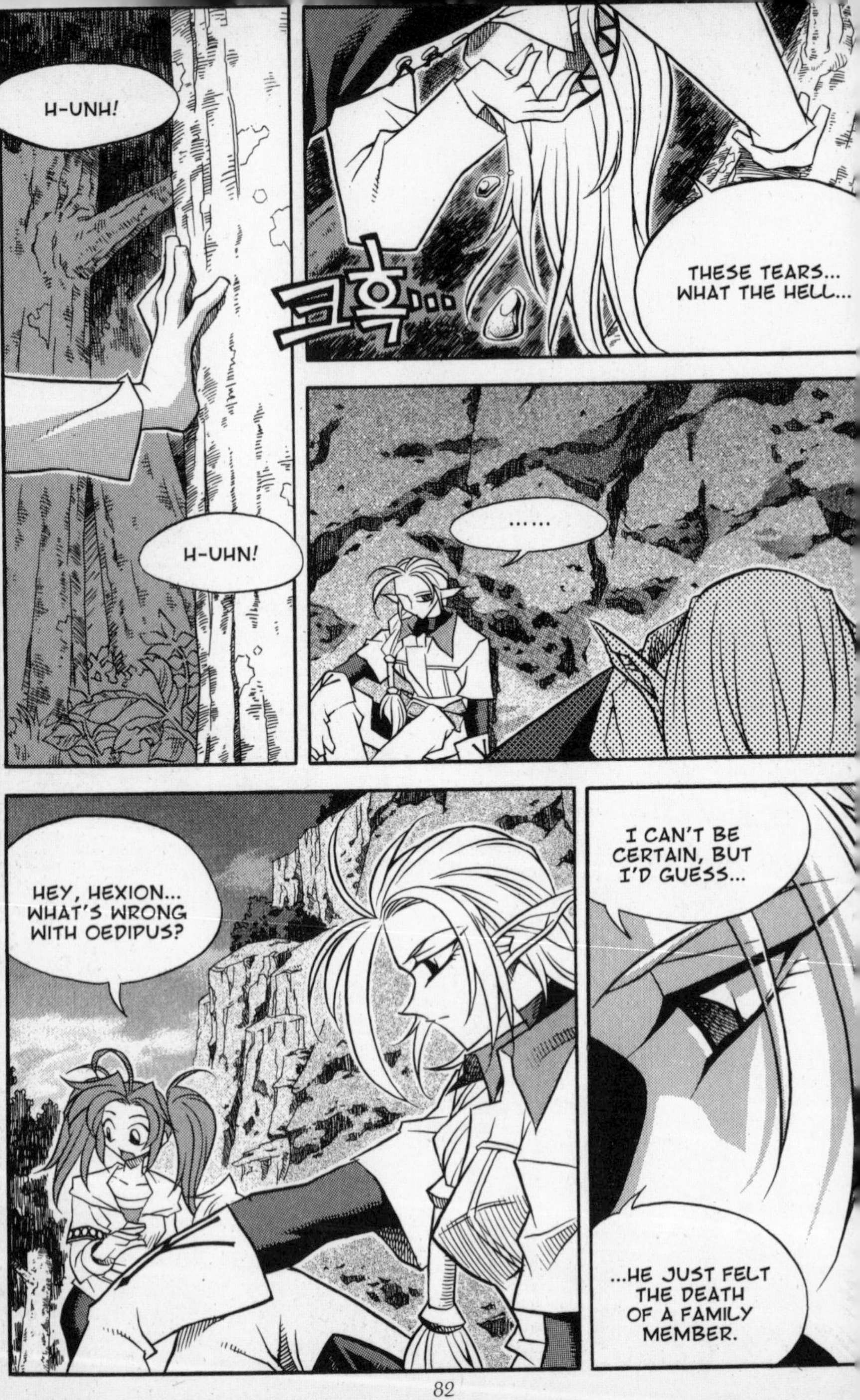
H-UNH!
H-UHN!
크흑...
THESE TEARS... WHAT THE HELL...
......
HEY, HEXION... WHAT'S WRONG WITH OEDIPUS?
I CAN'T BE CERTAIN, BUT I'D GUESS...
...HE JUST FELT THE DEATH OF A FAMILY MEMBER.

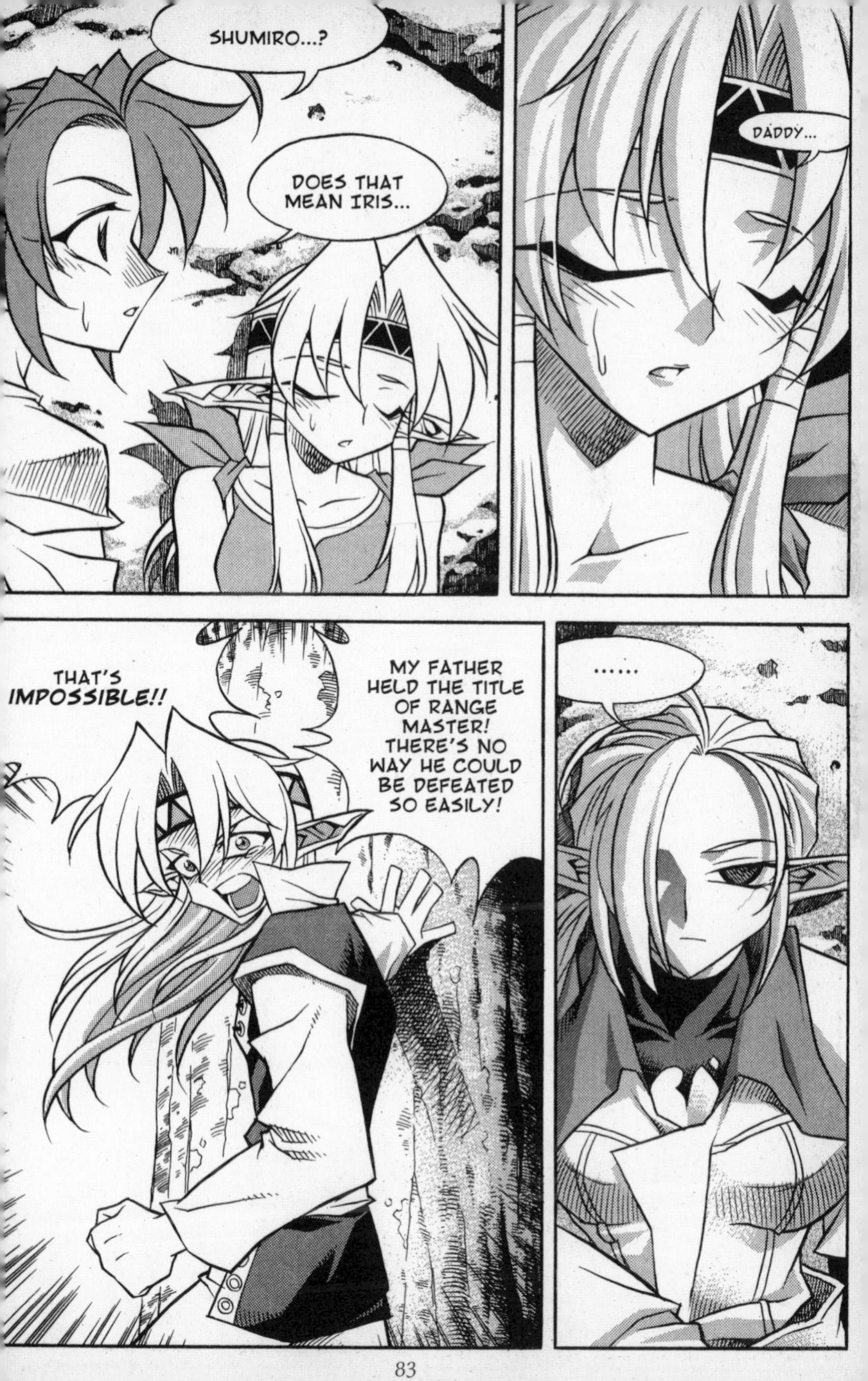
SHUMIRO...?
DOES THAT MEAN IRIS...
DADDY...
THAT'S IMPOSSIBLE!!
MY FATHER HELD THE TITLE OF RANGE MASTER! THERE'S NO WAY HE COULD BE DEFEATED SO EASILY!
......

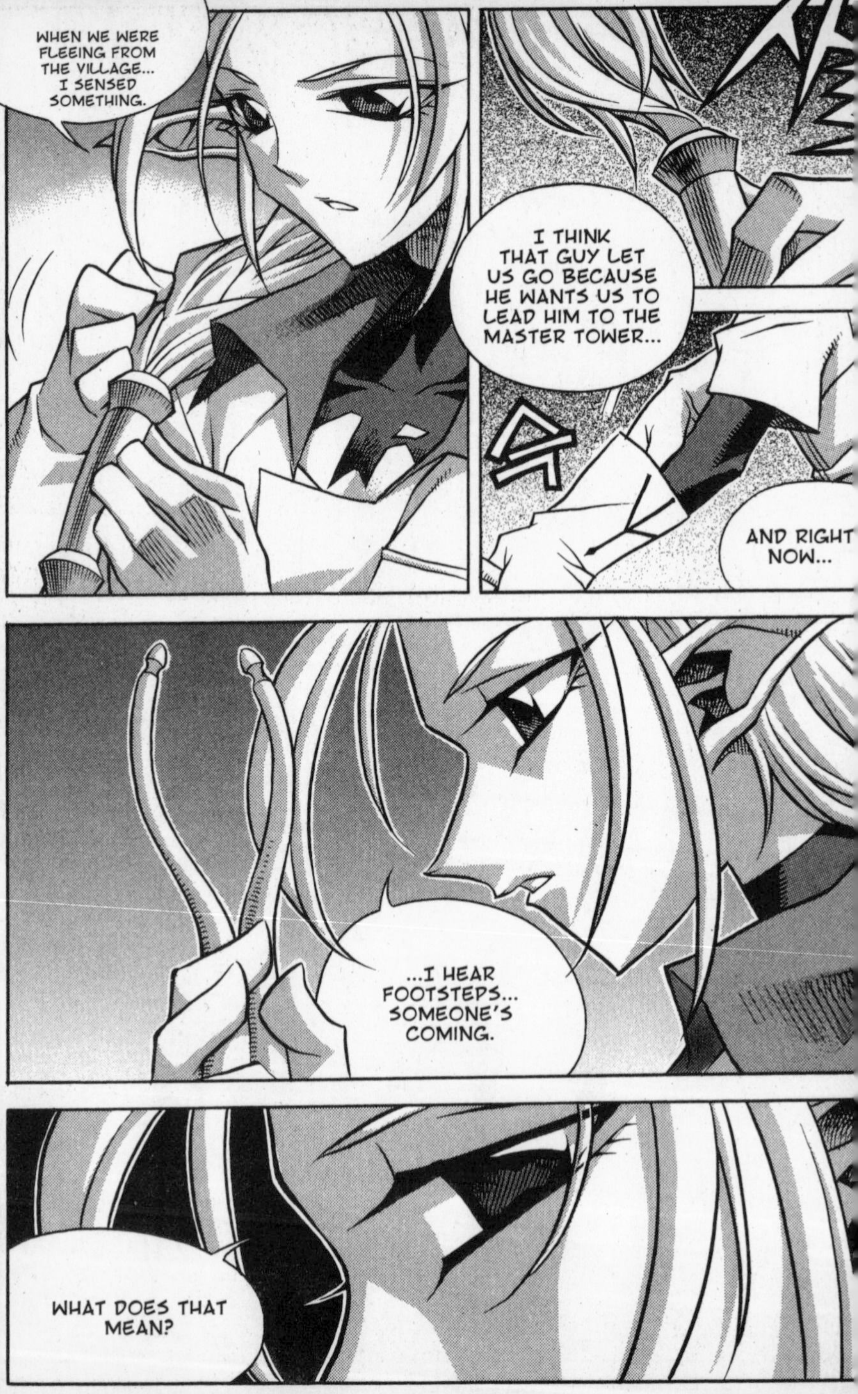
WHEN WE WERE FLEEING FROM THE VILLAGE... I SENSED SOMETHING.
I THINK THAT GUY LET US GO BECAUSE HE WANTS US TO LEAD HIM TO THE MASTER TOWER...
AND RIGHT NOW...
...I HEAR FOOTSTEPS... SOMEONE'S COMING.
WHAT DOES THAT MEAN?

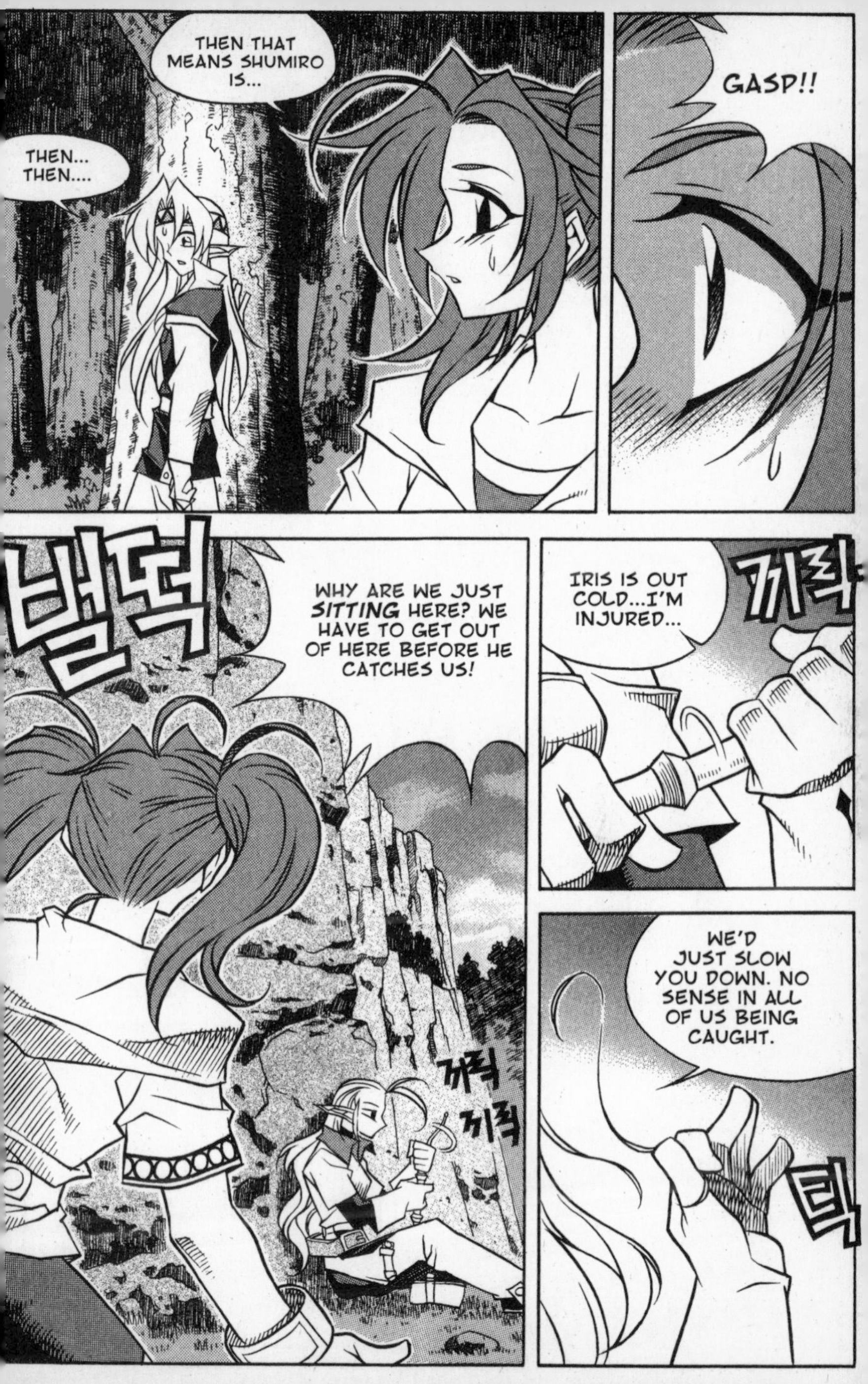
THEN THAT MEANS SHUMIRO IS...
THEN... THEN....
GASP!!
벌떡
WHY ARE WE JUST *SITTING* HERE? WE HAVE TO GET OUT OF HERE BEFORE HE CATCHES US!
끼적
끼적
IRIS IS OUT COLD...I'M INJURED...
WE'D JUST SLOW YOU DOWN. NO SENSE IN ALL OF US BEING CAUGHT.

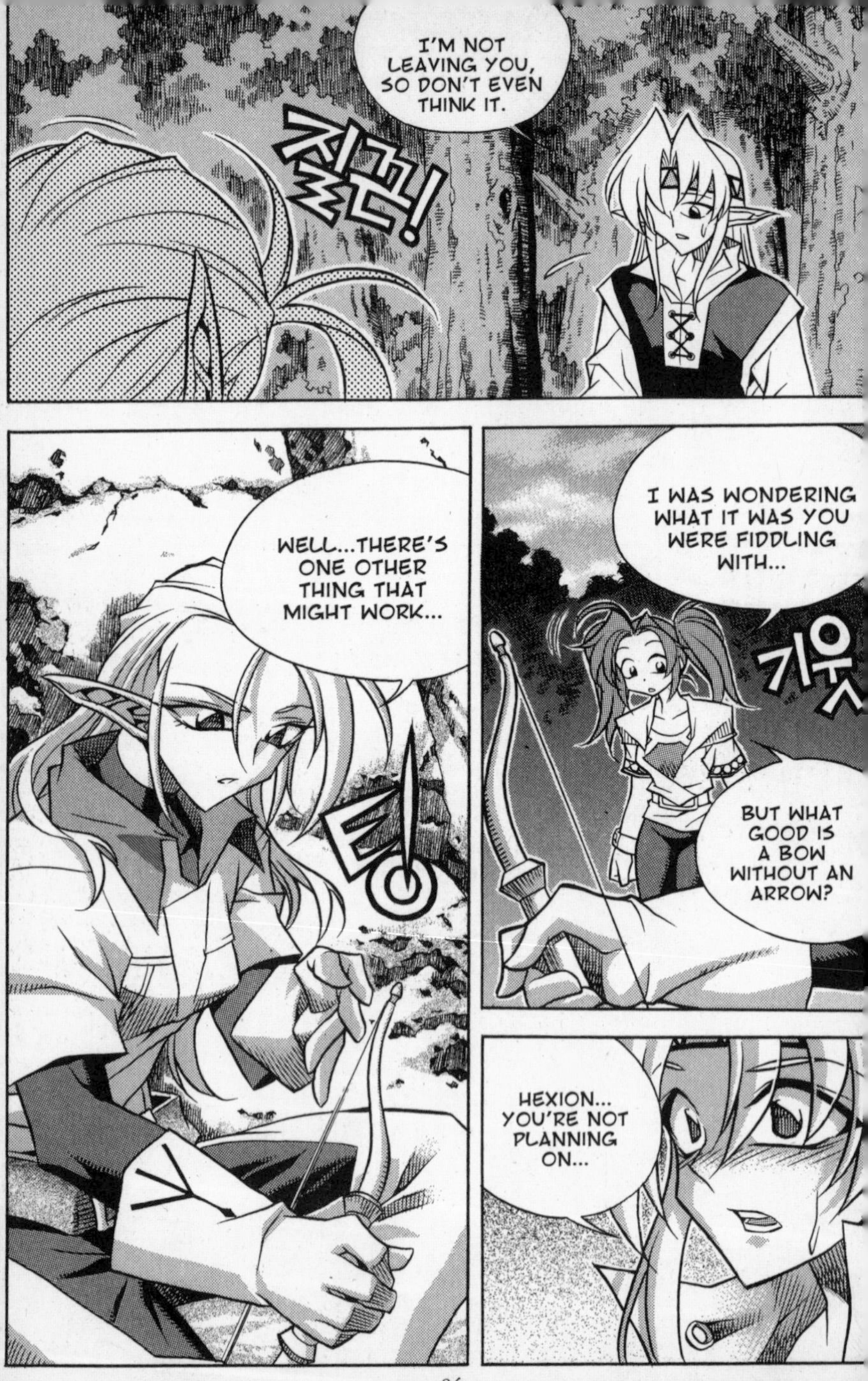
I'M NOT LEAVING YOU, SO DON'T EVEN THINK IT.
WELL...THERE'S ONE OTHER THING THAT MIGHT WORK...
I WAS WONDERING WHAT IT WAS YOU WERE FIDDLING WITH...
BUT WHAT GOOD IS A BOW WITHOUT AN ARROW?
HEXION... YOU'RE NOT PLANNING ON...

DON'T WORRY. I WAS SAVING THE ARROW FOR LAST.

HOW ARE YOU GONNA MAKE AN ARROW OUT OF THAT PIECE OF HAIR?

IT WON'T BE AS EFFECTIVE AS IRIS' MAGIC BOW...BUT IT'LL DO.

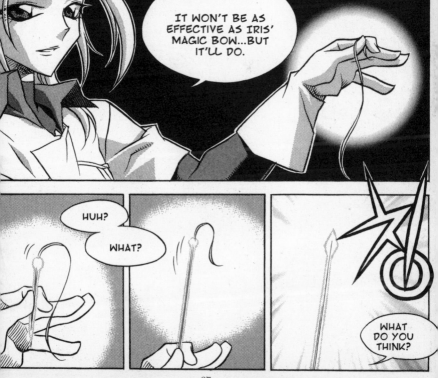

HUH?

WHAT?

WHAT DO YOU THINK?

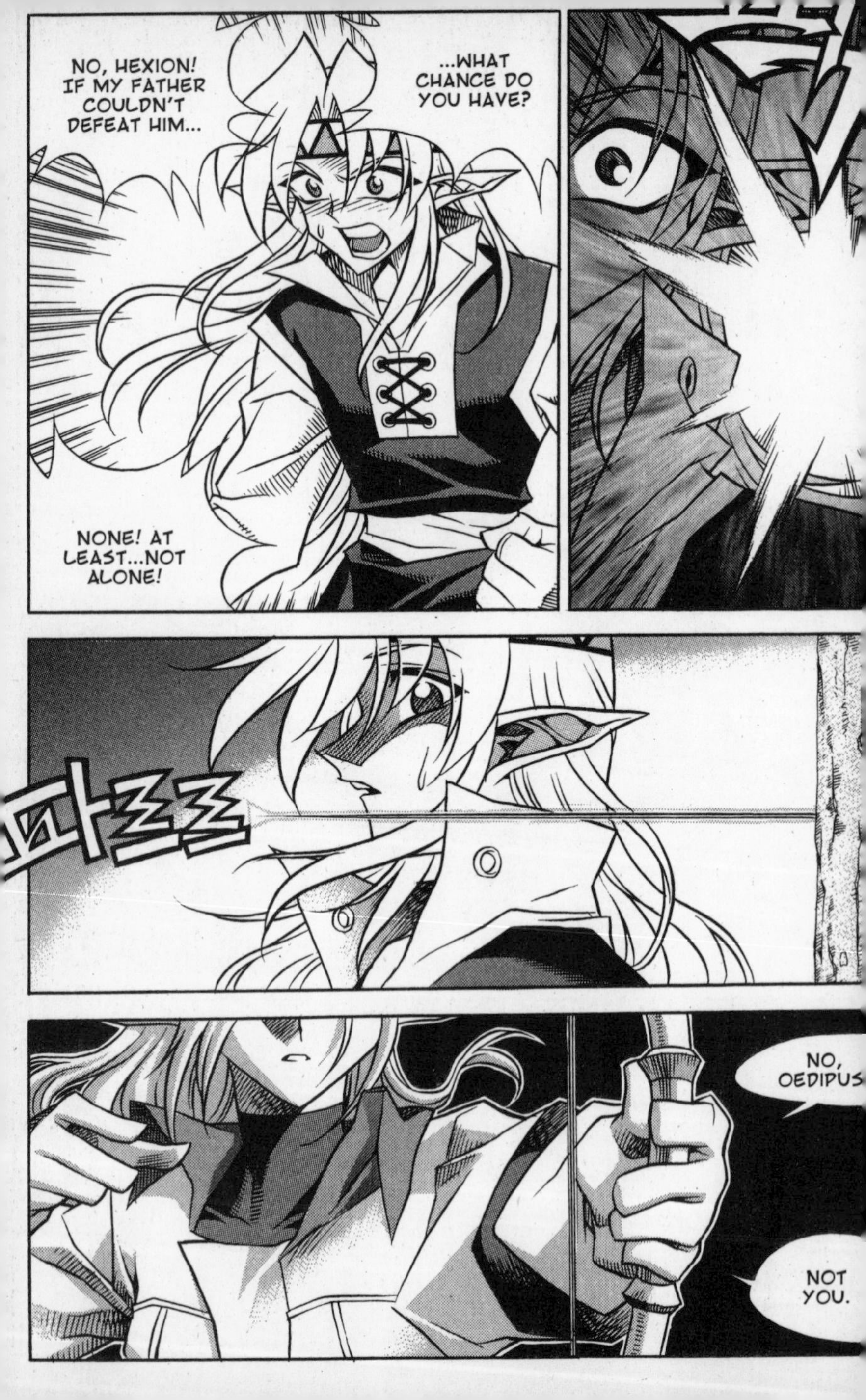
NO, HEXION! IF MY FATHER COULDN'T DEFEAT HIM...
...WHAT CHANCE DO YOU HAVE?
NONE! AT LEAST...NOT ALONE!
NO, OEDIPUS
NOT YOU.

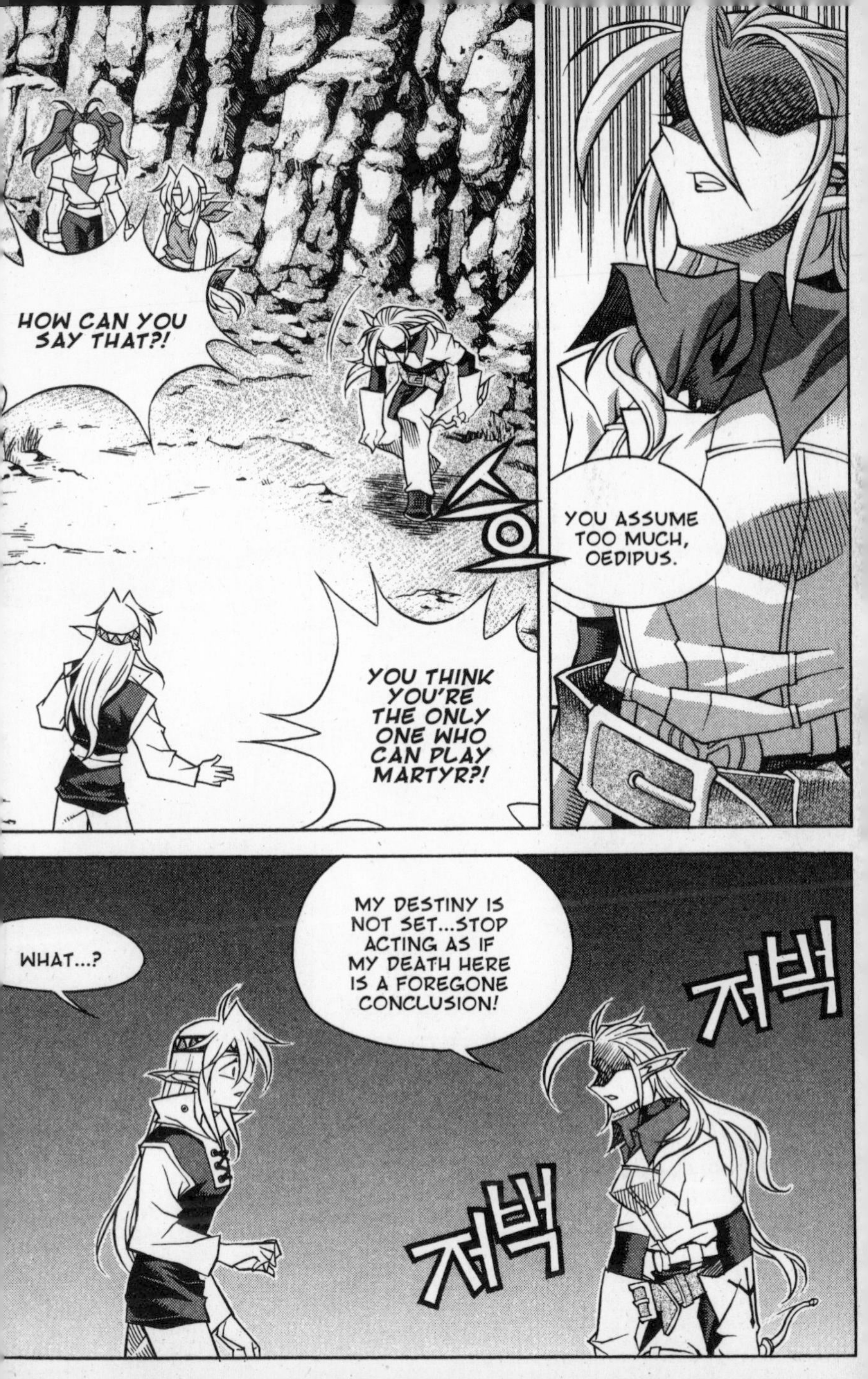
HOW CAN YOU SAY THAT?!
YOU THINK YOU'RE THE ONLY ONE WHO CAN PLAY MARTYR?!
YOU ASSUME TOO MUCH, OEDIPUS.
WHAT...?
MY DESTINY IS NOT SET...STOP ACTING AS IF MY DEATH HERE IS A FOREGONE CONCLUSION!
저벅
저벅

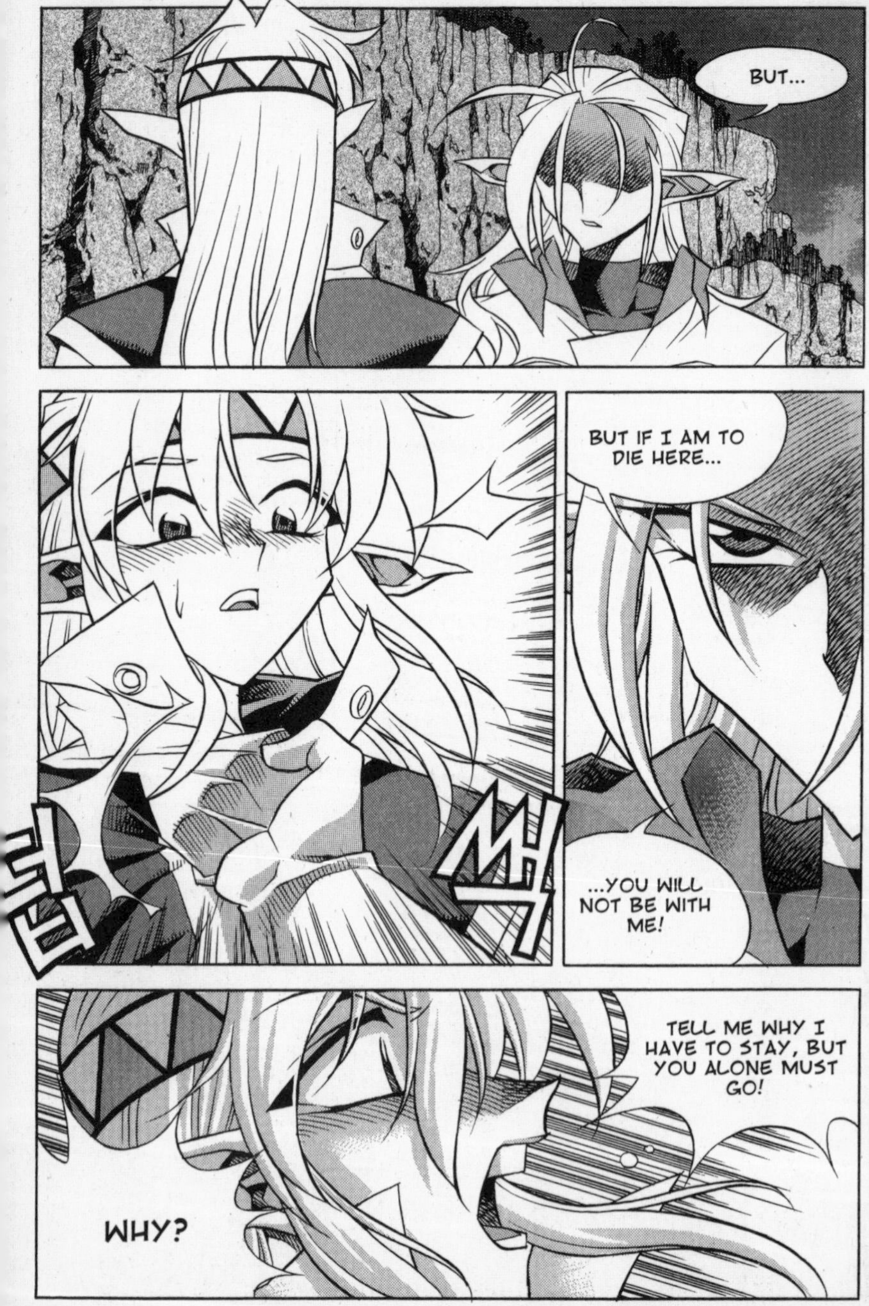
BUT...
BUT IF I AM TO DIE HERE...
...YOU WILL NOT BE WITH ME!
TELL ME WHY I HAVE TO STAY, BUT YOU ALONE MUST GO!
WHY?

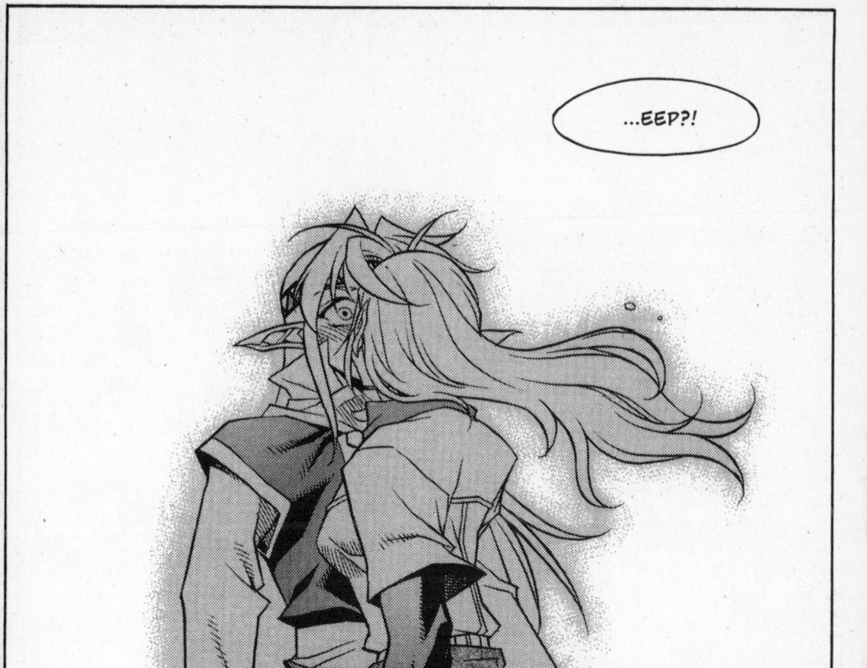
...EEP?!

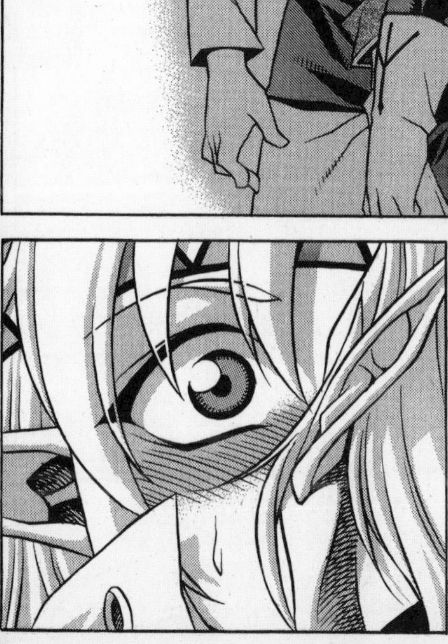

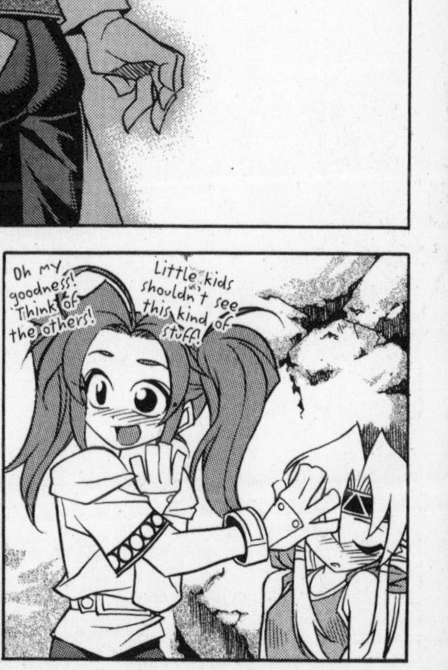
Oh my goodness! Think of the others!
Little kids shouldn't see this kind of stuff!

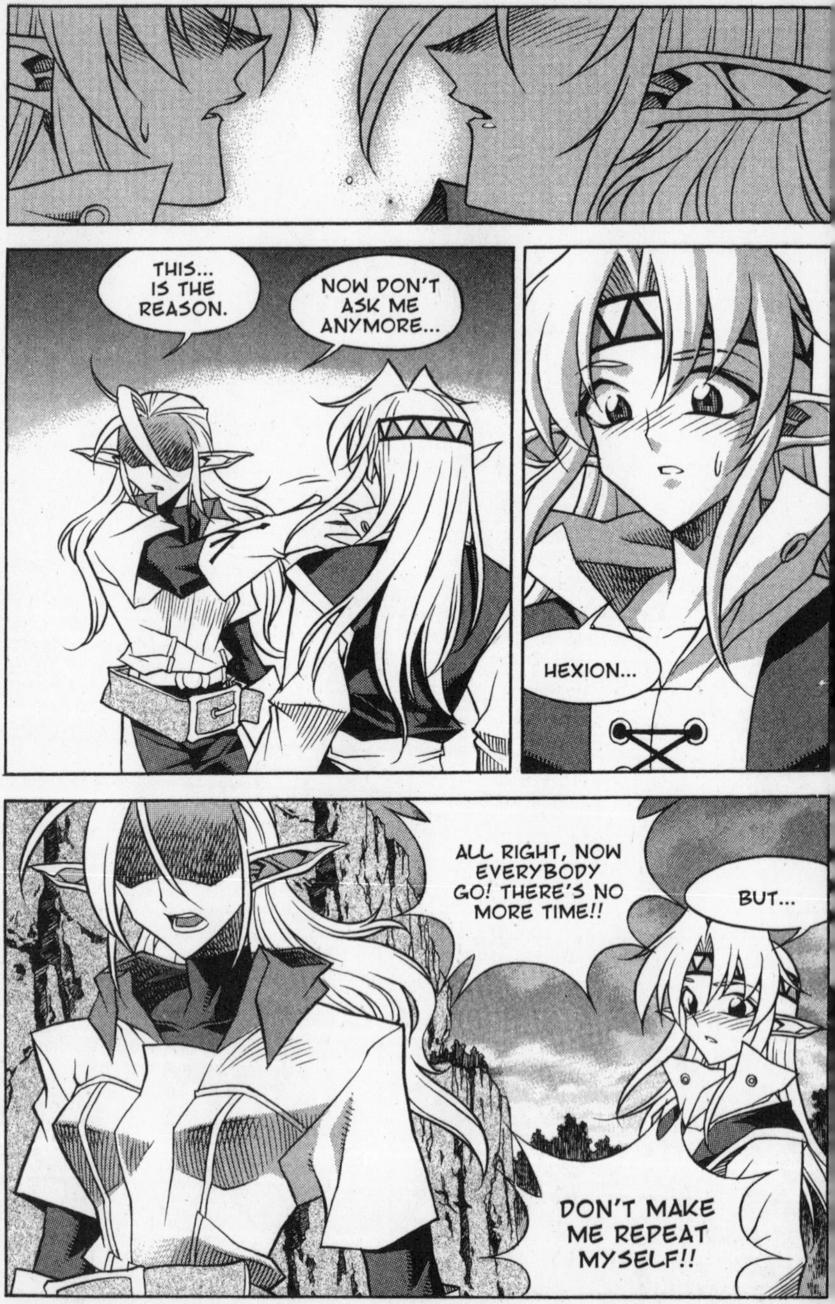
THIS... IS THE REASON.
NOW DON'T ASK ME ANYMORE...
HEXION...
ALL RIGHT, NOW EVERYBODY GO! THERE'S NO MORE TIME!!
BUT...
DON'T MAKE ME REPEAT MYSELF!!

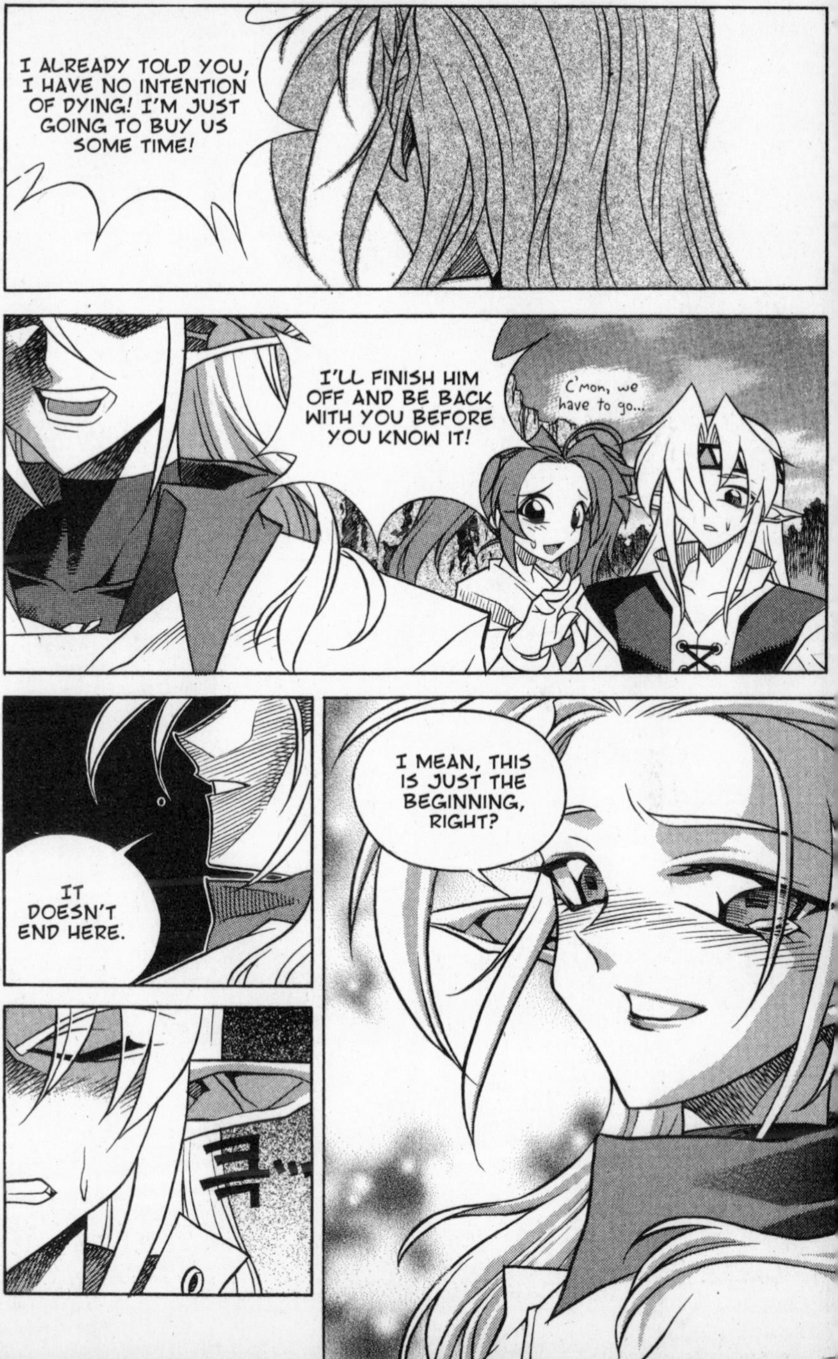
I ALREADY TOLD YOU, I HAVE NO INTENTION OF DYING! I'M JUST GOING TO BUY US SOME TIME!
I'LL FINISH HIM OFF AND BE BACK WITH YOU BEFORE YOU KNOW IT!
C'mon, we have to go...
IT DOESN'T END HERE.
I MEAN, THIS IS JUST THE BEGINNING, RIGHT?

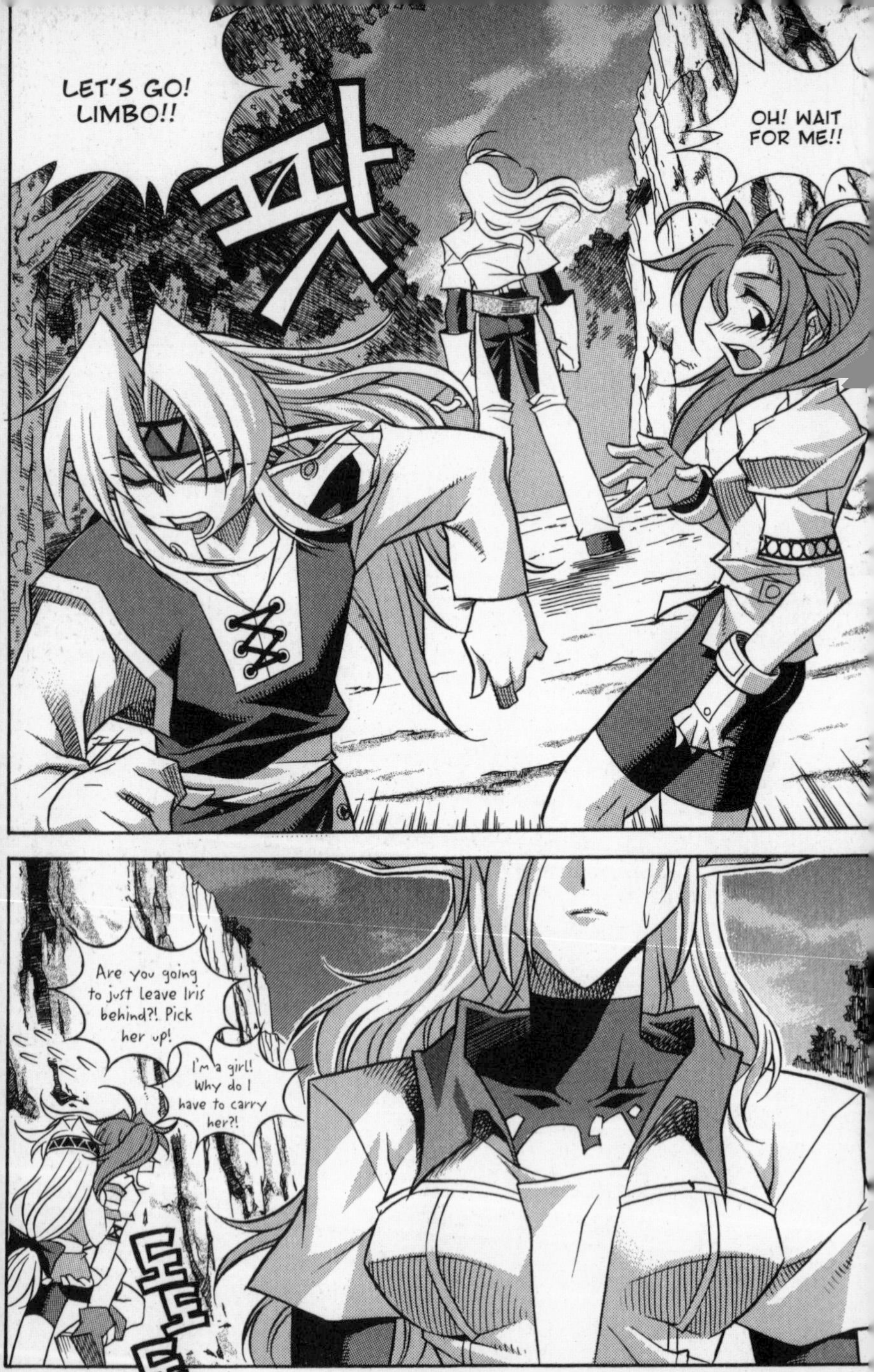
LET'S GO! LIMBO!!
OH! WAIT FOR ME!!
Are you going to just leave Iris behind?! Pick her up!
I'm a girl! Why do I have to carry her?!

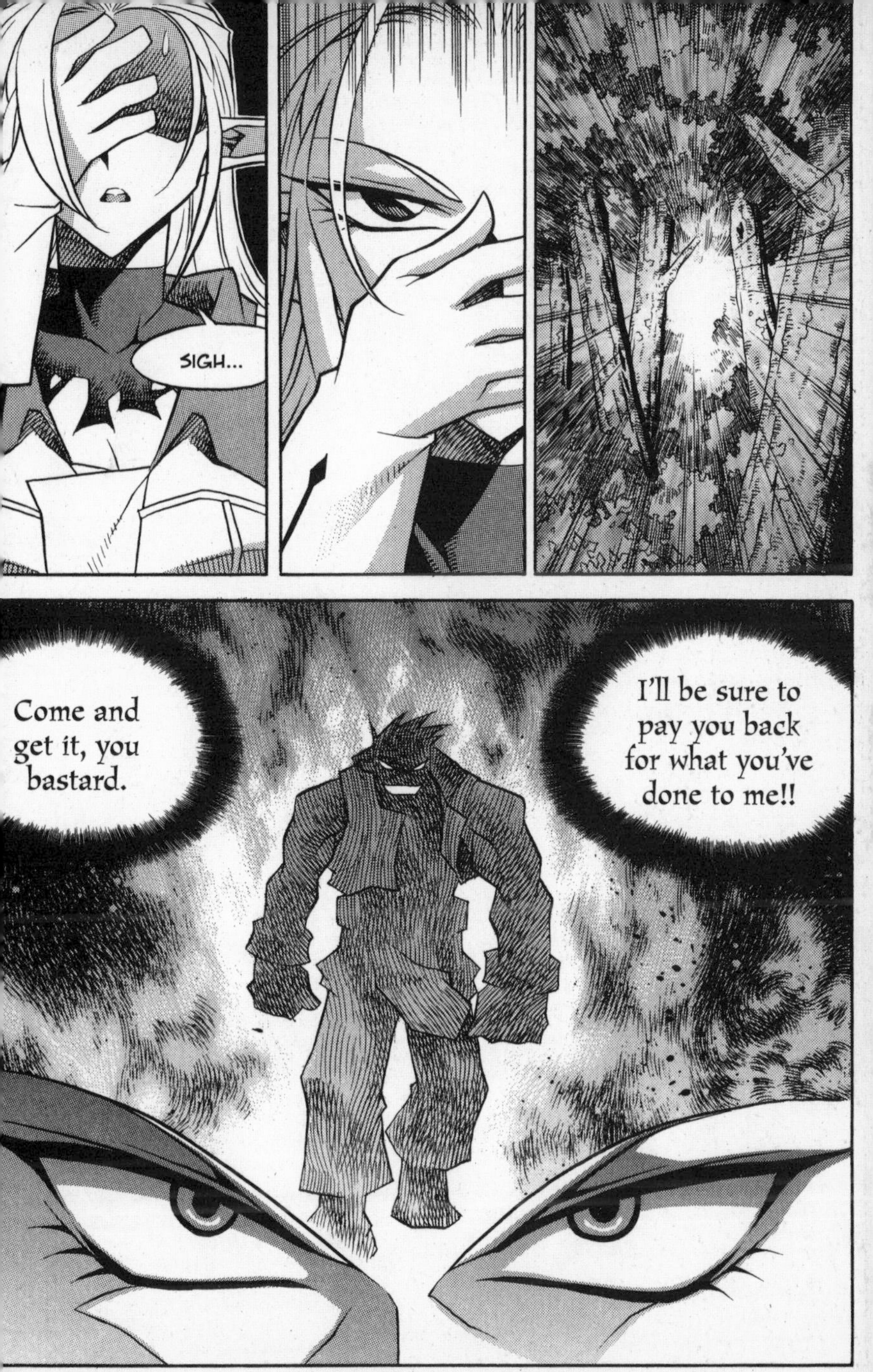
SIGH...
Come and get it, you bastard.
I'll be sure to pay you back for what you've done to me!!

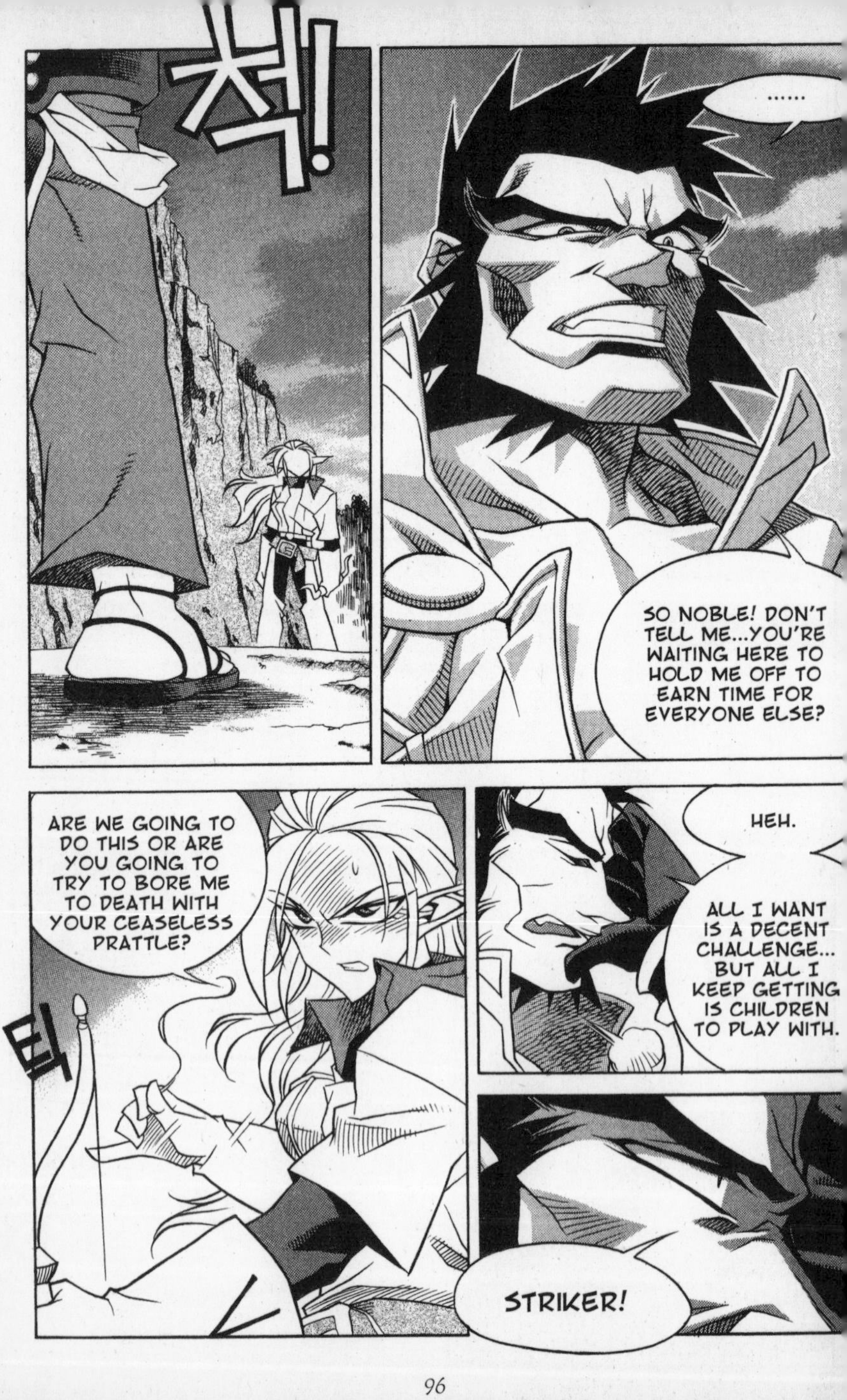
척!
......
SO NOBLE! DON'T TELL ME...YOU'RE WAITING HERE TO HOLD ME OFF TO EARN TIME FOR EVERYONE ELSE?
ARE WE GOING TO DO THIS OR ARE YOU GOING TO TRY TO BORE ME TO DEATH WITH YOUR CEASELESS PRATTLE?
HEH.
ALL I WANT IS A DECENT CHALLENGE... BUT ALL I KEEP GETTING IS CHILDREN TO PLAY WITH.
STRIKER!

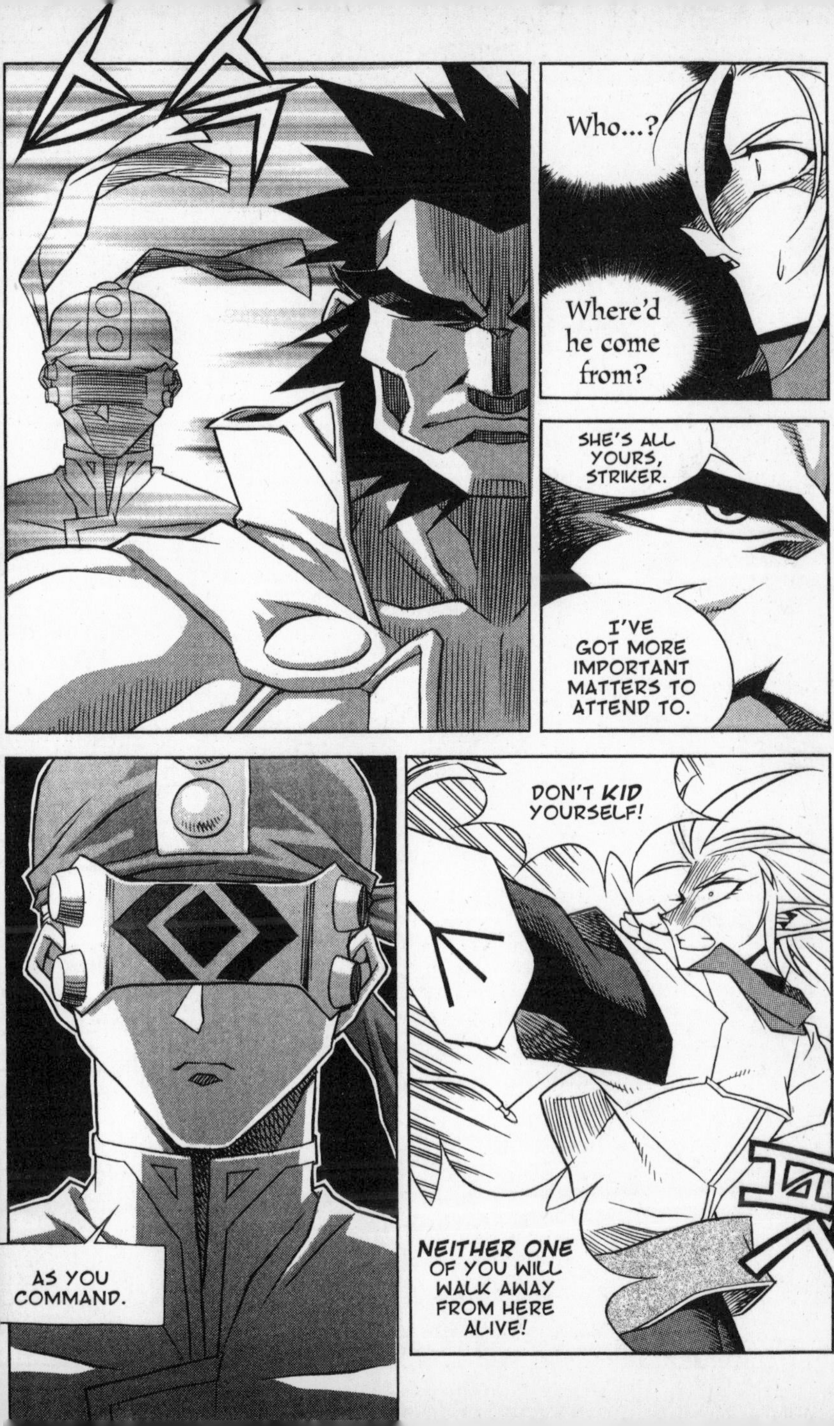
Who...?
Where'd he come from?
SHE'S ALL YOURS, STRIKER.
I'VE GOT MORE IMPORTANT MATTERS TO ATTEND TO.
AS YOU COMMAND.
DON'T KID YOURSELF!
NEITHER ONE OF YOU WILL WALK AWAY FROM HERE ALIVE!

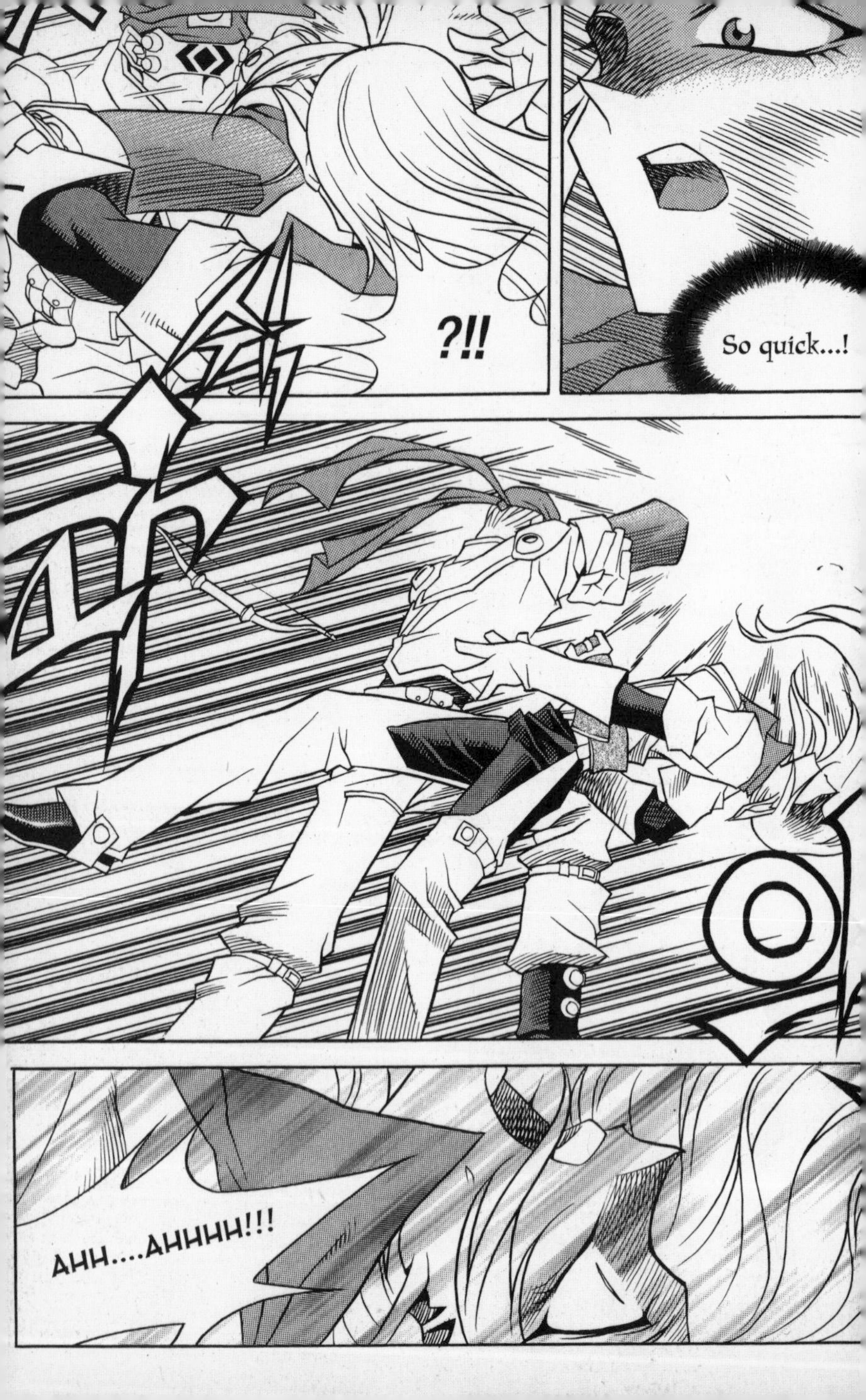
?!!
So quick...!
AHH....AHHHH!!!

Quest 64

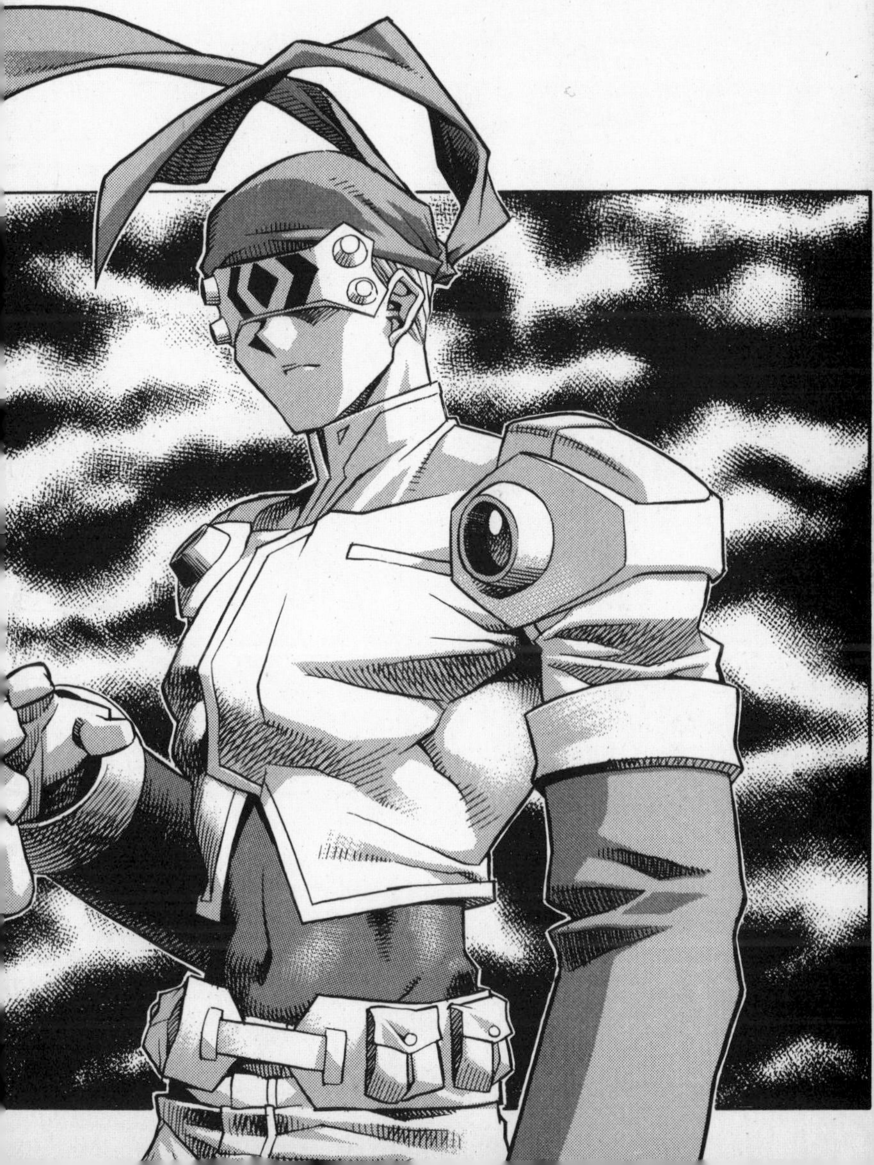

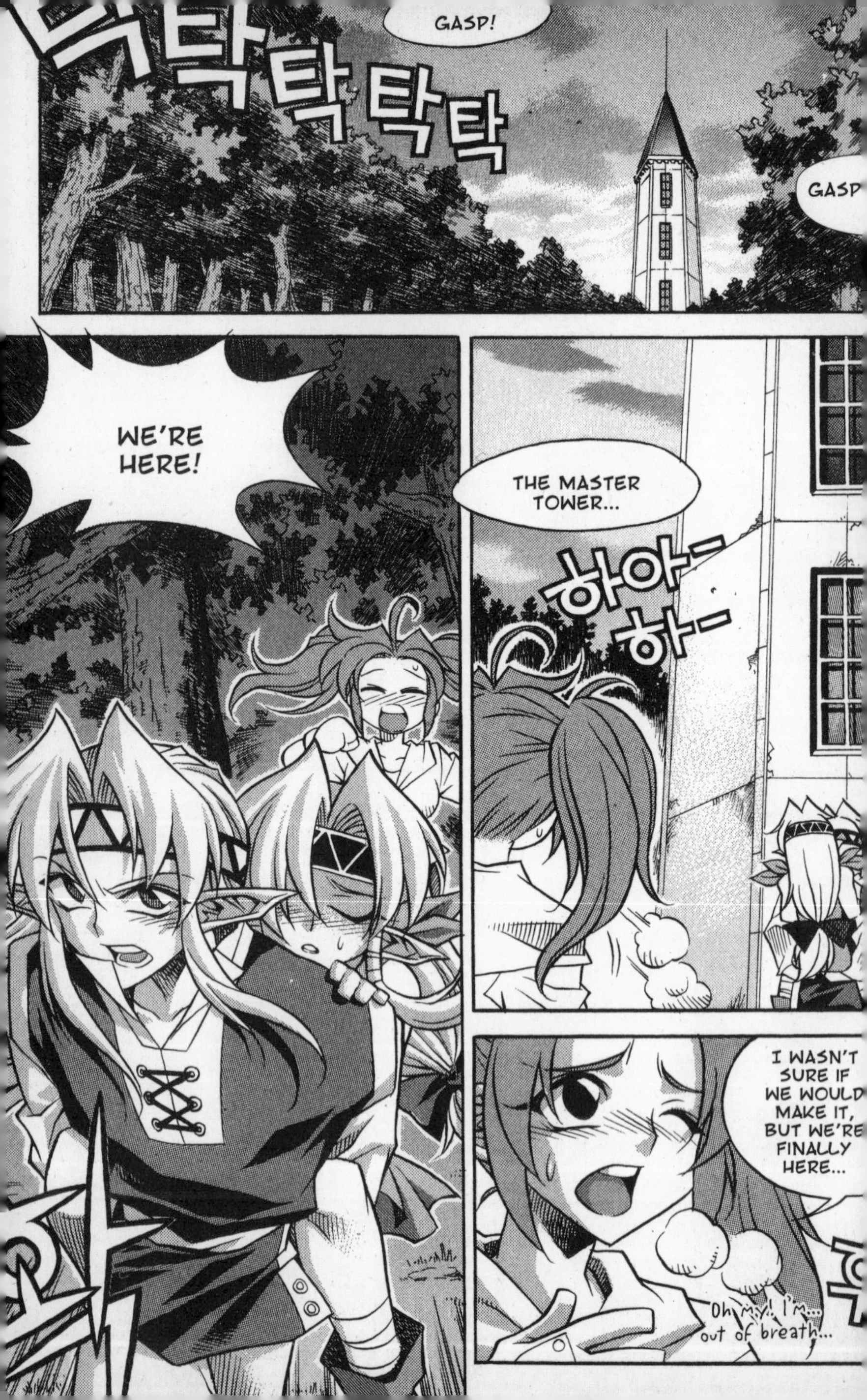

탁탁탁탁
GASP!
GASP
WE'RE HERE!
THE MASTER TOWER...
하아- 하-
I WASN'T SURE IF WE WOULD MAKE IT, BUT WE'RE FINALLY HERE...
Oh my! I'm... out of breath...

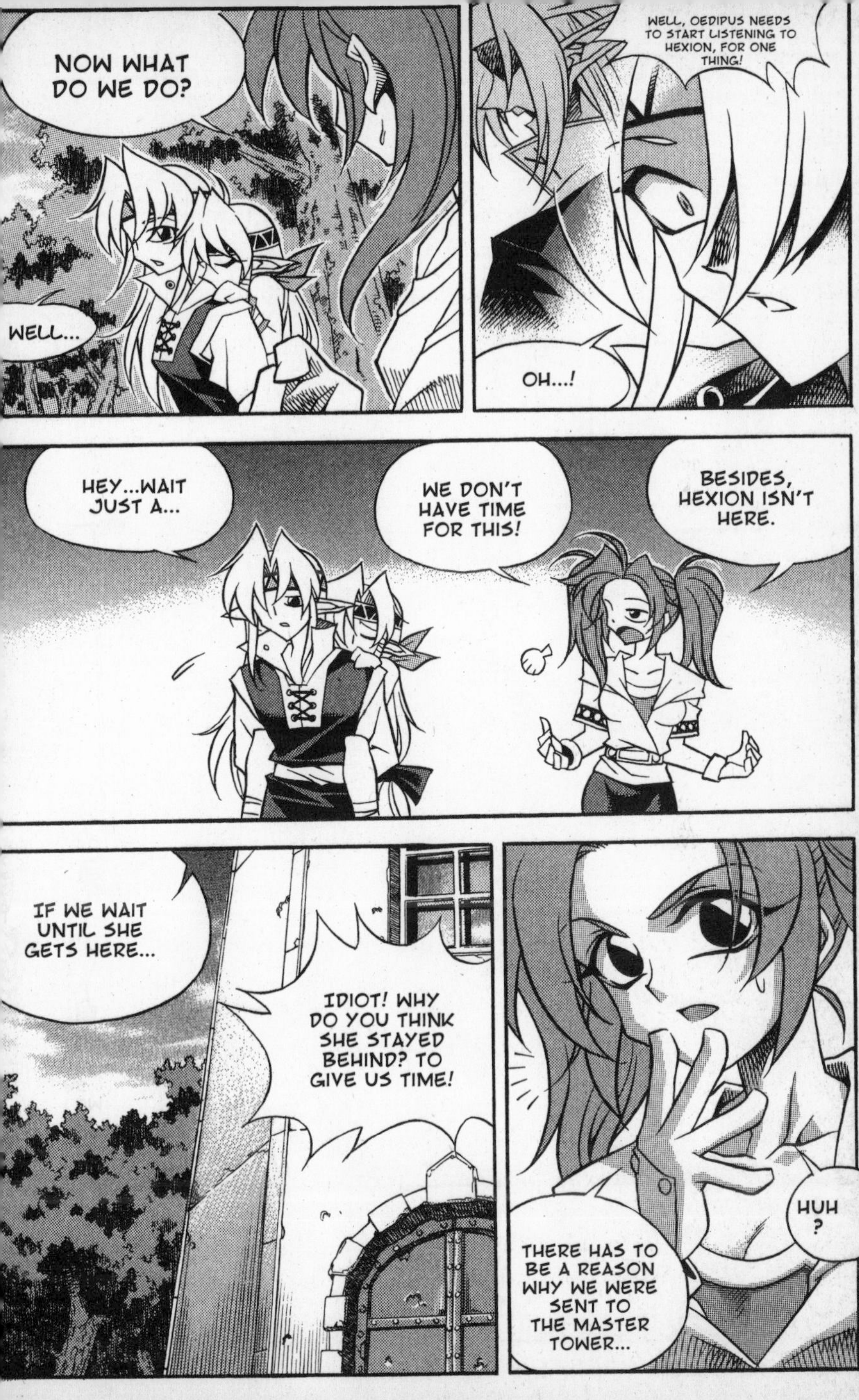
NOW WHAT DO WE DO?
WELL...
WELL, OEDIPUS NEEDS TO START LISTENING TO HEXION, FOR ONE THING!
OH...!
HEY...WAIT JUST A...
WE DON'T HAVE TIME FOR THIS!
BESIDES, HEXION ISN'T HERE.
IF WE WAIT UNTIL SHE GETS HERE...
IDIOT! WHY DO YOU THINK SHE STAYED BEHIND? TO GIVE US TIME!
HUH?
THERE HAS TO BE A REASON WHY WE WERE SENT TO THE MASTER TOWER...

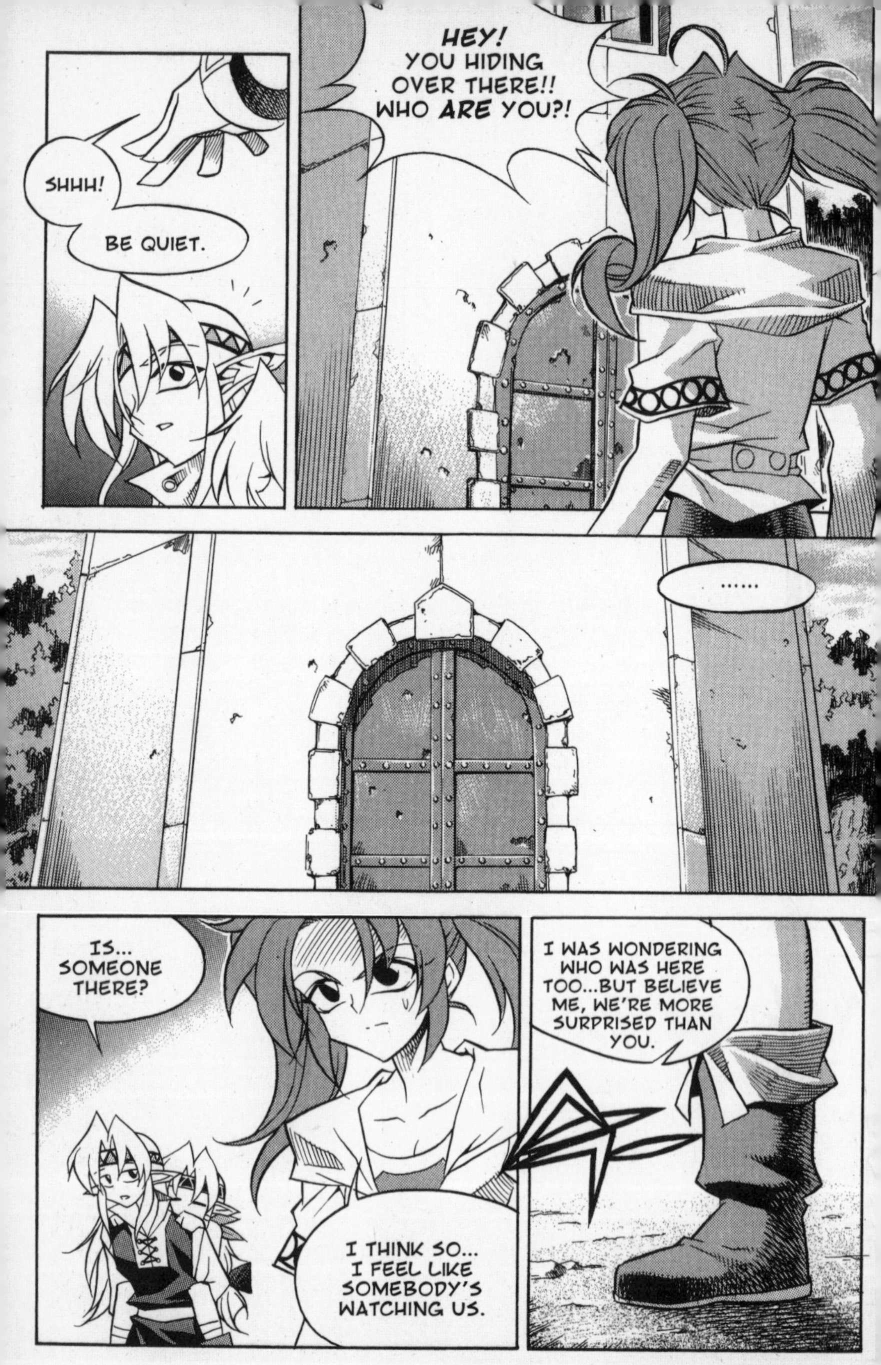
SHHH!
BE QUIET.
HEY! YOU HIDING OVER THERE!! WHO ARE YOU?!
......
IS... SOMEONE THERE?
I THINK SO... I FEEL LIKE SOMEBODY'S WATCHING US.
I WAS WONDERING WHO WAS HERE TOO...BUT BELIEVE ME, WE'RE MORE SURPRISED THAN YOU.

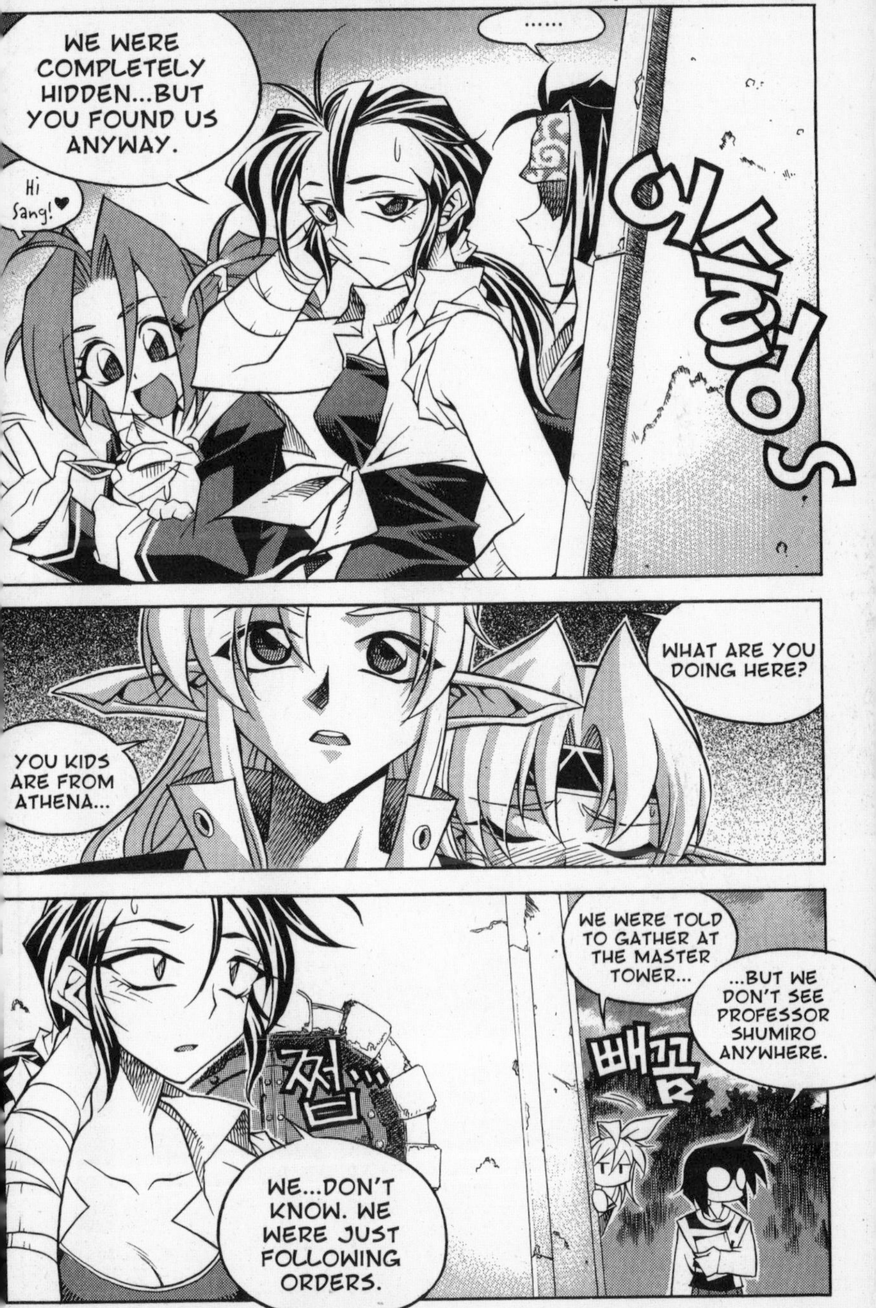
WE WERE COMPLETELY HIDDEN...BUT YOU FOUND US ANYWAY.
Hi Sang!♥
......
어슬렁
YOU KIDS ARE FROM ATHENA...
WHAT ARE YOU DOING HERE?
쩝...
WE...DON'T KNOW. WE WERE JUST FOLLOWING ORDERS.
WE WERE TOLD TO GATHER AT THE MASTER TOWER...
...BUT WE DON'T SEE PROFESSOR SHUMIRO ANYWHERE.
빼꼼

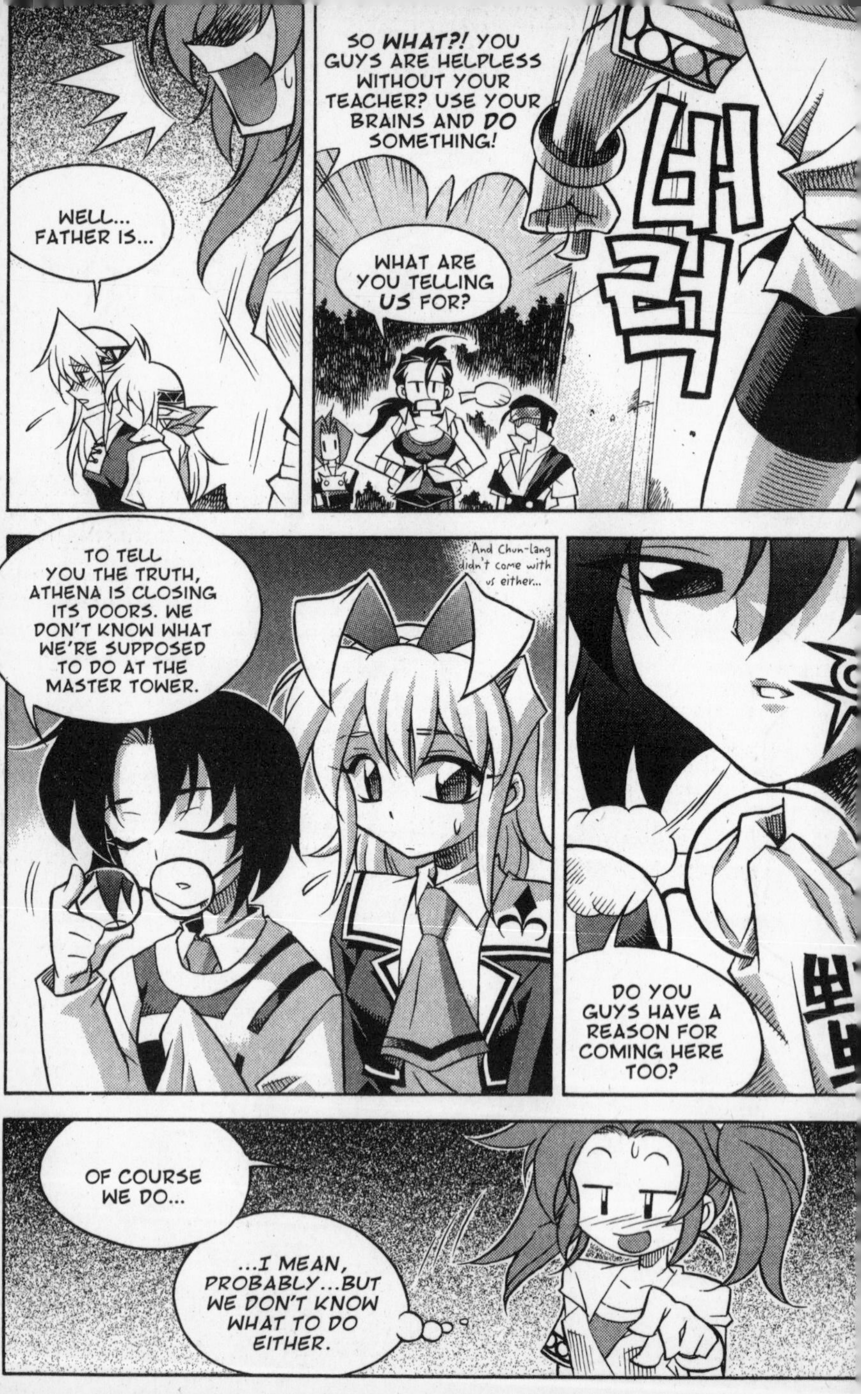
WELL... FATHER IS...
SO WHAT?! YOU GUYS ARE HELPLESS WITHOUT YOUR TEACHER? USE YOUR BRAINS AND DO SOMETHING!
WHAT ARE YOU TELLING US FOR?
TO TELL YOU THE TRUTH, ATHENA IS CLOSING ITS DOORS. WE DON'T KNOW WHAT WE'RE SUPPOSED TO DO AT THE MASTER TOWER.
And Chun-lang didn't come with us either...
DO YOU GUYS HAVE A REASON FOR COMING HERE TOO?
OF COURSE WE DO...
...I MEAN, PROBABLY...BUT WE DON'T KNOW WHAT TO DO EITHER.

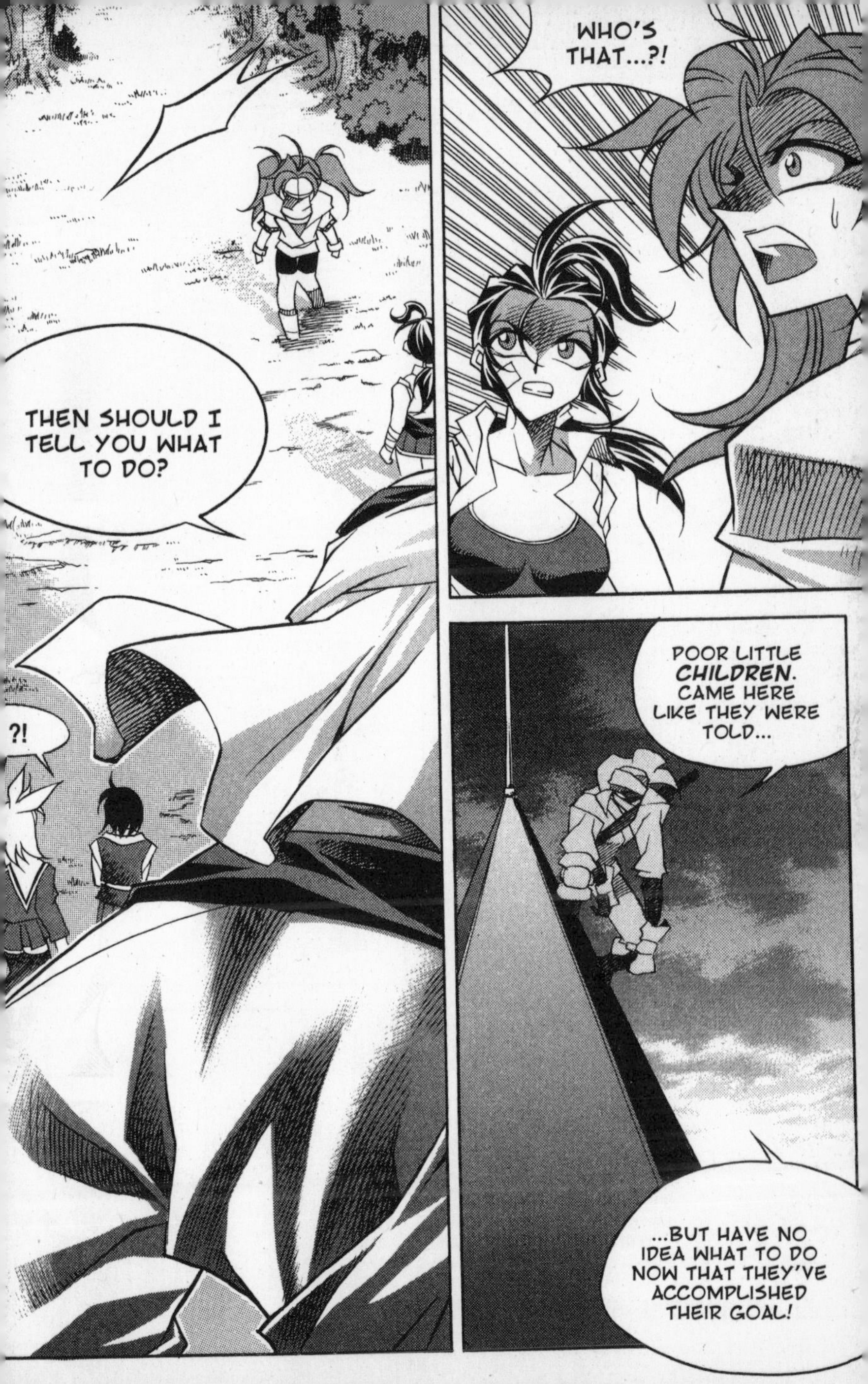
THEN SHOULD I TELL YOU WHAT TO DO?
?!
WHO'S THAT...?!
POOR LITTLE CHILDREN. CAME HERE LIKE THEY WERE TOLD...
...BUT HAVE NO IDEA WHAT TO DO NOW THAT THEY'VE ACCOMPLISHED THEIR GOAL!

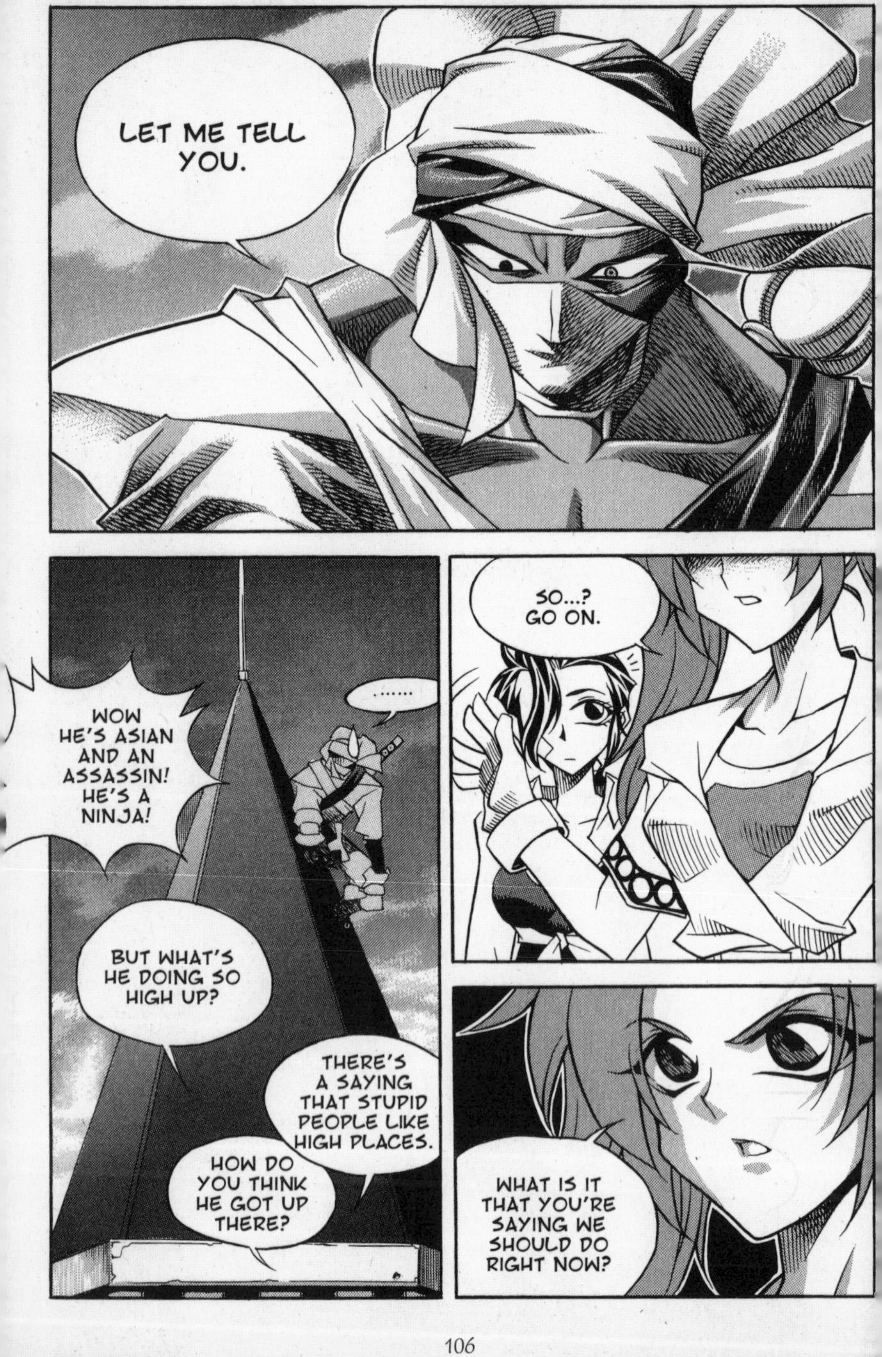
LET ME TELL YOU.
WOW HE'S ASIAN AND AN ASSASSIN! HE'S A NINJA!
....
BUT WHAT'S HE DOING SO HIGH UP?
THERE'S A SAYING THAT STUPID PEOPLE LIKE HIGH PLACES.
HOW DO YOU THINK HE GOT UP THERE?
SO...? GO ON.
WHAT IS IT THAT YOU'RE SAYING WE SHOULD DO RIGHT NOW?

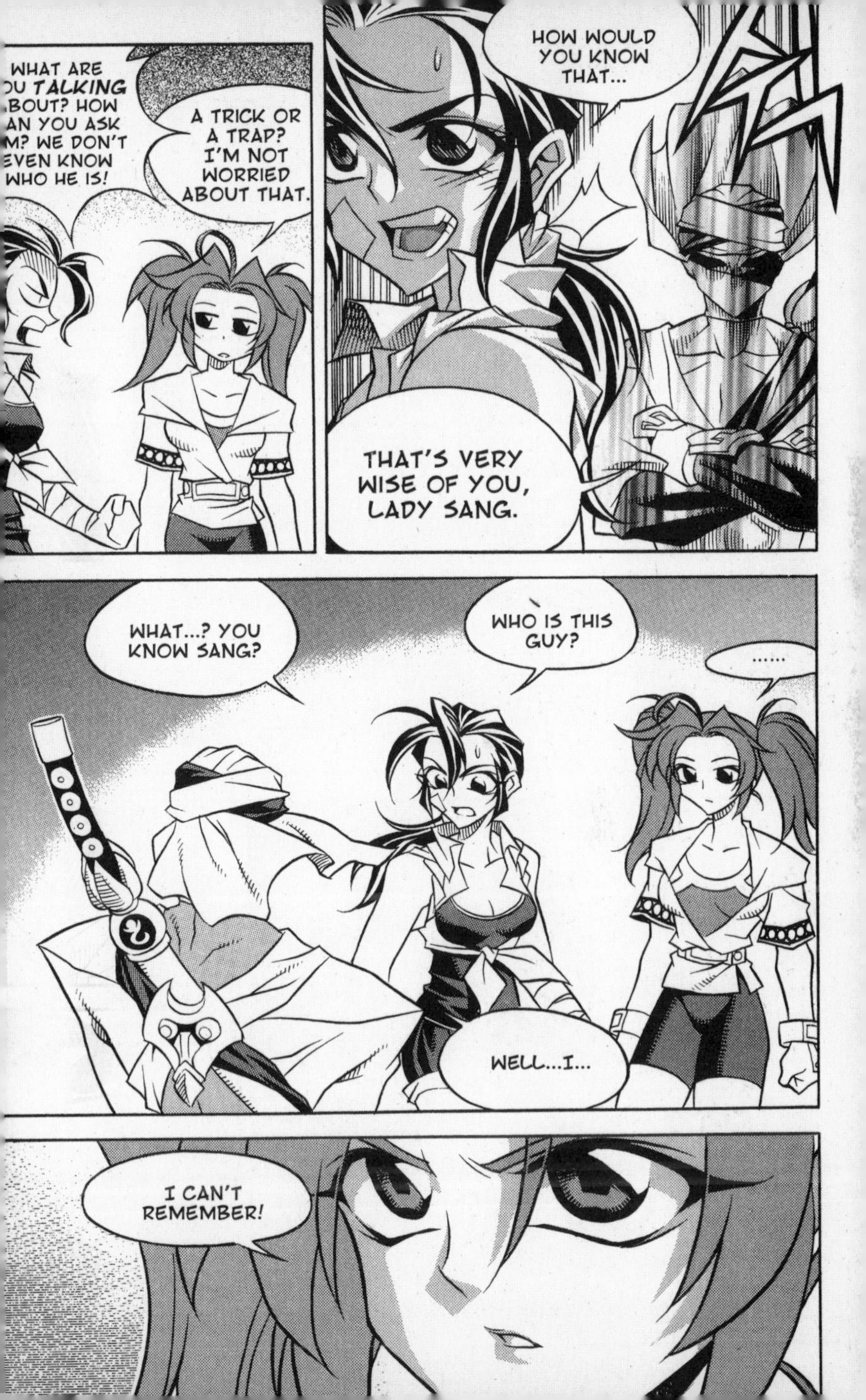
WHAT ARE
OU TALKING
BOUT? HOW
AN YOU ASK
M? WE DON'T
EVEN KNOW
WHO HE IS!
A TRICK OR A TRAP? I'M NOT WORRIED ABOUT THAT.
HOW WOULD YOU KNOW THAT...
THAT'S VERY WISE OF YOU, LADY SANG.
WHAT...? YOU KNOW SANG?
WHO IS THIS GUY?
......
WELL...I...
I CAN'T REMEMBER!

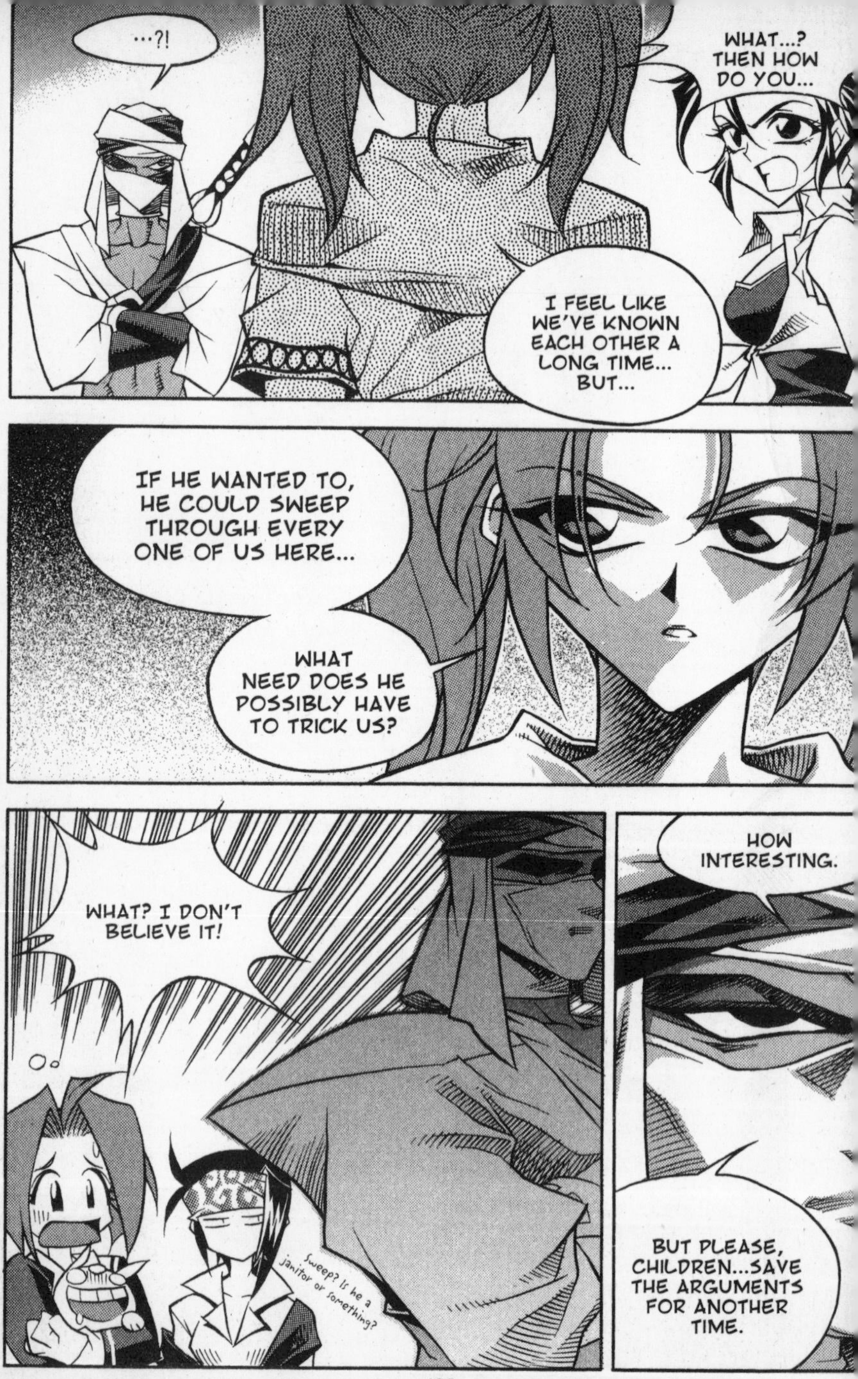

...?!
WHAT...? THEN HOW DO YOU...
I FEEL LIKE WE'VE KNOWN EACH OTHER A LONG TIME... BUT...
IF HE WANTED TO, HE COULD SWEEP THROUGH EVERY ONE OF US HERE...
WHAT NEED DOES HE POSSIBLY HAVE TO TRICK US?
WHAT? I DON'T BELIEVE IT!
Sweep? Is he a janitor or something?
HOW INTERESTING.
BUT PLEASE, CHILDREN...SAVE THE ARGUMENTS FOR ANOTHER TIME.

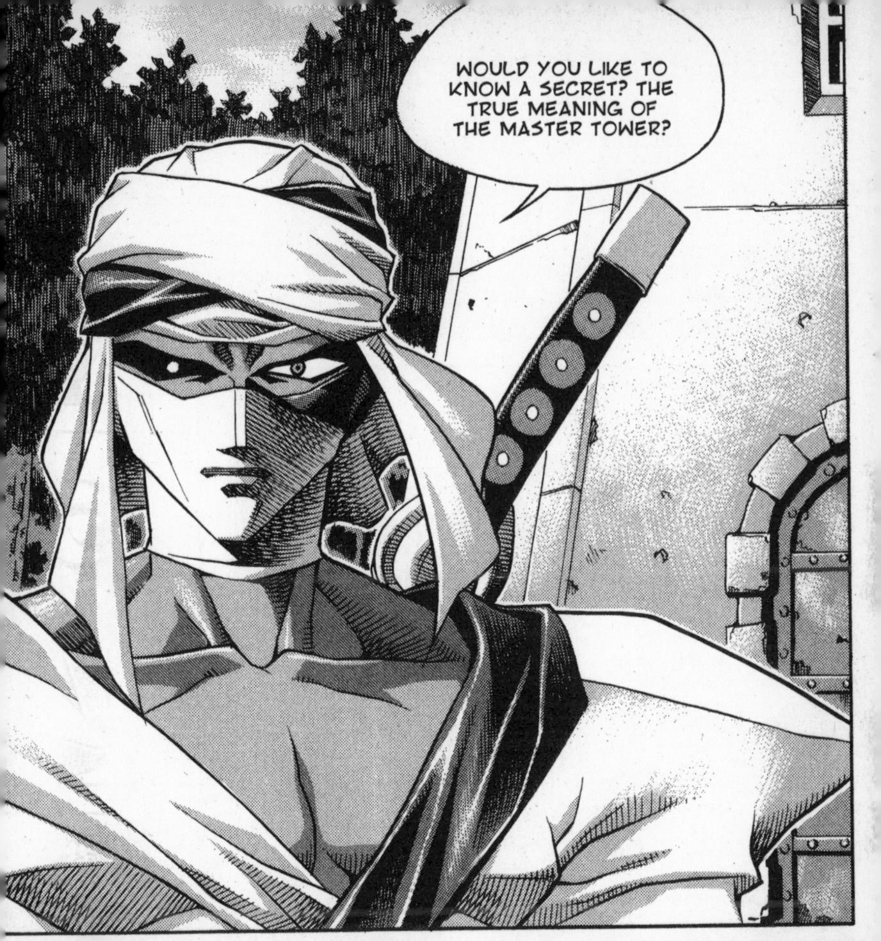
WOULD YOU LIKE TO KNOW A SECRET? THE TRUE MEANING OF THE MASTER TOWER?
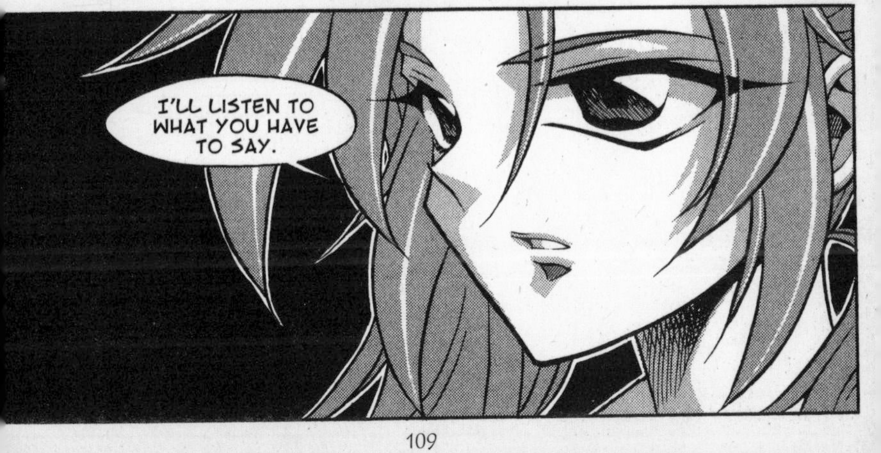
I'LL LISTEN TO WHAT YOU HAVE TO SAY.

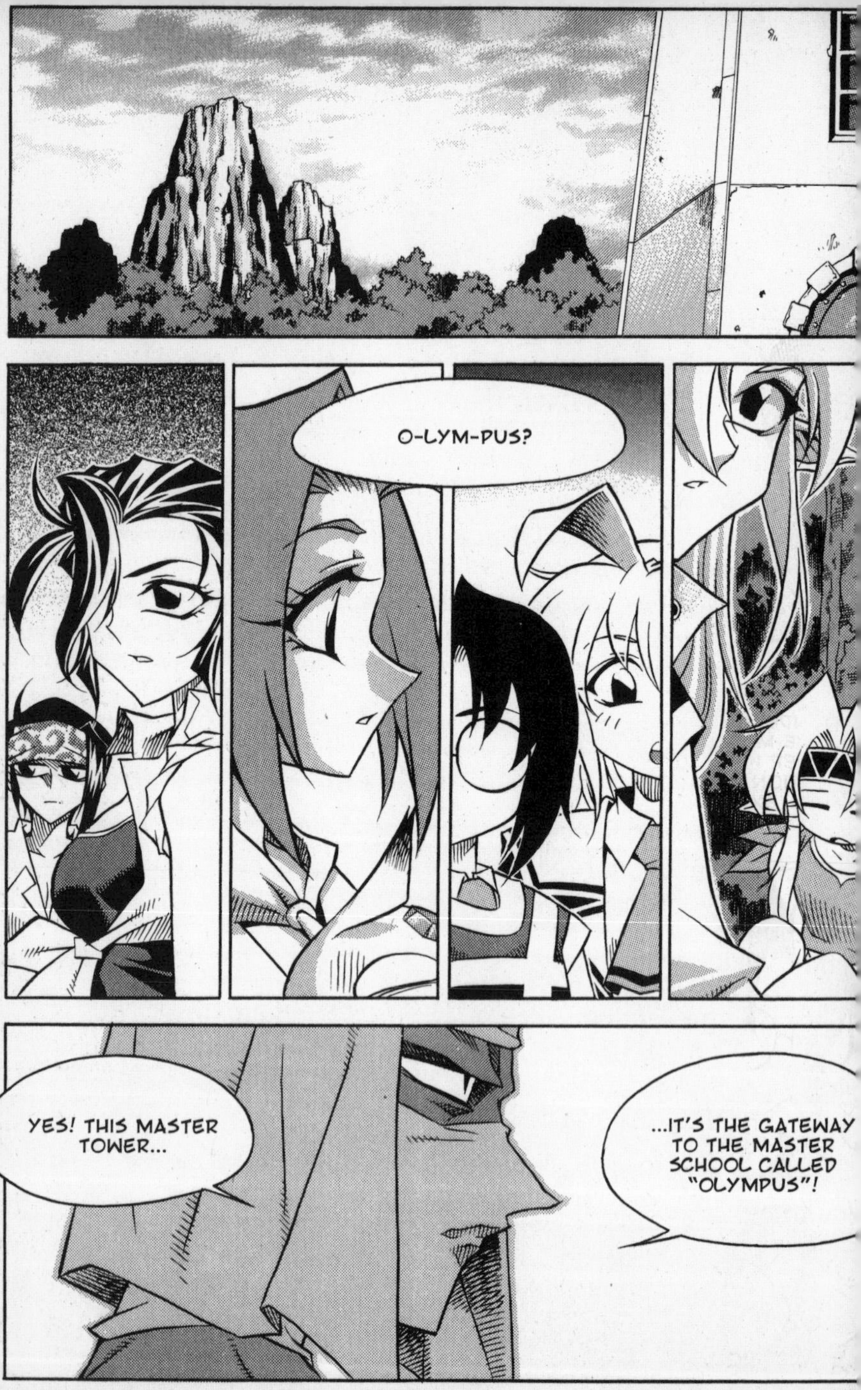
O-LYM-PUS?
YES! THIS MASTER TOWER...
...IT'S THE GATEWAY TO THE MASTER SCHOOL CALLED "OLYMPUS"!

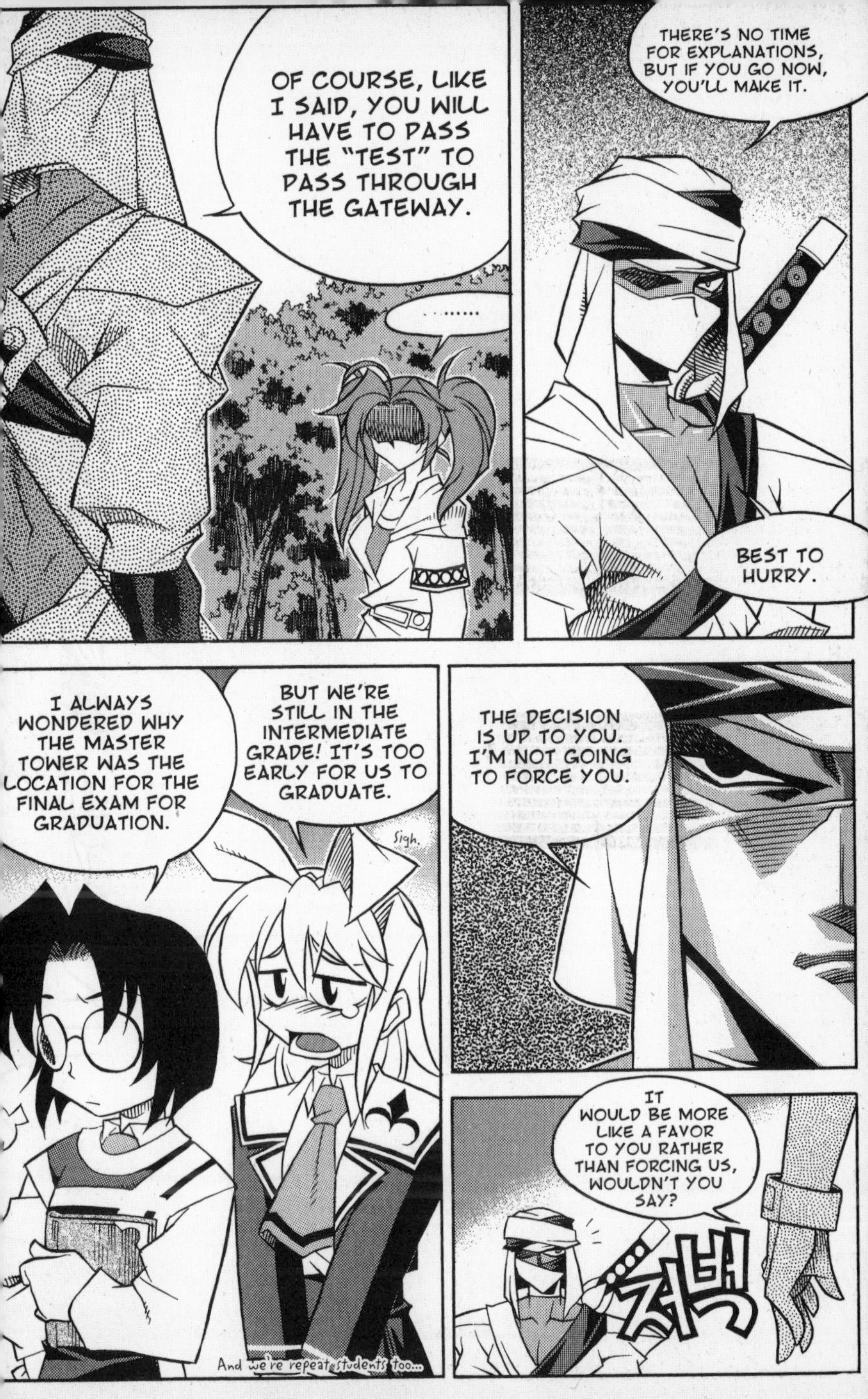
OF COURSE, LIKE I SAID, YOU WILL HAVE TO PASS THE "TEST" TO PASS THROUGH THE GATEWAY.
....
THERE'S NO TIME FOR EXPLANATIONS, BUT IF YOU GO NOW, YOU'LL MAKE IT.
BEST TO HURRY.
I ALWAYS WONDERED WHY THE MASTER TOWER WAS THE LOCATION FOR THE FINAL EXAM FOR GRADUATION.
BUT WE'RE STILL IN THE INTERMEDIATE GRADE! IT'S TOO EARLY FOR US TO GRADUATE.
Sigh.
And we're repeat students too...
THE DECISION IS UP TO YOU. I'M NOT GOING TO FORCE YOU.
IT WOULD BE MORE LIKE A FAVOR TO YOU RATHER THAN FORCING US, WOULDN'T YOU SAY?
저벅

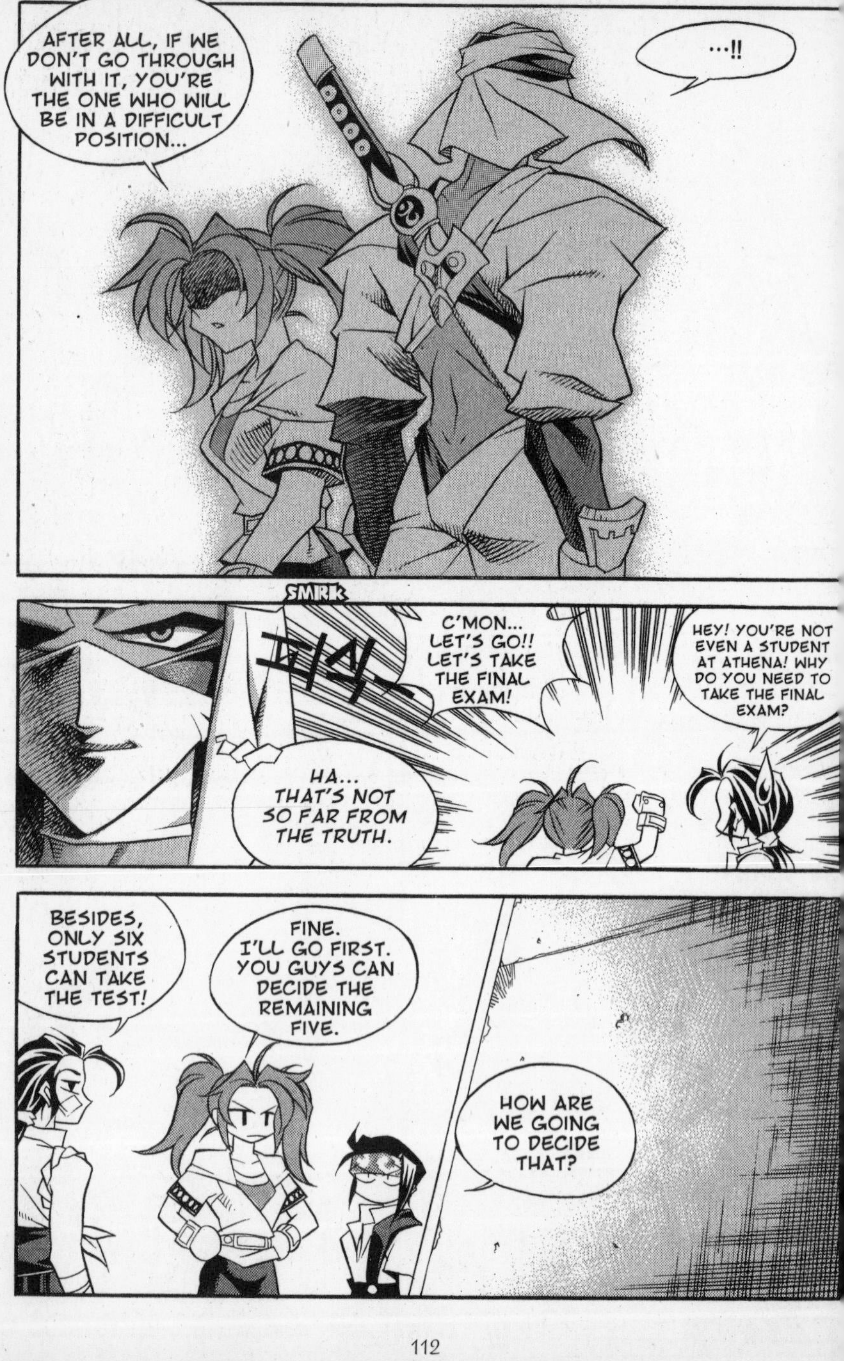
AFTER ALL, IF WE DON'T GO THROUGH WITH IT, YOU'RE THE ONE WHO WILL BE IN A DIFFICULT POSITION...
...!!
SMRK
피식-
C'MON... LET'S GO!! LET'S TAKE THE FINAL EXAM!
HEY! YOU'RE NOT EVEN A STUDENT AT ATHENA! WHY DO YOU NEED TO TAKE THE FINAL EXAM?
HA... THAT'S NOT SO FAR FROM THE TRUTH.
BESIDES, ONLY SIX STUDENTS CAN TAKE THE TEST!
FINE. I'LL GO FIRST. YOU GUYS CAN DECIDE THE REMAINING FIVE.
HOW ARE WE GOING TO DECIDE THAT?

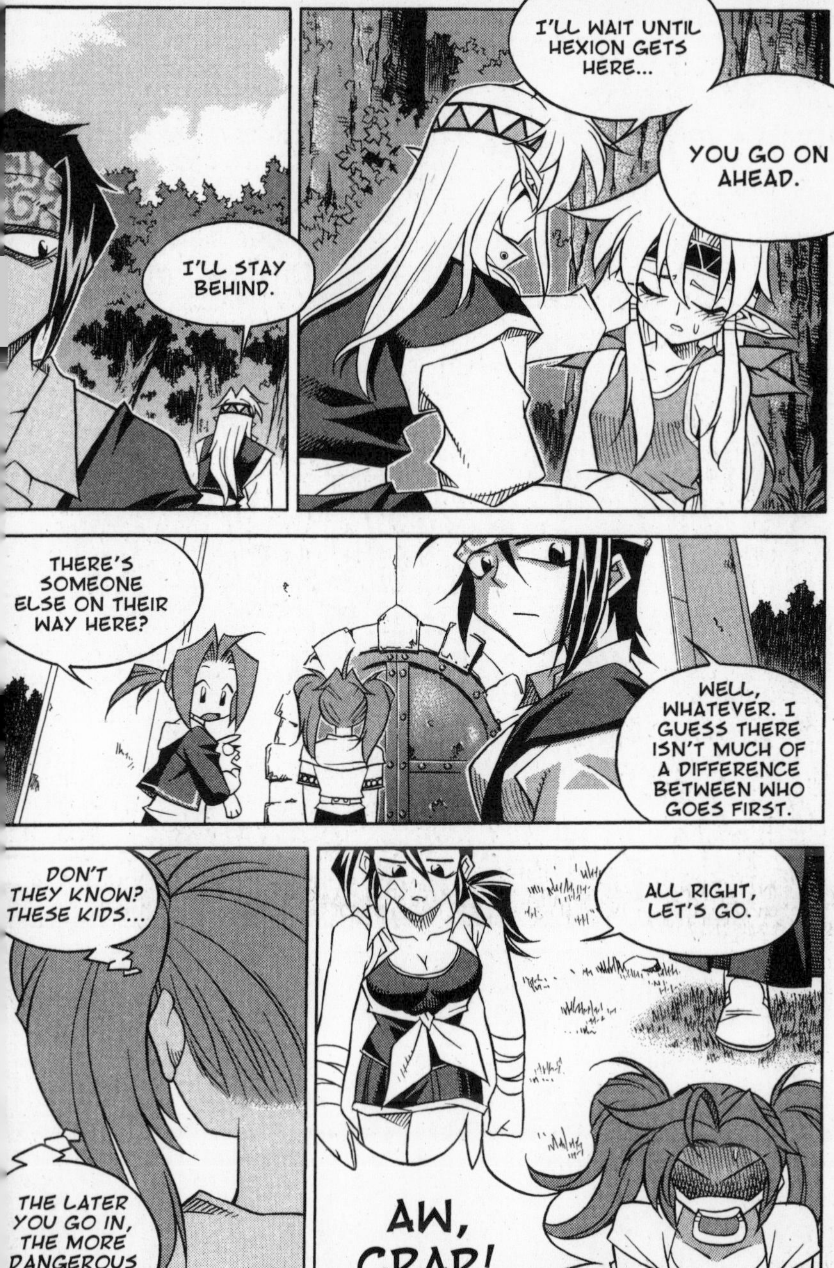
I'LL STAY BEHIND.
I'LL WAIT UNTIL HEXION GETS HERE...
YOU GO ON AHEAD.
THERE'S SOMEONE ELSE ON THEIR WAY HERE?
WELL, WHATEVER. I GUESS THERE ISN'T MUCH OF A DIFFERENCE BETWEEN WHO GOES FIRST.
DON'T THEY KNOW? THESE KIDS...
THE LATER YOU GO IN, THE MORE DANGEROUS IT IS...
ALL RIGHT, LET'S GO.
AW, CRAP!

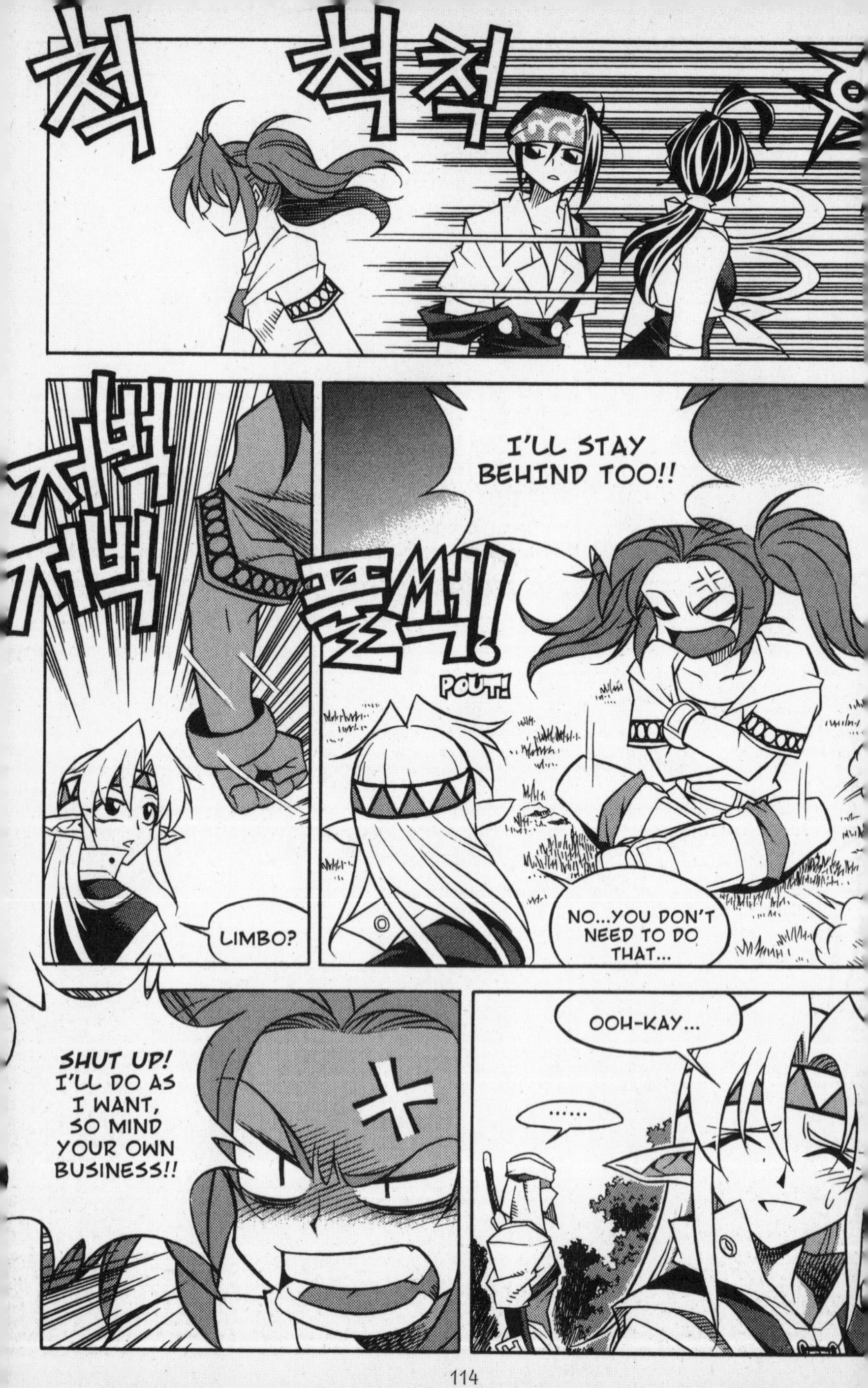
척 척척
저벅 저벅
LIMBO?
I'LL STAY BEHIND TOO!!
풀썩!
POUT!
NO...YOU DON'T NEED TO DO THAT...
SHUT UP! I'LL DO AS I WANT, SO MIND YOUR OWN BUSINESS!!
OOH-KAY...
......

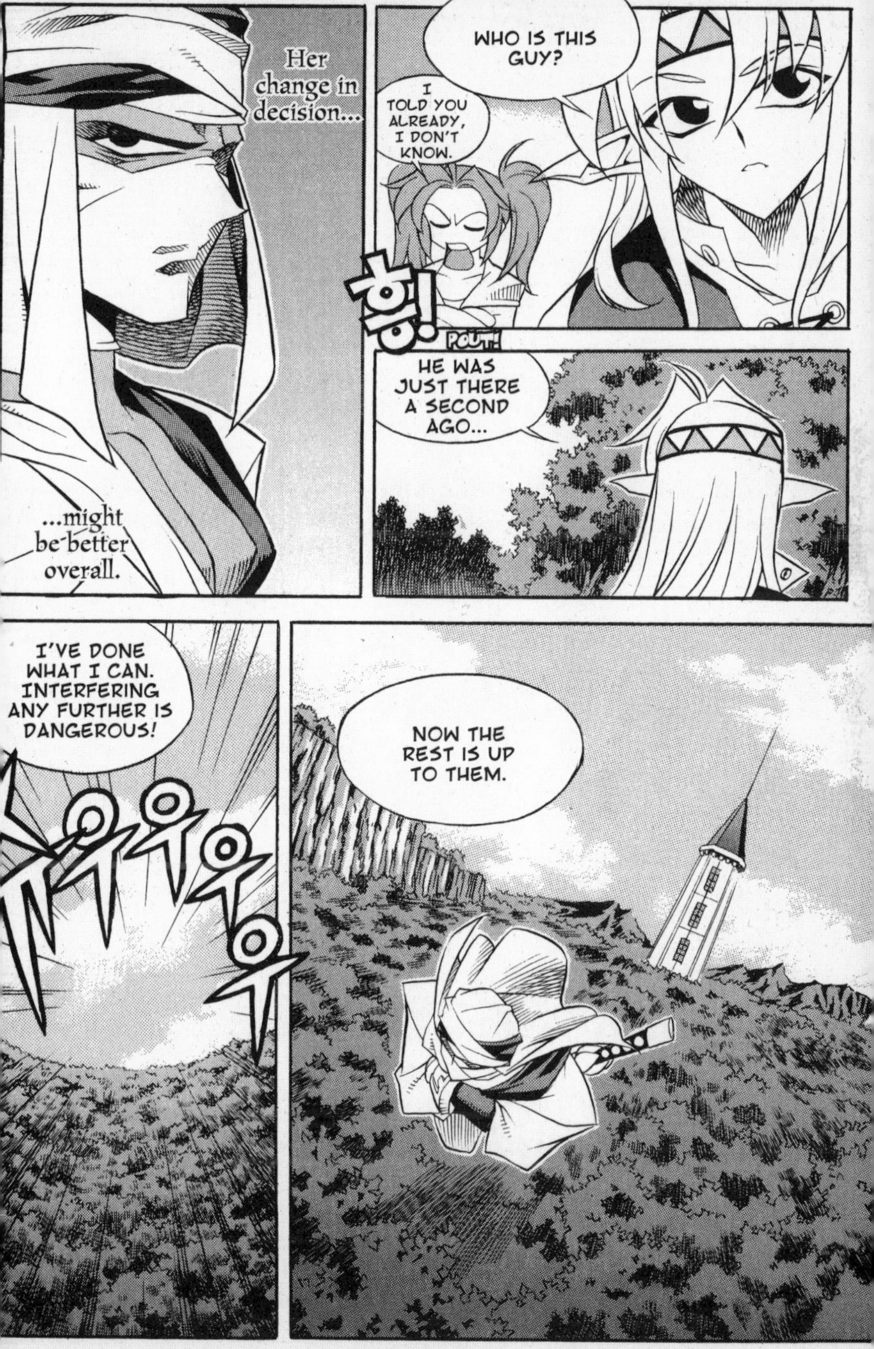
Her change in decision...
...might be better overall.
WHO IS THIS GUY?
I TOLD YOU ALREADY, I DON'T KNOW.
흥!
POUT!
HE WAS JUST THERE A SECOND AGO...
I'VE DONE WHAT I CAN. INTERFERING ANY FURTHER IS DANGEROUS!
NOW THE REST IS UP TO THEM.

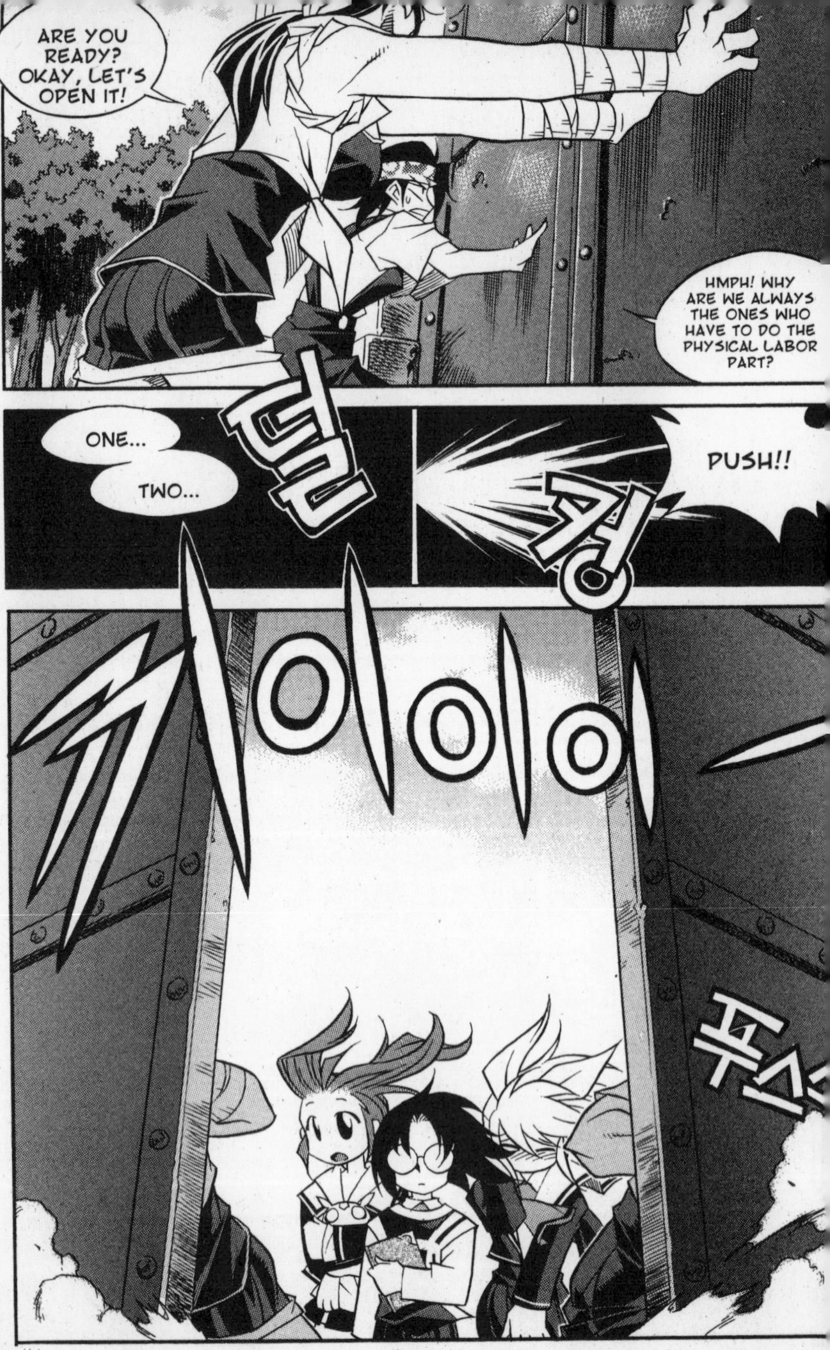
ARE YOU READY? OKAY, LET'S OPEN IT!
HMPH! WHY ARE WE ALWAYS THE ONES WHO HAVE TO DO THE PHYSICAL LABOR PART?
ONE...
TWO...
PUSH!!

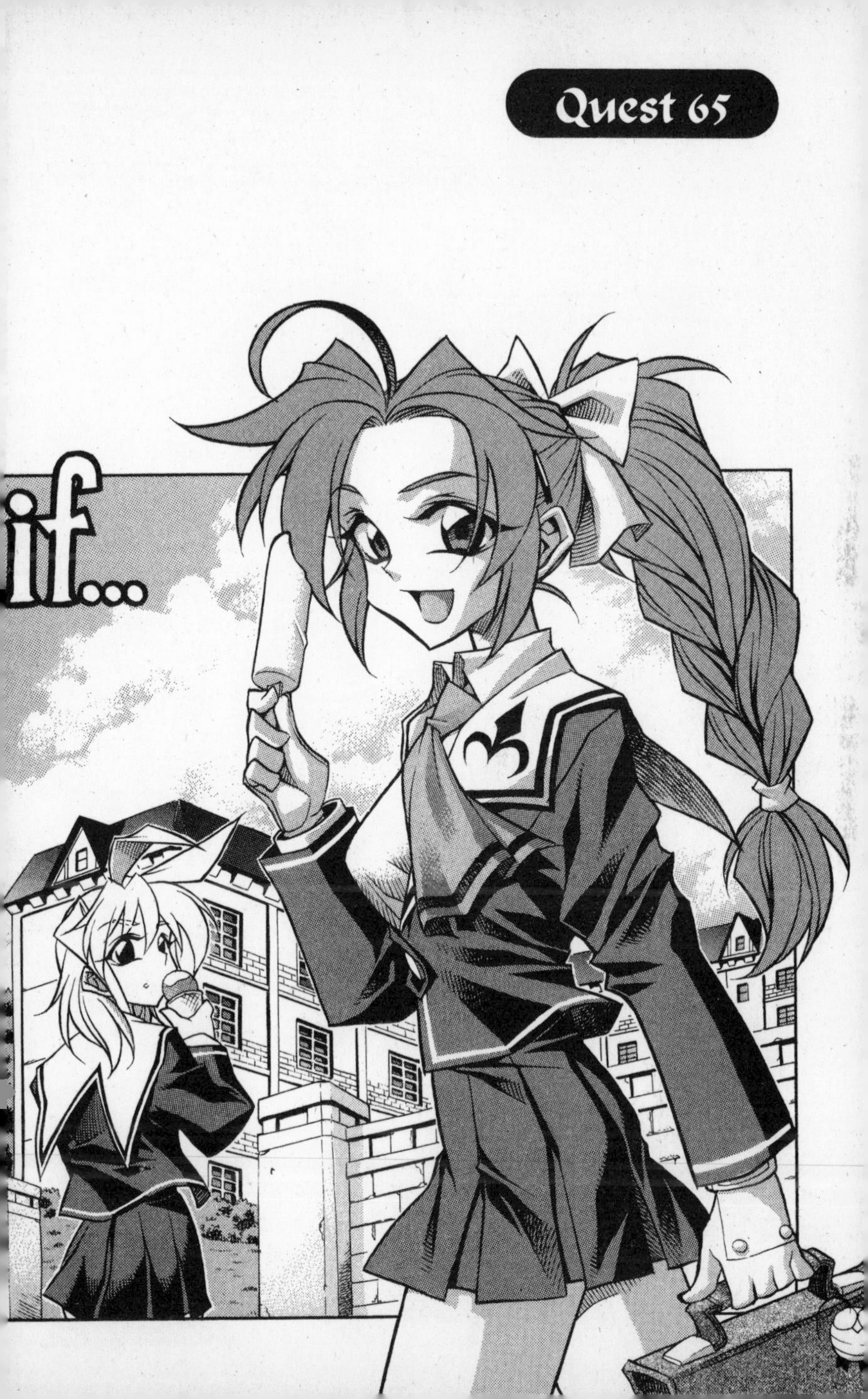
Quest 65
if...

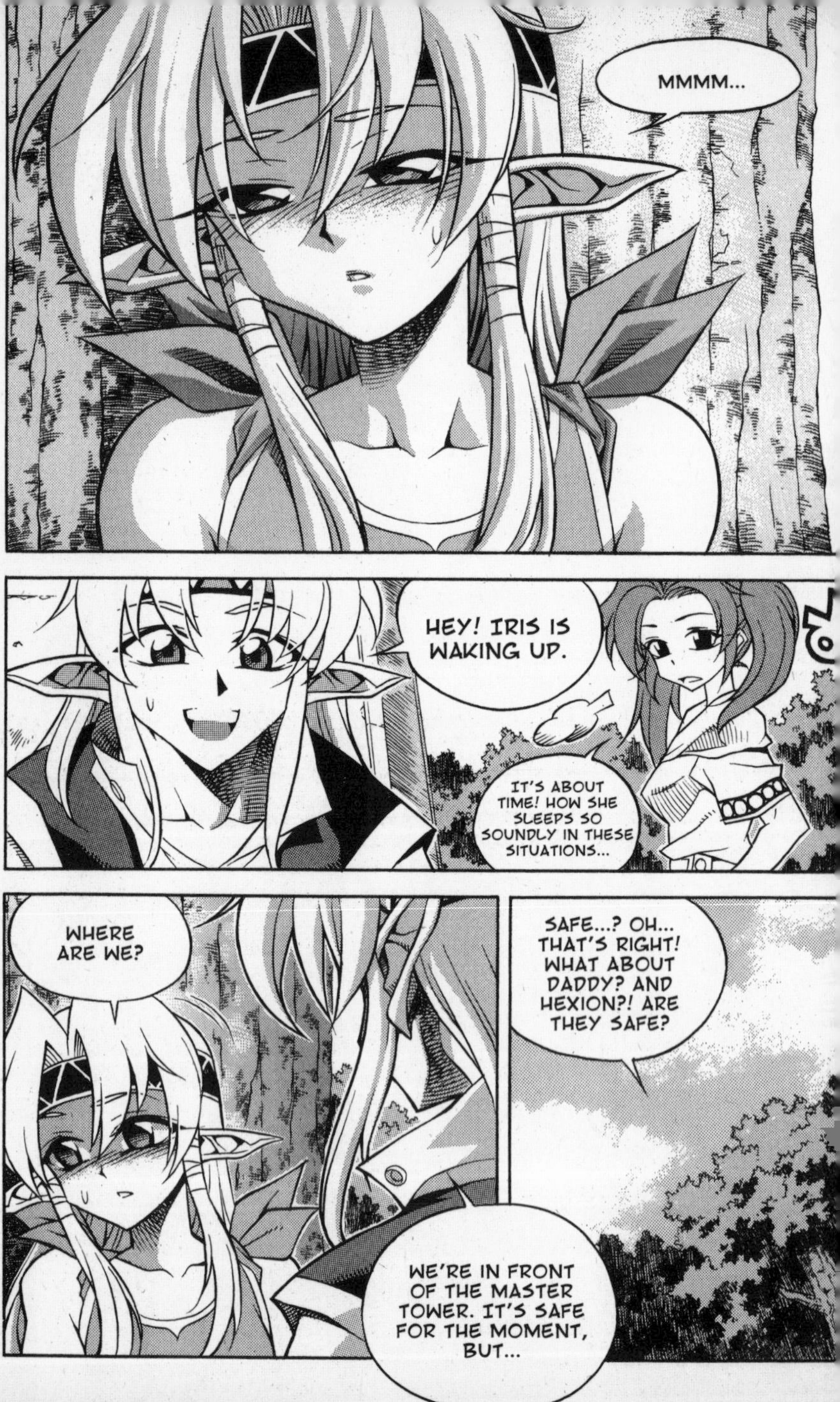
MMMM...
HEY! IRIS IS WAKING UP.
IT'S ABOUT TIME! HOW SHE SLEEPS SO SOUNDLY IN THESE SITUATIONS...
WHERE ARE WE?
WE'RE IN FRONT OF THE MASTER TOWER. IT'S SAFE FOR THE MOMENT, BUT...
SAFE...? OH... THAT'S RIGHT! WHAT ABOUT DADDY? AND HEXION?! ARE THEY SAFE?

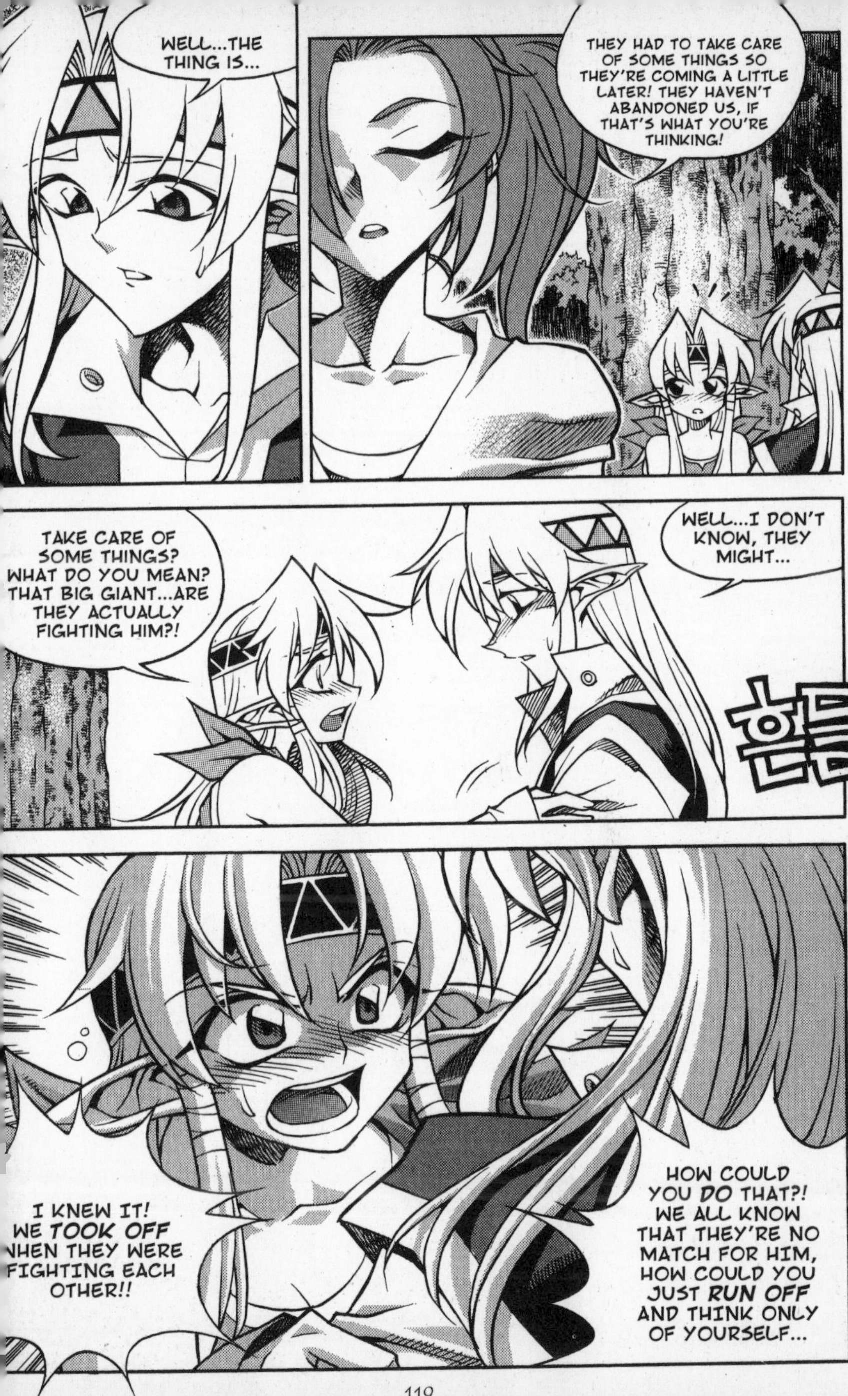
WELL...THE THING IS...
THEY HAD TO TAKE CARE OF SOME THINGS SO THEY'RE COMING A LITTLE LATER! THEY HAVEN'T ABANDONED US, IF THAT'S WHAT YOU'RE THINKING!
TAKE CARE OF SOME THINGS? WHAT DO YOU MEAN? THAT BIG GIANT...ARE THEY ACTUALLY FIGHTING HIM?!
WELL...I DON'T KNOW, THEY MIGHT...
흔들
I KNEW IT! WE *TOOK OFF* WHEN THEY WERE FIGHTING EACH OTHER!!
HOW COULD YOU *DO* THAT?! WE ALL KNOW THAT THEY'RE NO MATCH FOR HIM, HOW COULD YOU JUST *RUN OFF* AND THINK ONLY OF YOURSELF...

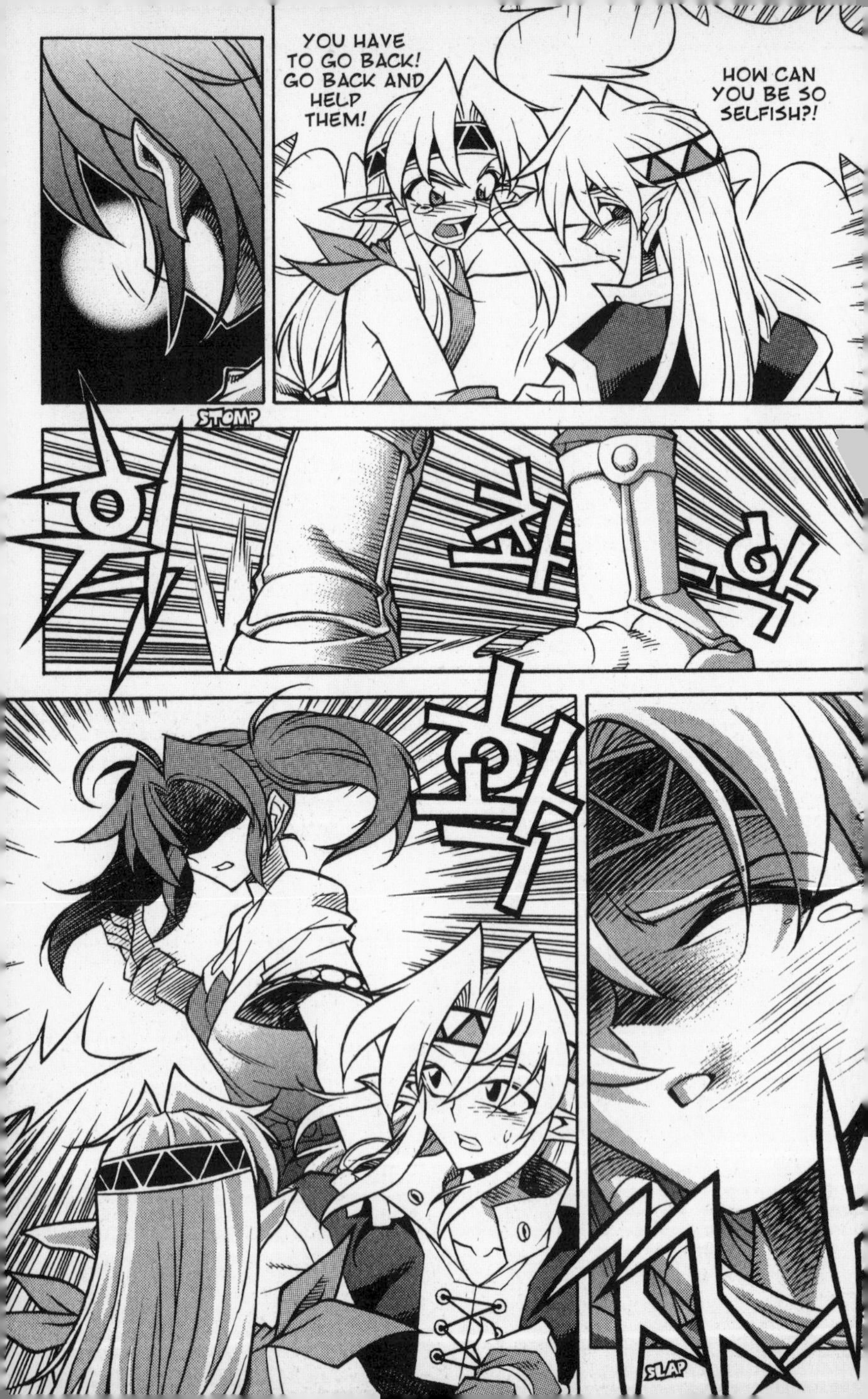
YOU HAVE TO GO BACK! GO BACK AND HELP THEM!
HOW CAN YOU BE SO SELFISH?!
STOMP
SLAP

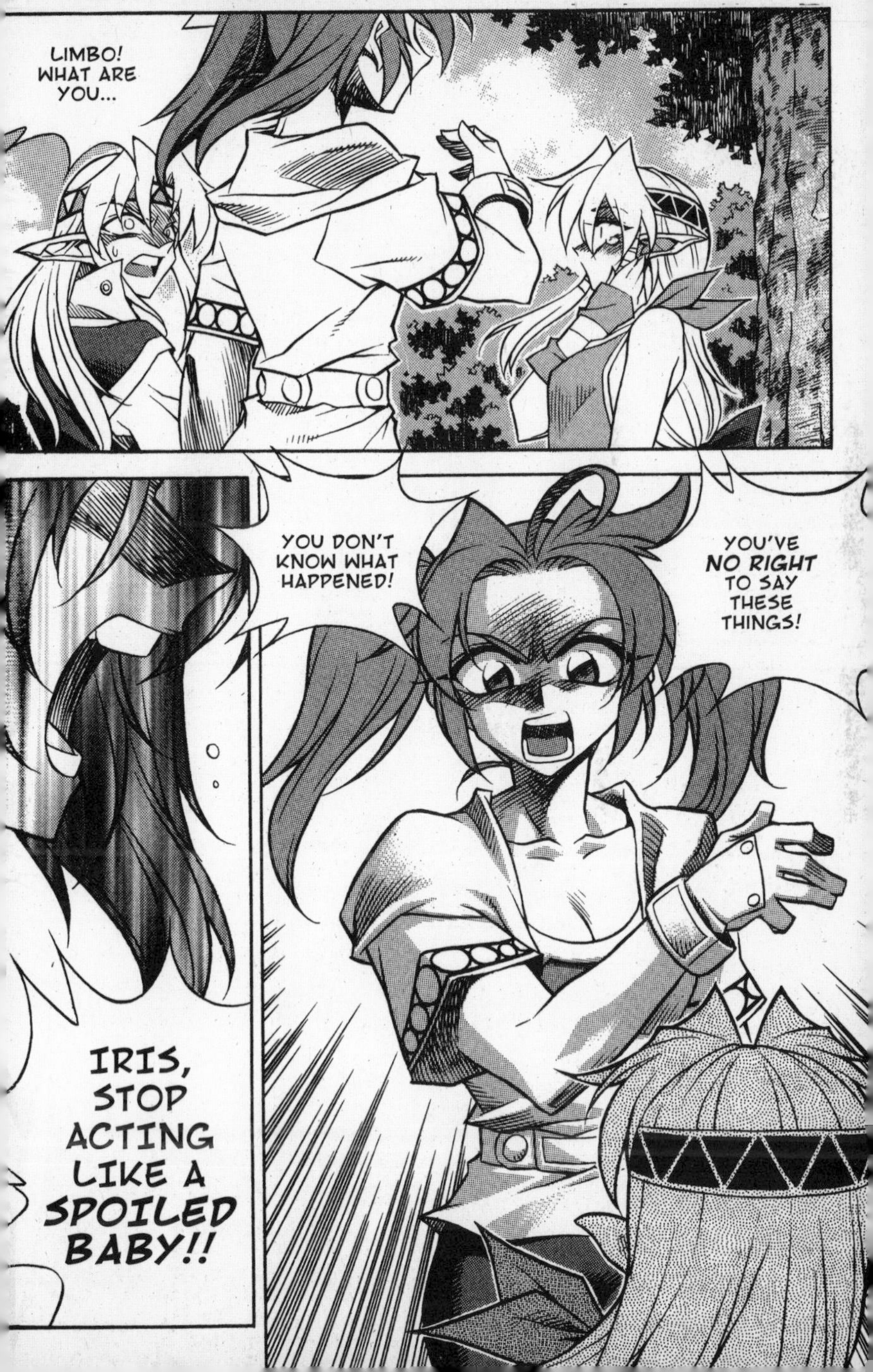
LIMBO! WHAT ARE YOU...
YOU DON'T KNOW WHAT HAPPENED!
YOU'VE NO RIGHT TO SAY THESE THINGS!
IRIS, STOP ACTING LIKE A SPOILED BABY!!

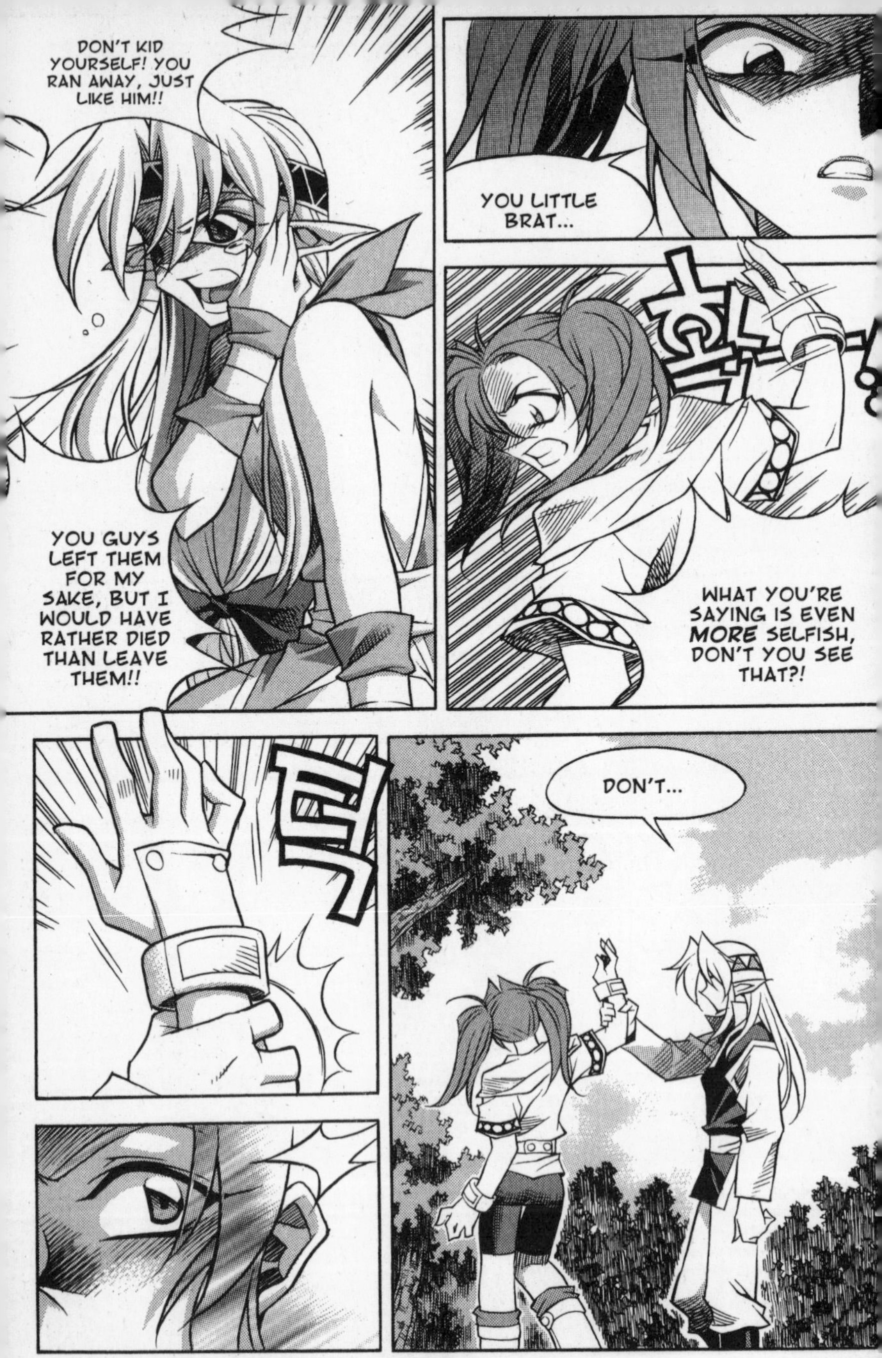
DON'T KID YOURSELF! YOU RAN AWAY, JUST LIKE HIM!!
YOU GUYS LEFT THEM FOR MY SAKE, BUT I WOULD HAVE RATHER DIED THAN LEAVE THEM!!
YOU LITTLE BRAT...
WHAT YOU'RE SAYING IS EVEN MORE SELFISH, DON'T YOU SEE THAT?!
DON'T...

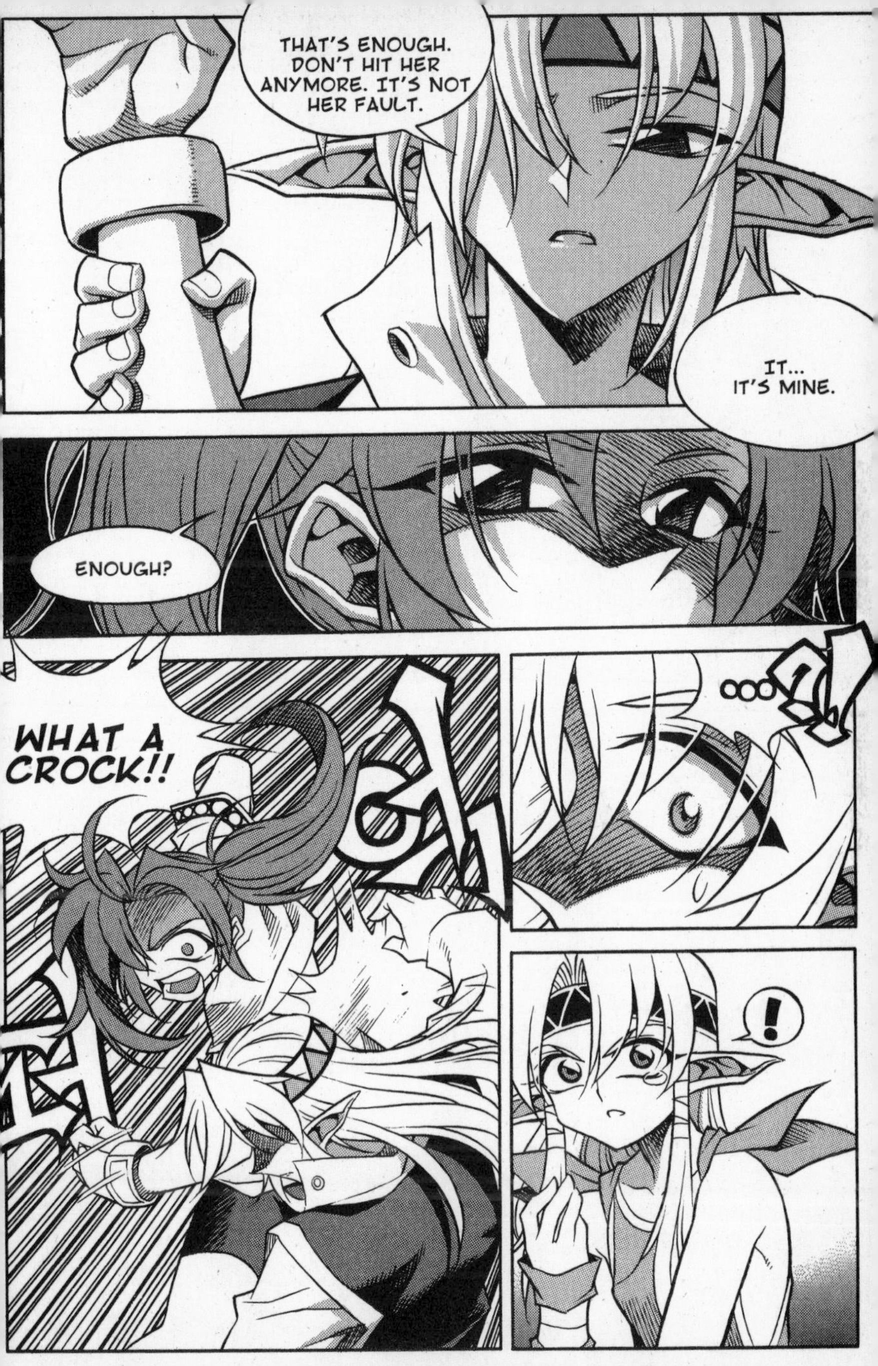
THAT'S ENOUGH. DON'T HIT HER ANYMORE. IT'S NOT HER FAULT.
IT... IT'S MINE.
ENOUGH?
WHAT A CROCK!!
...?!
!

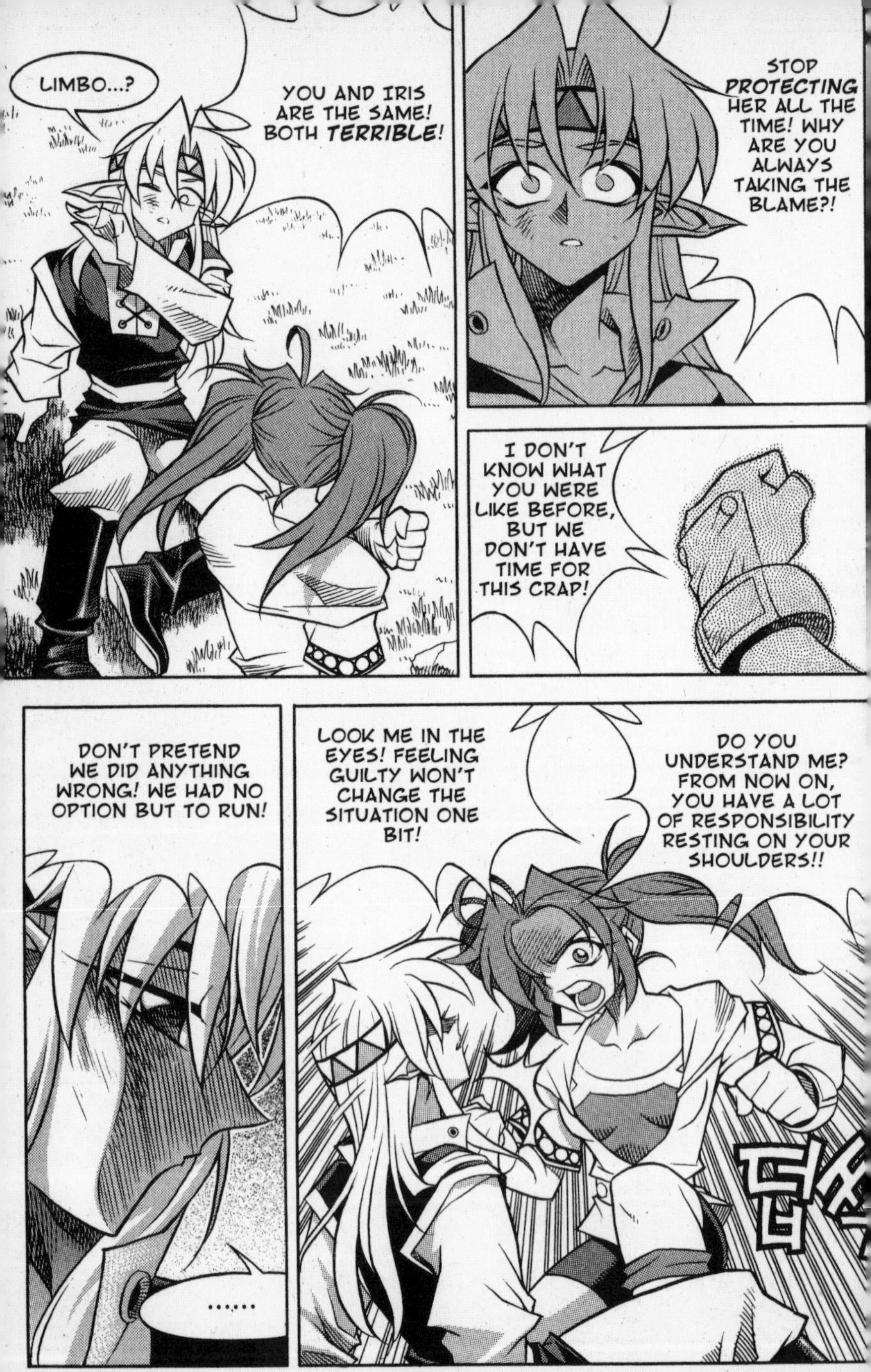
LIMBO...?
YOU AND IRIS ARE THE SAME! BOTH TERRIBLE!
STOP PROTECTING HER ALL THE TIME! WHY ARE YOU ALWAYS TAKING THE BLAME?!
I DON'T KNOW WHAT YOU WERE LIKE BEFORE, BUT WE DON'T HAVE TIME FOR THIS CRAP!
DON'T PRETEND WE DID ANYTHING WRONG! WE HAD NO OPTION BUT TO RUN!
...,...
LOOK ME IN THE EYES! FEELING GUILTY WON'T CHANGE THE SITUATION ONE BIT!
DO YOU UNDERSTAND ME? FROM NOW ON, YOU HAVE A LOT OF RESPONSIBILITY RESTING ON YOUR SHOULDERS!!

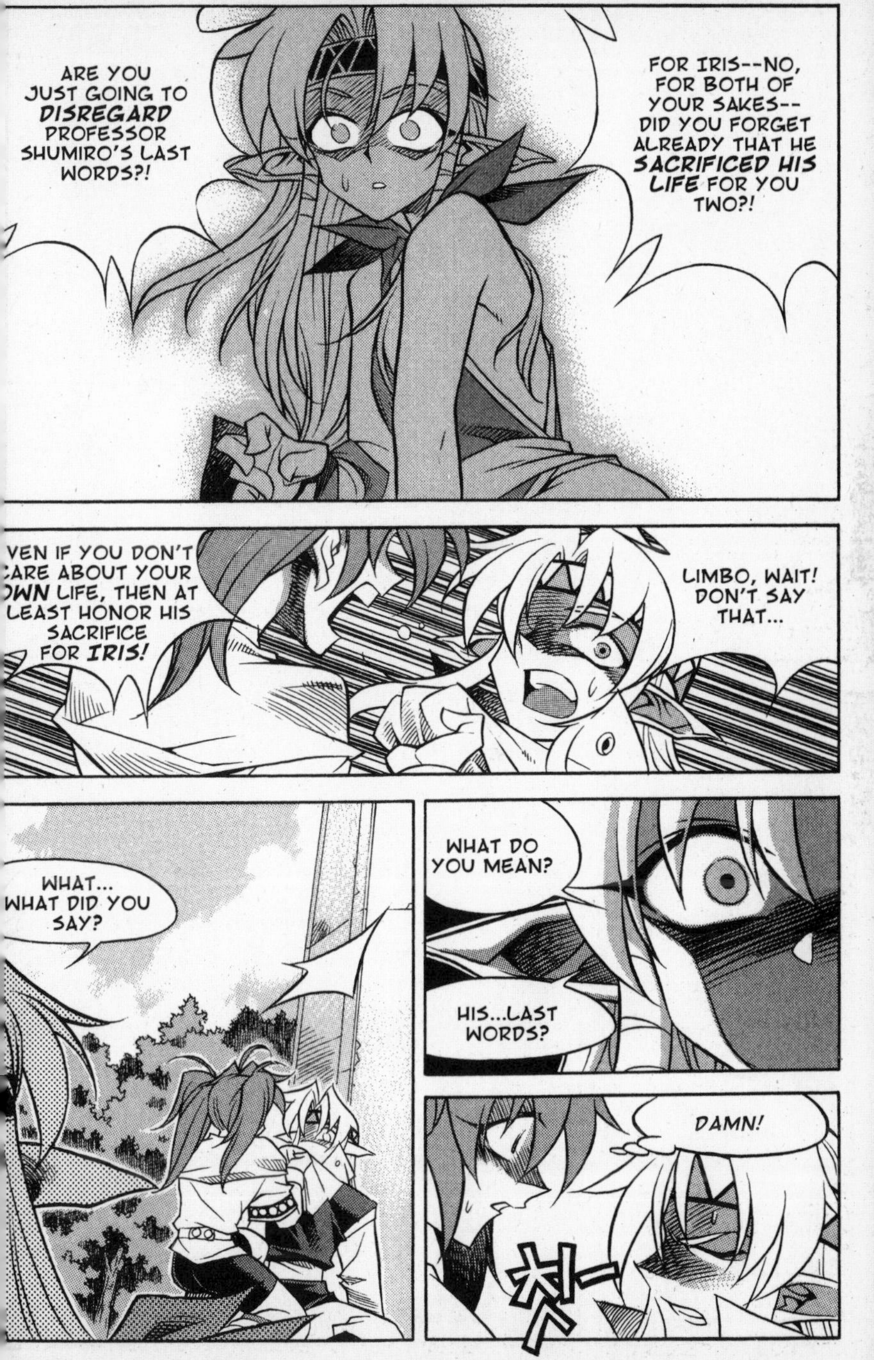
ARE YOU JUST GOING TO DISREGARD PROFESSOR SHUMIRO'S LAST WORDS?!
FOR IRIS--NO, FOR BOTH OF YOUR SAKES--DID YOU FORGET ALREADY THAT HE SACRIFICED HIS LIFE FOR YOU TWO?!
VEN IF YOU DON'T CARE ABOUT YOUR OWN LIFE, THEN AT LEAST HONOR HIS SACRIFICE FOR IRIS!
LIMBO, WAIT! DON'T SAY THAT...
WHAT... WHAT DID YOU SAY?
WHAT DO YOU MEAN?
HIS...LAST WORDS?
DAMN!

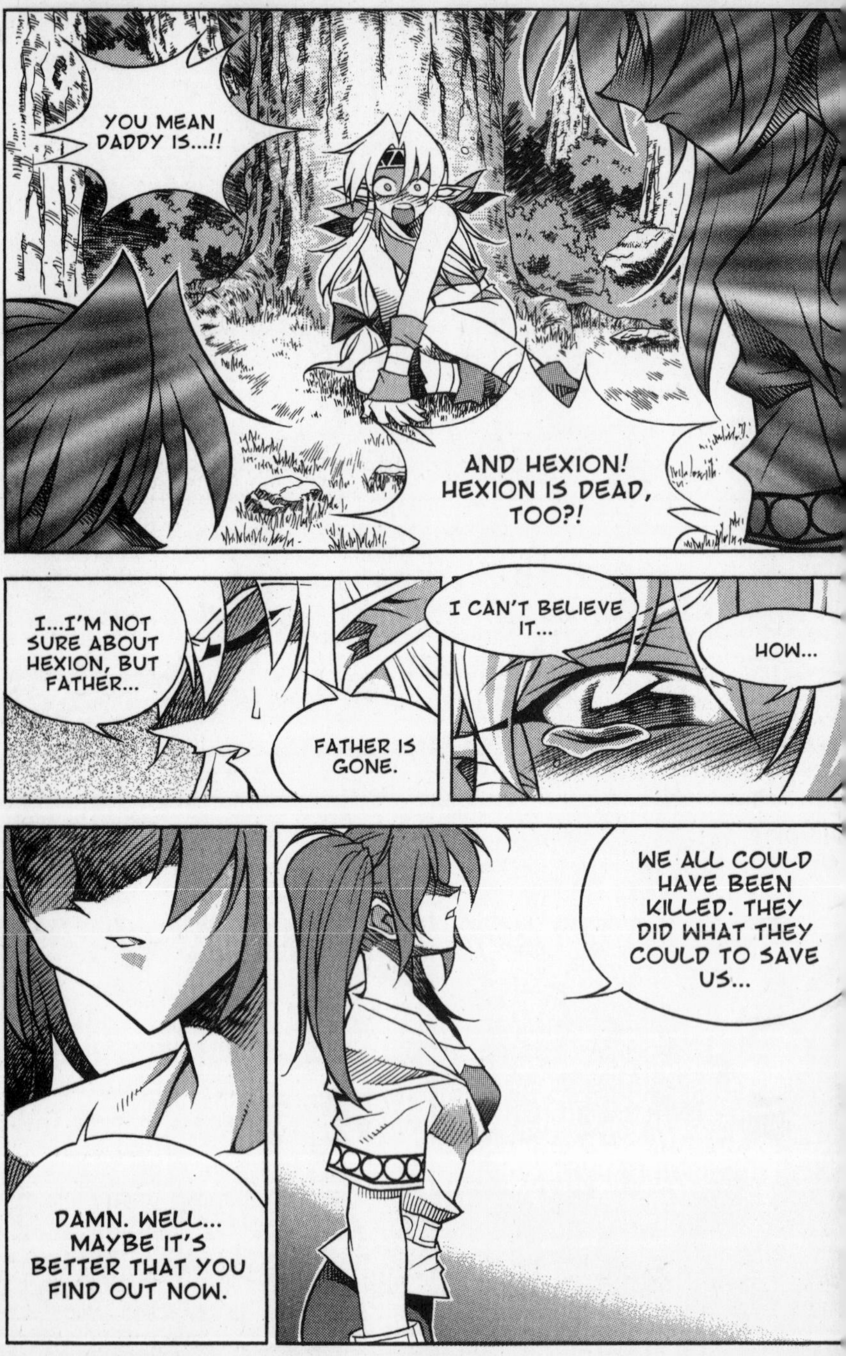
YOU MEAN DADDY IS...!!
AND HEXION! HEXION IS DEAD, TOO?!
I...I'M NOT SURE ABOUT HEXION, BUT FATHER...
FATHER IS GONE.
I CAN'T BELIEVE IT...
HOW...
DAMN. WELL... MAYBE IT'S BETTER THAT YOU FIND OUT NOW.
WE ALL COULD HAVE BEEN KILLED. THEY DID WHAT THEY COULD TO SAVE US...

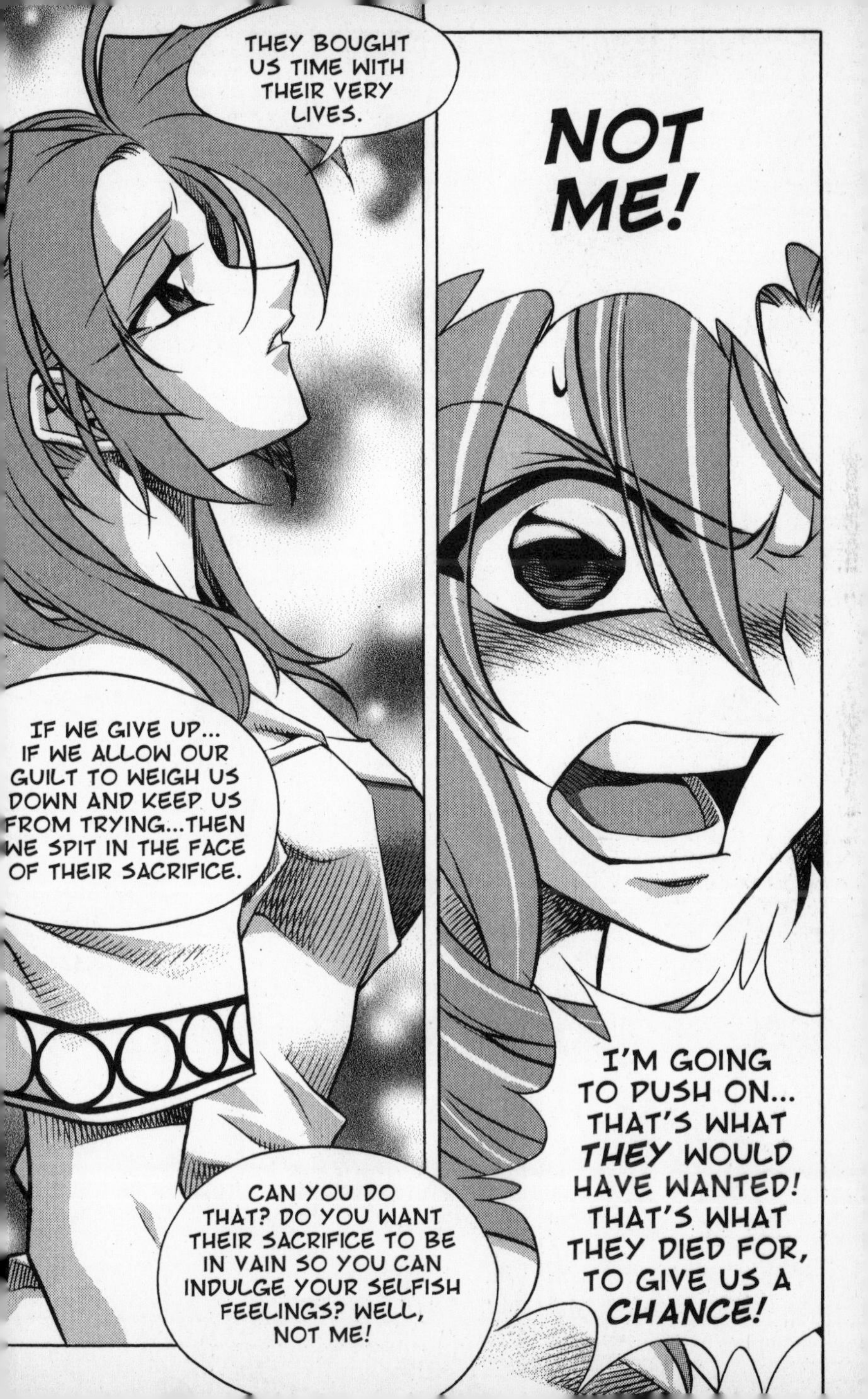
THEY BOUGHT US TIME WITH THEIR VERY LIVES.
IF WE GIVE UP... IF WE ALLOW OUR GUILT TO WEIGH US DOWN AND KEEP US FROM TRYING...THEN WE SPIT IN THE FACE OF THEIR SACRIFICE.
CAN YOU DO THAT? DO YOU WANT THEIR SACRIFICE TO BE IN VAIN SO YOU CAN INDULGE YOUR SELFISH FEELINGS? WELL, NOT ME!
NOT ME!
I'M GOING TO PUSH ON... THAT'S WHAT *THEY* WOULD HAVE WANTED! THAT'S WHAT THEY DIED FOR, TO GIVE US A *CHANCE!*

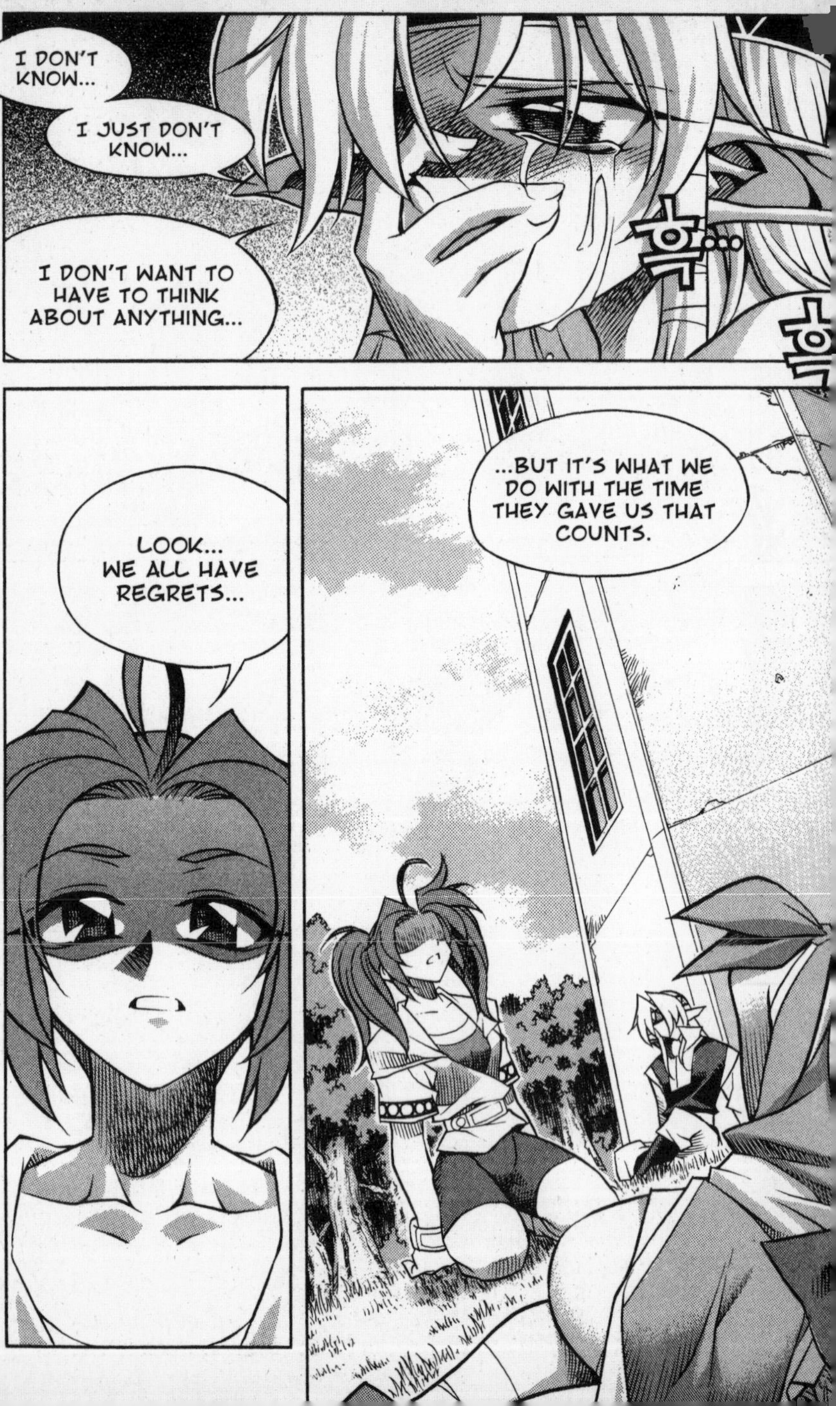
I DON'T KNOW...
I JUST DON'T KNOW...
I DON'T WANT TO HAVE TO THINK ABOUT ANYTHING...
흑...
흐흑
LOOK... WE ALL HAVE REGRETS...
...BUT IT'S WHAT WE DO WITH THE TIME THEY GAVE US THAT COUNTS.

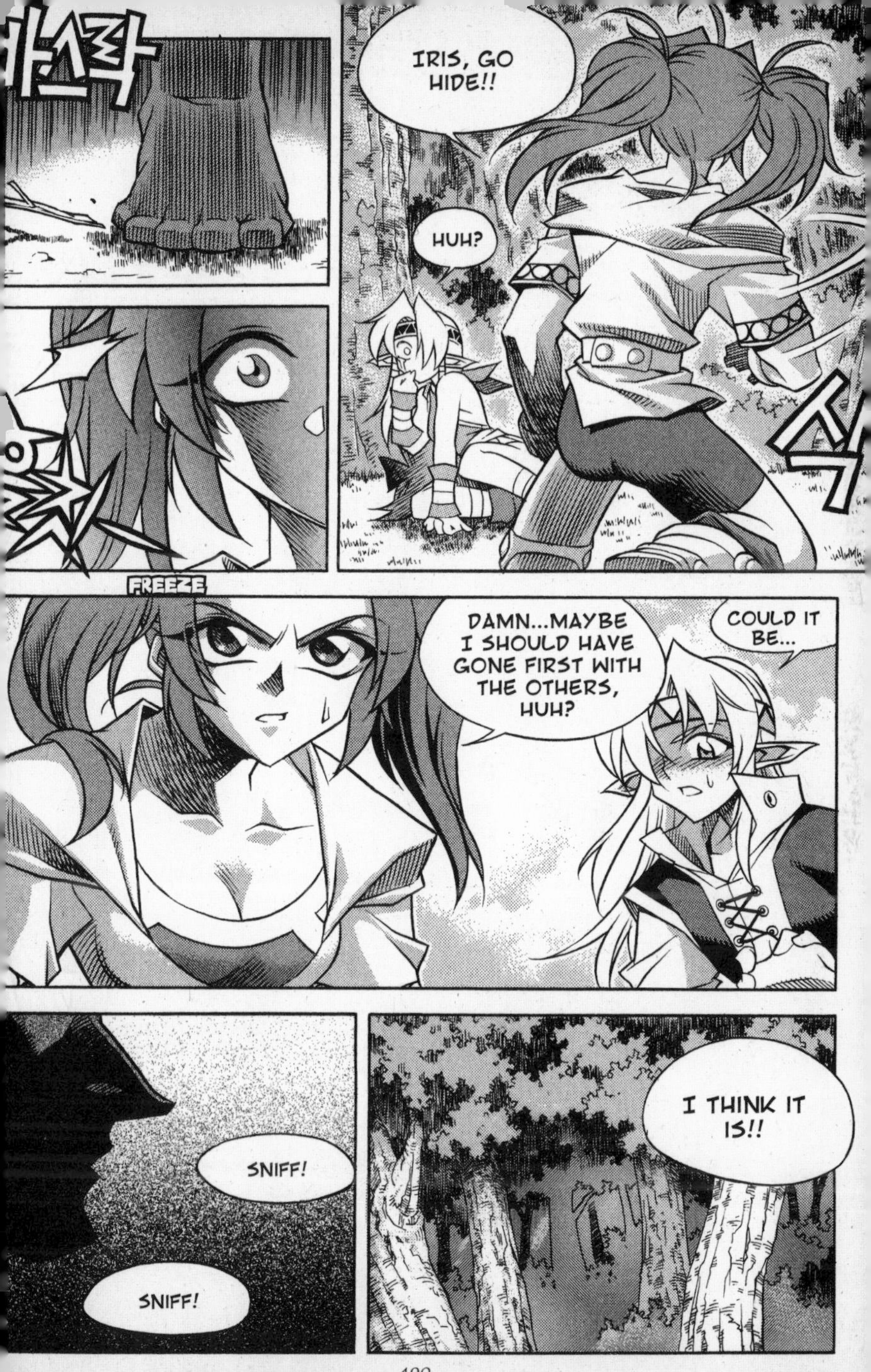
IRIS, GO HIDE!!
HUH?
FREEZE
DAMN...MAYBE I SHOULD HAVE GONE FIRST WITH THE OTHERS, HUH?
COULD IT BE...
SNIFF!
SNIFF!
I THINK IT IS!!

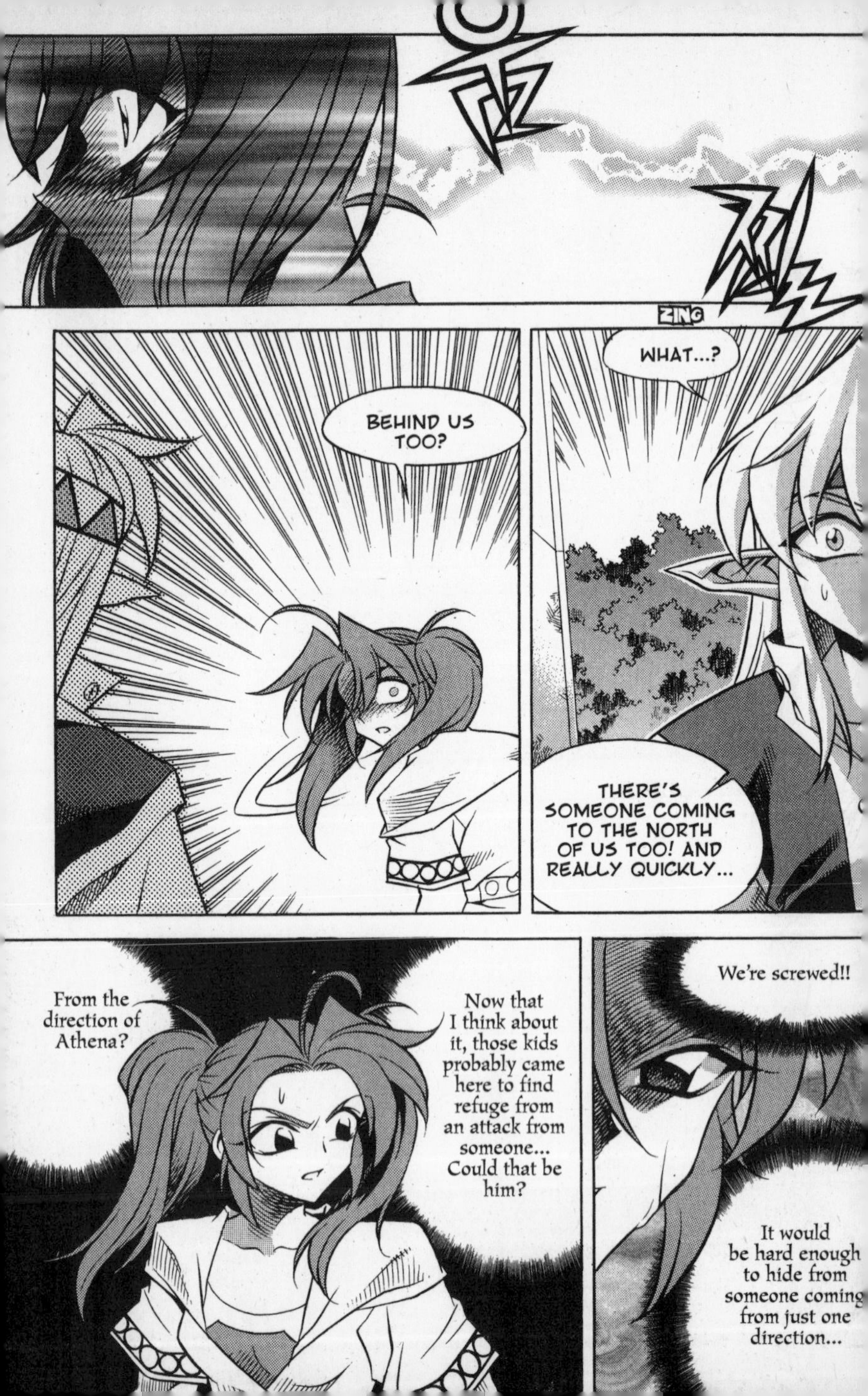
ZING
BEHIND US TOO?
WHAT...?
THERE'S SOMEONE COMING TO THE NORTH OF US TOO! AND REALLY QUICKLY...
From the direction of Athena?
Now that I think about it, those kids probably came here to find refuge from an attack from someone... Could that be him?
We're screwed!!
It would be hard enough to hide from someone coming from just one direction...

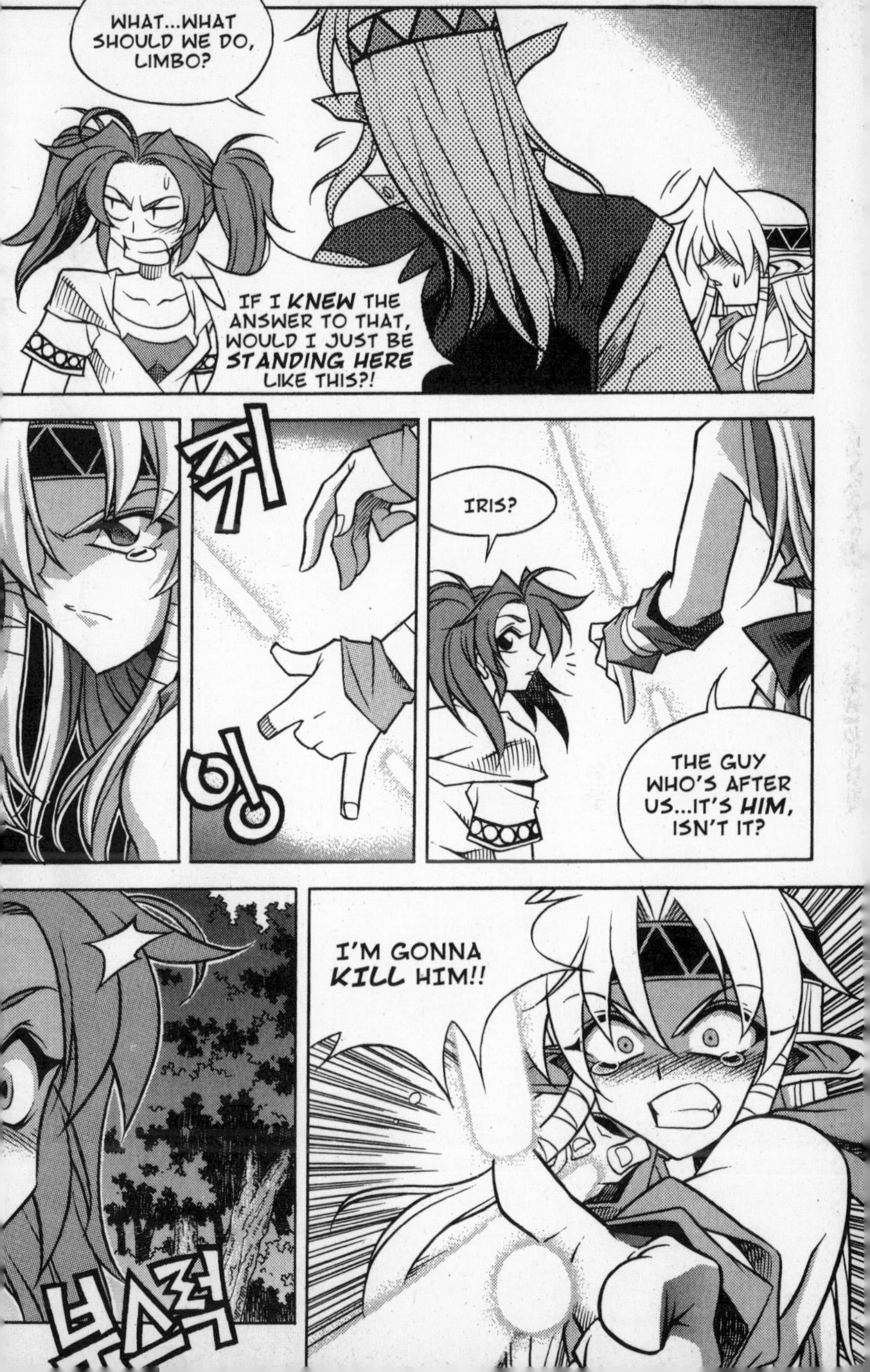
WHAT...WHAT SHOULD WE DO, LIMBO?
IF I *KNEW* THE ANSWER TO THAT, WOULD I JUST BE ***STANDING HERE*** LIKE THIS?!
IRIS?
THE GUY WHO'S AFTER US...IT'S ***HIM***, ISN'T IT?
I'M GONNA ***KILL*** HIM!!

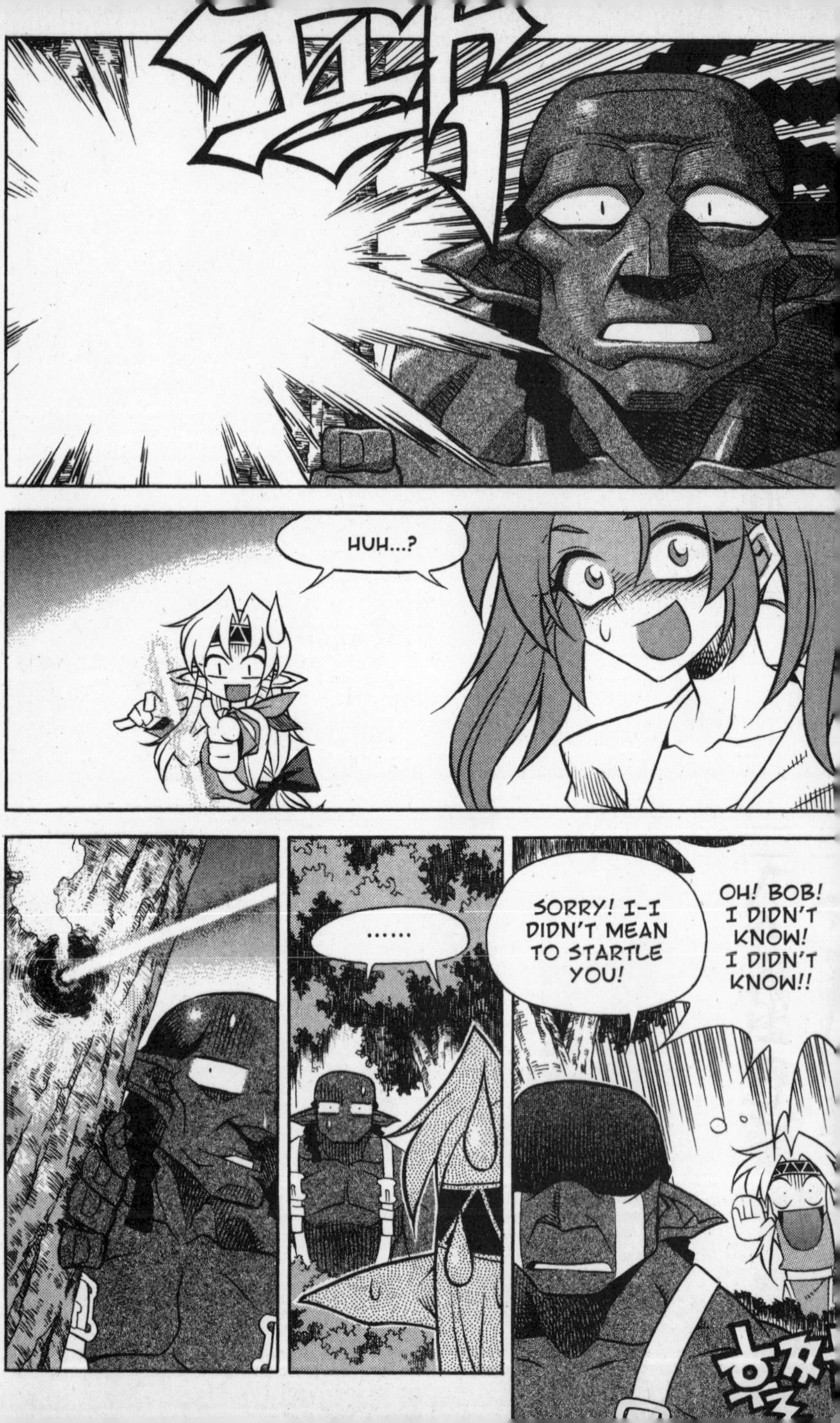
HUH...?
......
SORRY! I-I DIDN'T MEAN TO STARTLE YOU!
OH! BOB! I DIDN'T KNOW! I DIDN'T KNOW!!

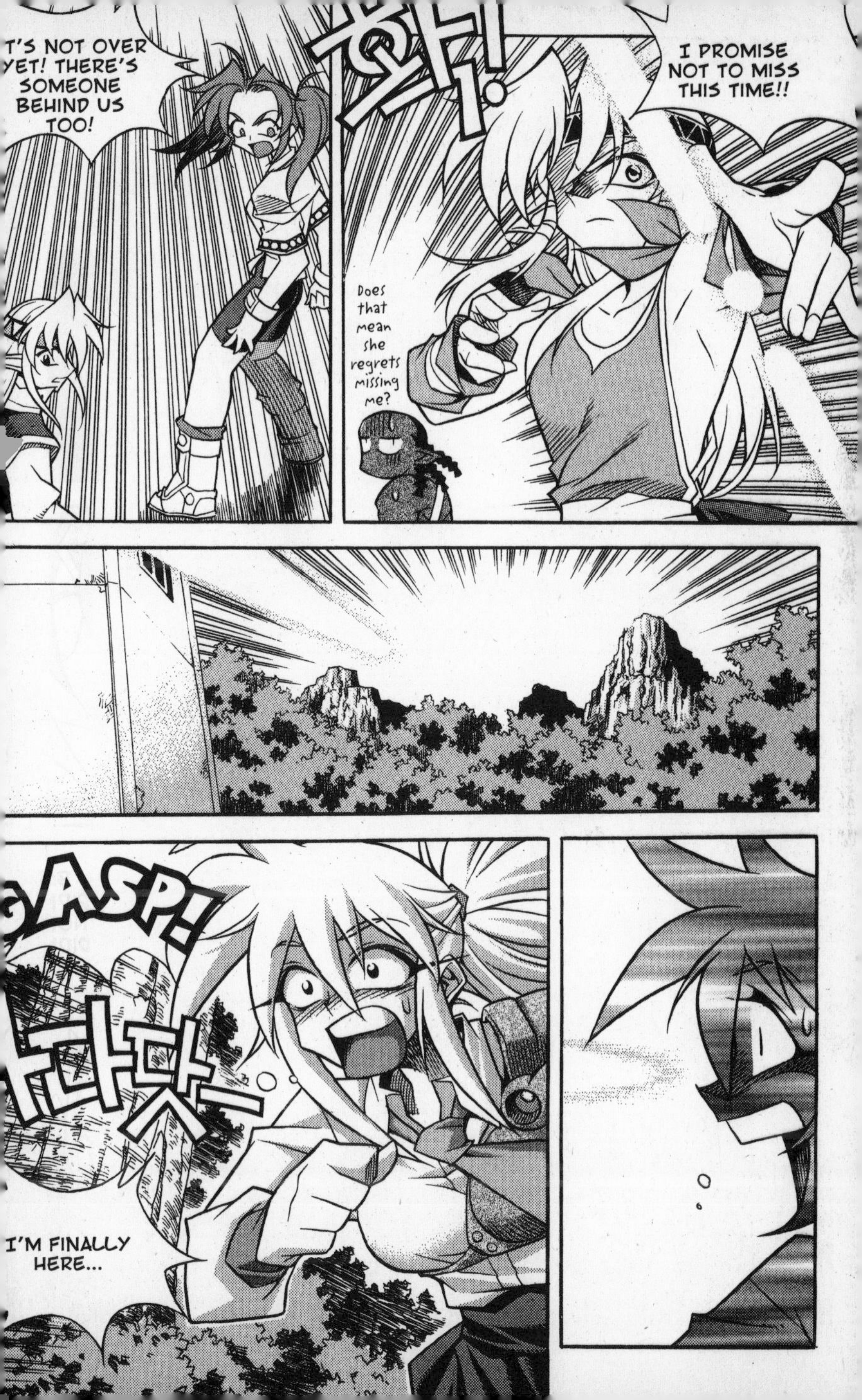

T'S NOT OVER YET! THERE'S SOMEONE BEHIND US TOO!
I PROMISE NOT TO MISS THIS TIME!!
Does that mean she regrets missing me?
GASP!
I'M FINALLY HERE...

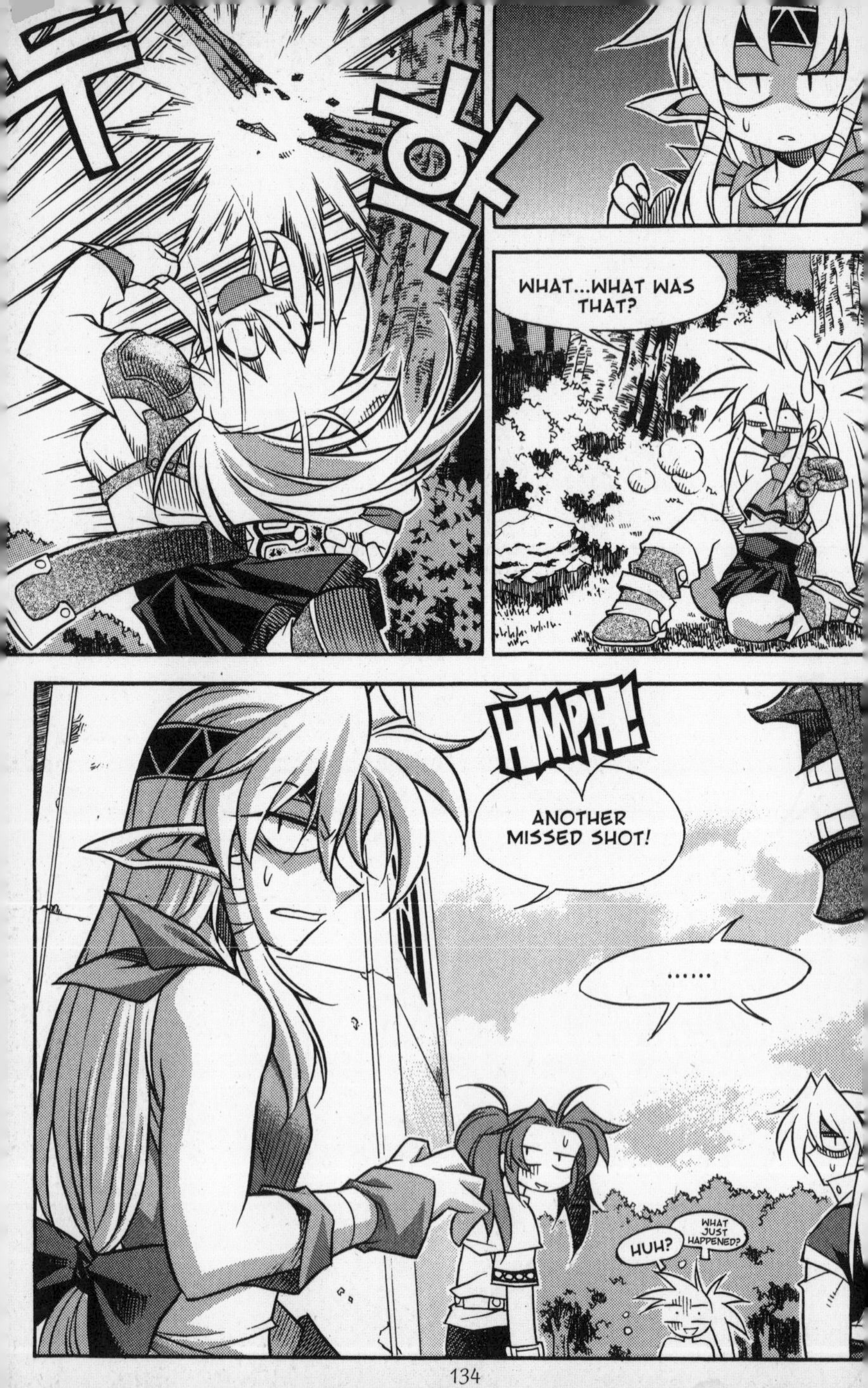
WHAT...WHAT WAS THAT?
HMPH!
ANOTHER MISSED SHOT!
......
HUH?
WHAT JUST HAPPENED?

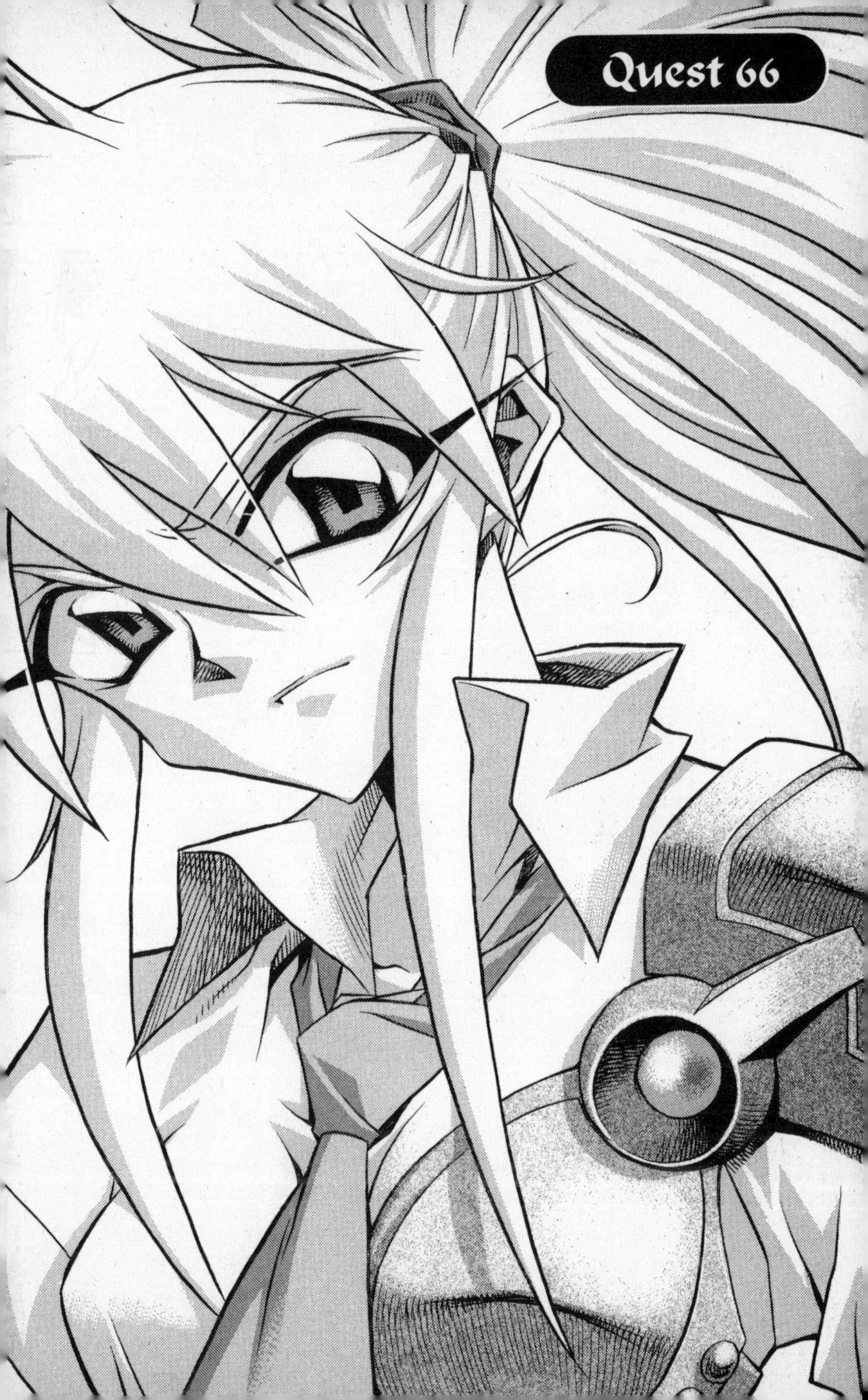
Quest 66

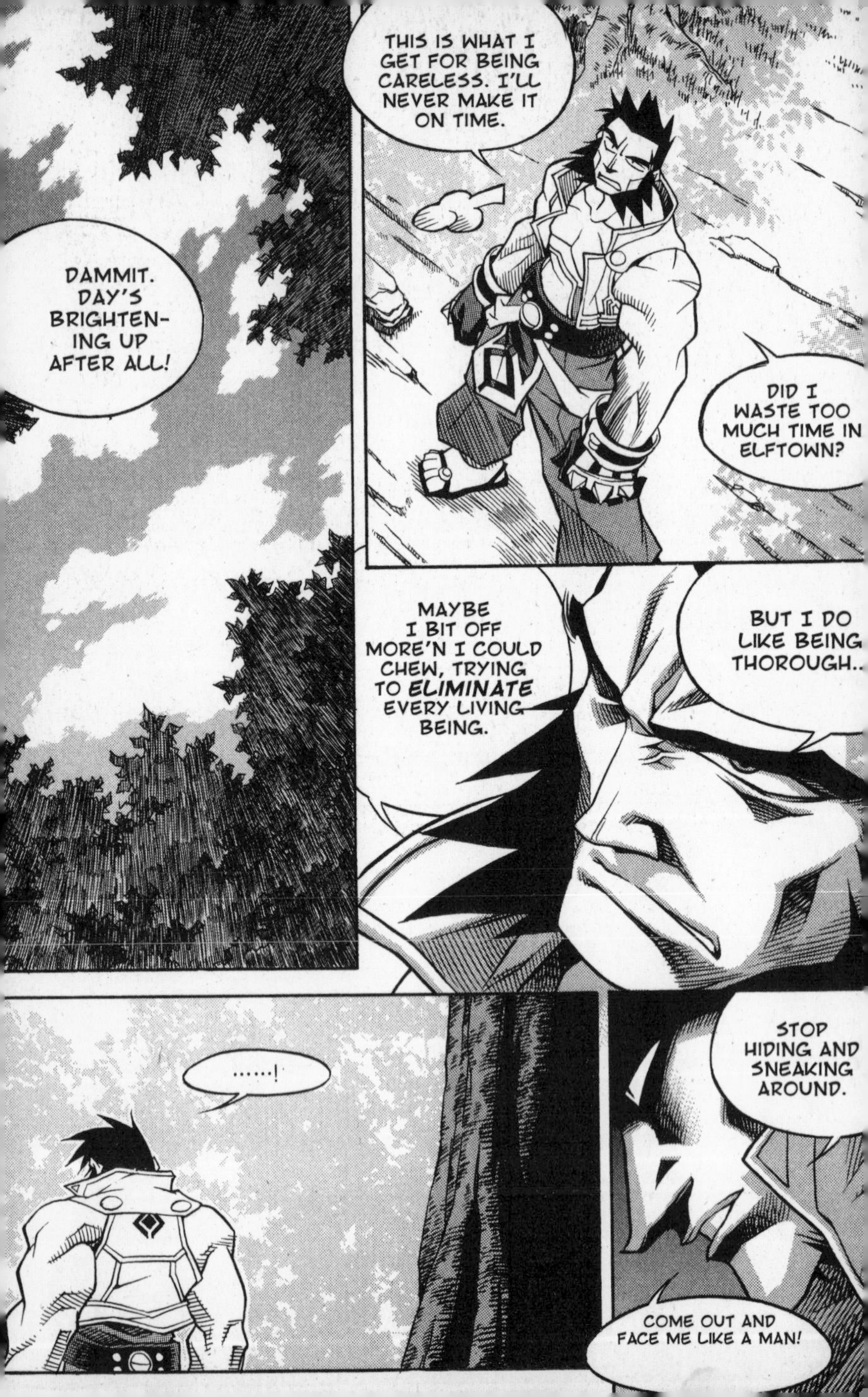
DAMMIT. DAY'S BRIGHTEN-ING UP AFTER ALL!
THIS IS WHAT I GET FOR BEING CARELESS. I'LL NEVER MAKE IT ON TIME.
DID I WASTE TOO MUCH TIME IN ELFTOWN?
MAYBE I BIT OFF MORE'N I COULD CHEW, TRYING TO *ELIMINATE* EVERY LIVING BEING.
BUT I DO LIKE BEING THOROUGH..
......!
STOP HIDING AND SNEAKING AROUND.
COME OUT AND FACE ME LIKE A MAN!

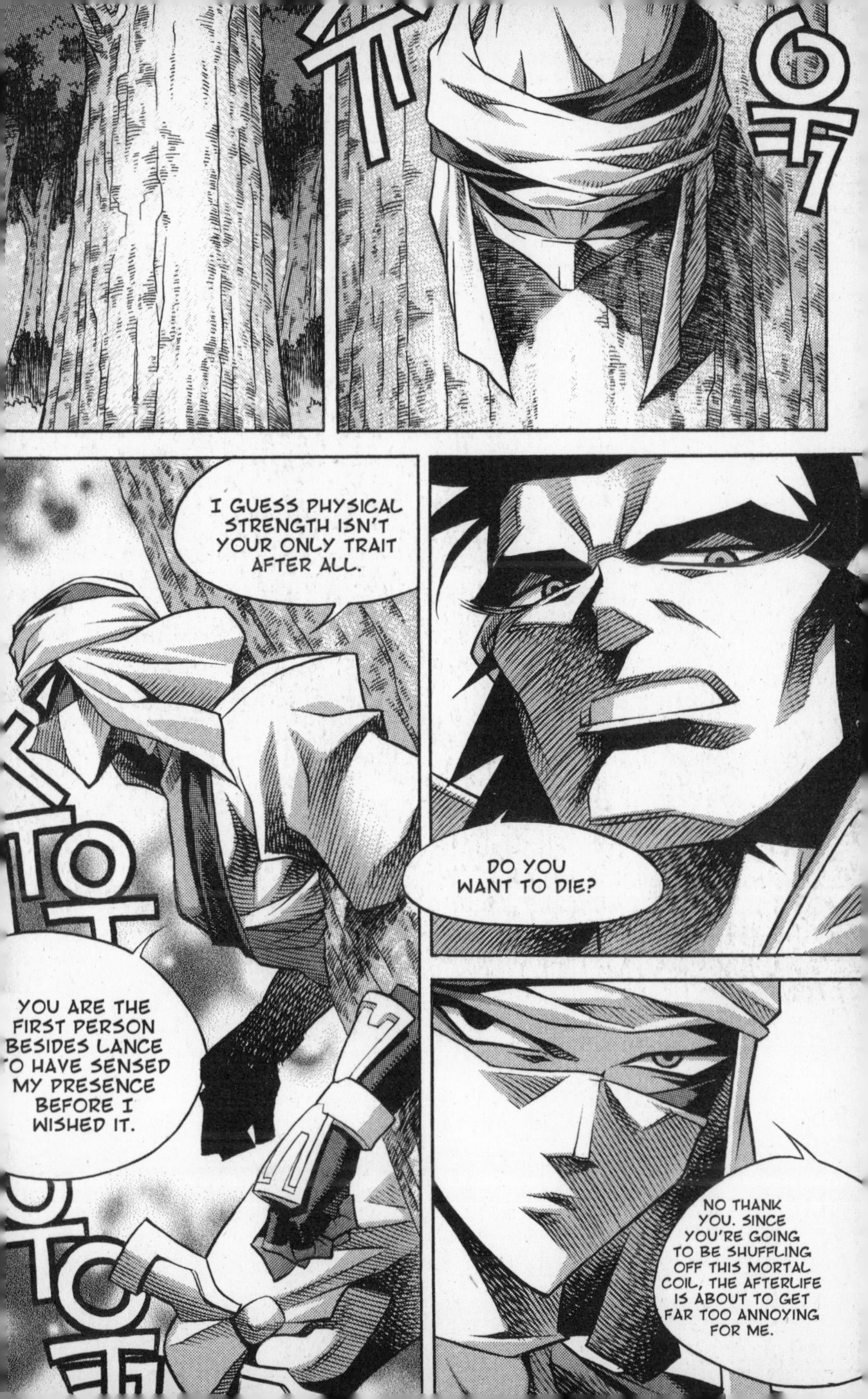
I GUESS PHYSICAL STRENGTH ISN'T YOUR ONLY TRAIT AFTER ALL.
DO YOU WANT TO DIE?
NO THANK YOU. SINCE YOU'RE GOING TO BE SHUFFLING OFF THIS MORTAL COIL, THE AFTERLIFE IS ABOUT TO GET FAR TOO ANNOYING FOR ME.
YOU ARE THE FIRST PERSON BESIDES LANCE TO HAVE SENSED MY PRESENCE BEFORE I WISHED IT.

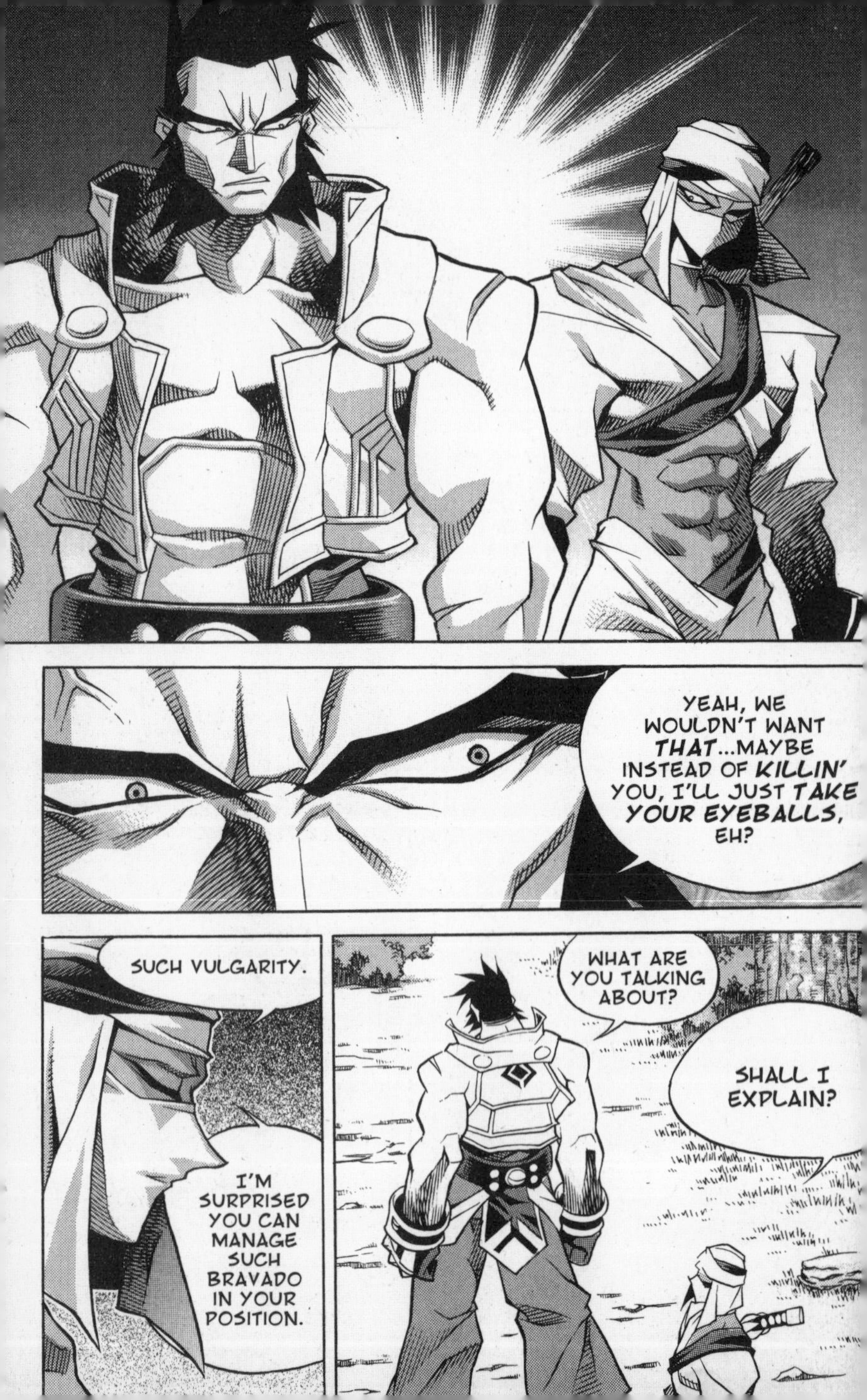
YEAH, WE WOULDN'T WANT THAT...MAYBE INSTEAD OF KILLIN' YOU, I'LL JUST TAKE YOUR EYEBALLS, EH?
SUCH VULGARITY.
I'M SURPRISED YOU CAN MANAGE SUCH BRAVADO IN YOUR POSITION.
WHAT ARE YOU TALKING ABOUT?
SHALL I EXPLAIN?

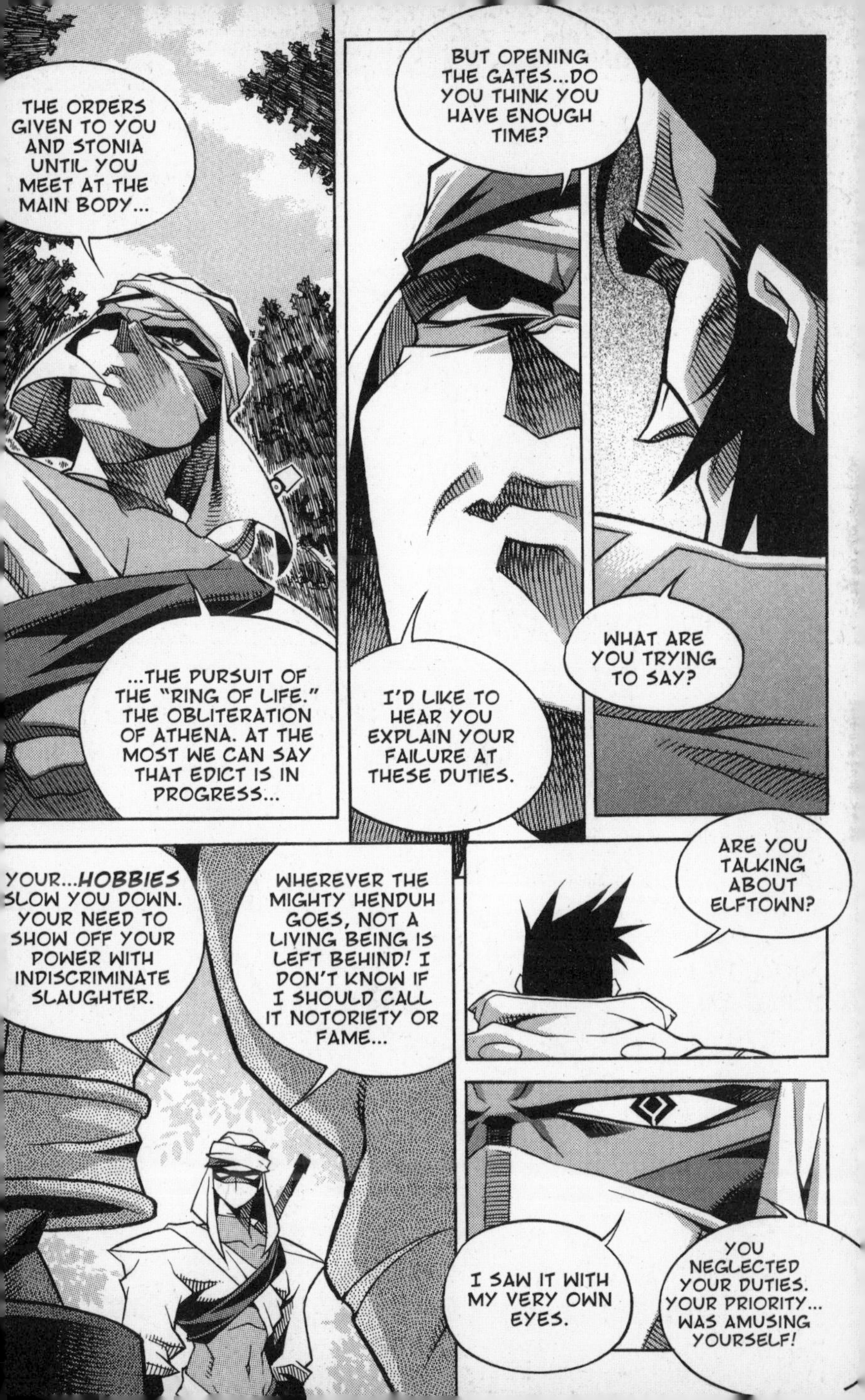
THE ORDERS GIVEN TO YOU AND STONIA UNTIL YOU MEET AT THE MAIN BODY...
...THE PURSUIT OF THE "RING OF LIFE." THE OBLITERATION OF ATHENA. AT THE MOST WE CAN SAY THAT EDICT IS IN PROGRESS...
BUT OPENING THE GATES...DO YOU THINK YOU HAVE ENOUGH TIME?
I'D LIKE TO HEAR YOU EXPLAIN YOUR FAILURE AT THESE DUTIES.
WHAT ARE YOU TRYING TO SAY?
YOUR...**HOBBIES** SLOW YOU DOWN. YOUR NEED TO SHOW OFF YOUR POWER WITH INDISCRIMINATE SLAUGHTER.
WHEREVER THE MIGHTY HENDUH GOES, NOT A LIVING BEING IS LEFT BEHIND! I DON'T KNOW IF I SHOULD CALL IT NOTORIETY OR FAME...
ARE YOU TALKING ABOUT ELFTOWN?
I SAW IT WITH MY VERY OWN EYES.
YOU NEGLECTED YOUR DUTIES. YOUR PRIORITY... WAS AMUSING YOURSELF!

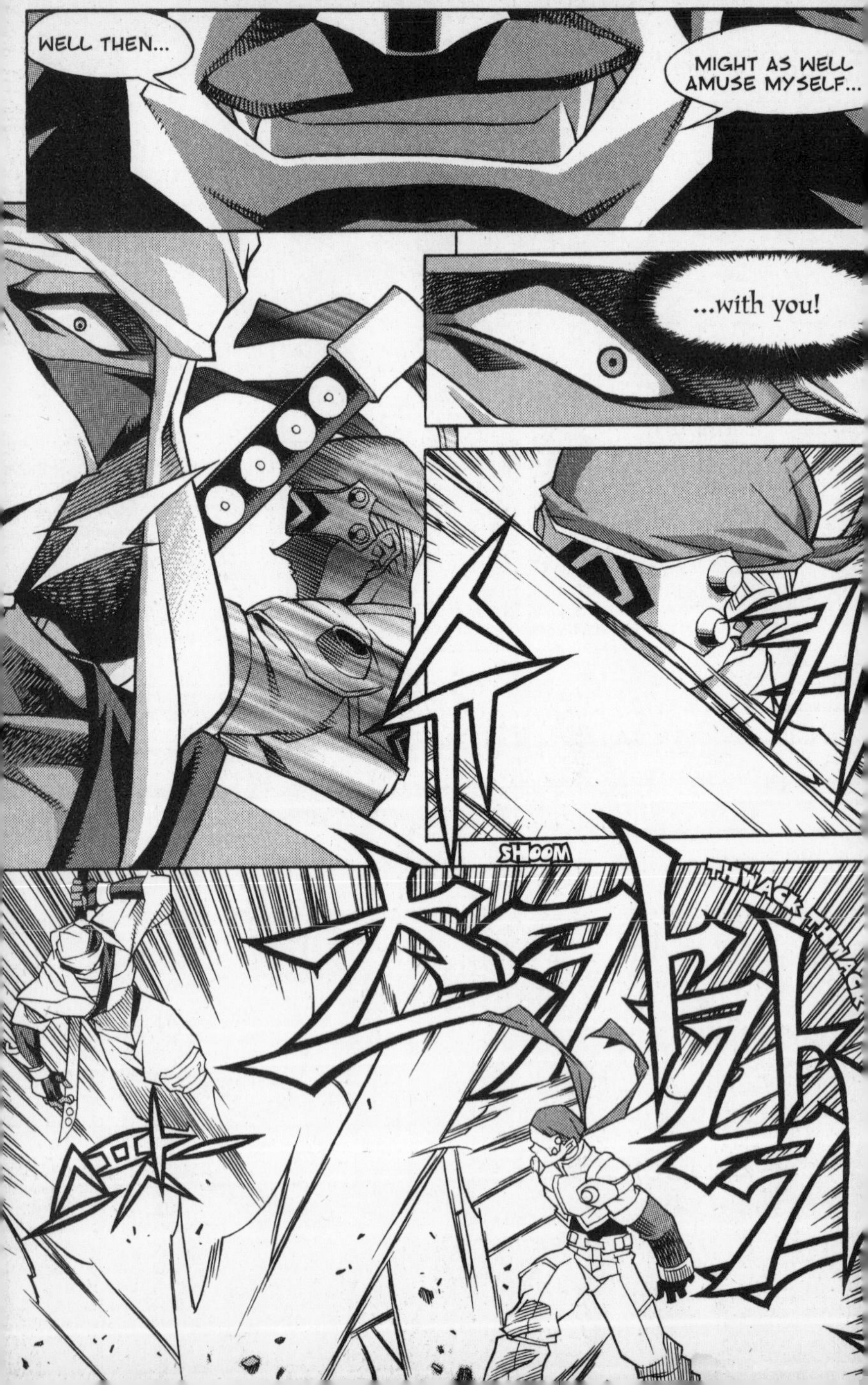
WELL THEN...
MIGHT AS WELL AMUSE MYSELF...
...with you!
SHOOM
THWACK THWACK

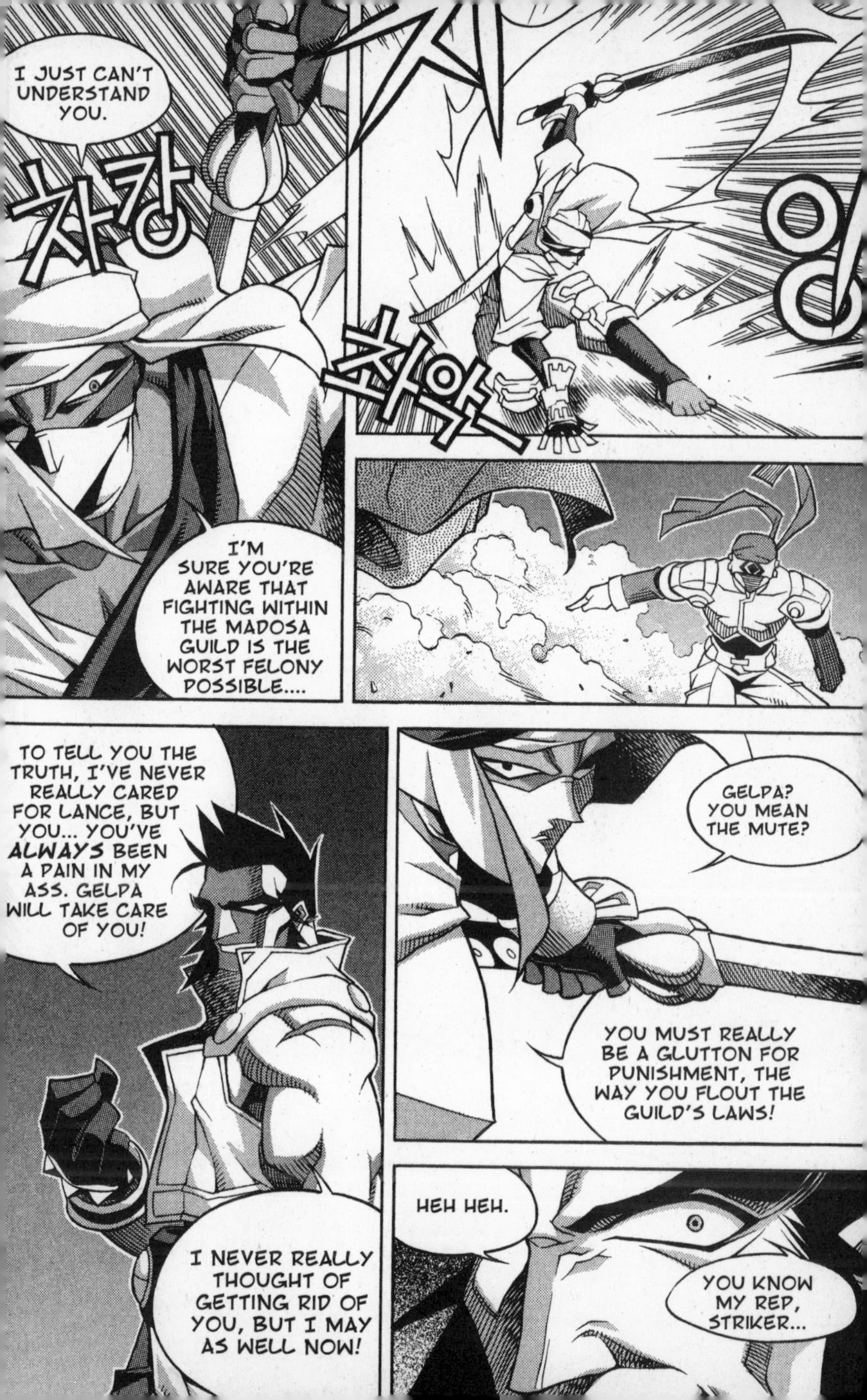
I JUST CAN'T UNDERSTAND YOU.
차캉
I'M SURE YOU'RE AWARE THAT FIGHTING WITHIN THE MADOSA GUILD IS THE WORST FELONY POSSIBLE....
차악
TO TELL YOU THE TRUTH, I'VE NEVER REALLY CARED FOR LANCE, BUT YOU... YOU'VE *ALWAYS* BEEN A PAIN IN MY ASS. GELPA WILL TAKE CARE OF YOU!
I NEVER REALLY THOUGHT OF GETTING RID OF YOU, BUT I MAY AS WELL NOW!
GELPA? YOU MEAN THE MUTE?
YOU MUST REALLY BE A GLUTTON FOR PUNISHMENT, THE WAY YOU FLOUT THE GUILD'S LAWS!
HEH HEH.
YOU KNOW MY REP, STRIKER...

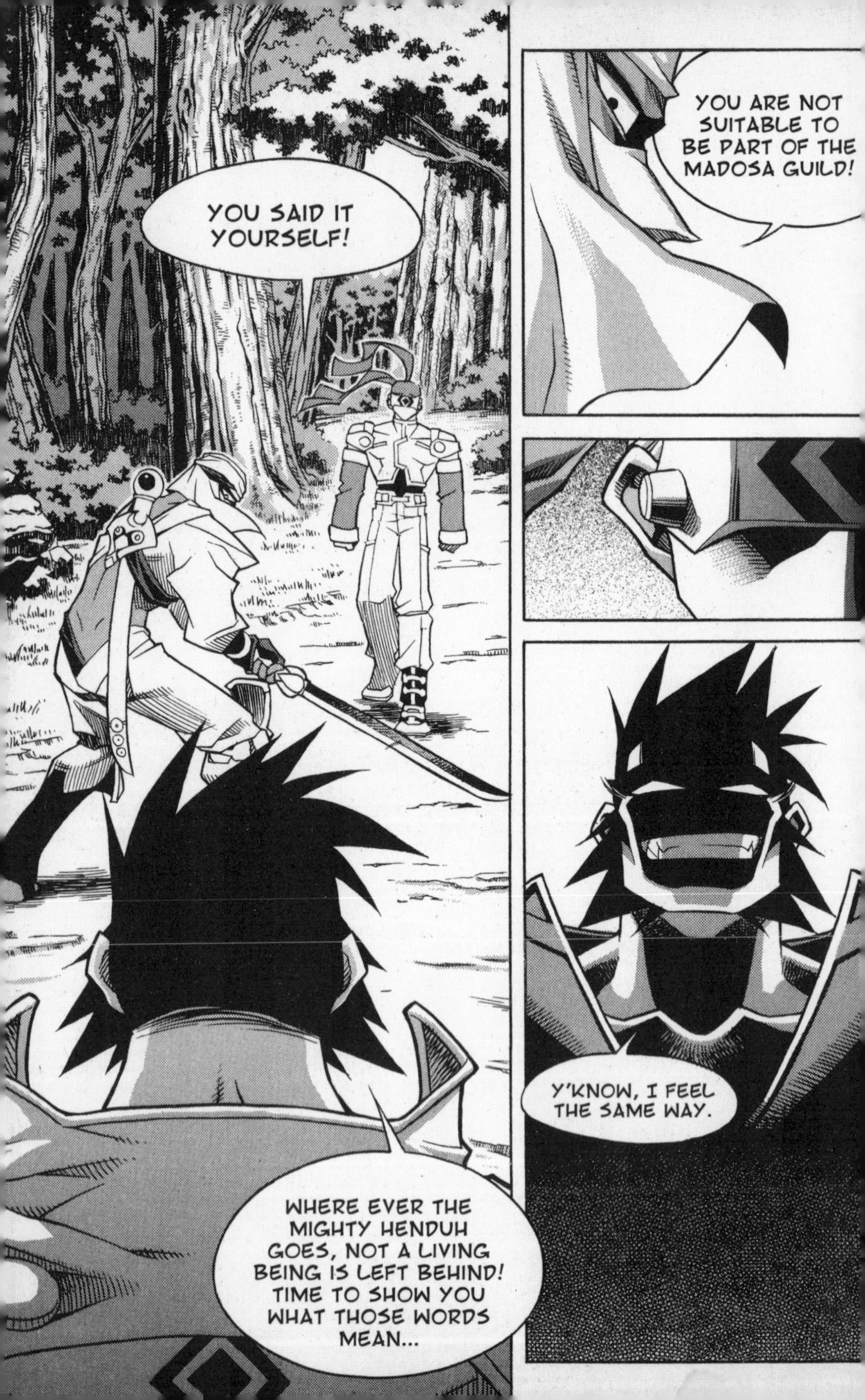
YOU SAID IT YOURSELF!
WHERE EVER THE MIGHTY HENDUH GOES, NOT A LIVING BEING IS LEFT BEHIND! TIME TO SHOW YOU WHAT THOSE WORDS MEAN...
YOU ARE NOT SUITABLE TO BE PART OF THE MADOSA GUILD!
Y'KNOW, I FEEL THE SAME WAY.

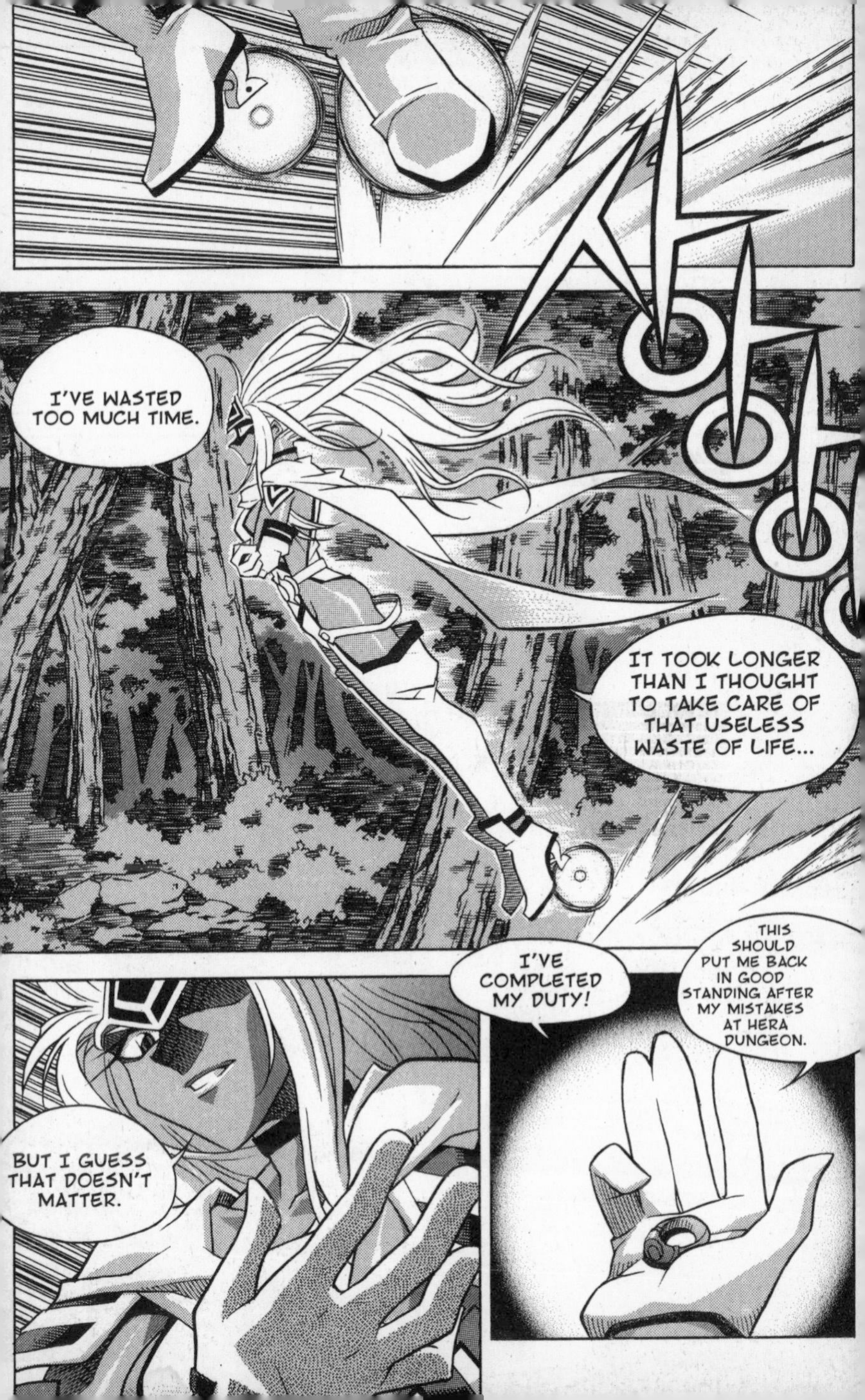
I'VE WASTED TOO MUCH TIME.
IT TOOK LONGER THAN I THOUGHT TO TAKE CARE OF THAT USELESS WASTE OF LIFE...
BUT I GUESS THAT DOESN'T MATTER.
I'VE COMPLETED MY DUTY!
THIS SHOULD PUT ME BACK IN GOOD STANDING AFTER MY MISTAKES AT HERA DUNGEON.

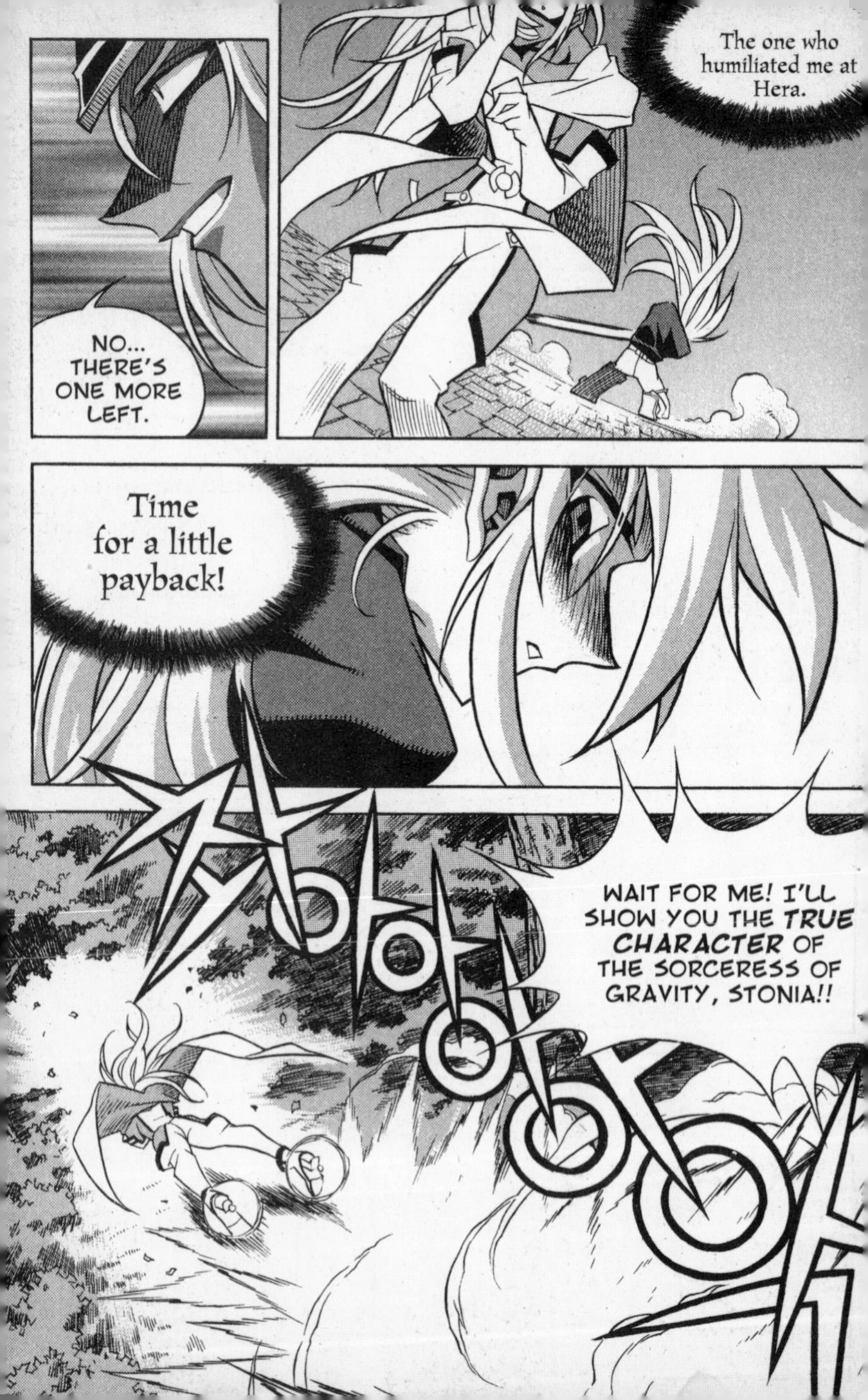

NO... THERE'S ONE MORE LEFT.
The one who humiliated me at Hera.
Time for a little payback!
WAIT FOR ME! I'LL SHOW YOU THE TRUE CHARACTER OF THE SORCERESS OF GRAVITY, STONIA!!

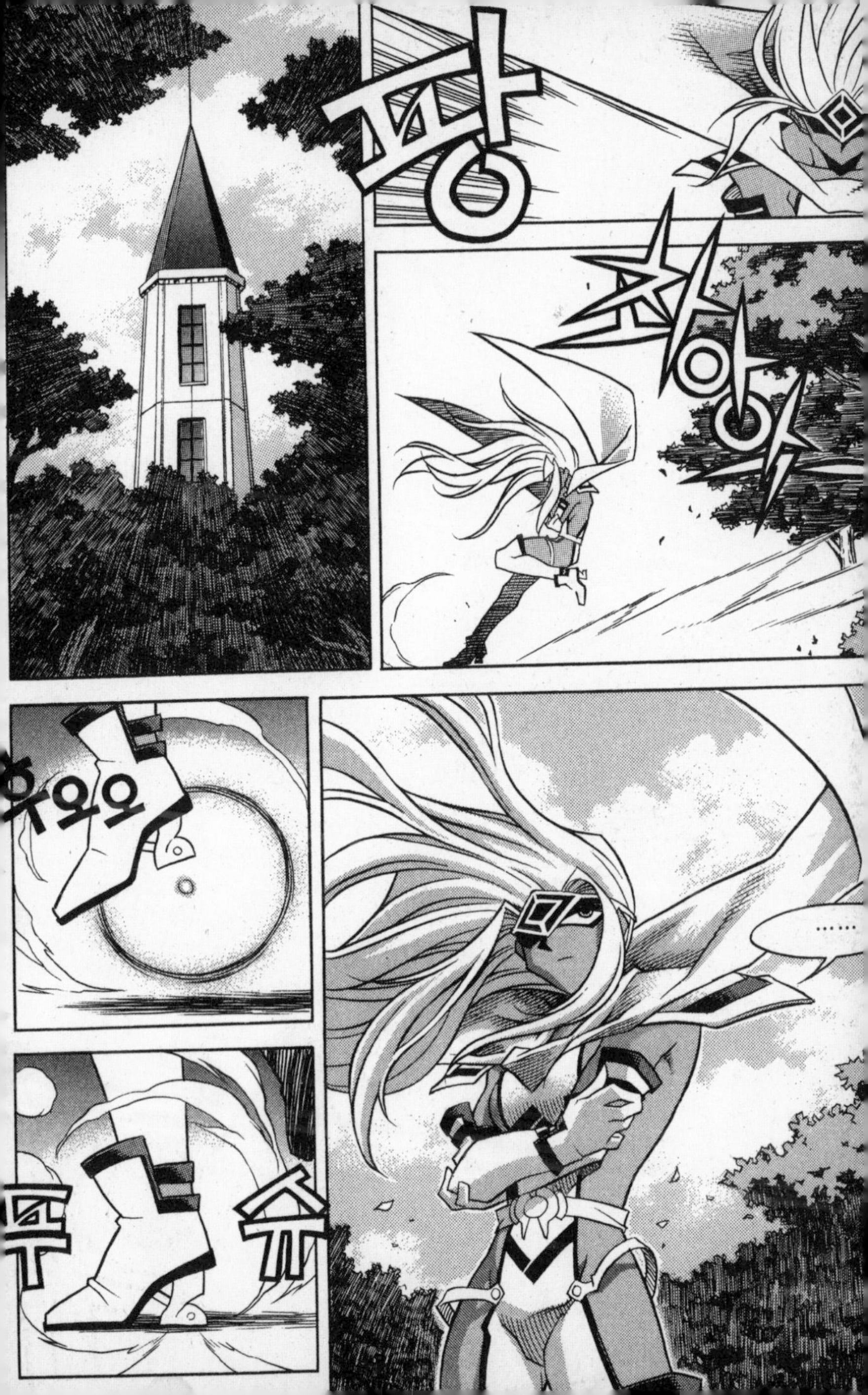

팡
후오오
……

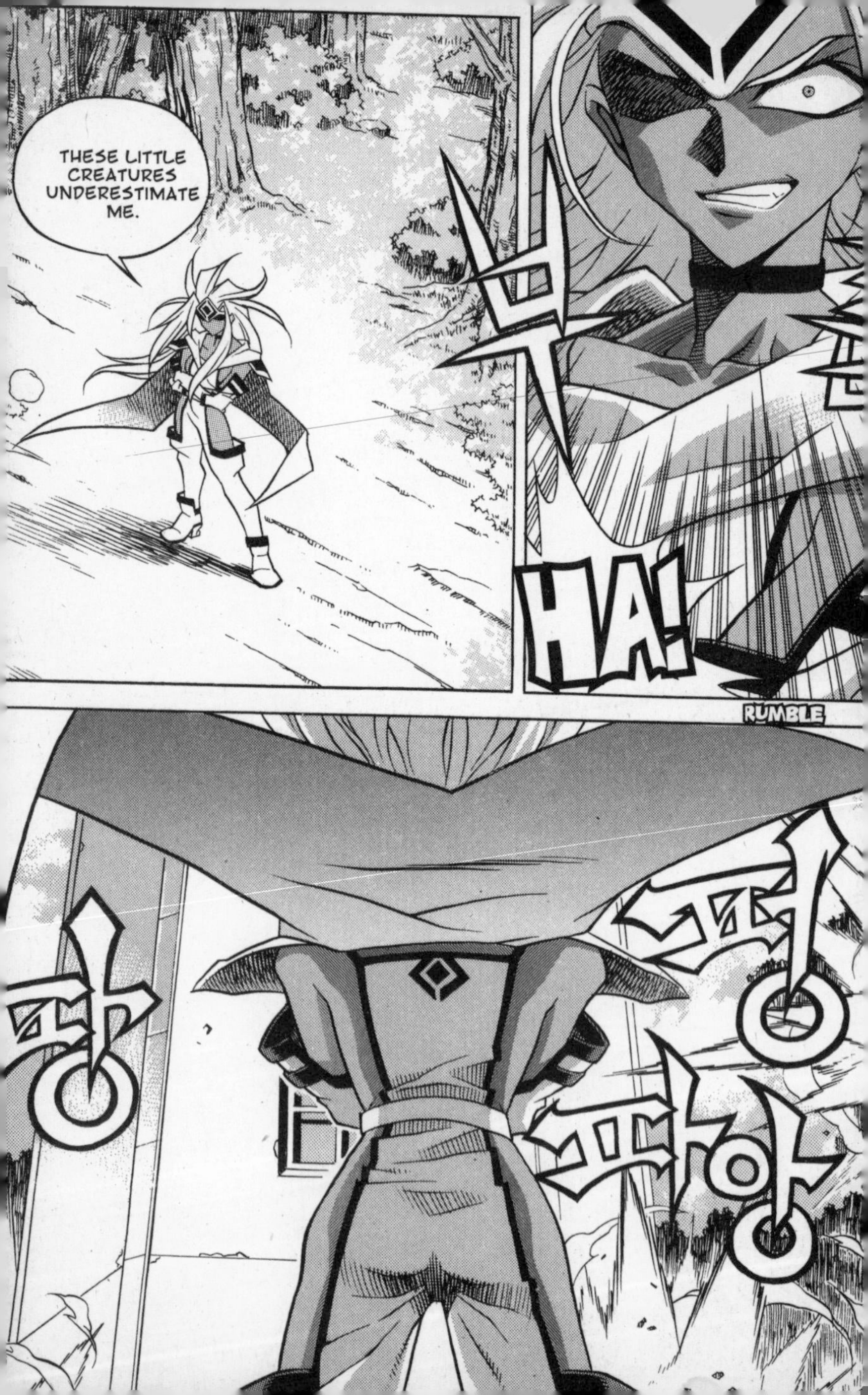
THESE LITTLE CREATURES UNDERESTIMATE ME.
HA!
RUMBLE

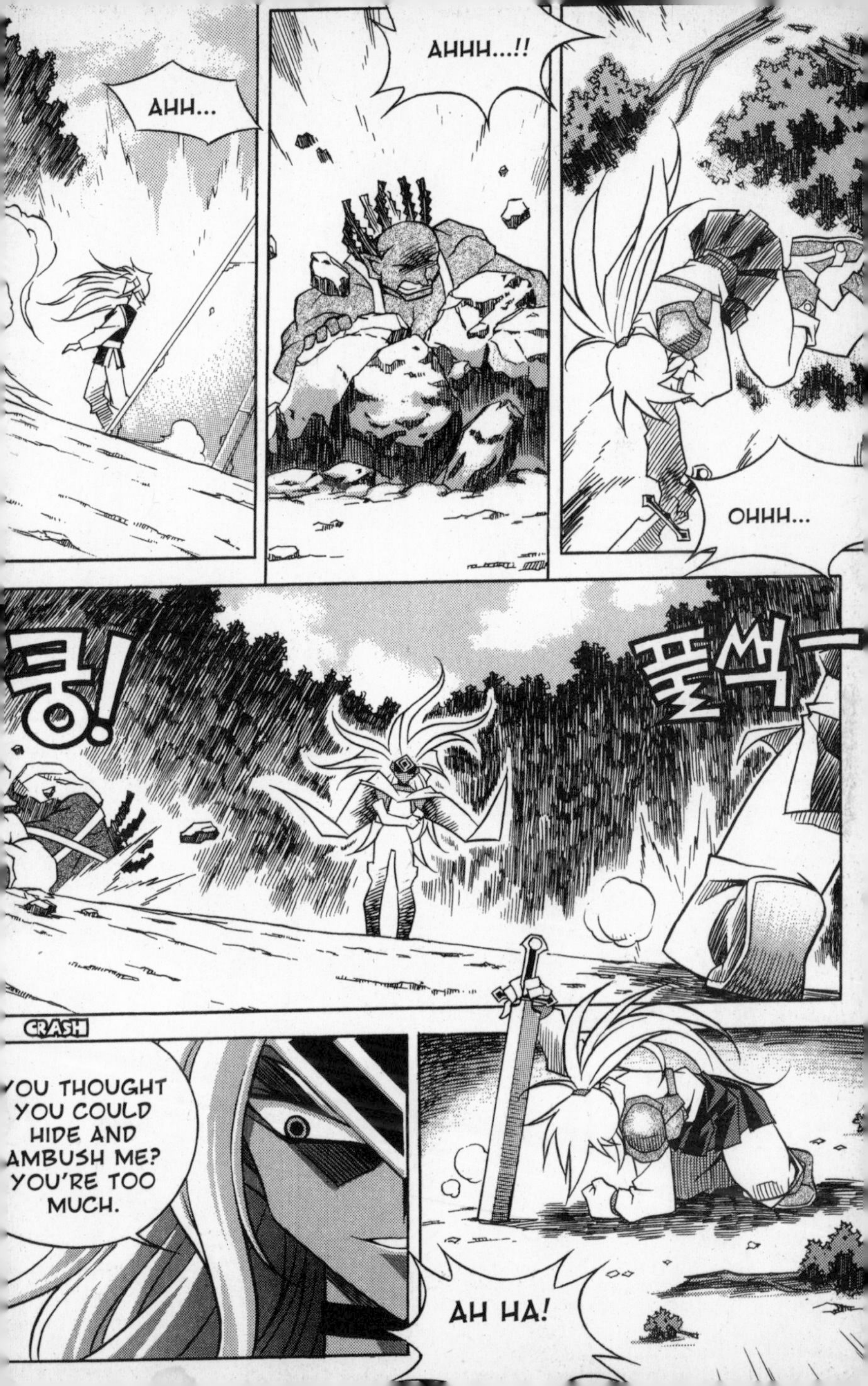
AHH...
AHHH...!!
OHHH...
쿵!
털썩ㅡ
CRASH
YOU THOUGHT YOU COULD HIDE AND AMBUSH ME? YOU'RE TOO MUCH.
AH HA!

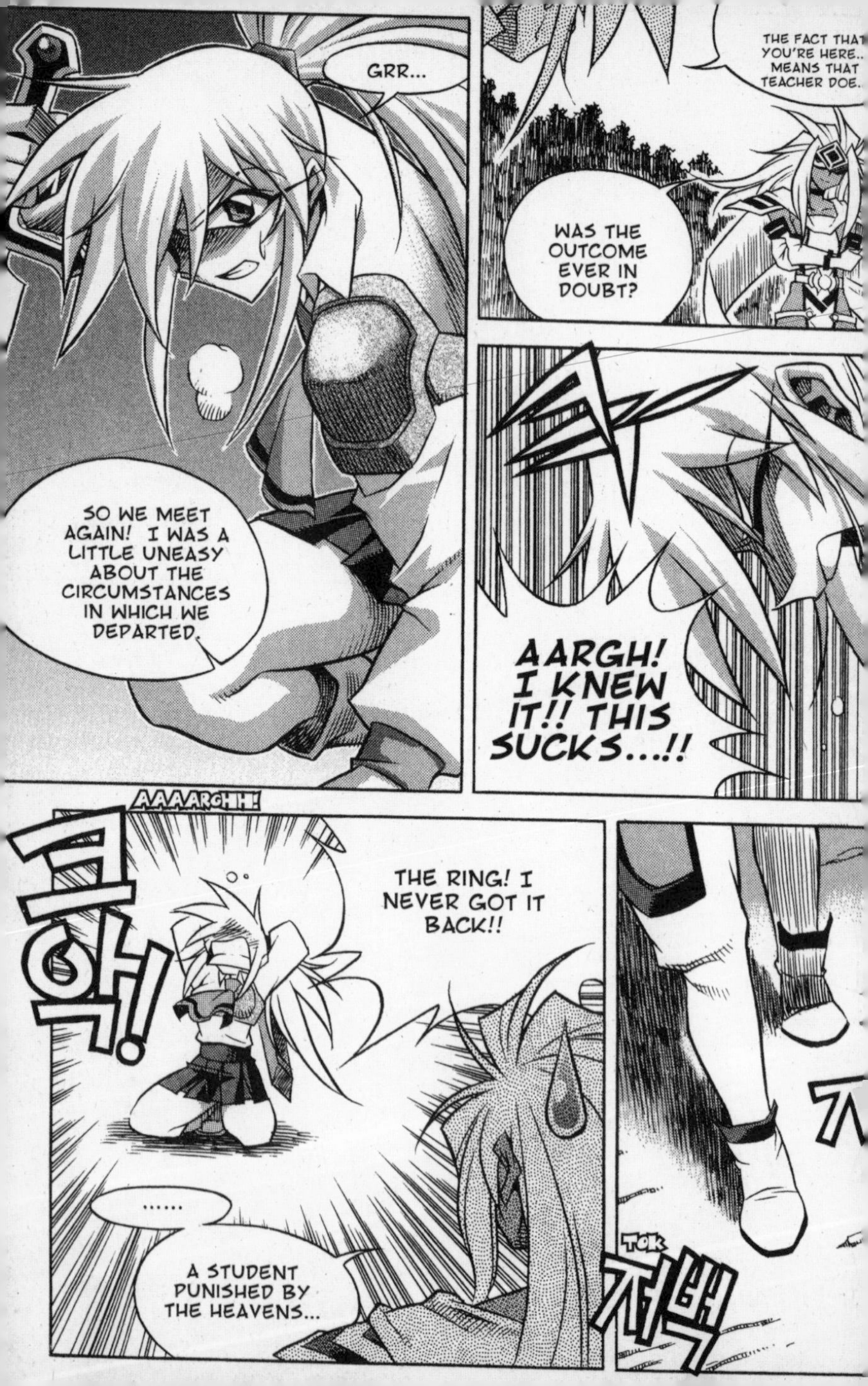
GRR...
SO WE MEET AGAIN! I WAS A LITTLE UNEASY ABOUT THE CIRCUMSTANCES IN WHICH WE DEPARTED.
THE FACT THAT YOU'RE HERE.. MEANS THAT TEACHER DOE..
WAS THE OUTCOME EVER IN DOUBT?
AARGH! I KNEW IT!! THIS SUCKS...!!
AAAARGHH!
크아!
THE RING! I NEVER GOT IT BACK!!
......
A STUDENT PUNISHED BY THE HEAVENS...
TOK

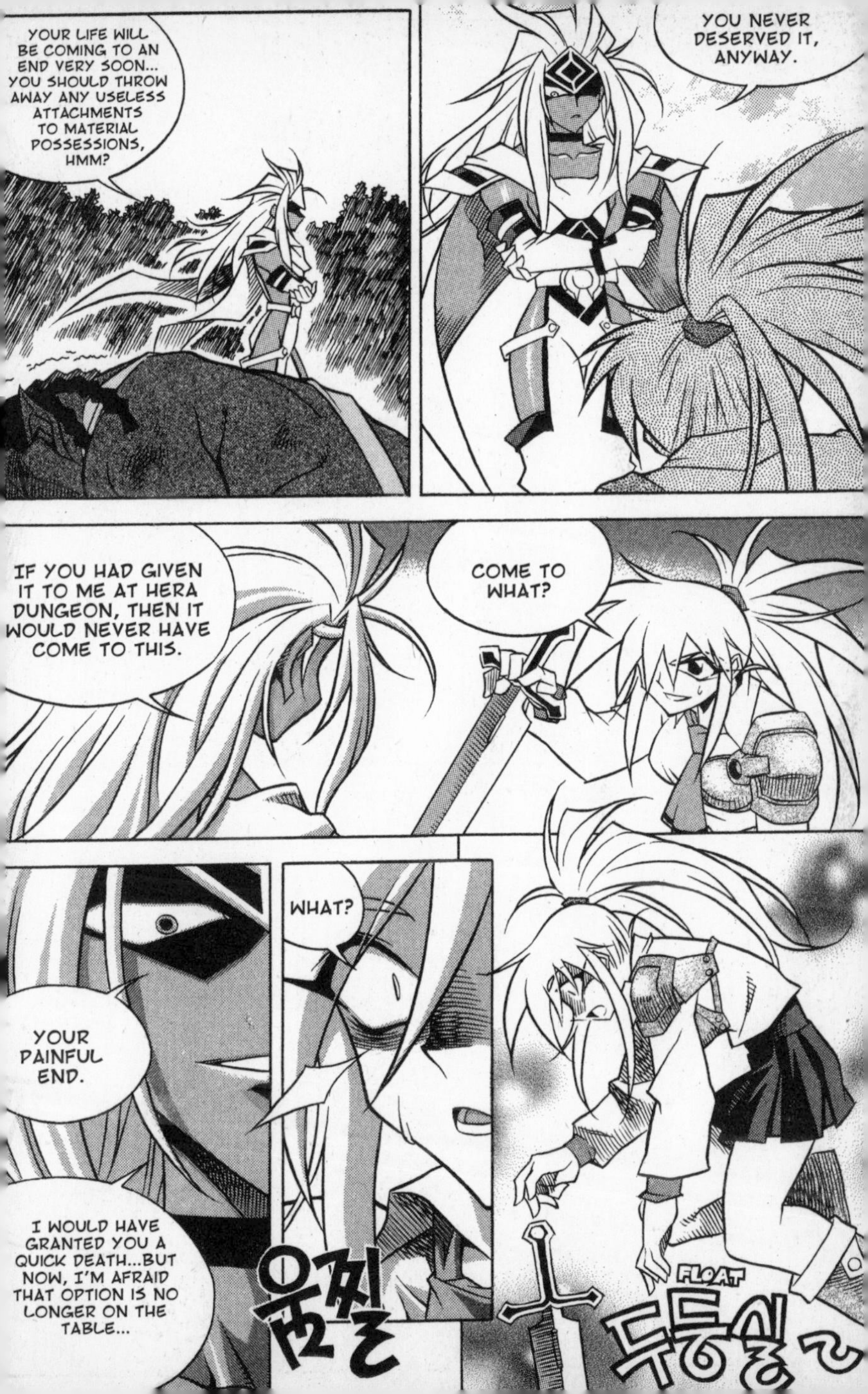
YOUR LIFE WILL BE COMING TO AN END VERY SOON... YOU SHOULD THROW AWAY ANY USELESS ATTACHMENTS TO MATERIAL POSSESSIONS, HMM?
YOU NEVER DESERVED IT, ANYWAY.
IF YOU HAD GIVEN IT TO ME AT HERA DUNGEON, THEN IT WOULD NEVER HAVE COME TO THIS.
COME TO WHAT?
YOUR PAINFUL END.
I WOULD HAVE GRANTED YOU A QUICK DEATH...BUT NOW, I'M AFRAID THAT OPTION IS NO LONGER ON THE TABLE...
WHAT?
FLOAT

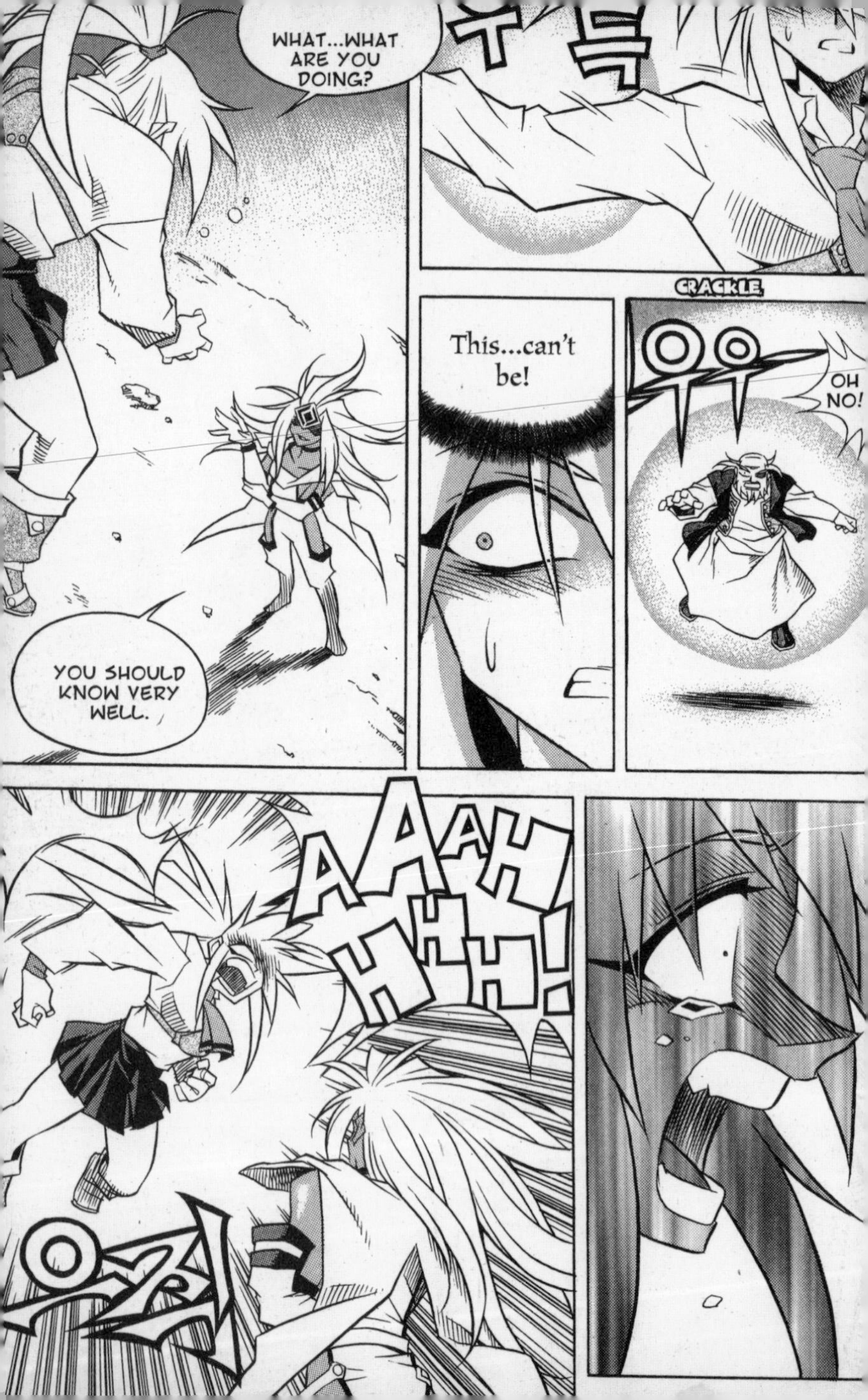
WHAT...WHAT ARE YOU DOING?
YOU SHOULD KNOW VERY WELL.
This...can't be!
CRACKLE
OH NO!
AAAHHHH!

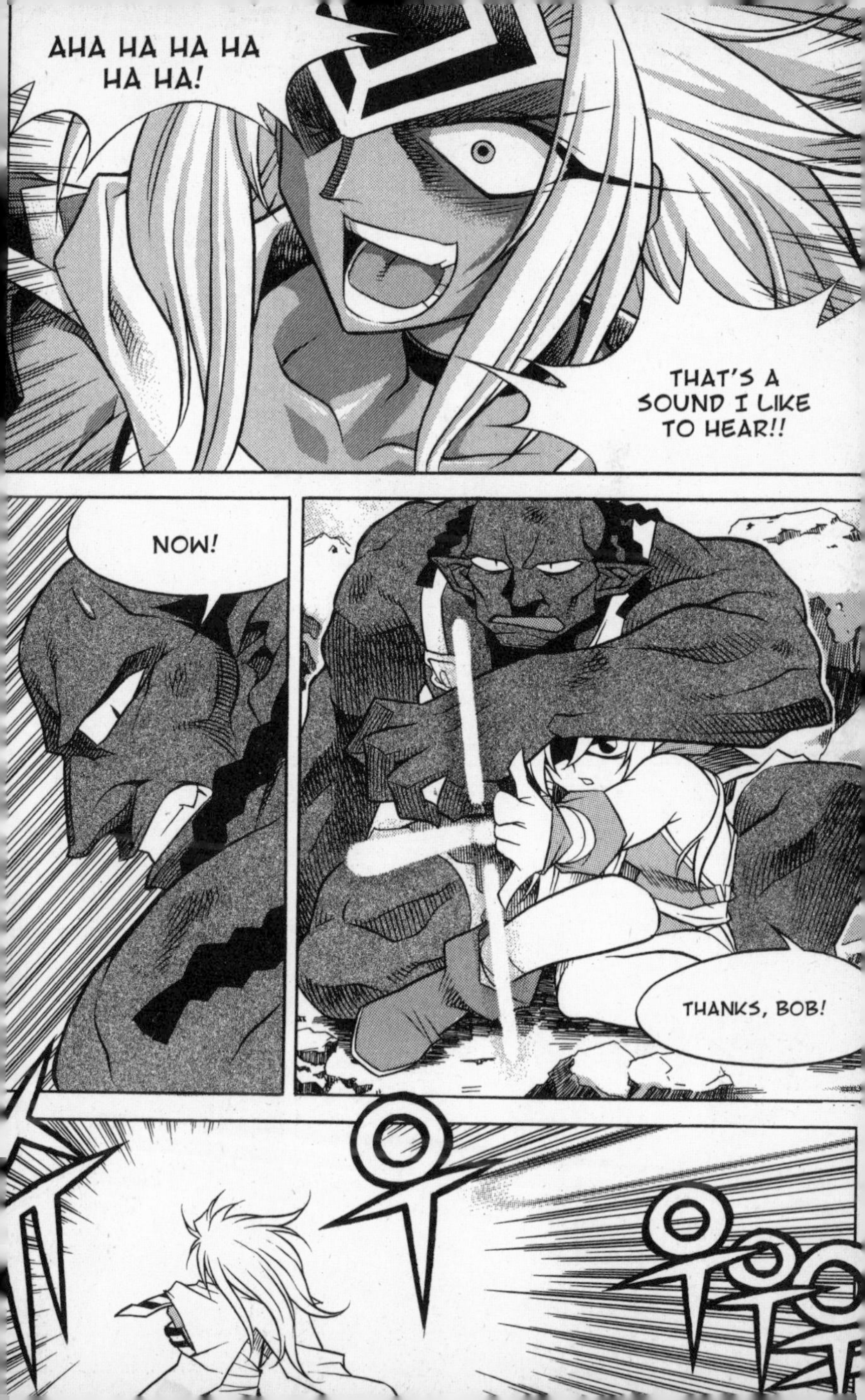
AHA HA HA HA HA HA!
THAT'S A SOUND I LIKE TO HEAR!!
NOW!
THANKS, BOB!

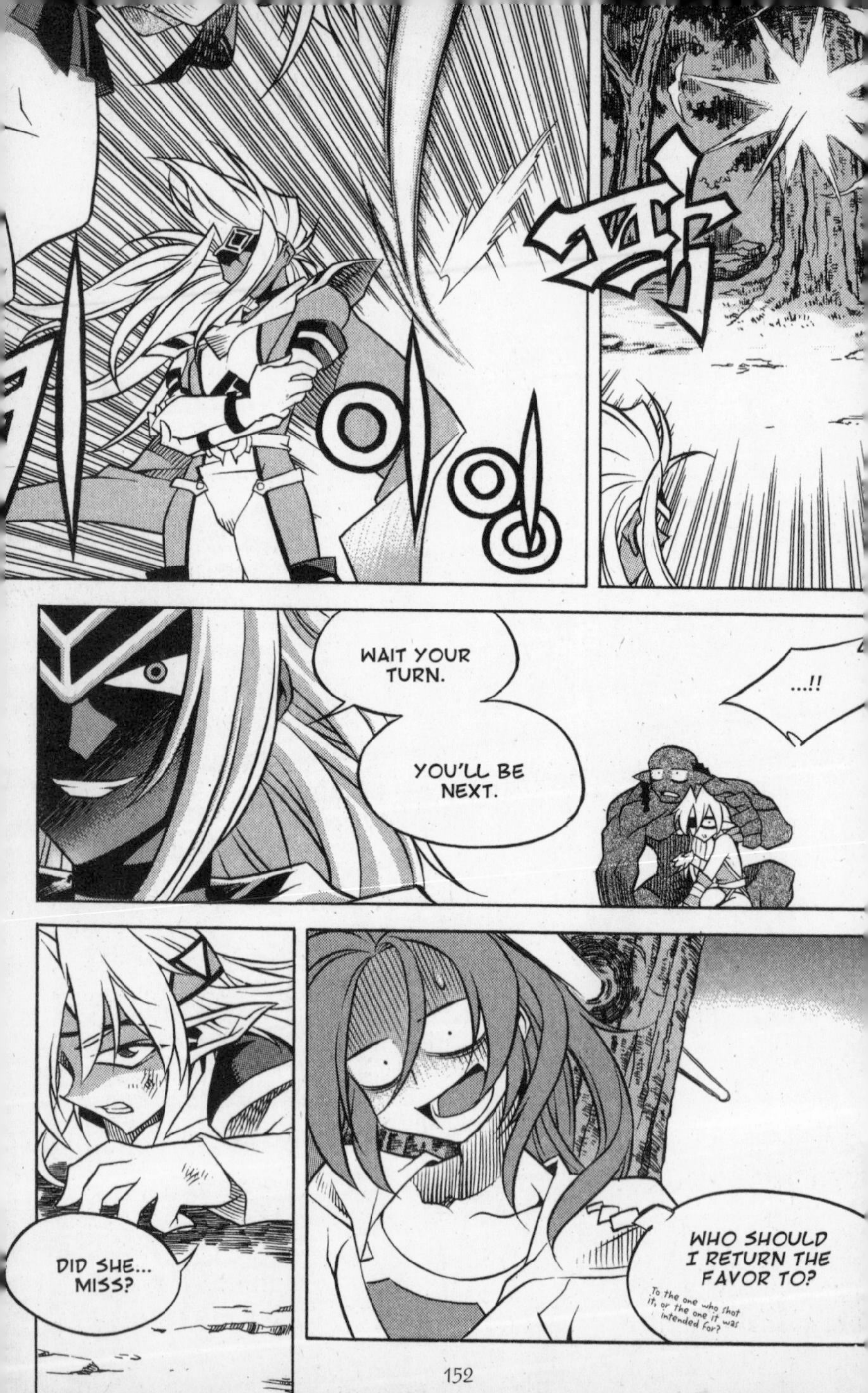
WAIT YOUR TURN.
YOU'LL BE NEXT.
...!!
DID SHE... MISS?
WHO SHOULD I RETURN THE FAVOR TO?
To the one who shot it, or the one it was intended for?

Quest 67

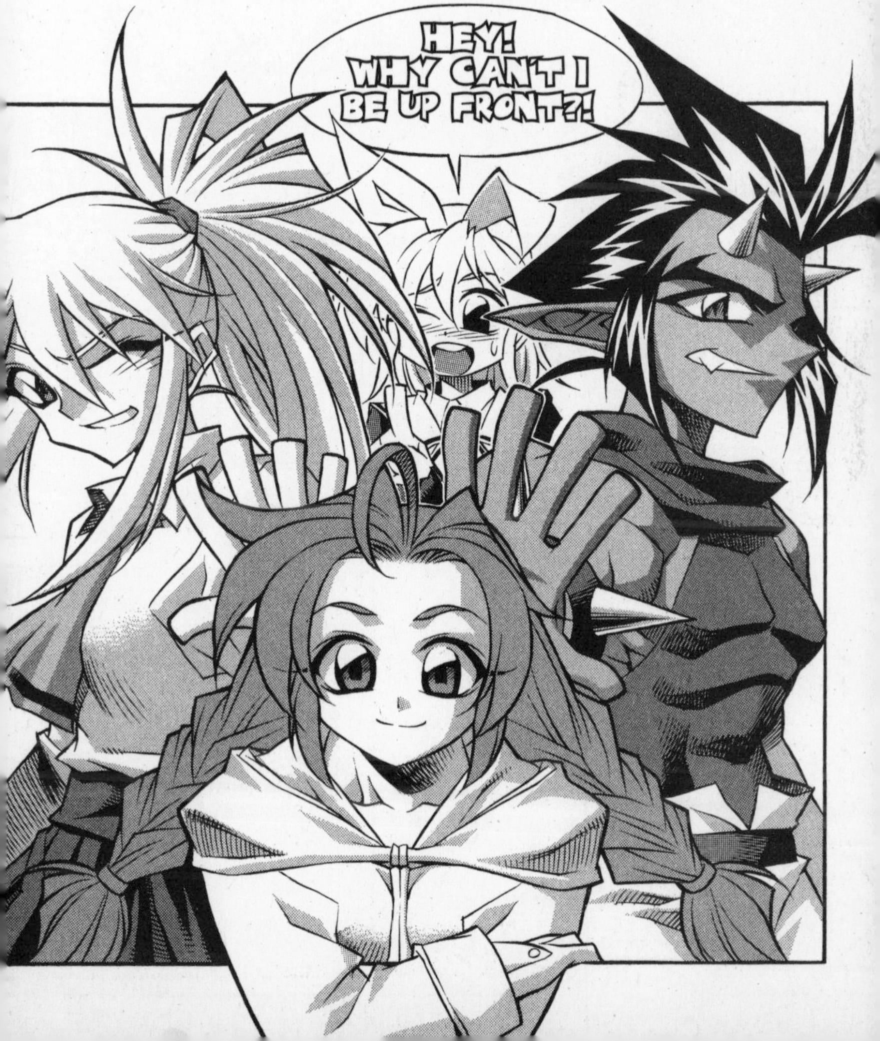
HEY! WHY CAN'T I BE UP FRONT?!

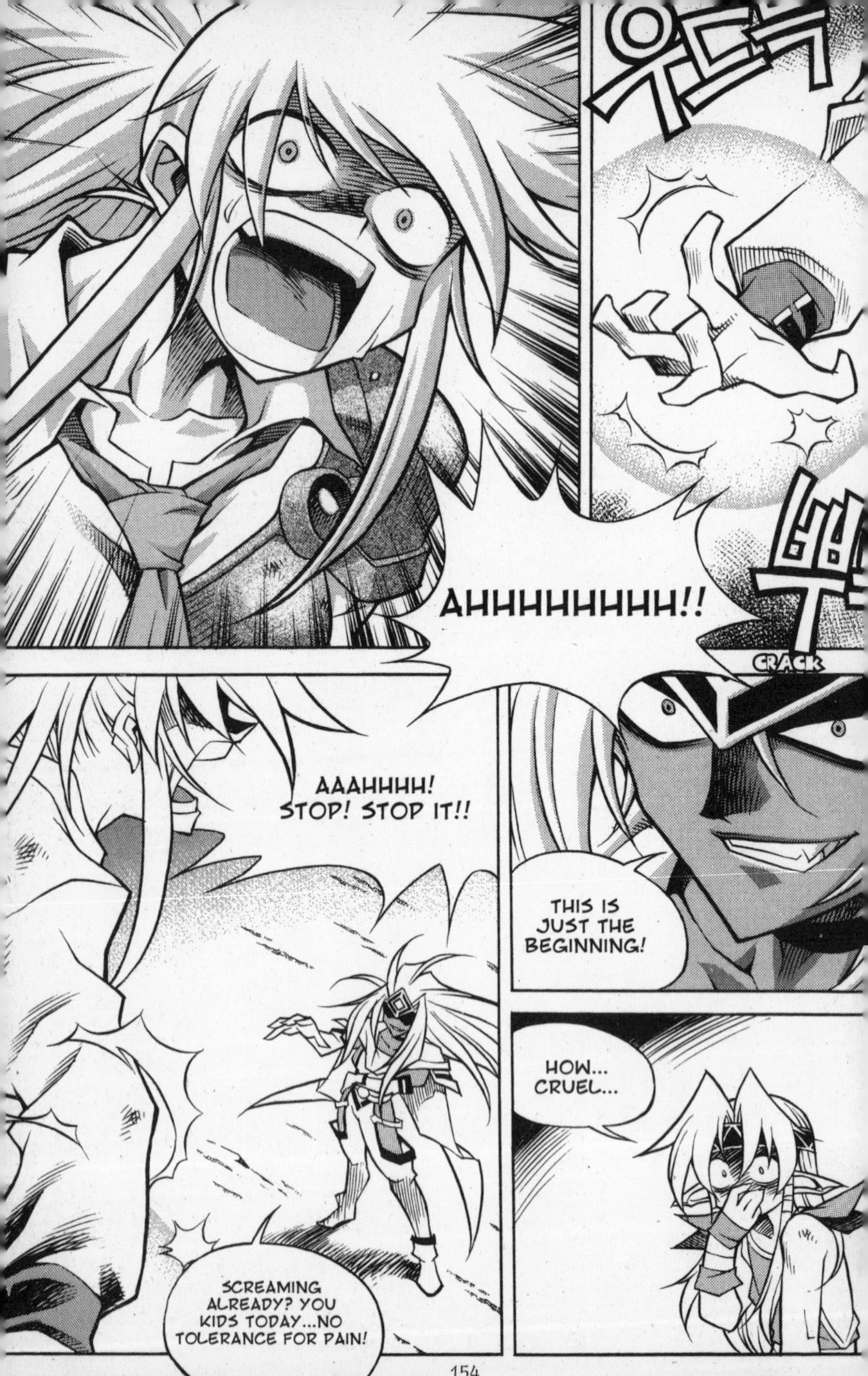
AHHHHHHHH!!
CRACK
AAAHHHH! STOP! STOP IT!!
SCREAMING ALREADY? YOU KIDS TODAY...NO TOLERANCE FOR PAIN!
THIS IS JUST THE BEGINNING!
HOW... CRUEL...

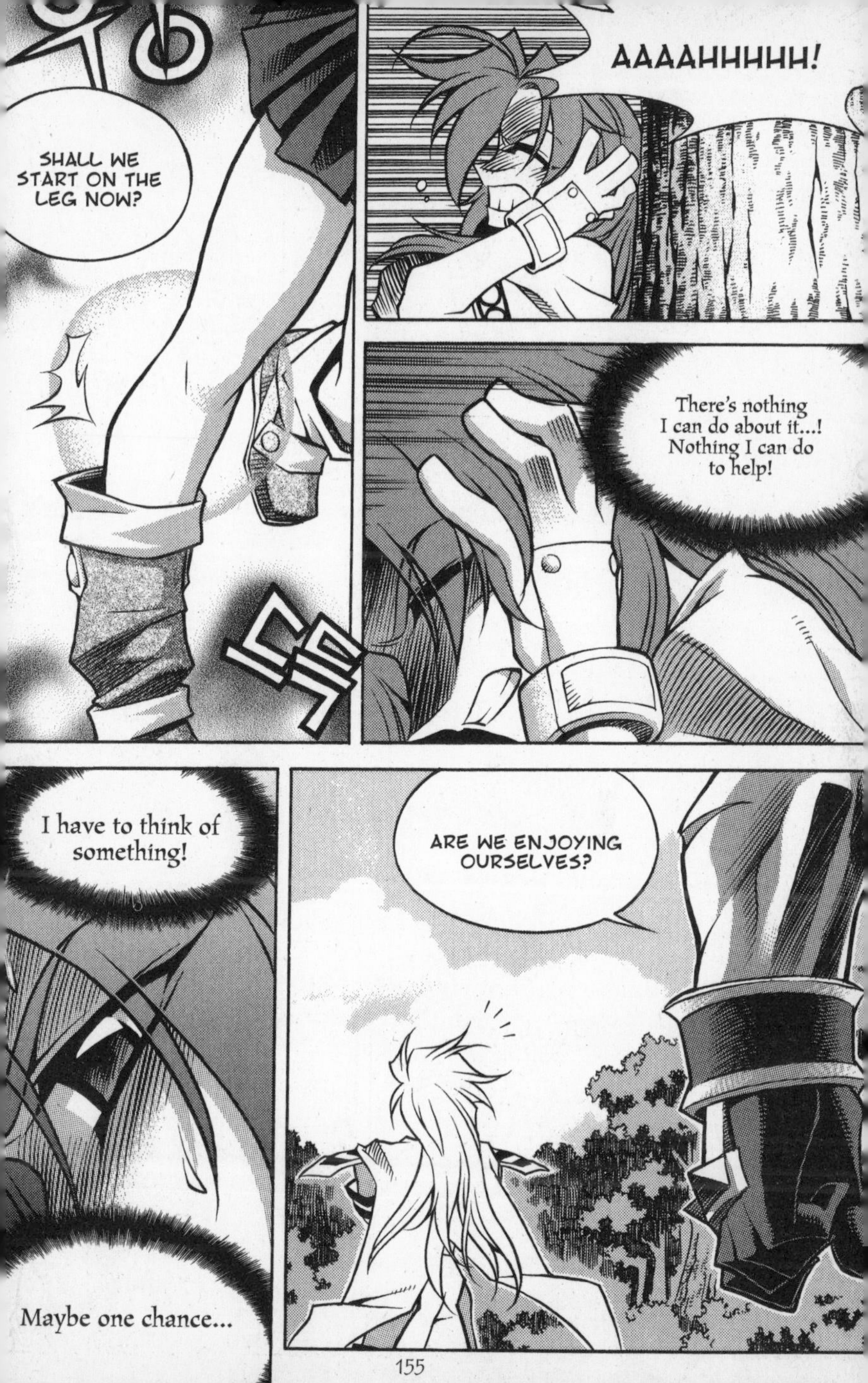
SHALL WE START ON THE LEG NOW?
AAAAHHHHH!
There's nothing I can do about it...! Nothing I can do to help!
I have to think of something!
Maybe one chance...
ARE WE ENJOYING OURSELVES?

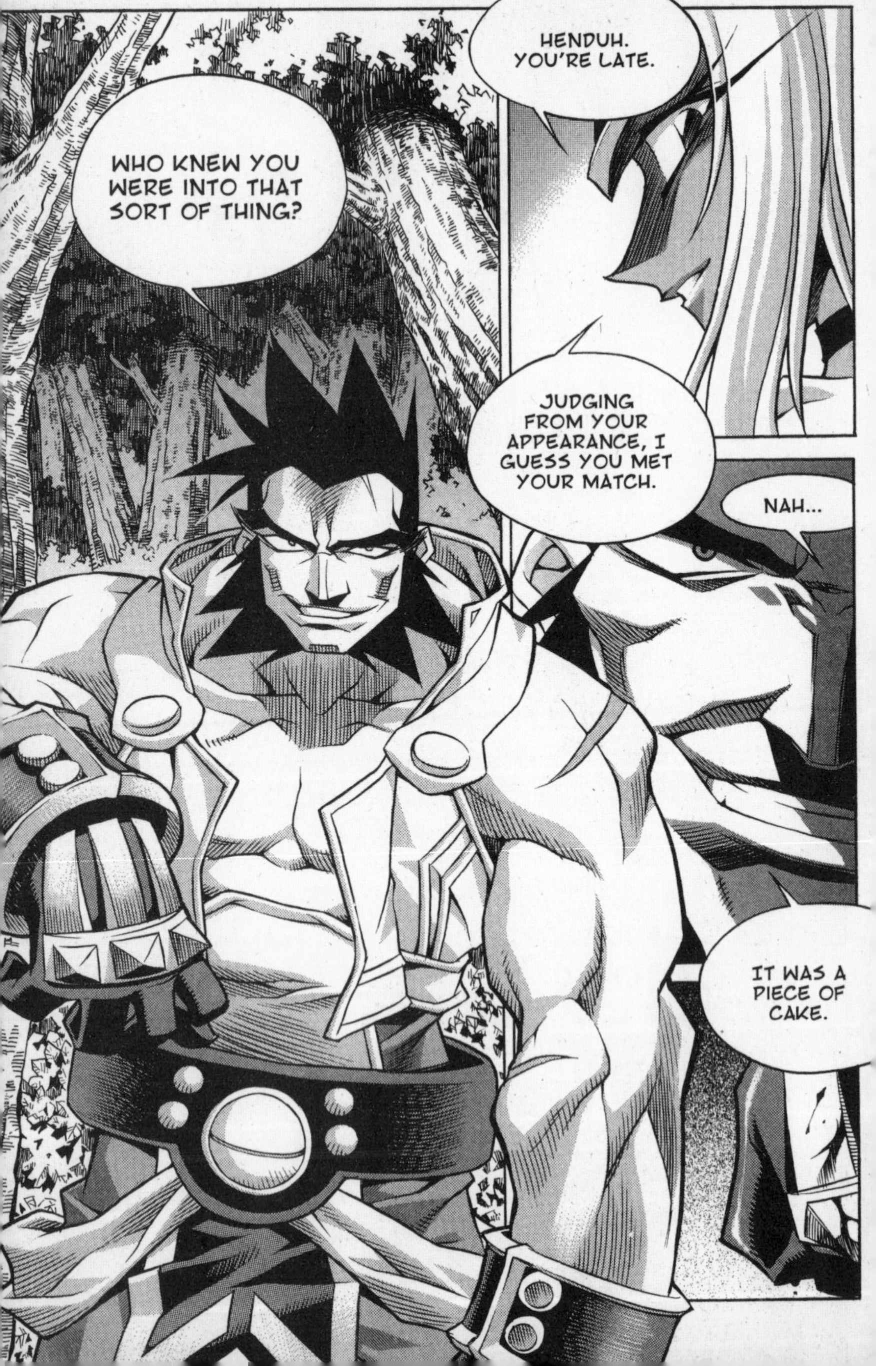
WHO KNEW YOU WERE INTO THAT SORT OF THING?
HENDUH. YOU'RE LATE.
JUDGING FROM YOUR APPEARANCE, I GUESS YOU MET YOUR MATCH.
NAH...
IT WAS A PIECE OF CAKE.

Dammit! As if things weren't bad enough! Where did he come from?!

HOW DID YOU DO?

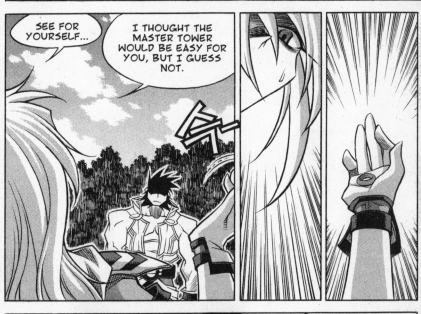

SEE FOR YOURSELF...

I THOUGHT THE MASTER TOWER WOULD BE EASY FOR YOU, BUT I GUESS NOT.

I GOT...HUNG UP. TOOK ME A LITTLE LONGER THAN I EXPECTED...

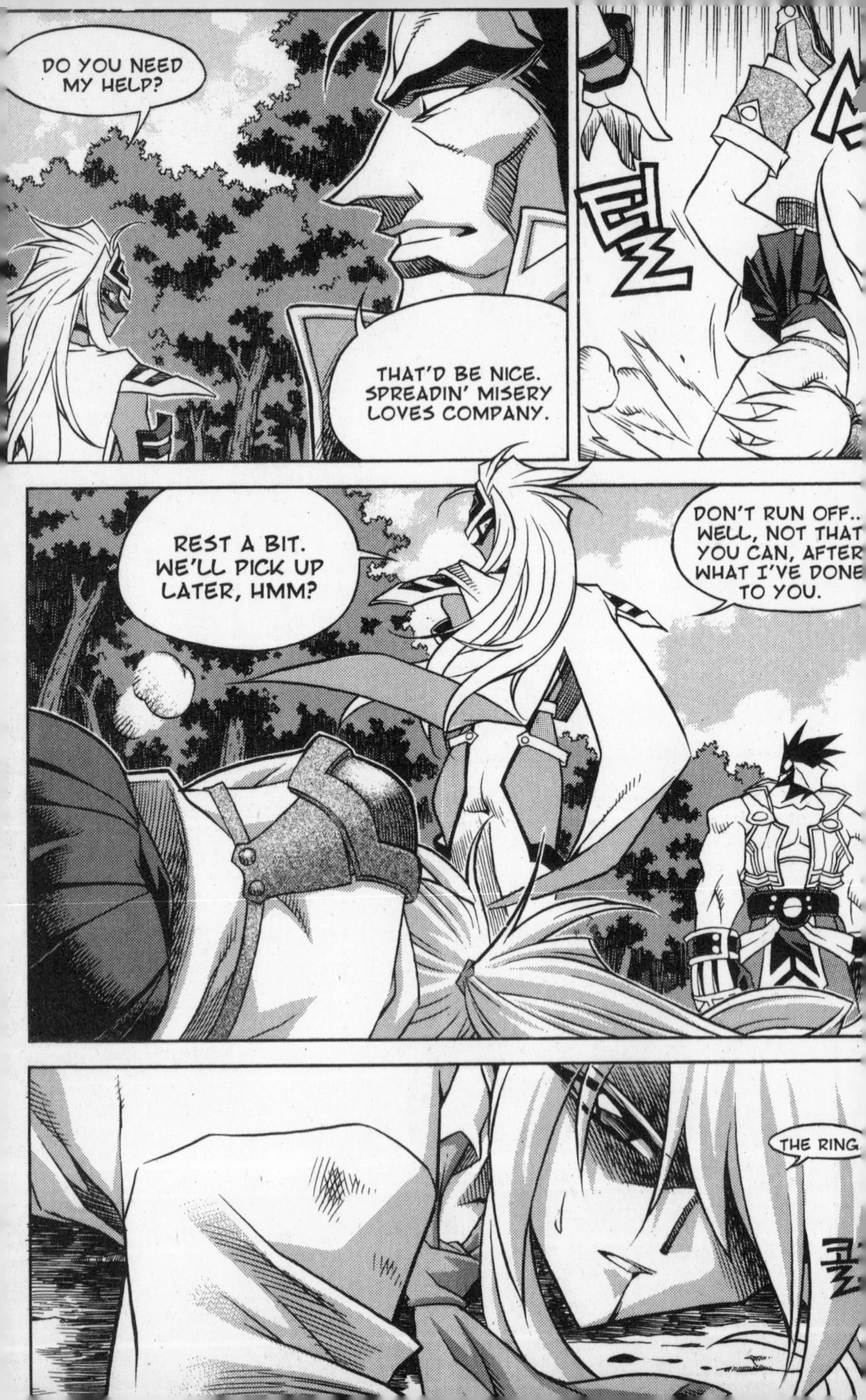
DO YOU NEED MY HELP?
THAT'D BE NICE. SPREADIN' MISERY LOVES COMPANY.
REST A BIT. WE'LL PICK UP LATER, HMM?
DON'T RUN OFF... WELL, NOT THAT YOU CAN, AFTER WHAT I'VE DONE TO YOU.
THE RING

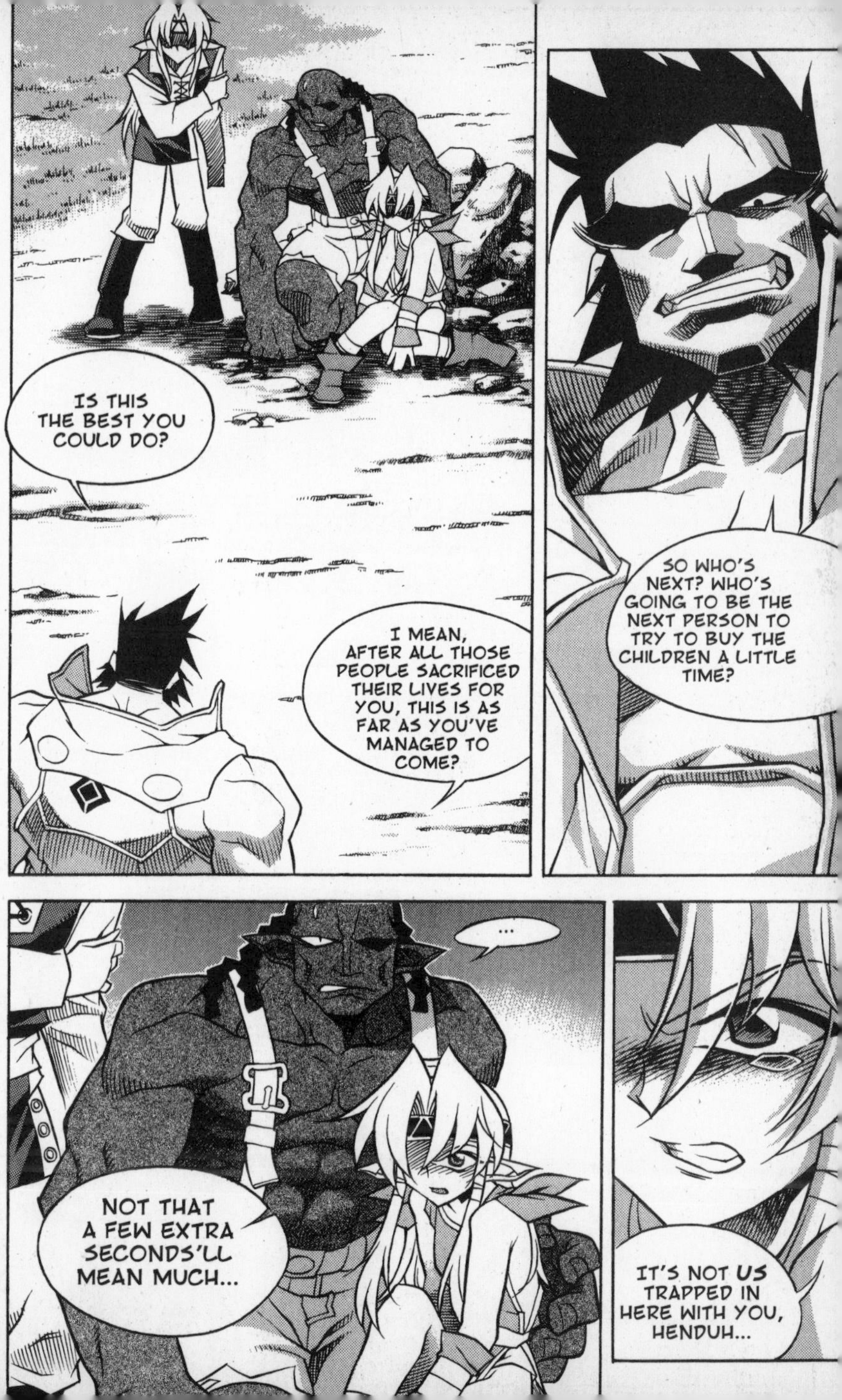
IS THIS THE BEST YOU COULD DO?
I MEAN, AFTER ALL THOSE PEOPLE SACRIFICED THEIR LIVES FOR YOU, THIS IS AS FAR AS YOU'VE MANAGED TO COME?
SO WHO'S NEXT? WHO'S GOING TO BE THE NEXT PERSON TO TRY TO BUY THE CHILDREN A LITTLE TIME?
...
NOT THAT A FEW EXTRA SECONDS'LL MEAN MUCH...
IT'S NOT **US** TRAPPED IN HERE WITH YOU, HENDUH...

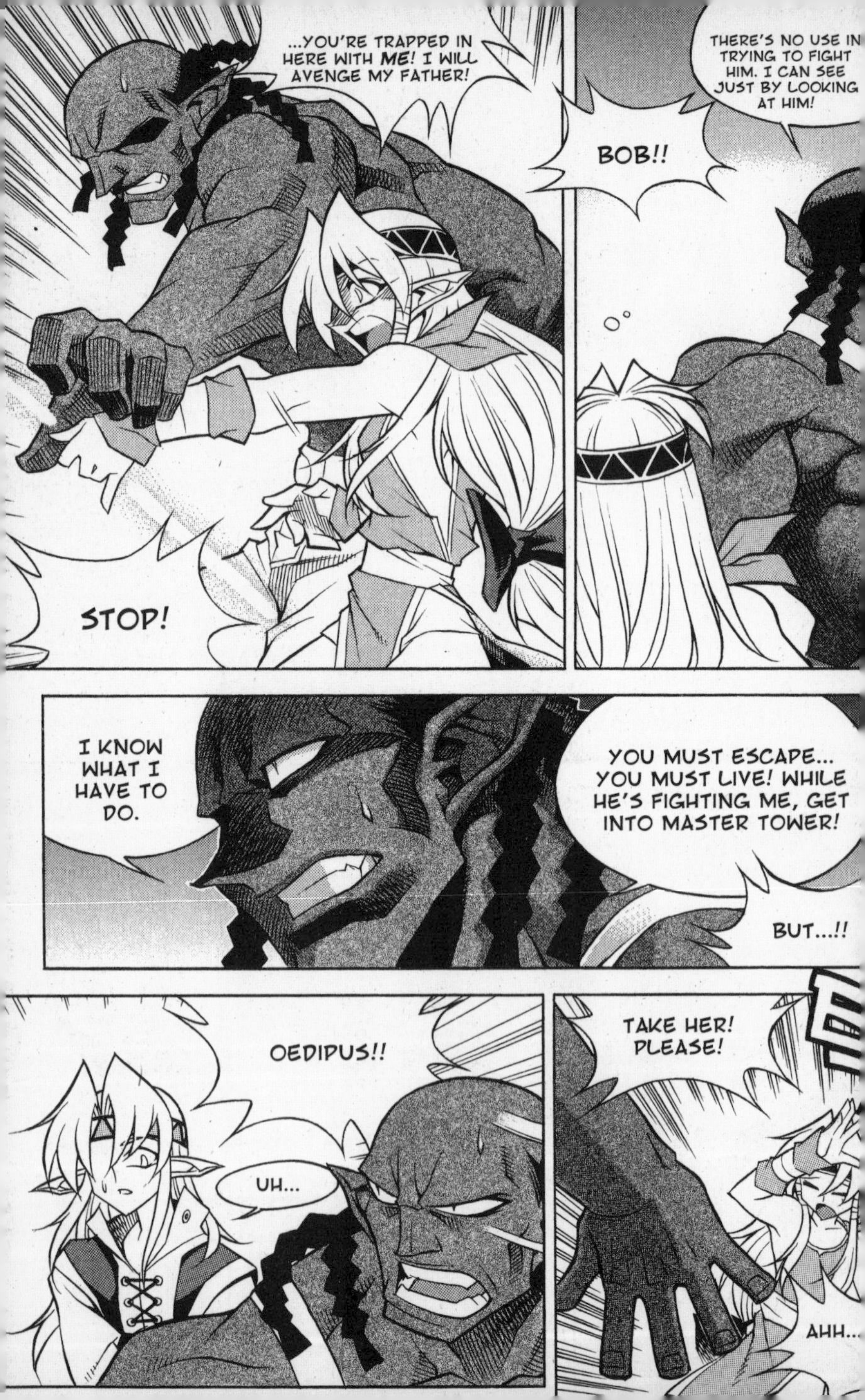
...YOU'RE TRAPPED IN HERE WITH ME! I WILL AVENGE MY FATHER!
STOP!
THERE'S NO USE IN TRYING TO FIGHT HIM. I CAN SEE JUST BY LOOKING AT HIM!
BOB!!
I KNOW WHAT I HAVE TO DO.
YOU MUST ESCAPE... YOU MUST LIVE! WHILE HE'S FIGHTING ME, GET INTO MASTER TOWER!
BUT...!!
OEDIPUS!!
UH...
TAKE HER! PLEASE!
AHH...

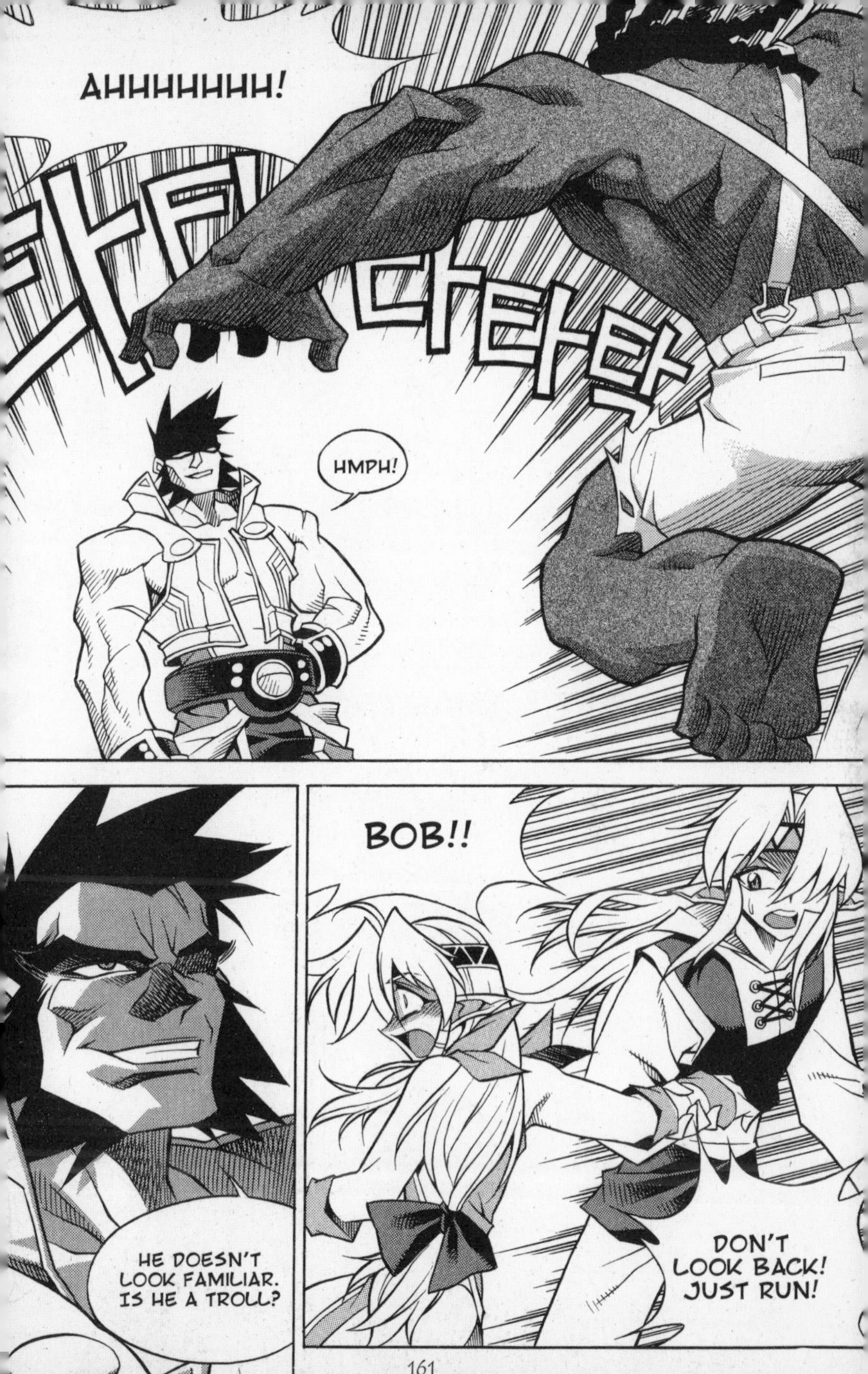
AHHHHHHH!
HMPH!
HE DOESN'T LOOK FAMILIAR. IS HE A TROLL?
BOB!!
DON'T LOOK BACK! JUST RUN!

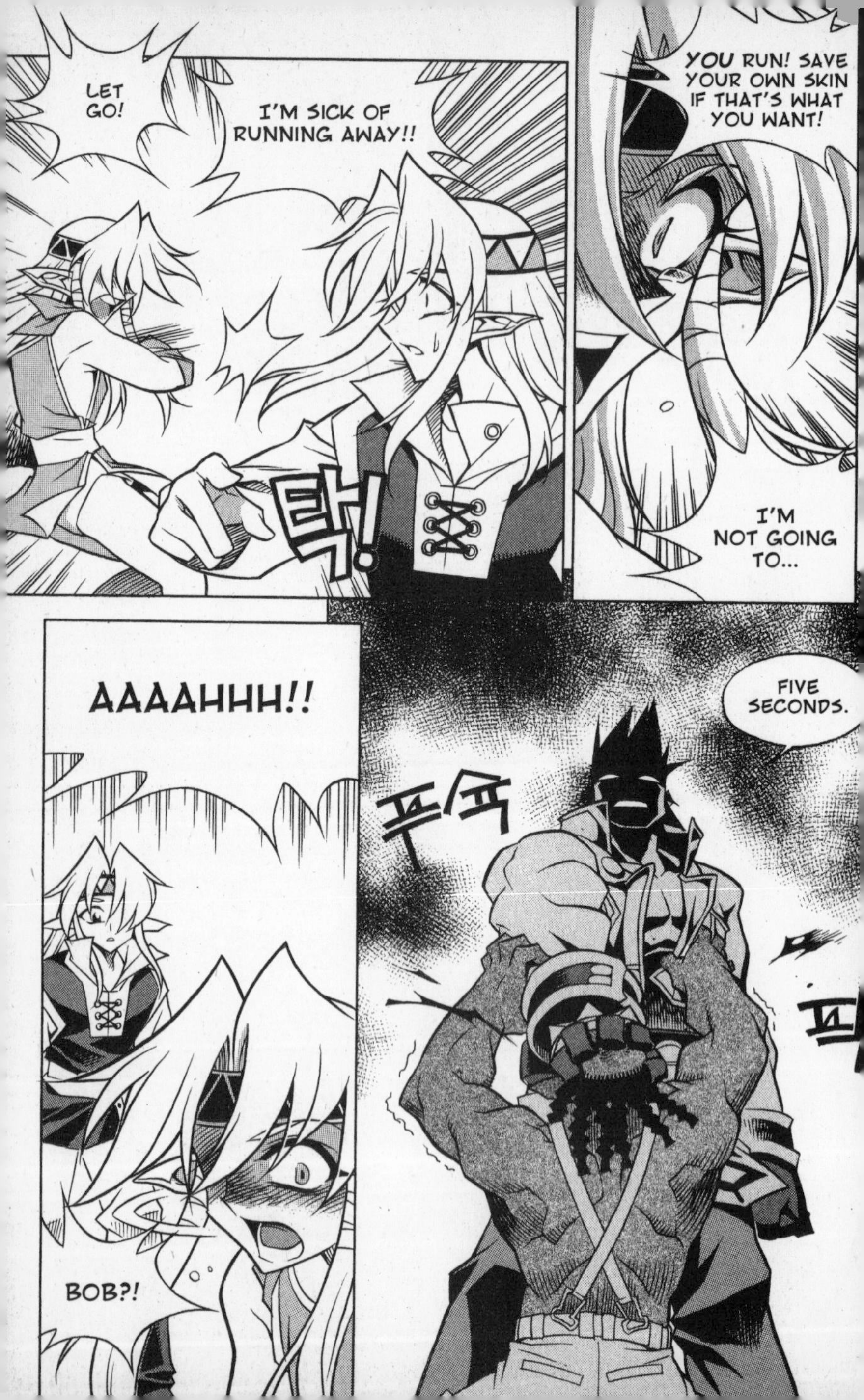
LET GO!
I'M SICK OF RUNNING AWAY!!
탁!
YOU RUN! SAVE YOUR OWN SKIN IF THAT'S WHAT YOU WANT!
I'M NOT GOING TO...
AAAAHHH!!
BOB?!
FIVE SECONDS.
푸슉

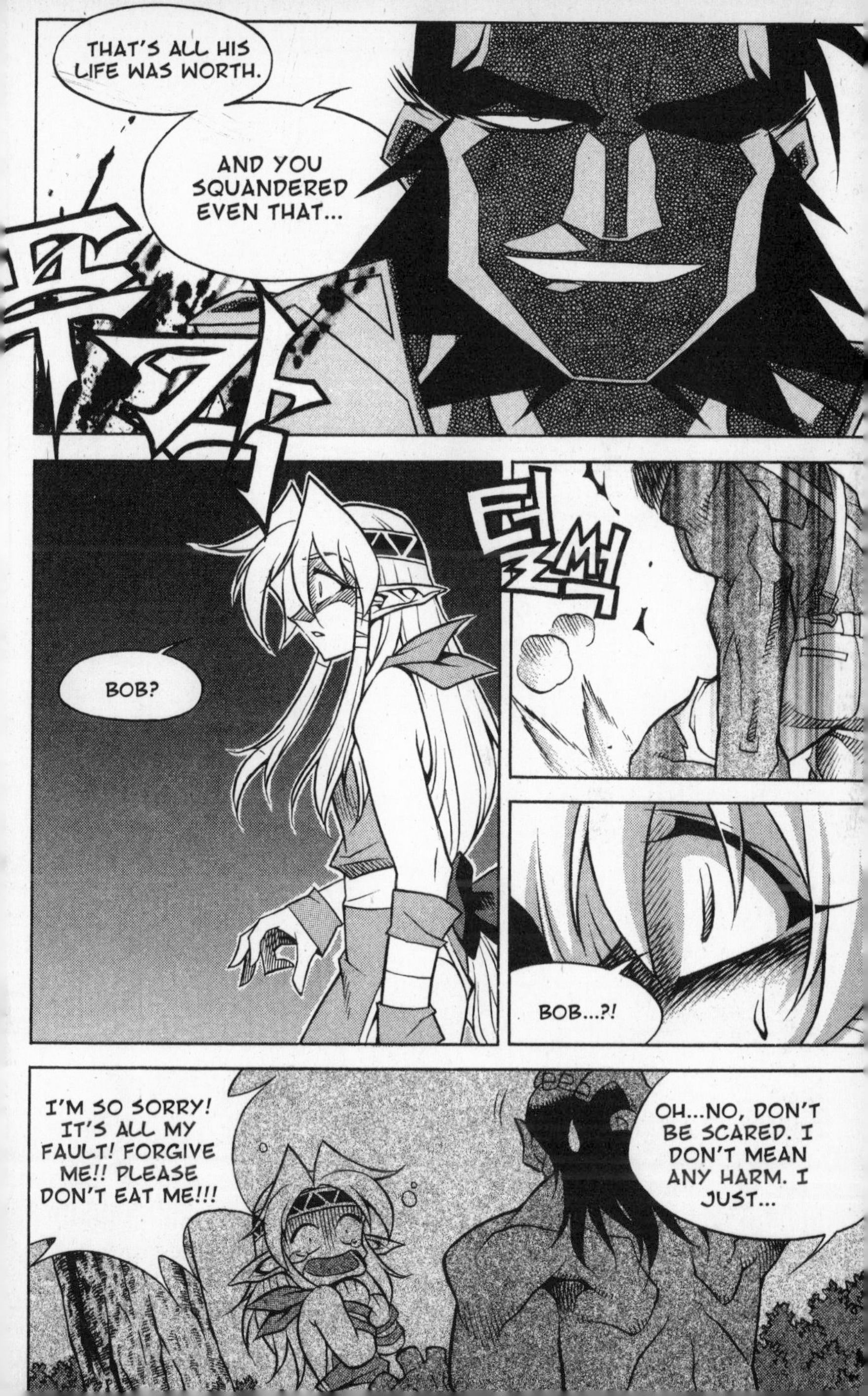
THAT'S ALL HIS LIFE WAS WORTH.
AND YOU SQUANDERED EVEN THAT...
BOB?
BOB...?!
I'M SO SORRY! IT'S ALL MY FAULT! FORGIVE ME!! PLEASE DON'T EAT ME!!!
OH...NO, DON'T BE SCARED. I DON'T MEAN ANY HARM. I JUST...

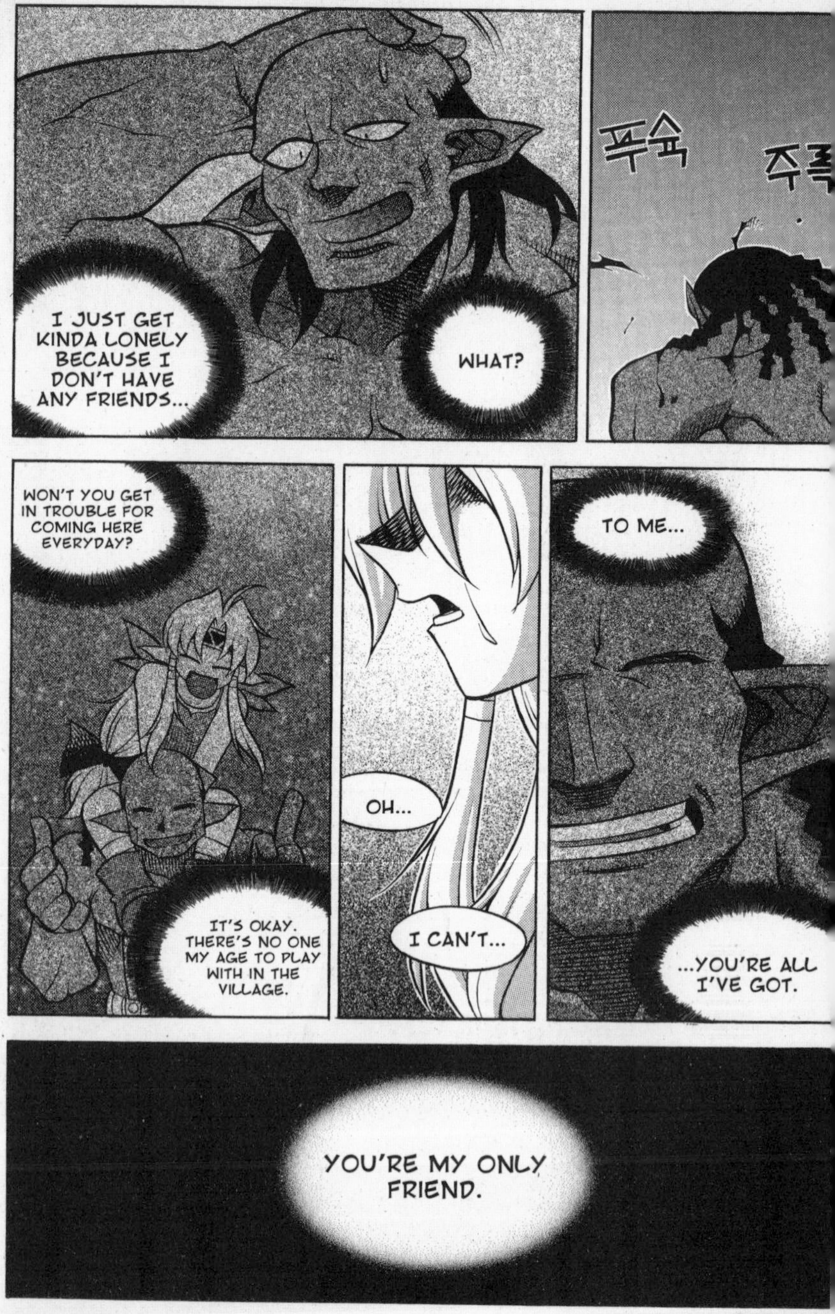
I JUST GET KINDA LONELY BECAUSE I DON'T HAVE ANY FRIENDS...
WHAT?
푸슉
주륵
WON'T YOU GET IN TROUBLE FOR COMING HERE EVERYDAY?
IT'S OKAY. THERE'S NO ONE MY AGE TO PLAY WITH IN THE VILLAGE.
OH...
I CAN'T...
TO ME...
...YOU'RE ALL I'VE GOT.
YOU'RE MY ONLY FRIEND.

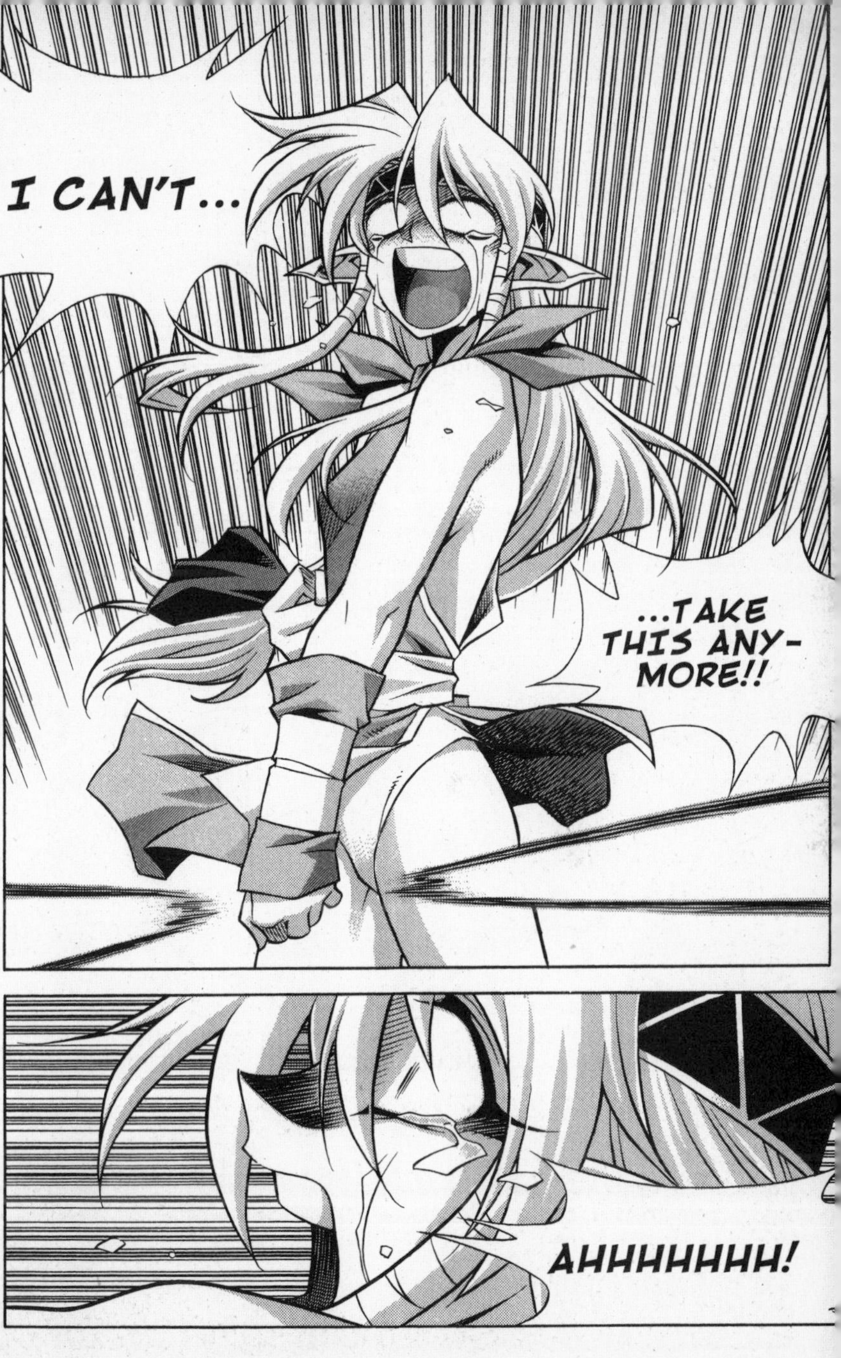
I CAN'T...
...TAKE THIS ANY-MORE!!
AHHHHHHH!

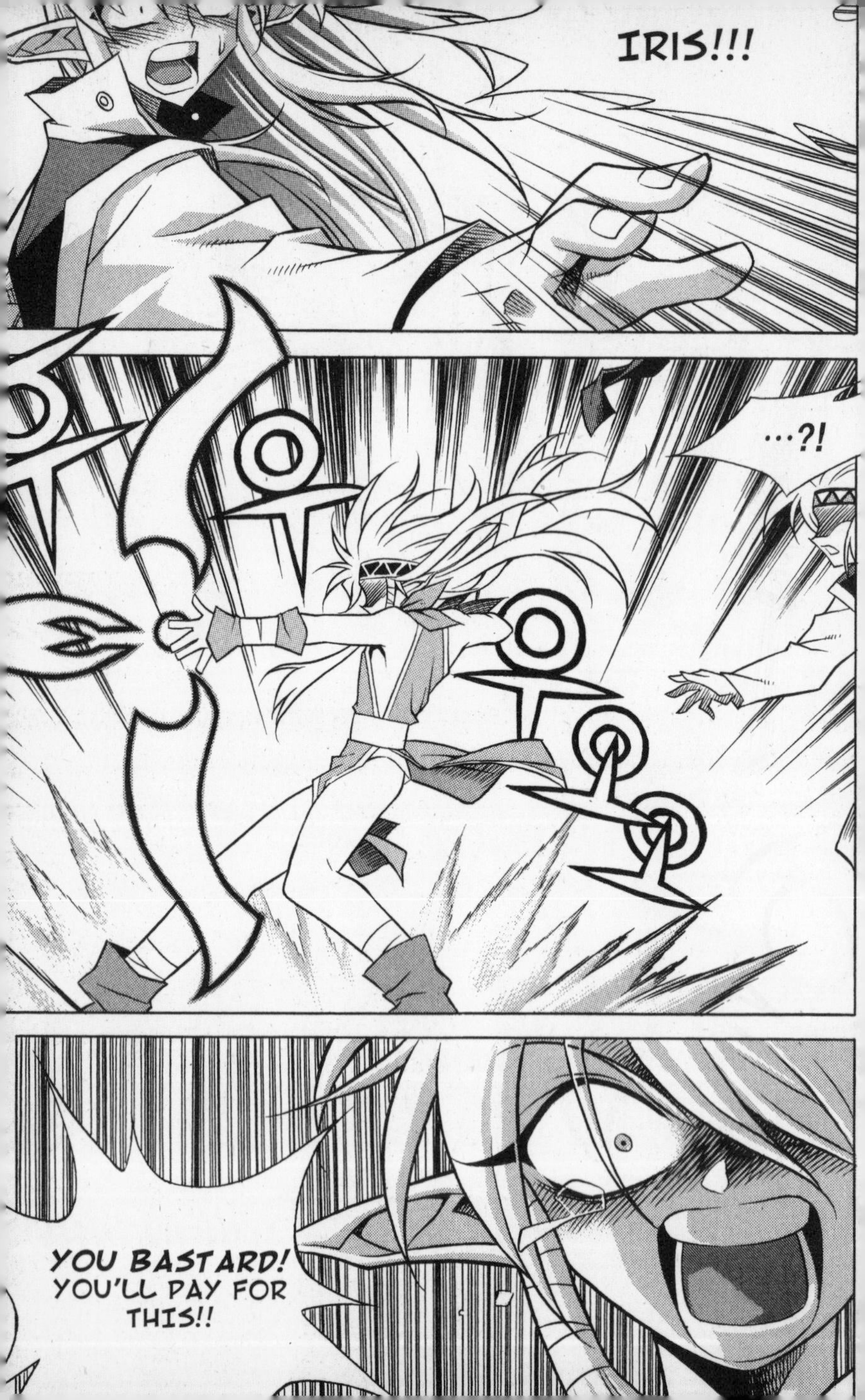
IRIS!!!
...?!
YOU BASTARD! YOU'LL PAY FOR THIS!!

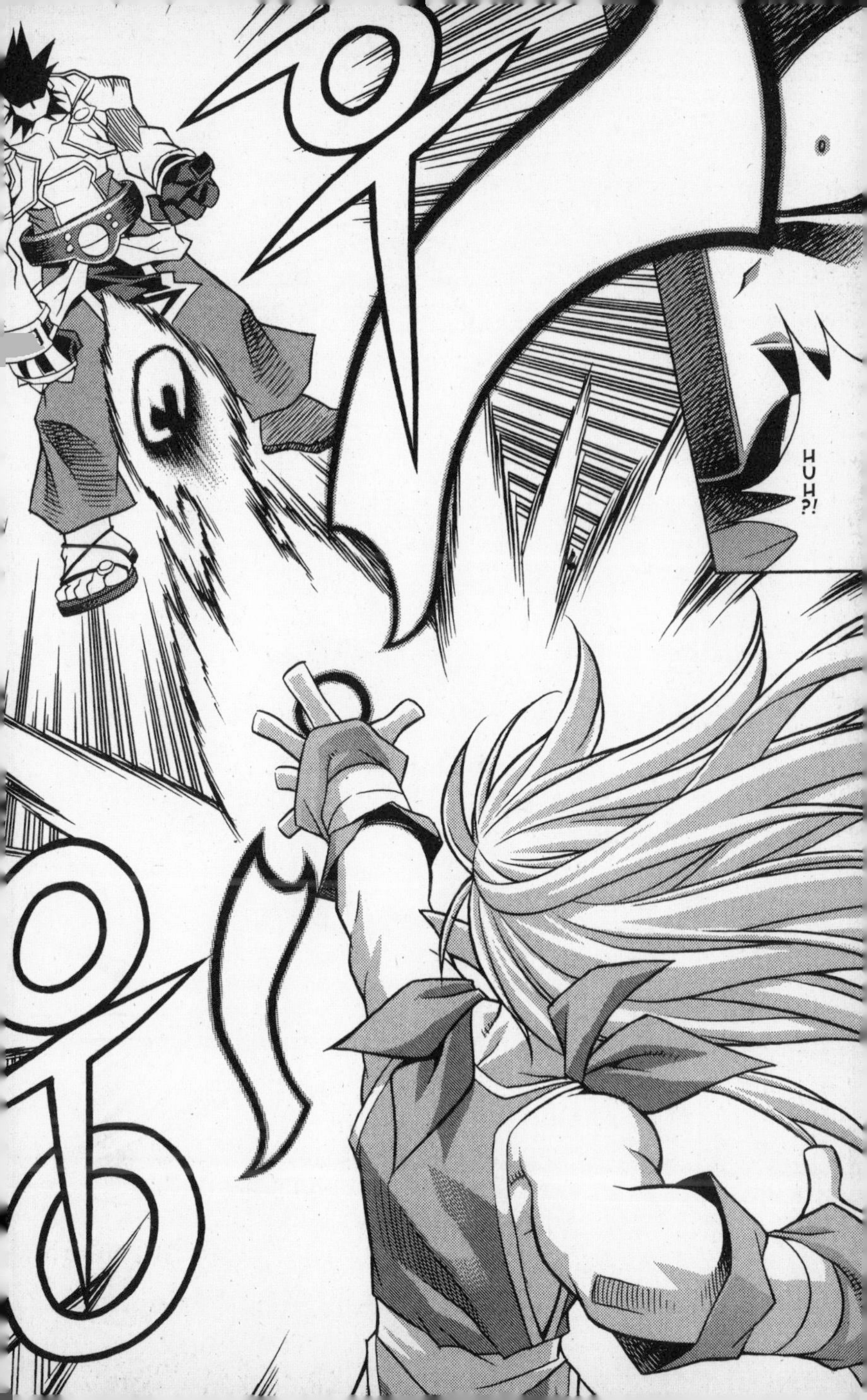
HUH?!

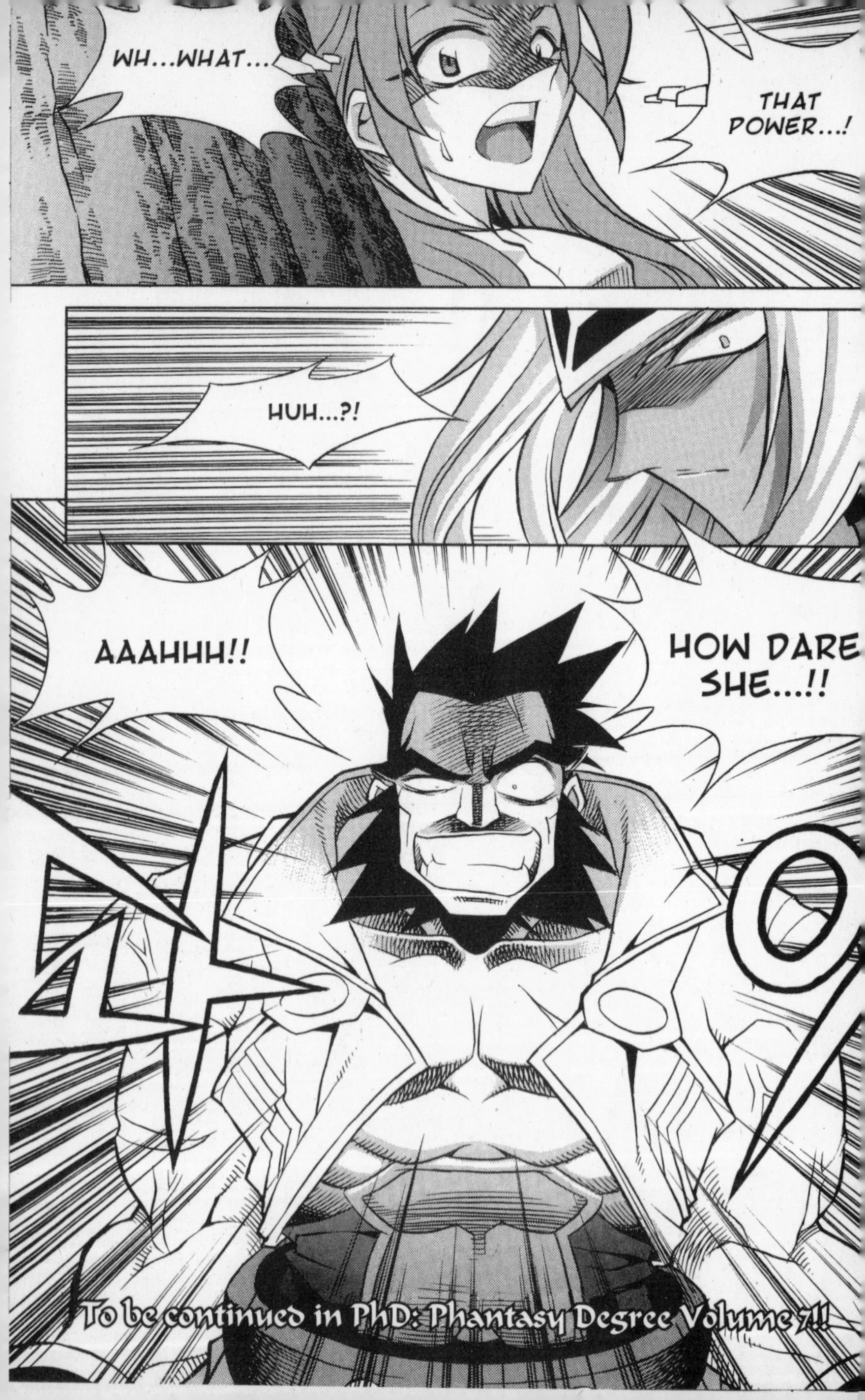
WH...WHAT...
THAT POWER...!
HUH...?!
AAAHHH!!
HOW DARE SHE...!!
To be continued in PhD: Phantasy Degree Volume 7!!

In the Next Volume of...

PhD
PHANTASY DEGREE

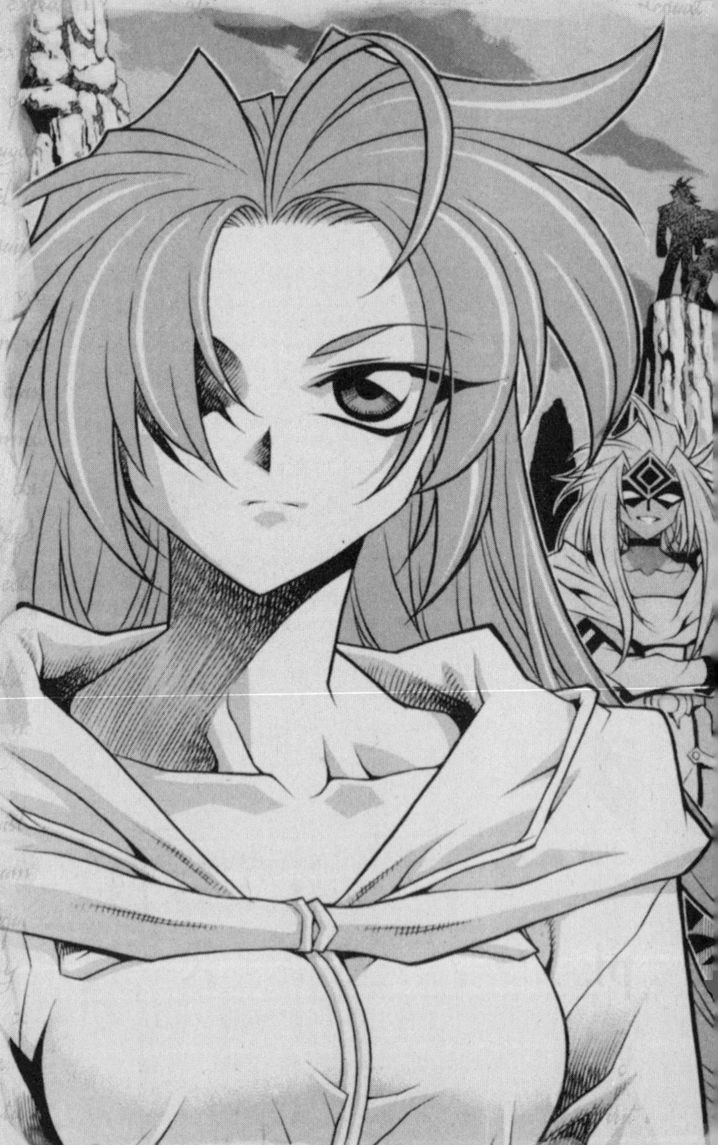

Available October 2006

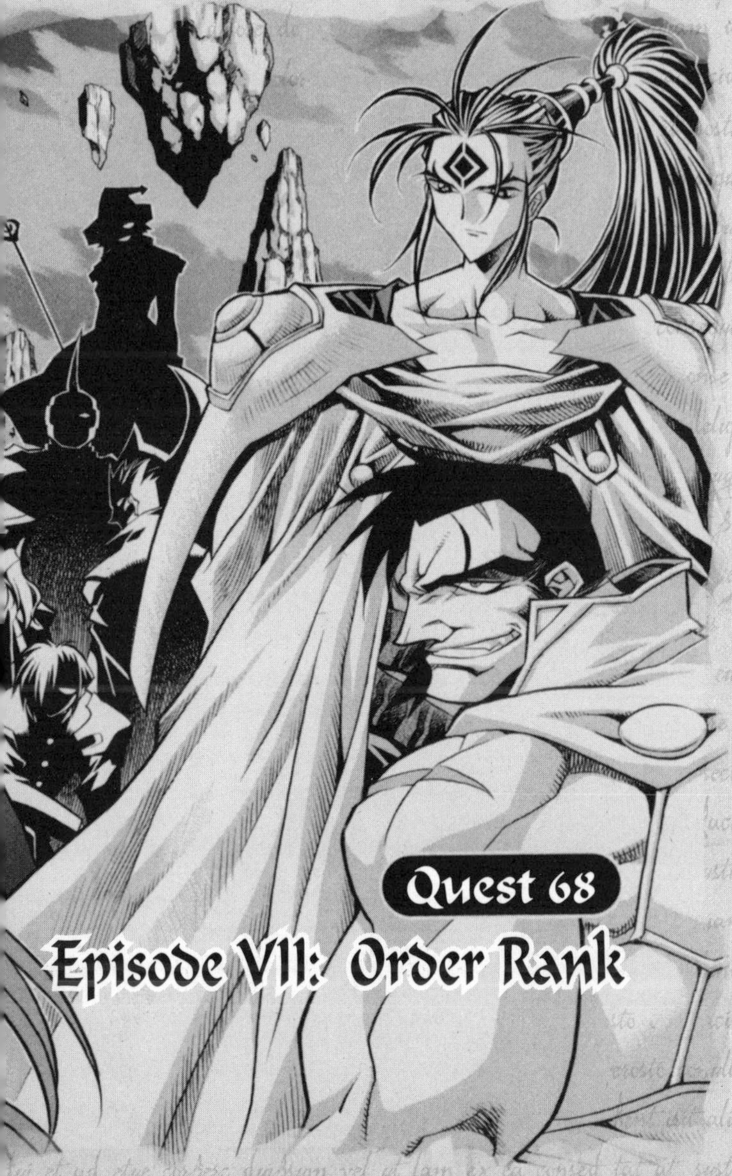
Quest 68
Episode VII: Order Rank

BLADE of HEAVEN
™

THE ULTIMATE CLASH IS ABOUT TO BEGIN.

When Soma, a human, is accused of stealing the Heaven King's Sword, the otherwordly order is knocked out of balance. Heavenly beings and demons clash for ultimate supremacy. The hope for salvation rests with Soma, the heavenly princess, and the Blade of Heaven—each holds the key to preventing all Hell from breaking loose!

TEEN
AGE 13+

The manga that inspired the hit anime!

RAVE MASTER ™

Three Heroes.
Two Quests.
One Destiny.

www.TOKYOPOP.com

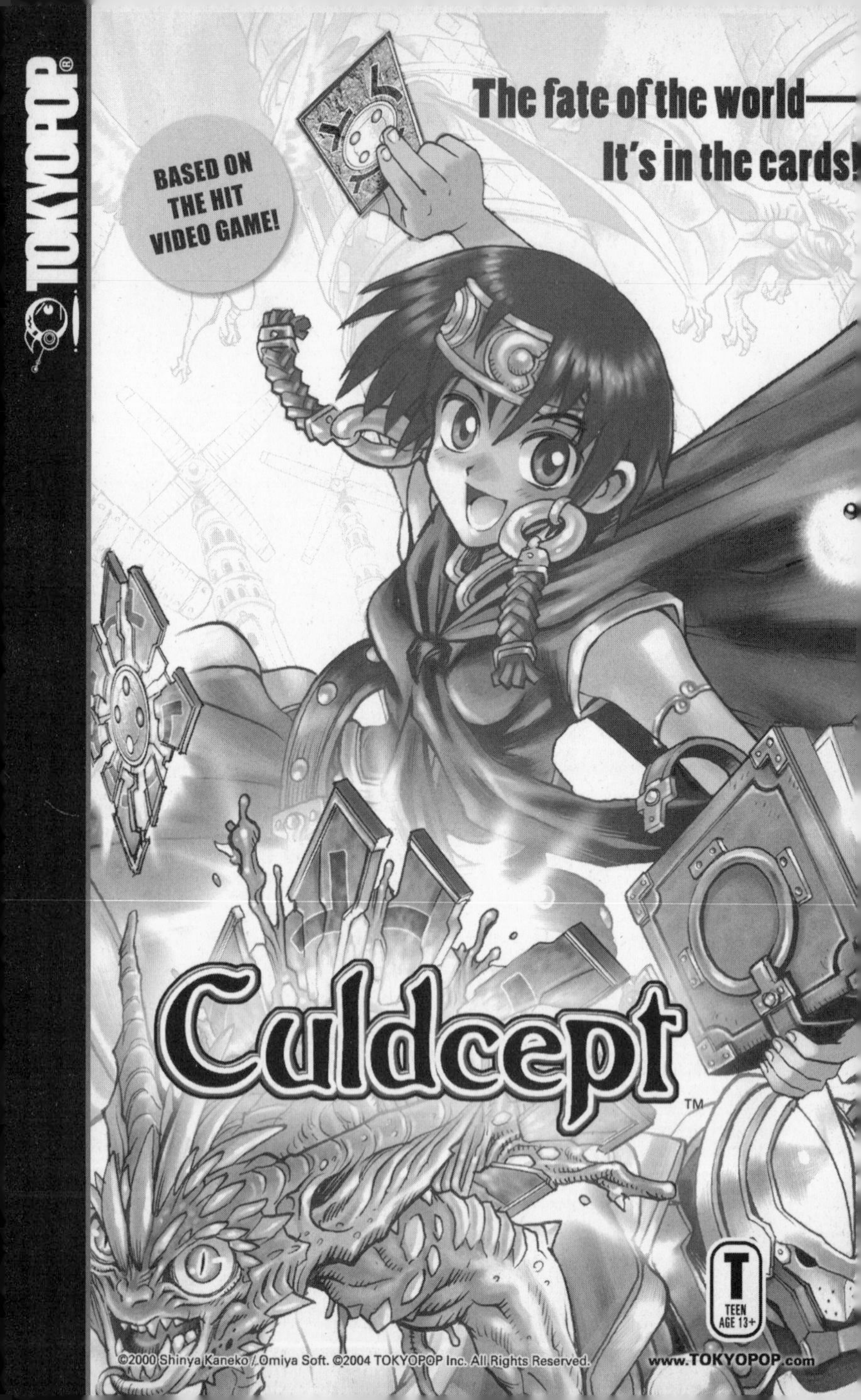
TOKYOPOP
The fate of the world—
It's in the cards!
BASED ON THE HIT VIDEO GAME!
Culdcept™
T TEEN AGE 13+
©2000 Shinya Kaneko / Omiya Soft. ©2004 TOKYOPOP Inc. All Rights Reserved.
www.TOKYOPOP.com

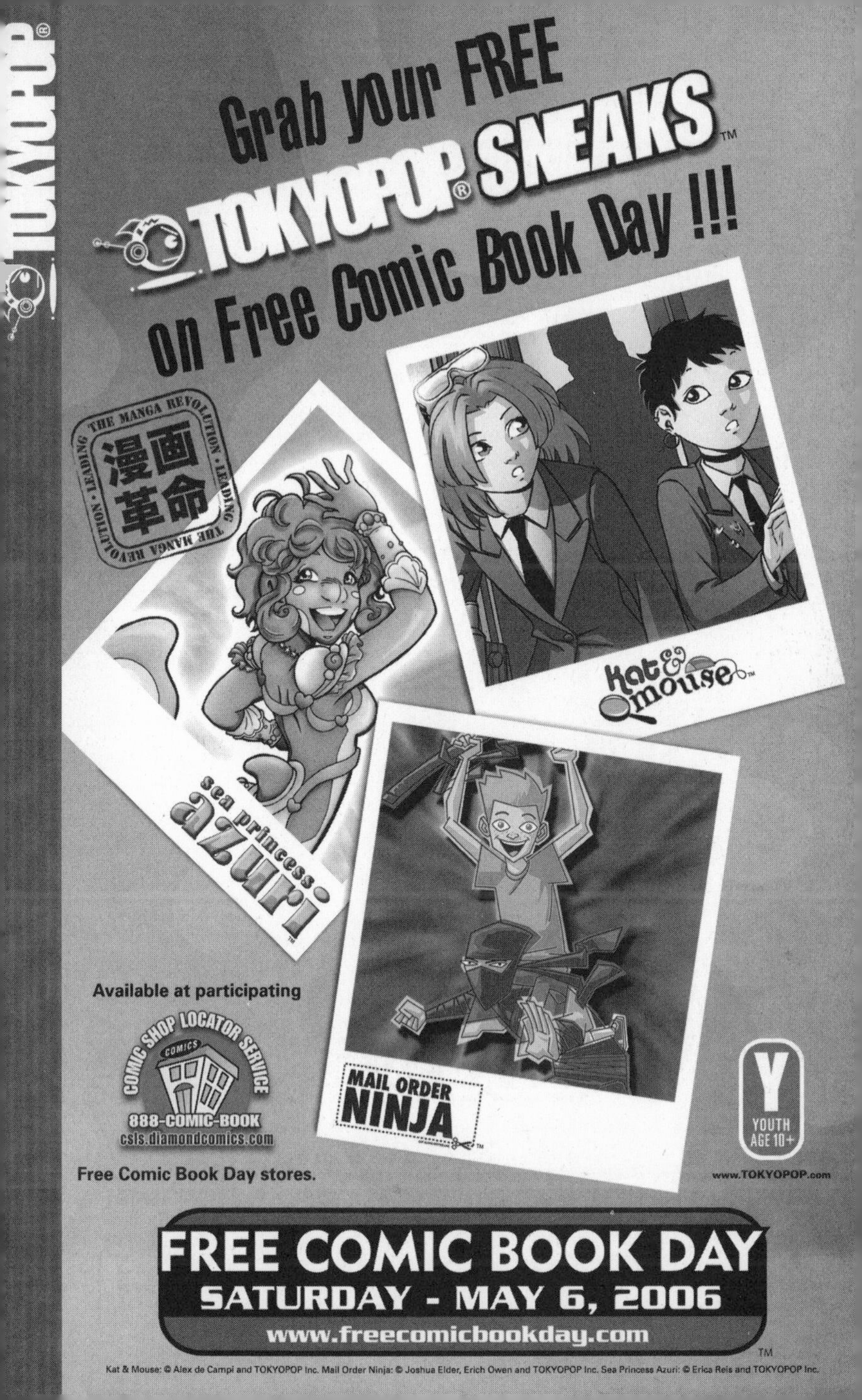
TOKYOPOP
Grab your FREE
TOKYOPOP® SNEAKS™
on Free Comic Book Day !!!
THE MANGA REVOLUTION · LEADING THE MANGA REVOLUTION · LEADING
漫画革命
Kat & mouse™
sea princess azuri™
MAIL ORDER NINJA™
Available at participating
COMIC SHOP LOCATOR SERVICE
COMICS
888-COMIC-BOOK
csls.diamondcomics.com
Free Comic Book Day stores.
Y
YOUTH
AGE 10+
www.TOKYOPOP.com
FREE COMIC BOOK DAY
SATURDAY - MAY 6, 2006
www.freecomicbookday.com
TM
Kat & Mouse: © Alex de Campi and TOKYOPOP Inc. Mail Order Ninja: © Joshua Elder, Erich Owen and TOKYOPOP Inc. Sea Princess Azuri: © Erica Reis and TOKYOPOP Inc.

SHRINE OF THE MORNING MIST

BY HIROKI UGAWA

When the spirit world suddenly shifts out of balance, it's up to sisters Kurako, Yuzu and Tama to save us—but first they must get through their family drama.

FANTASY

T TEEN AGE 13+

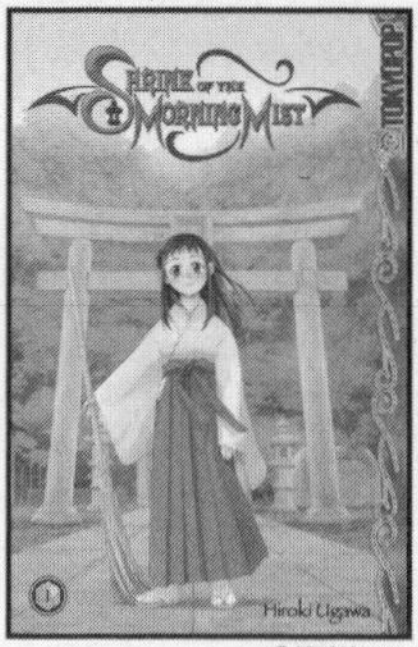
TOKYOPOP
SHRINE OF THE MORNING MIST
1
Hiroki Ugawa

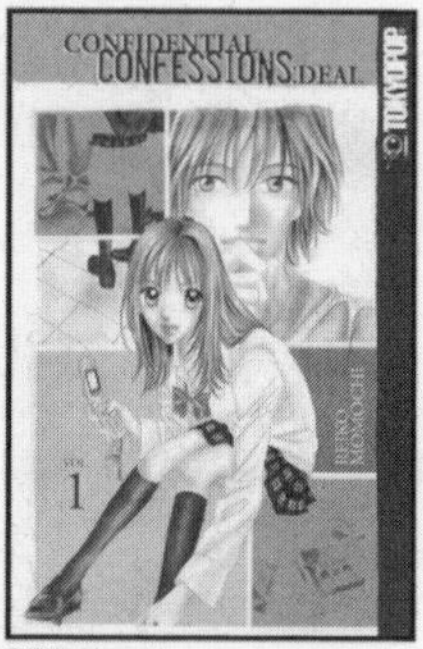
CONFIDENTIAL CONFESSIONS:DEAI
TOKYOPOP
REIKO MOMOCHI
VOL 1

CONFIDENTIAL CONFESSIONS -DEAI-

BY REIKO MOMOCHI

In this unflinching portrayal of teens in crisis, silence isn't always golden...

DRAMA

OT OLDER TEEN AGE 16+

DEATH JAM

BY JEON SANG YOUNG

Muchaca Smooth is an assassin with just one shot to make it big!

ACTION

OT OLDER TEEN AGE 16+

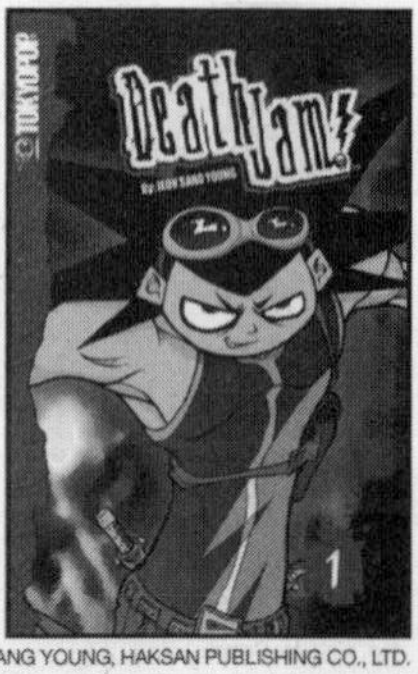
TOKYOPOP
Death Jam
1

© PEACH-PIT, GENTOSHA COMICS INC.

ROZEN MAIDEN
BY PEACH-PIT

Welcome to the world of *Rozen Maiden* where a boy must enter an all-new reality to protect and serve a living doll!

From the creators of *DearS*!

BOYS OF SUMMER
BY CHUCK AUSTEN AND HIROKI OTSUKA

Just because you strike out on your first attempt at scoring with a girl doesn't mean you won't end up hitting a home run!

© Chuck Austen and TOKYOPOP Inc.

© Alex de Campi and TOKYOPOP Inc.

KAT & MOUSE
BY ALEX DE CAMPI AND FEDERICA MANFREDI

When science whiz Kat teams up with computer nerd Mouse, bullies and blackmailers don't stand a chance!

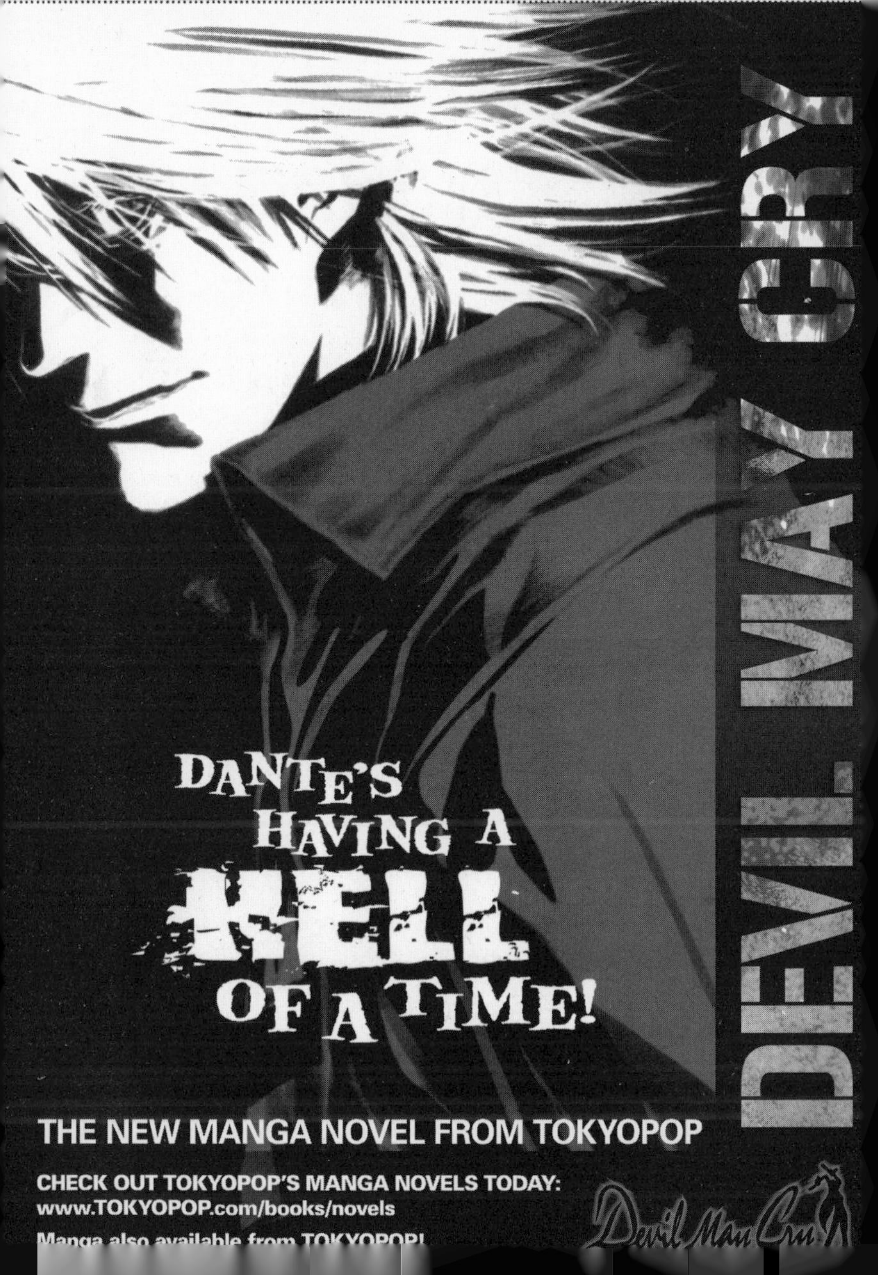
DEVIL MAY CRY
DANTE'S HAVING A HELL OF A TIME!
THE NEW MANGA NOVEL FROM TOKYOPOP
CHECK OUT TOKYOPOP'S MANGA NOVELS TODAY:
www.TOKYOPOP.com/books/novels
Manga also available from TOKYOPOP!
Devil May Cry

Dear Diary,
I'm starting to feel

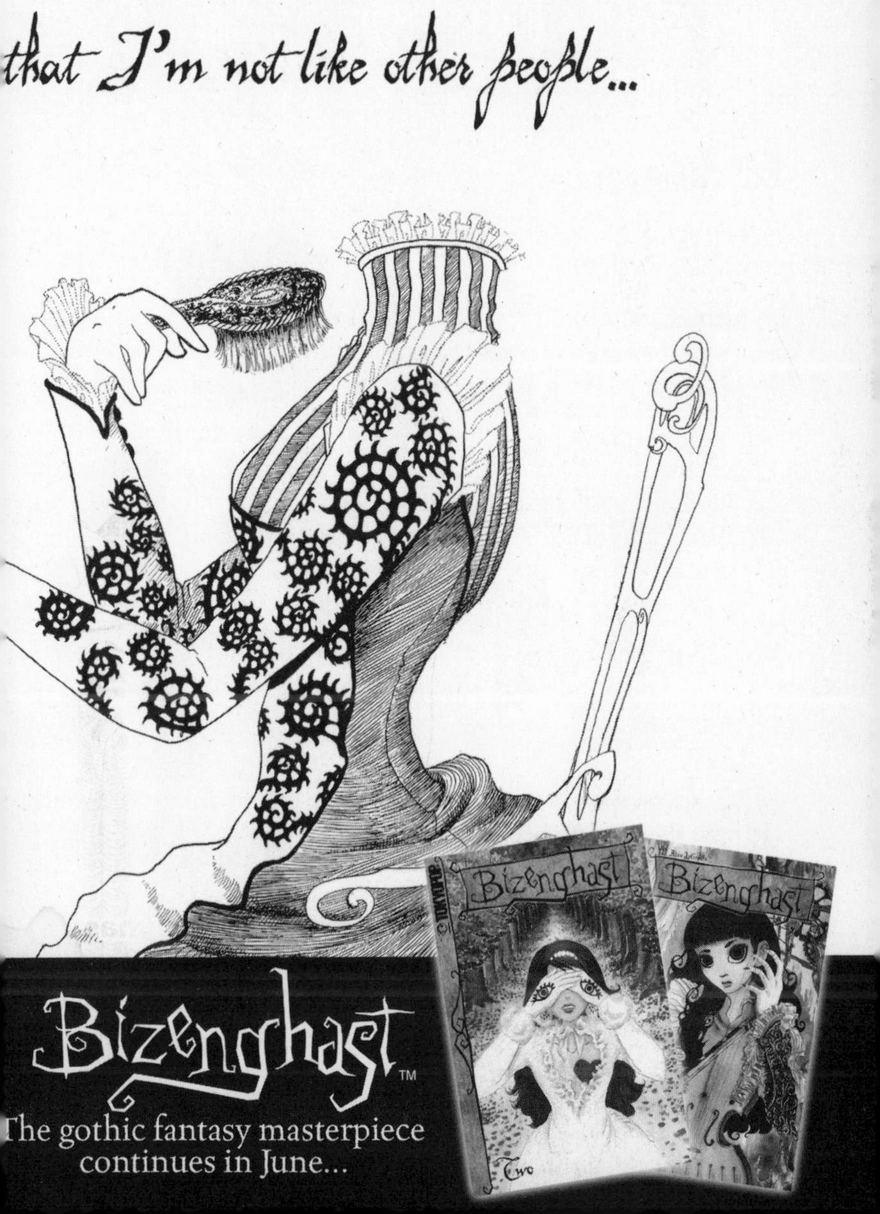
that I'm not like other people...
Bizenghast
Bizenghast
TOKYOPOP
Two
Bizenghast™
The gothic fantasy masterpiece
continues in June...

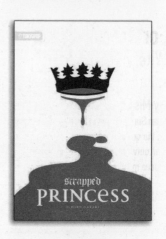